The Comprehensive Guide To
Fish
Locators

The Comprehensive Guide To
Fish
Locators
by Babe Winkelman

Published by
Babe Winkelman Productions, Inc.
Brainerd, Minnesota

Author	Babe Winkelman
Editor	Mark Strand
Artwork	Duane Ryks/John Norlin/Charles Dunemann
Photography	Mark Strand/Charles Dunemann
Cover Design	Duane Ryks/John Norlin
Layout	Duane Ryks
Keyline	Sandra Ryks
Typesetting	Sentinel Printing
Printing	Sentinel Printing

Published by Babe Winkelman Productions
P.O. Box 407, 213 N.W. 4th St., Brainerd, MN 56401

Printed in the United States of America

First edition, 1987
Library of Congress Catalog
Card Number 87-051209

ISBN 0-915405-06-7

Library of Congress Cataloguing in
Publication Date

Winkelman, Babe
The Comprehensive Guide to Fish Locators

Brainerd, Minnesota: Babe Winkelman Productions, Inc.
ISBN 0-915405-06-7

It is with love, respect and admiration that I dedicate this book:

to Carl Lowrance, one of the world's first scientific fishermen, and to his family, who backed and helped him while he did the tireless research and development that brought sonar to the average inland fisherman;

to all the great and foresighted fishermen who embraced Carl's sonar technology in the beginning, and helped convince the fishing public that it was the wonderful invention it was;

to my wife Charlie and daughters Tanya, Jennifer, Jasmine, Donielle and MacKenzie—who continue to provide the love and understanding that makes us a united family;

to the people of our company, who have taken so many burdens off my back and returned the faith I had in them;

and once again to my Creator, who continues to bless me, and all of you, with special days on the water.

ACKNOWLEDGEMENTS

Starting with my original *Fish Locators* course as a foundation, and forming a complete and solid work that includes the latest advancements in sonar technology, was the job I gave to Mark Strand. He has done his usual grand work. This book would not be what it is if not for his writing and photographic talents, and hard work.

Ray Eng, another accomplished and trusted member of my staff, filled in many factual holes with his research skills.

Duane Ryks, whose name appears on every book I've ever produced, once again spent many hours pouring over the manuscript to ensure that it says all we want it to. Duane also supervised the illustration and design work, and the look of this book shows again why I wanted him to run part of my company a few years back.

John Norlin and Charlie Dunemann, a pair of creative artists, make the principles of sonar pop out at you with their illustrations.

Sandy Ryks, another old hand who gets better with every job, did another masterful bit of keylining that gives the book its clean, professional appearance.

There were so many who gave unselfishly of their time as we assembled the facts that make this book a complete guide. Darrell Lowrance, Thayne Smith, Kim Mitchell, Phil Williams, Mike Render, John Floro and a host of others at Eagle Electronics helped immeasurably in clarifying questions about the way sonar works and the direction it is heading.

Jim Wentworth, owner of Fish Lectronics, a sonar repair expert who has seen it all from the beginning, answered every question we had about installing and caring for sonar, despite being up to his elbows in customer's units. *Everybody* goes to Jim when their sonar needs a tune-up. Read his words of wisdom, and you'll know why.

Don Pereira, Dennis Schupp, Dennis Anderson, Jim Lilienthal, Tim Brastrup, Carl Bublitz and Joe Geis are all educated and gifted public servants with the Minnesota Department of Natural Resources. They painted a clear picture of how their work can benefit you as an angler, in the chapter on fishing a new lake.

There are so many great fishermen on my Research Team who added insight, but I want to mention John Christianson, Wayne Ekelund, Larry Sletten, and Larry Pressnall. I'd hate to be a fish if all those guys were in one boat!

Thanks also to Bill Diedrich, promotion manager for Ferguson-Keller Associates for helping with photography sessions; to Rod Romine, Koden representative, and Dan Chesky, Marine Electric, for their technical input. And, finally, a thanks to all the sonar manufacturers who shared information about their product offerings and sonar in general, that gives this book a well-rounded persepctive.

TABLE OF CONTENTS

FOREWORD

It's really a sense of what's right and wrong, more than the desire to impress other people, that drives most fishermen. The very thought of getting our butts kicked by an animal with "a brain the size of a pea" spurs us to develop help for the limited reach of our senses.

We can't see into the water, except in clear, shallow areas, and that's a large part of what makes fishing a mystery. Our eyes work just fine when it comes to seeing parallel to the surface, and that's what makes it easy to watch a guy like Babe Winkelman haul in fish after fish while you wonder whether his last one was a bass or a walleye.

Getting an opportunity to share the boat with a master, though, can change your luck dramatically. It's been a number of years since I started fishing with people who never look up to carry on a conversation, much less survey their surroundings. To the elite angler, the direction the boat is traveling relative to visible objects doesn't mean much. They concern themselves with an entire underwater dimension that lesser fishermen haven't come to know: the structure, bottom density, cover and yes, fish, present *in* the water.

Of all the fishermen I have come to know, Babe Winkelman sits in a solitary position as the thinking man's professional. When he really gets on a roll, he operates at a level only masters can relate to, that can make him seem esoteric even to fellow pros. He was tired of looking parallel to the water's surface while Carl Lowrance, the sonar pioneer, was still working on the first portable unit for the freshwater angler. Babe was mentally ready to accept such an instrument when it came, embraced it and stretched its potential before most folks realized such a gadget existed.

Many walleyes ago, Babe learned the science of modern fishing sonar, and what it offers you as a recreational or serious fisherman. The machines available today add more reach to our human senses than the ones Babe learned on, yet almost none of us understand their limitations and promise. Yes, we buy them and have them installed, probably more out of a sense of what today's fishing machine is supposed to look like than anything else. We use them to tell us when the water is too deep to see into, and therefore gather no more solid fishing information than we used to. I know how it was for me. As a kid, I was a hotshot fisherman for a long time before I learned how to use a depth finder. That probably explains why it took me so long to wise up.

If you haven't learned the wonders of sonar, don't wait any longer. Even though he understands more about the subject than we ever will, Babe Winkelman has retained the ability to explain it to us. This book can teach you to join the power of modern sonar with your own two eyes; to look into the water and find how understandable and fascinating the other dimension of fishing can be. It will show you how much fun sonar can be all by itself, and open forever a new chapter in the world's most wonderful lifetime sport.

The things he has taught me have made my fishing a lot more fun. Read this book, and let him do the same for you.

—Mark Strand
Mgr., Photo/Journalism Dept.
Babe Winkelman Productions, Inc.

Chapter 1
An Introduction

Everything should be made as simple
as possible but not simpler
   —**Albert Einstein**

I have my theories on why fishing is as popular as it is. For hours on end, little children will stare into the waters of an aquarium, studying the fish. Fish are wonderful to watch. They glide so easily, and they have a beauty to them that is *different*.

We relish any chance, I think, to get a good look at fish with our own eyes, because the chances come only so often. Most of the time, the fish's underwater world is something we can only imagine, a dark and mysterious void harder to understand than outer space. It's right here on our planet, and we spend a few weeks every summer staring into it as far as we can from the safety of a boat, but we don't really understand much about it.

Other things, we can see with our eyes and make educated guesses about. A patch of woods isn't nearly as mysterious as the waters of our favorite lake or river, because in a few hours we can have tromped through the entire thing, and looked over every inch of that patch of woods with our own eyes. We can *know* what the woods look like.

What's down there in the water, though?

Anglers since the beginning have wondered the same thing. If you've spent any amount of time re-hashing a day of fishing, you have heard about every theory and wive's tale ever told. *The northern pike aren't biting at this time of year because they lost their teeth. The fish are there, but this cold front just has them turned off. Or, how about this one...I just can't understand it. The fish were here yesterday...*

Understanding the world of the fish is what my life has been all about, really. Yes, I have other interests, like you do. I love going to the movies, and taking my kids on the rides at the amusement center. I wouldn't trade my family, and the other parts of my day, for anything. But if I could just crack, once and for all, where the walleyes go when...

I'm supposed to be one of the guys who has all the answers about fishing. I know a lot about where fish go at different times of the year, and how to catch fish when a lot of other people can't. But what about the times when I don't catch anything, even though I'm trying as hard as I can, using every bit of information and skill I have?

Fish and fishing are a complicated business. We can't pretend to know everything about what goes on under the water, but we try. We have five certified scuba divers on the staff of Babe Winkelman Productions, myself included. We are all serious fishermen. We spend time *in* the fish's world, and those sessions are where some of the information we offer comes from. But we leave more unanswered questions every time we discover something new.

Oh well, I guess that keeps alive the interest and curiosity of fishermen everywhere. We make it our business to help people peer into the water and understand what fish do, and how to catch more. As long as people stare into the water and ask questions, we'll be able to make a living selling a few answers.

When you can't see into the water (and many lakes, rivers and reservoirs are so off-colored that scuba diving becomes nothing more than blindly feeling along the bottom), sonar can be your eyes. If you have a curiosity about fish, sonar can tell you so much. It can make your time as a fisherman fuller and more enjoyable. Fishing without sonar is like trying to see into the water with your own eyes. You can't see very far, or very much.

Whether you're a beginning or seasoned angler, there is much to wonder at in the underwater world of the fish. That, in itself, is much of the enchantment of the sport of fishing.

I'll never understand why the same guy who spends weeks scouting a five-mile area to determine what the deer are doing so he's in the right place come opening day of deer season, drives out in his boat and looks around, says "hey, this looks like a good spot," and drops his anchor. Does that make sense to you?

About as much as hunting with a blindfold on.

Modern fishing sonar allows us to "hunt" fish. It takes time, I know, to get good at interpreting the signals sonar shows us, and to be able to say, "okay, I know that I am over the tip of that point, and out to my right it drops off very steeply and I know the walleyes tend to hold right along the area where it starts to break."

But getting that good at using sonar is what this book is all about. In a way, it's what my company is all about. I have dedicated the past years of my life to helping others understand how to catch fish, and using sonar properly is a cornerstone skill to that end.

For some reason, many people get psyched out by the thought of how hard it will be for them to "see" into the fish's world through the aid of sonar. Actually, it is the same process as looking at anything above the water's surface; it just takes experience to be able to decipher the signals the sonar unit sends us.

Let's get one thing straight. Modern sonar is not a "fish finder." It will not find fish for us. We still need to understand the basic habits of fish, the types of places they tend to concentrate during different seasons, in order to put our boat in the right place at the right time. When *we* find fish, the sonar unit simply shows us what *we've* found. A sonar unit is not a fishing guide. A sonar unit does not know where to take you to catch fish. You still need to know that.

But, boy can it show you what you've found!

As I've said, fishing is a complicated subject. To learn to really use sonar takes time on your part. Time to learn how sonar works, so you can know the limitations and the possiblities; time to master the possibilities.

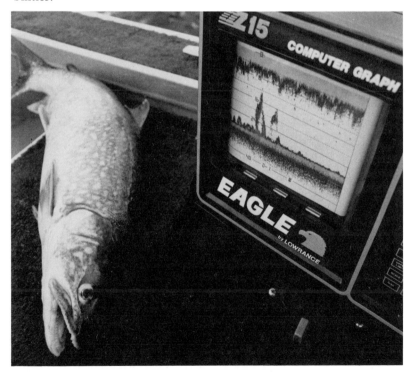

A sonar unit can't find fish for us; it can only show us what we have found. A fisherman must understand the species of fish he wants to catch, and be able to present a lure to the fish.

The technology in modern sonar has made the units capable of functioning almost on their own. They only need you to turn them on, in the most basic sense. Many fishermen will be fooled by that lure, buy an "automatic" sonar unit, turn it on and head out over the fish's world mentally unarmed. Yes, an automatic sonar unit will produce good images under some conditions. But which ones? When should you take such a unit out of automatic and run it in manual mode? What do all those signals on the screen represent?

It reminds me so much of the age of automatic cameras. Sure, armed with an automatic camera, a complete amateur can make a properly exposed photograph, *under certain conditions*. But what about the lighting situations which fool an automatic camera? And, even if a picture is properly exposed, is it a good picture? To assume that an automatic camera makes a beginner a photographer is to belittle the years that serious photographers have spent honing their compositional and lighting skills, of learning "when to go click," as they say.

It's the same story in the sonar arena. An automatic sonar unit will not take the place of time spent studying how sonar works, and how to understand sonar signals. Sonar is a wonderful tool, but let's respect the time it takes to get good at using it. Let's respect the time-honored art of fishing, and yet grab for the technology that helps us take our understanding of fish to a new level.

Let's take time to master the possibilities.

Just like a basketball player is forced by the coach to spend time working on basic skills, you must find time to practice using your sonar unit. The athlete takes each thing a step at a time at the beginning of his or her career: learning to dribble the ball, to make various kinds of passes, to work together with teammates, to condition the human body for intense competition, to shoot the ball into the basket from various positions on the floor.

Fishermen, for some reason, think it's different with their sport. It's not. You need to learn to cast and tie knots, and you have to learn what the different families of fishing lures are and what species of fish they are used for. You need to study the basic habits and seasonal movements of the fish you want to catch.

And, you need to practice using your sonar in order to understand what it is showing you. Sometimes, you need to spend time practicing with your sonar and *not fishing* at all. Don't basketball players, even experienced professionals, spend time practicing their shooting and dribbling without constantly playing in a game? How do you think they get to be as good as they are?

People who want to do well at anything spend time learning the basic skills. If you want to be a good fisherman, become as good as you can at using sonar. You won't be sorry.

Yes, the parade of new technology will continue to march into winter sports shows all over the country. Every year, four-color advertisements will herald the arrival of a new day in fishing sonar. This is good, as long as the advancements are meaningful and useful to you as a fisherman. But realize one very important thing: no matter what bells

Figure 1—It takes time to become proficient with sonar. Dig in to the study of how it works, and then practice with your sonar unit on the water. It will make your fishing more fun, not more complicated!

and whistles they add to a sonar unit, no matter whether it displays information to you on a flasher dial, on paper, with liquid crystal, video or lazer beams, the way the information got to the screen will remain the same.

That is why the information in this book about how sonar works, and how to use it, will never become outdated. Don't fear that you have spent your money on a sonar book you will have to th row out when next year's models hit the shelves. Read this information, learn it and keep it somewhere handy so you can teach yourself to get the most out of the wonderful thing they call fishing sonar.

Let me tell you a story about one of the best fishermen I know. In the middle of his life, he quit his job in the big city and moved to Minnesota. He did this for one reason and one reason only: so he could fish every day all summer, after and before work, and on the weekends.

After he got settled into his house, I gave him a couple days and then called him to see how he was getting along.

"So," I began, "how do you like these Minnesota lakes?"

"Fantastic," he answered, enthusiasm spilling through the phone lines. "I've been out every day since I got here and I like what I see so far."

"Have you caught any good fish?" I asked.

"I haven't fished yet," he answered. "It's taking me awhile to get to know these lakes with my locator."

This man, as I said, is one of the best fishermen I know.

I rest my case.

Chapter 2
The history of sonar

I was at a sports show in 1979, walking up and down the rows of products and resort booths, talking to people and finding out what was new. I have a habit of listening out of one ear to what other fishermen are saying, so I couldn't help but pick up a conversation one booth over, concerning how to interpret graph paper readings.

Paper graphs were being used by only a small minority of fishermen. In fact, at that time they were considered so deadly that some politicians were trying to get their use in fishing situations banned! But, it was a strange time in the evolution of sonar. That small minority of hardcore graph users was starting to stretch the truth a bit about what those units were capable of telling them.

"Now, you see these big hooks?" the expert said to his buddy. "Those are chinooks. And you see these markings down here? Those are lake trout."

Oh boy. Here was a guy, who hadn't even made the graph tape in question, boldly proclaiming what species of fish were on the paper. How was that poor beginner ever going to understand how to use graphs, when he wasn't even given the out-of-bounds markers? I suspect similar stories were being told in many other locations about that time, and probably still are.

Sonar units aren't capable of distinguishing species of fish. They can give you a relative indication of a fish's size, whether it is schooled up or alone, and how close it is to baitfish and structure. But as for whether it's a lake trout or a chinook or a smallmouth bass, male or female? No way. Yes, a good fisherman—who knows what type of areas certain species of fish hold in—can make an educated guess that "those are *probably* lake trout." But only on the basis of information used in conjunction with the sonar unit, not solely from information displayed on the screen.

Anglers who expect too much from sonar will never appreciate its truly astounding capabilities. Before Carl Lowrance and his two sons laid the groundwork and then developed modern fishing sonar, lakes were "mapped out" by fishermen who bounced heavy weights off the bottom. That way, in a few weeks, they could get a very rough idea of the depths of various portions of *one* lake. Not very fun, precise or efficient.

To get an appreciation for how far we have come with sonar techno-logy, and what these units *can* do that is so extraordinary, we have to look back to the beginning.

And it's not far back, even to the very beginning.

Just a few short years ago, during the pre-sonar age, "serious" fishing meant casting for hours at visible cover, hoping to catch a decent fish.

Actually, the military had been using early sonar units for doing crude mapping, and for ocean navigation, years before the units became available to the inland fisherman. What it took for sonar to come to the average freshwater angler was, well, a fishing family and its revolutionary impatience.

To understand what I mean by "revolutionary impatience," you need to recall or learn of the mainstream of fishing thought in the 1940s and 50s. Fishing, in those days, was not a quazi-science like it is today. There were no fancy bass boats or any of the electronic fishing devices that hang today like ornaments from the deck of every serious angler's floating fish attacker. Americans were wrapped up in other serious business, like winning and staying out of wars. Fishing was a virgin recreational activity, not much changed from the days of Izaak Walton.

In the mid-South, in fact, "serious" fishing, which in essence meant casting for hours at untold miles of shoreline stumps, hoping to intercept a black bass, was something reserved for macho men with strong forearms and weak minds. Families, when they fished, sat in one place for hours and angled peacefully for crappies, white bass or catfish. If you didn't like sitting still for so long, you quit fishing and went for a drive in the car. Prevailing opinion, reinforced by the only solid evidence anglers had, said you anchored at a known fish hotspot (somewhere you'd caught fish before), and "waited for them to bite."

The Carl Lowrance family was no different from any other. Except for one thing: Mrs. Lowrance and the kids weren't buying the old notion. 'Are you sure the fish are here?' she would ask her husband. 'How do you know?' one of the kids would inquire.

After feeling badgered for a time, Carl Lowrance began to wonder, too. It was the beginning of a revolution that would change sportfishing forever.

Carl's mind grew restless for the answers to the fishing puzzles. Maybe there is something better we could be doing, he thought, a way to guarantee we are fishing where fish are. He became serious, you might say, about becoming a better fisherman.

Identifying a problem never solves it, of course. This was a complex subject, that was going to require a lot of research to even begin to understand. The Lowrance family went right to the heart of the matter—into the fish's world.

A restless mind looks for answers, and when the entire Lowrance family searched for a way to know fish were present where they were fishing, a whole new era of angling was the result. Carl Lowrance, shown here in a rare photo from the "early days," certainly found the bass home on this trip!

Carl purchased complete sets of scuba gear and an air compressor. The eyes for his research would belong to his two sons, Darrell and Arlen. You might think it took some bribing to get the boys into the water for hours and hours of observation, but that was far from the case. All through their younger years, the sons were serious swimmers and competitive springboard divers, who raised their own money (matched equally by their father's) for snorkeling gear.

They grabbed at the chance to see what the heck was down there.

Carl occasionally dived with the boys, in fact, but ear trouble forced him to give it up. The Lowrances were some of the first divers in the Midwest, joining the Kansas City Frogmen club soon after it was formed. They got their basic instruction from the Frogmen, then became serious and accomplished divers who spent a lot of time under water, all in the pursuit of knowledge about fish movements and behavior.

"It was a fascinating period," recalls Darrell Lowrance. "Arlen and I would spend a lot of time moving along various structures, and were quite surprised in many cases to not find fish in spots you would normally expect them to be. During and after fishing trips, the three of us would spend hours talking about what we knew, and making guesses about what we didn't. Our observations enabled us to come up with some of the earliest theories on structure fishing.

"I'll never forget the first time we ever saw a school of big black bass. It was on Bull Shoals Reservoir. (Because it was the clearest lake near their Joplin, MO home, Bull Shoals was the Lowrance's main 'study lake.' But they also spent a lot of time on Tenkiller and the Honey Creek arm of Grand Lake, among others.) Down in about 15 feet of water we came onto a bunch of fish that looked to be all about six or eight pounds. We couldn't believe it. At that time, it was the rare hero who caught a six or eight pound bass, and here were a whole bunch of them! Bass weren't supposed to be schooling fish. Everybody told us that bass were loners, that they found their favorite stump in shallow water and sat and guarded that stump for the rest of their lives. And if *we* didn't believe what we saw, we were sure nobody else would believe us, either.

"But what also got to us was that we could return to that exact spot the next day and there wouldn't be any fish! Our diving was uncovering some things about fish behavior that challenged everything we'd ever heard or read. It made us realize how many factors must influence fish location, and made us realize that the whole study of fishing was more complicated than we even thought."

As pioneers before them have discovered, the Lowrances became aware that they had opened the lid on a huge untapped puzzle. Every answer they came up with raised 10 new questions. But they also did a lot of thinking about something else: it wasn't going to prove efficient in the long run to have a pair of divers following the boat around, relaying information on water depth, bottom composition, amount of cover, and presence or absence of fish.

The diving observations of the Lowrances made them realize that many times, even in areas you would expect to find fish, there would be "none at home."

"We had come up with a lot of ideas and theories concerning fish schooling and fish habits, but we still didn't have an answer to the big question on our minds. My father kept coming back to the concept of a device that would be able to show us fish, so we wouldn't have to spend so much time fishing where there weren't any fish. He wanted to have some kind of instrument that would allow him to move around a structure until he found a place where at least the fish were 'home.' That way, he could fish with more piece of mind, knowing fish were in the vicinity. Then, he could spend his time worrying about whether he was using the right colored lure and things like that."

It has always been this spirit of inventiveness, this desire to "build a better mousetrap" that has led to great advances. In the case of fishing sonar, it was no different. Carl Lowrance didn't rest until he was out there fishing with one of those devices.

"We were generally aware that there was sonar for depth sounding," said Darrell, "and we had gotten all the literature on the various units that at that time were being used in the ocean. We located a boat that had a depth-sounding machine on board, and went out on it for a demonstration. We could see rough bottom contours, but we couldn't see anything that we were satisfied were fish.

"In fact, all the manuals that came with sonar devices in those days said that it was basically impossible to see fish. They said that *if* you passed over a large school of large fish, you might get an indistinct blob or flashing—most of them were flashers—on the display."

As you may have gathered from the core of the early intent, the Lowrances set out to create a "fish finder" more than a "structure finder." They wanted something to show them fish, because they assumed they could find the fish's likely locations.

21

No doubt they could, on lakes they already knew. But what about lakes they'd never been to before? What about future generations of anglers, who would learn to fish lakes they'd never seen before? Today, even with ultra-sophisticated sonar units, we often use sonar primarily for helping us locate areas of the lake that should hold fish—and only secondarily for finding fish.

In the mid 1950s, the Lowrances stood a breath away from developing an instrument that would change fishing forever, in more ways than they could know.

Once they had a firm idea of the type of machine they wanted to develop, the Lowrances sat down and did their scientific homework.

"We did quite a bit of just basic study and research," Darrell Lowrance said. "We got our hands on everything we could find concerning the propogation of sound through water. When I talk about sound in this sense, I am speaking of ultrasonic sound (above the range of human hearing). We learned that the commercial type sonar being used for depth-finding purposes in the ocean were commonly 28-50 kilohertz in frequency.

"Now, as we also learned, being of this relatively low frequency, these early sonar units were adequate for what they were being used for, but would not be particularly good for inland freshwater fishing. The lower frequencies meant that early sonar units had what we now term poor resolution. They had a very long pulse width, or sound wave, which was helpful for getting the signal through very deep water and back to the receiver. You see, these units were built for use in water up to and deeper than 1,000 feet. But, because of such long pulse widths, these units would blend fish, baitfish, weeds, and the bottom signal together if they were within about five to six feet of each other!

"With this type of unit, most fish blended with the bottom reading and simply appeared as one more hump on the bottom contour, and suspended fish, even large fish, if they were within five or six feet of other fish or a group of baitfish, just showed up as an indistinct cloud or blob. So, in designing our units—which were intended for relatively shallower water and specifically for fishing—we wanted to be able to show individual fish, as well as exact bottom contours, and their exact depths. We decided to go to a much higher frequency of 200 kilohertz. That's about 10 times higher than the human ear can hear.

"Because of the higher frequency, we were able to use a much smaller transducer, with much smaller crystals. In fact, we went to a piezoelectric crystal, the first of its type to be used for depth sounding. At the time, transducers were very large and made with the old wire-wound, magneto, restrictive type design."

The smaller transducers, with their high frequency, put out an extremely short sound wave, or pulse length. Even with their early units, the Lowrances were able to separate fish from the bottom or from other fish as long as they were more than six inches apart!

But, having the idea and the technology to develop high-frequency sonar for the freshwater fisherman was one thing. There was the small matter of making it lightweight and portable.

Fishing sonar has come a long way in a short time, since the days the Lowrances were studying everything they could get their hands on that could help them develop a unit for the average fisherman. Today, there are many manufacturers of sonar units, offering everything from flashers to paper graphs, liquid crystal and video.

"The small boats being commonly used for fishing at that time," Darrell said, "were open aluminum boats without the fancy 12-volt battery systems on board that you see so much these days. So, it was necessary for us to build a small sonar instrument that had low power consumption, that could work off of small dry-cell batteries.

"The way we accomplished this was by designing a circuit that used transistors rather than vacuum tubes. That was the breakthrough that made it possible to have a small, portable sonar for inland fishing boats."

In the summer of 1957, they started theorizing and working on the design of a small, portable sonar unit for the inland fisherman. But there were two more obstacles, and big ones they were.

Number one, they had to take their concepts and theories and build them into a machine that would do what they wanted it to—show individual fish and their exact depth (along with the exact depth of the bottom).

They took their ideas to a tiny company on the West Coast. From that plant came the very first Lowrance sonar unit, housed in a blue, chipped fiberglass case. There were only 1,000 of these made, and many didn't work. Many of those that did were damaged in shipping, because the fiberglass case couldn't withstand much bouncing around.

After about six months of this frustration, the Lowrances switched their manufacturing contract to a large firm that began building sonar units in a grey steel casing. A small number of the grey units were made before they began painting the housings red, and the early "Red Box" was born.

But these units didn't fare any better than the fiberglass ones did, according to Darrell Lowrance. Despite the almost indestructible case, the electronic components were of poor quality, and many of the sets didn't even light up when turned on.

Faced with growing impatience over these quality control and distribution problems, the Lowrances decided in 1959 that they would have to build the units themselves if they were going to get what they wanted. They went to work over the summer, and by fall, the first sonar unit that actually *worked* was being introduced to anglers.

This time, the case was military grade aluminum. The color was green. And anyone at all familiar with the history of fishing sonar has heard of the "Green Box."

"Finally," Darrell Lowrance said, "we had a unit that worked. They worked great. We were fanatics about quality. They all got checked at every step, and each unit had a burn-in test." (Faulty electronics usually go bad within a short time. To test for defective parts, a machine is turned on and left running for a number of hours. This is still done to a measured percentage of units at the factory today, ensuring that there are no statistically significant defaults in the manufacturing process.)

So, the Lowrances were out on the market with their dream machine. It did what they wanted it to do. It sounds like the ending to a happy story, but this one's far from over. By this time, Carl Lowrance had sold off three successful trucking and produce businesses, and borrowed money against virtually every other possession he had. On top of that, the heavy losses suffered through the early manufacturing and delivery troubles left them in a huge financial hole.

Still, it would have been an easy climb out, except for one last thing. The final obstacle, one they hadn't considered, was the feeling among the public that this "fish finder" was a hoax. *What do you mean, something that sends sound waves down through the water? And the sound waves are something that we can't hear? Oh, I see. Yeah, right. Who are these guys?*

You get the idea. And if you were one of the doubters, don't you feel silly now?

"My father's least favorite saying," Darrell Lowrance remembers, "is that one that says 'if you build a bettter mousetrap the world will beat a path to your door.' We were beating a path to the fishermen's doors and they wouldn't let us in. I can remember working in the sporting goods departments of Sears stores, demonstrating the sonar equipment to customers. Many of them would just come up and laugh, saying we were trying to pull their legs. At times, we felt like the old medicine wagon barkers.

"With a new concept like this, we found it very difficult to change people's habits. They were used to fishing a certain way, and they just didn't believe these things were going to work. The guides saw them as a threat, and the local fishing heros hoped they wouldn't work, so they could continue to keep their fishing secrets to themselves."

Stretched to the breaking point financially, the Lowrances had to come up with a plan, or their dream would soon go up in smoke. Their sonar units were selling for $150 or more in 1959-60, which was far and away the most expensive item—save for fancy shotguns and rifles—in any sporting goods inventory. They identified two key markets, Minneapolis, Minnesota and Dallas, Texas. Here, they felt, were high numbers of fishermen per capita, with a reputation for being somewhat innovative in their fishing techniques.

Fanatical about quality, the Lowrance name, and now Eagle as well, has become synonymous with reliable performance to a throng of serious fishermen.

The Lowrance's strategy was to take the owner or buyer of better sporting goods stores out on the water, and teach them to use the Green Box. They hoped it would lead to the enthusiastic selling of their product.

"We found that they realized what these things could do, once we showed them," Darrell said. "The owners would buy a unit for themselves, but felt the product was too expensive for their customers. Most wouldn't stock any, so the sales we got were from the owner showing his personal unit to customers, and then taking special orders if the customer wanted one."

It was a long, slow road. A trip to New York in the early 1960s by Carl and his wife helped turn public attitude in their favor. He stayed until he had met with the fishing editors from *Sports Afield, Field & Stream, Outdoor Life* and *True* magazines. He left each of them a unit, showed them how to use it, and tried to impress upon them how he felt the machine was going to change fishing for the better, if the fishermen would just learn to believe in it and use it.

Positive editorial support was critical for convincing skeptical fishermen that the newfangled gadget being touted by the Lowrances would actually help them in their fishing.

The resulting favorable press, along with slowly climbing sales, helped Lowrance Electronics show its first profit, of about $2,000, in 1964. By then, the fishing habits of many serious anglers had been reformed forever. The enjoyment of their invention had begun almost immediately, though, for the Lowrances themselves. Because they were so familiar with the technology and capabilities of sonar, they were the first to find the joys of electronic fishing.

"It was exciting," remembers Darrell, speaking about their own fishing with the new devices. "We of course tested our units, and spent a lot of time scuba diving to verify what we saw on the flasher dial. We sure didn't mean for this thing to be a secret, but I guess we were the only ones taking advantage of it for a long time."

There were many discoveries along the way, but one really stands out in Darrell's memory.

"One thing that was really something," he said, "was the time we were fishing in front of the dam on Grand Lake, in 1958. We left the dam and started crossing the middle of the lake, heading for a nearby cove. Way out in the middle of the lake (it was actually right over the old river channel), we started seeing blips, from about 8-12 feet down. We could go a long ways and they would still be there. We circled back into them and started fishing, and almost immediately began catching white bass. Until then, *nobody ever* fished out in the middle of the lake. We couldn't believe what we had found. Since then, we have found this to be one of the most reliable summer patterns on reservoirs all over the South, for white bass, crappies and even channel catfish.

"To this day, it's one of my father's favorite methods of fishing."

I don't have to wonder why.

About this same time, a young Minnesota kid was trying his heart out to learn how to fish, and to understand what goes on under the visible surface of the water. To him, the idea of a machine that would instantly display depth and bottom density, and even show fish, was worth more than anything else he could think of at the moment. He was an early believer, you might say. If that sonar machine could do half of what they said it could, it didn't matter what the price was.

That's why, in 1959, a kid named Babe Winkelman was one of the first in line to buy the Lowrance Red Box.

Chapter 3
Sonar 101: Understanding how it works

The Principles of Sonar.

No matter how we try to disguise the name for this chapter, it ends up sounding like one of those classes you would get out of if you could find a way.

In fact, I learned at a very early age to avoid anything that had the word "principle" in it anywhere. It reminds me of getting to the first day of Little League baseball practice and having the coach tell us we're "not going to play a game for the first three years. You guys are going to be working on the fundamentals until you're old enough to shave."

It makes you want to quit before you ever start.

Learning to catch fish with sonar involves learning how sonar works. But I promise, you can digest this chapter before you need to change your socks.

Let's make this as much fun as possible. Pretend we are milling around the halls, waiting for our class, Principles of Sonar 101, to start. We are all serious fishermen, and even though we realize we need to learn the "technical crap," we are anxious to skip right to the good stuff.

After a few minutes, Professor Kilohertz comes around the corner to unlock the door. Before he can even get the key in the lock, the first question comes flying at him from the crowd:

"What I really want to know," the student asks, "is whether I should buy a flasher, liquid crystal, paper graph, video, or what. They all seem to work so differently, and I'm confused as to which would be best for my kind of fishing."

The distinguished Professor Kilohertz, who had predicted this question would arise at some point, is ready with an answer.

"My dear boy," he begins, "first of all, let's get one thing straight. All the various modes of sonar display you just mentioned, the flashers, paper graphs, liquid crystals, videos, and even digital displays, work in precisely the same manner. SONAR is SONAR. Every type of machine on the market operates on the same principles of sending sound waves down into the water, picking up some that bounce back to the surface, and then displaying the signals to you in some form.

"The way the modes differ is in how they display the signals to you. That's the only way they differ significantly. Now, different brands or models can vary in the quality of their sonar performance, but let's not get into that. So, you see, they all show you the same information, more or less. Flashers might be more difficult for the beginner to decipher, but there are many experienced fishermen who prefer them. Graphs, liquid crystals and videos draw you a 'picture' of what's below you, that is easier for many people to understand. But, some liquid crystals have very crude displays that can be confusing.

"The fact remains, however, that all are SOund NAvigation and Ranging (SONAR) devices, meaning that there is only one *type* of unit. There are different display modes, but they are all sonar units, they all work the same way. By the way, for everybody's benefit, we will get deeply into this topic, to help all of you choose the right unit for your type of fishing, in chapter 4."

The guy who asked the question is now staring down, counting the floor tiles. Everybody else is glad they didn't open their mouth yet. The rest of us look at each other with the old "yeah, I knew that" nod of assurance.

The Professor, meanwhile, wiggles the key, opens the door, turns on the lights, and we are soon learning everything we need to know about how sonar works. And, as everybody knows, sonar is sonar.

It's time to buckle down and concentrate.

Power: a critical consideration

If a unit doesn't send out a signal with enough power, nothing else really matters.

You can compare power considerations in a sonar unit's transmitter to the power of a small local, vs. powerful regional, radio station. In town, a small local station comes in loud and clear. But as soon as you get past the outskirts of town, you get interference from various electrical sources, such as electrical lines, power lines, phone lines and every other thing. There gets to be so much static that eventually you can't even hear the signal. You can be listening to your favorite song and it'll sound like a bad bus ride.

A low-power sonar unit presents the same problem to the fisherman. To continue the analogy, let's say you are struggling along, trying to keep a low-power radio station tuned in because you happen to like the song, or are trying to listen to the ballgame. As you reach the limits of the station's broadcast range, interference makes it almost impossible to keep the sound coming through. To compensate, you turn the volume knob way up on your radio. You can still hear the song, but barely—and the increased volume of all the static makes listening a real chore.

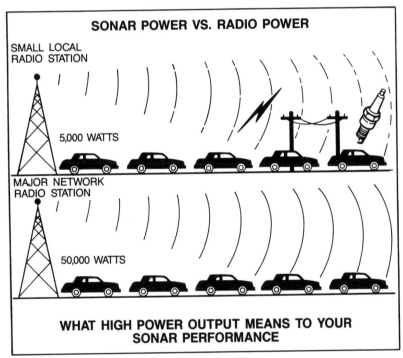

Figure 2—Just like low-power radio stations are only capable of producing clear broadcasts over a limited range, low-power sonar units provide acceptable performance only in shallow water and under ideal conditions. Interference from a variety of sources drowns sonar performance, just as it does radio signals, unless the source of the desired signal is strong.

You literally can't decifer the strains, or the individual instruments. If you know the song you can "sort of" hear what it is, but what if you were listening to it for the first time?

If you switch over and begin listening to a big, powerful radio station, the signal will be loud and clear. In fact, if you don't turn the volume down, it will blast you into the back seat! With the large station, which is acting as a more powerful transmitter, you can turn down the receiver—your radio—and get a clear, crisp signal with almost no unwanted interference.

Now, isn't that nice? Even if you haven't heard the song before, you can listen to it, understand the words, and hear the various instruments clearly.

Believe me, it isn't any different with fishing sonar units. A powerful transmitter will allow the unit to penetrate even mid-range and deeper water, helping the receiver pick up a clear signal of what's down there: the bottom, weeds, rock humps, fish, baitfish, you name it.

Just as a powerful, clear signal from a radio station makes it easy to study and understand a new song, a powerful and clear signal from a sonar unit makes it possible to study and understand the world of the fish—even on a lake you have never fished before.

RMS vs peak-to-peak power ratings

But the whole topic of power can get very confusing when shopping for a sonar unit. How much power is enough? It's a complicated subject, because the power of the transmitter won't mean much if the unit has a poor receiver. You have got to have a matched set of quality sending and receiving components in order to have a good sonar unit.

Beware of the two separate power ratings you will see on sonar brochures and boxes, peak-to-peak and RMS.

RMS, or *Root Means Square*, is a measure of the average amount of power available for use by the unit, in equivalent DC output. This is the only number that means anything. Peak-to-peak power ratings are nothing more than a sales gimmick thrust upon the poor consumers (and the honest sonar manufacturers) by huckster companies looking for something good to say about poor products. Ignore peak-to-peak power ratings.

How sonar works

Basically, what a sonar unit does is send a sound wave to the bottom of the lake. Now, if the unit doesn't send a strong enough signal to get to the bottom and bounce back up to the sonar unit, it can't do a good job of displaying what's down there. Make sense? Therefore, a low-power sonar unit can be compared to that low-power radio station.

Microchip computer technology has probably been the thing that, above all else, has revolutionized sonar design and performance in the last few years. On the average, units are now smaller, more accurate, have better resolution, and contain many more features, because of microprocessors.

Basically, there are three parts to a sonar unit: the transmitter, transducer and receiver.

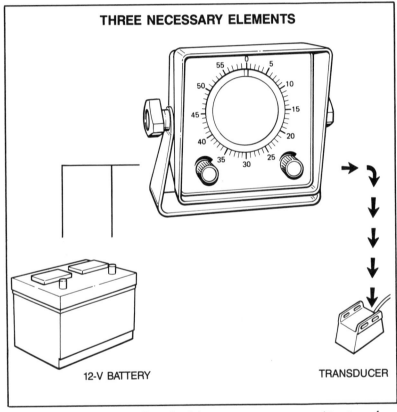

Figure 3—Sonar units are all made of three components: transmitter, transducer and receiver. The transmitter sends an electrical pulse to the transducer, which converts it to sound energy. The sound pulse is sent into the water, where some of it reflects off objects denser than water and returns to the transducer. The returning echoes strike the transducer, which connverts them back to electrical energy, and sends them to the receiver. The receiver, like a car radio, amplifies the signal and displays it on your unit.

First, the transmitter draws an electrical signal from its 12-volt power source, be it the small lantern batteries found in portable locators, or the big marine battery systems common in fishing boats. The transmitter then sends the electrical charge down the line to the transducer.

The transducer is actually a small crystal made of a plate of silver on the top, and on the bottom. When the electrical charge hits the plates of silver, the plates expand and contract in a convex-concave pattern. This expansion-contraction cycle causes the silver to "ring." In the process, the electrical impulse is converted into sound waves that can travel through the water.

There is a housing around the transducer on three sides, which forces the sound waves to go out only through the bottom. The sound waves are sent into the water (Fig. 4). As they travel toward the lake bottom, the signal expands (explaining why your sonar signal covers more bottom area the deeper it goes).

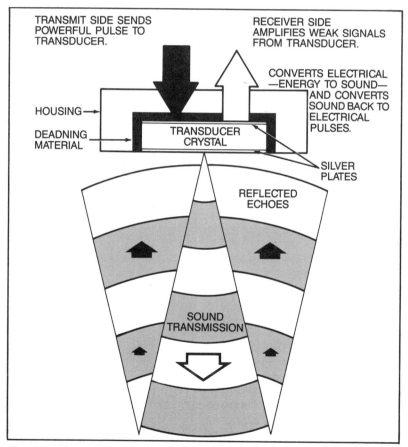

Figure 4—Your sonar unit is not going to perform well if it doesn't have both a powerful transmitter and sensitive receiver. This we might call "total system performance." The quality of the receiver is measured in its ability to gather and display the "tiny" signals, such as those bouncing back from a little baitfish.

You may think that a continous series of signals is being sent and received by the unit. But, believe it or not, one signal is sent down and received back before another is sent. It happens incredibly fast, about 10 times per second on the average! That is really cookin'.

How the pulses "find" targets

Whenever the sound impulses hit anything more dense than water, either the bottom or an object (including fish!), some of them get reflected back and received by the transducer.

(In fact, that brings us to a definition: anything that is dense enough to reflect the sound impulses sent out by the sonar unit is called a *target*. Targets are such things as fish, baitfish, plankton, submerged brush, weeds, etc. Throughout the book, you will see the term target, so you should know what it means.)

Now, if you have been following carefully, you'll realize that those are reflected *sound* waves coming back to the transducer. Your sonar unit is not capable of displaying sound waves for you. They have to be converted back into electrical impulses. This is done by the transducer. Then, the electrical charge is sent to the receiver, or signal processor, the third part of the sonar unit.

The amount of time it took for the signal to go down and bounce back to the transducer is calculated by the sonar unit, amplified by the receiver, and displayed on the screen or dial.

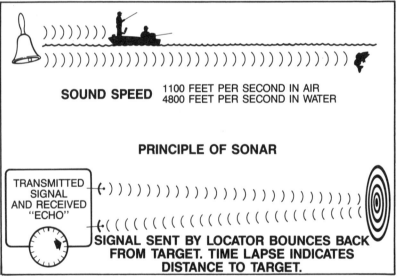

Figure 5—Sound travels at 4800 feet per second in water, four times faster than in air. When sound pulses strike anything of different density than water (such as fish or the bottom), an echo is reflected. Sonar units are able to accurately calculate the amount of time it takes for the return echoes to get to the unit, and therefore can display the depth of the bottom and objects between the surface and the bottom.

34

That describes how the unit "knows" the signal from a suspended fish is four feet off the bottom, the cloud of baitfish is scattered from six to eight feet off the bottom, and at exactly what depth the bottom is.

And it does it at an average speed, or *repetition rate* of 10 times every second!

(All sonar units work this way. Remember, no matter what display mode your sonar unit uses to show the information to you, be it on a flasher dial, paper graph, liquid crystal, video, or whatever else anybody invents in the meantime, the principle of sonar operation will forever remain the same.)

Are sonar signals loud enough to scare fish?

This is a good question! For years, the talk at the boat launching ramp and sports shows has gone back and forth. Many people believe that sonar signals scare fish.

Well, the answer is definitely NO. They don't scare fish. Sonar pulses are outside the range of a fish's hearing, just as an ultrasonic dog whistle is to humans.

Figure 6 shows an example of how this idea got started. Before we had sonar, we couldn't observe the reaction of fish as our boat came over them. Now, with picture-type sonar (paper graphs, liquid crystal and video), we can see how fish often get jumpy and scoot off to the side or into deeper water. Initially, fishermen assumed it was the sonar signals alerting the fish; in reality, it's the boat that causes the fish to react.

No matter what anybody tells you, it's impossible for that sonar unit to spook fish.

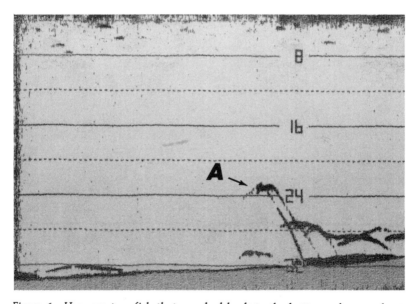

Figure 6—Here are two fish that spooked back to the bottom when my boat approached over them (A). It is the boat, not the sonar signals, that makes the fish jumpy.

Now that we understand how sonar works, let's take a look at how a sonar unit is able to distinguish among things that are fairly close together, and give you a separate display of each.

In other words, how is your unit able to show you that the bottom is at 22 feet, there is a fish of some kind holding a foot off the bottom, and there are baitfish about three feet above the big fish?

The answer is in the *resolution* of the unit.

Resolution, or the ability to separate targets, is determined by the length (sometimes referred to as width) of the pulse sent out by the sonar unit. As we mentioned, most modern sonar operates at a high frequency, around 200 kz. High frequency units emit short (narrow) pulses of sound, which enable the sonar unit to distinguish between targets which are much closer together than early sonar units could.

To determine the resolution of a given unit, find its pulse length. For instance, a unit like Eagle's Z-15 paper graph operates at 192 khz., which means it sends out 12-inch sound pulses. Now, divide the length of each sound pulse by two and you know how close two things can be and still get separated on the display of your unit.

In this case, the Eagle unit's "dead band" is six inches. It can separate a fish from the bottom reading as long as the fish is at least six inches off the bottom, and can show you two fish that are more than six inches apart as two separate fish rather than one "blended" reading. (Just for your information, resolution of most good flashers today is about four to six inches.)

The shorter the pulse length, the better the resolution. Manufacturers will vary on this, so be sure to check out the brand you are thinking of buying before making a decision.

On some of the new computerized paper graphs and liquid crystals, you can actually re-program the pulse length to get a sound pulse as thin as two inches, giving you resolution as fine as one inch!

There are tradeoffs, of course, when you do this. Making a sonar signal narrower also makes it less capable of penetrating deeper water, because it might "fizzle out" before getting to the bottom and back to your unit. But, the good news is that in normal fishing situations (water less than about 60 feet deep), you normally don't encounter this problem.

More good fishermen than you might expect take advantage of this feature. I do it all the time. If you can dial in a little more resolution, and it doesn't cost you any sonar performance, by all means do it. Shop for units that allow you to do this.

Basically, what I'm recommending for freshwater fishing applications is a high-frequency unit operating from 190-200 kHz. There are some very good units designed primarily for ocean fishing, and downrigger trolling on big inland waters like the Great Lakes, that operate at a lower frequency, normally about 50 kHz.

Lower frequency units send out a sound pulse that is longer (wider), and able to penetrate deep water better without *attenuating* or "fizzling

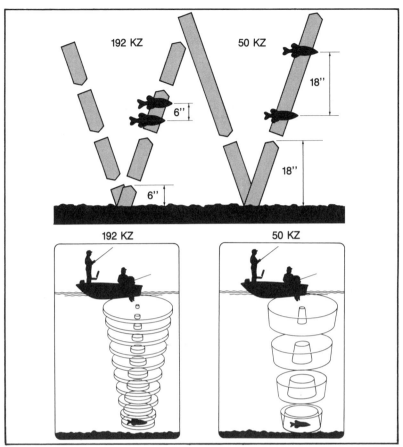

Figure 7—The "thickness" of each sound pulse is determined by the frequency of the unit. High frequency (normally about 200 KHz) units emit short, thin pulses; low frequency (about 50 KHz) units, long pulses. The high frequency units are able to distinguish between "targets" such as fish, or fish and the bottom, much better than low frequency units can.

out." These units are fitted with transducers that produce wide cone angles (more about this in a second), that allow downrigger trollers to track the depth of their lures, and even see fish. But realize that with that lower frequency and accompanying wider cone angle comes a tradeoff: less resolution. Think about that if you are buying a unit mostly for walleye and bass fishing, and only once or twice a year fish the big water, trolling with downriggers.

Many sonar engineers also believe that with lower frequency comes another performance tradeoff: difficulty suppressing unwanted interference. This is enough of a problem, by the way, that 50 kHz units do not operate well at high boat speeds—interference on the display becomes too much.

For most freshwater fishing applications, I'd recommend the higher-frequency units.

What is meant by cone angle?

Actually, we talk about cone angle, but the way the sound is sent out by the transducer is not really a cone-shaped pattern. In reality, it billows out from the transducer in an elliptical pattern, more resembling an inverted water balloon.

In our minds, we have grown accustomed to picturing something akin to an upside-down cone, and that's where the popular name cone angle comes from.

Actually, there is an optimum operating range, that does resemble the theoretical upside-down cone. As you can see in figure 8, the area of maximum sensitivity is approximately the portion of the signal that actually strikes the bottom.

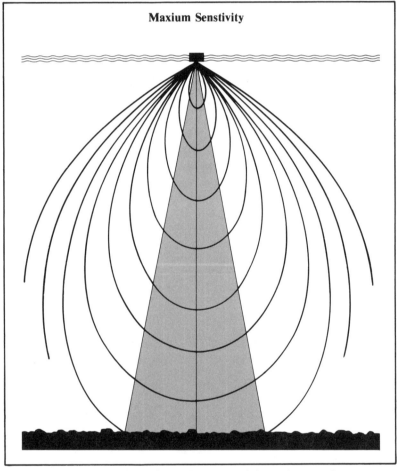

Maxium Senstivity

Figure 8—Actually, the sound impulses emitted from the transducer are not shaped like a cone at all, but more like a water balloon. Although the signal radiates far to all sides, the area of maximum sensitivity (shaded) is where your unit picks up most of the signals it displays to you.

The normal method for figuring and defining cone angle is to begin at a point directly beneath the boat (where the signal is strongest) and move out to all sides until you reach the point where the signal strength has been reduced by half.

The angle described by the outside edges of this "half strength" zone is what manufacturers call the cone angle—be it 8, 16, 20, 22, 45 degrees, or whatever.

The diameter of the crystal in the transducer, and the frequency of the sonar unit, both affect the cone angle. The diameter of the transducer is inversely proportional to the cone angle it naturally produces. In other words, smaller diameter transducers produce a wider cone angle, and larger transducers a narrower cone angle.

As I said, lower-frequency sonar units emit a wider sound pulse, that penetrates deep water well. But, because the pulse is wider, those units can't distinguish between sonar targets that are close together as well as narrower pulses can. Higher frequency sonar units send out narrow beams of signal, which do a great job of distinguishing between targets (fish, the bottom, weeds, etc.) that are close together.

Basically, with the high-frequency (190-200 kHz) units I have recommended for freshwater fishing, a one-inch transducer will give off a cone angle of about 22 degrees; a two-inch transducer, about eight degrees.

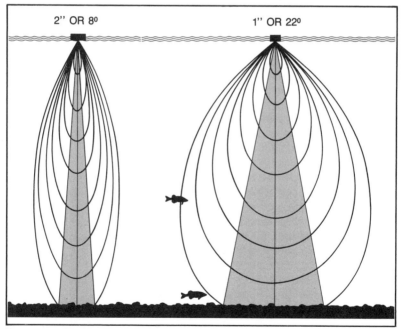

Figure 9—The standard method for measuring cone angle is to move out from the point of strongest signal (directly below the boat), until arriving at a signal strength half that amount. Basically, one-inch transducers reach that point at about 22 degrees, and two-inch transducers at about eight degrees, at least on high-frequency units.

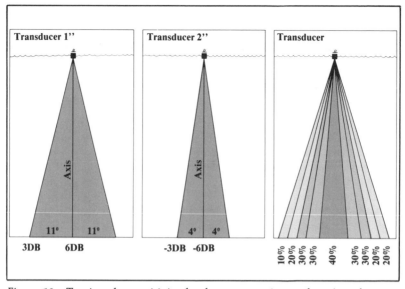

Figure 10—Turning the sensitivity knob up to maximum doesn't make your sonar unit more sensitive! As a matter of fact, when you turn the unit all the way up, the outer areas of the sound waves inevitably billow out and away, never reaching the lake bottom.

Remember now, these measurements are *definitions* of the cone angle. In the real world, the actual area your signal is strong enough to draw from varies depending on many factors, including bottom density.

If you are fishing over a super-hard bottom, for example, that one-inch transducer might be feeding you information from a wider-than-normal range, and you might be getting effectively a 35-degree cone angle or something. Is this better than seeing less of the bottom?

Yes and no.

In some instances, it can be a disadvantage to see more of the surrounding area. If you are showing fish on your flasher or graph, for example, and the unit is picking up signals from 35 or 40 degrees, it can be tougher than normal to zero in on exactly where those fish are in relation to your boat. And the same goes for finding little indentations in the bottom contour. The wider the cone angle, the less minute detail the readout can show you.

With all these factors considered, I would recommend a 20-22 degree cone angle transducer for most freshwater fishing conditions. The average angler after bass, walleyes, northerns, muskies, panfish, etc. will find these transducers give him a wide enough look at the bottom, while not being so wide as to show him too much information at once. It is really the best all-around choice for the kind of fishing most of us do.

When, however, is wider better? In the case of the recently-developed Eagle sonars which give you a 66-degree angle of viewing coverage, that's when! These liquid crystal sonars feed you a 22-degree view of the bottom (from directly below the boat), then another 22 degrees to each side from which fish can be seen. You can selectively scan left, center or right to determine which side of the boat fish are. This is a useful innovation in sonar technology that you should look at if you are shopping for a new unit.

You notice I haven't said much about the 8-degree cone. If you fish most of the time in less than 70-80 feet of water (and who doesn't, most of the time?), the 20-22 degree cone angle will be the best choice. If you fish most of the time deeper than that, you might be better off with the narrower beam offered by the 8-degree cone.

If you're fishing in about 15-30 feet of water, for example, where many people spend a great deal of time, the 22-degree cone will give you a wide enough look at the underwater surroundings to give you an idea of the contours, how many fish are down there, what the fish seem to be doing in reaction to what you are doing, etc. In those depths, the 8-degree cone proves to be too narrow, despite being excellent for showing little nooks and crannies in the bottom structure.

In a way, fishing shallow and medium depths with an 8-degree cone is like trying to read a billboard with a magnifying glass. Sure, you can see every grain in every letter, and you can see where the guys didn't put the paper on straight when they put the billboard together, but you can't read the message as well as if you step back and take a look with your naked eye.

In these cases, the 22-degree cone offers you a more "valuable and meaningful" look at the bottom.

But, run your boat out to 120 feet of water and start fishing with the 22-degree cone angle. In this case, the transducer might be gathering and showing you too much information and confusing you. In really deep water, an 8-degree cone might be a better choice.

So what if you spend a good deal of time doing both? Maybe your boat goes out on smaller lakes in search of bass and walleyes, and you also spend a few weeks a year trolling and jigging in very deep water. What do you do then? You can't very well have a sonar unit for both.

But you can have a transducer for both situations.

The answer to the need for "both" is to install a switching box and both 8- and 22-degree cone angle transducers in your boat. The switching box makes it a simple matter of flipping a switch to activate either transducer, and is an excellent solution to this dilemma.

Many good marine dealers, electronics dealers and boat repair outfits can advise you as to cost and feasibility of installing a switching box in your boat.

Another thing to think about are the new "dual frequency" and "dual beam" transducers available for some makes of sonar. In these, you have two different cone angles in the same transducer.

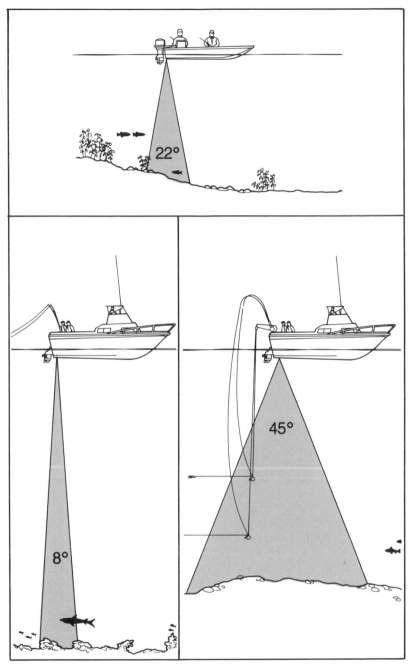

Figure 11—A 22-degree cone angle is preferred for most inland fishing. But, if you do a lot of ocean fishing or freshwater angling in water deeper than 100 feet, an eight-degree cone might work best for you. For downrigger trolling, you might consider a 45-degree cone angle unit that allows you to track downrigger balls and fish activity on your sonar unit.

About the only time I would recommend a 45-degree cone is for downrigger fishermen who want to take in a great deal of the bottom so they can track their downriggers, set lures to exact depths, and easily chart fish activity around their baits.

Remember, those wider cone angles might give you a view of a bigger area, but you sacrifice the ability to zero in on specifics! As with so many things in life, there are tradeoffs to be made in deciding how wide a cone angle to go with.

I think a chart would help us compare how much of the bottom, at various depths, different cone angles cover.

TABLE 1 — *Approximate coverage of various cone angles at different depths.*

8 Degree Cone		22 Degree Cone		45 Degree Cone	
Depth	Coverage	Depth	Coverage	Depth	Coverage
15'	2' diam. circle	15'	5' circle	15'	12.5' circle
30'	4' circle	30'	10' circle	30'	25' circle
60'	8' circle	60'	20' circle	60'	50' circle

Field tuning: seeing everything

Remember how power in a sonar unit is similar to power in a radio station? We are all familiar with turning the sound up or down on a radio, as we tune in more or less powerful stations, or as we pull off the freeway and stop at a stop sign. The highway noise is suddenly down to nothing, and the volume level that was comfortable going 55 m.p.h. with the windows rolled down now threatens to make you deaf in seconds!

What you do, when turning the volume up and down on your car radio, we can call *field tuning* the radio. It becomes second nature once you learn it. That way, you won't get scared when I tell you you need to learn to field tune your sonar unit for the different depths of water, bottom densities, etc. you encounter while fishing.

Field tuning, or adjusting the sensitivity (and sometimes suppression), is the thing that actually determines how effectively your unit is showing you what's down there at the moment.

Follow along with this discussion by looking at figure 13. As you can see, when you turn on the flasher, no matter how low, you will get a signal at zero. If you are over 20 feet of water, as we are in this example, it is pretty simple to turn up the sensitivity until you get a reading at the 20-foot mark on the flasher's scale.

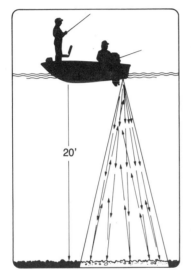 

Figure 13—It's not enough to turn up a flasher until you get just the bottom reading. Continue increasing the sensitivity until you get a second echo at twice the bottom depth. The lake bottom is 20 feet in this example, and the double echo shows up at 40 feet. Now, the unit is tuned to pick up the little signals, such as gamefish, baitfish, weeds and other cover.

To most anglers, this is where they stop. This is where they make their biggest mistake. Set to only this level, the sensitivity is too low to show the fisherman the incredible detail the unit is capable of showing them.

I don't know whether people are afraid of turning the "volume" up too high, get intimidated by all the "extra blips" they get when they do, or what, but most fishermen go along for years in this manner, using a very advanced sonar unit to show them only how deep the water is.

To me, it's like using a microwave oven for a clock.

To *properly* field tune the flasher in this example, the fisherman should continue to turn the sensitivity up until a "second echo" appears on the screen. A second echo is a reading at twice the bottom depth, that indicates you have turned up the gain (sensitivity and gain mean the same thing) high enough that your signal is getting to the bottom, bouncing back to the sonar unit, back down to the bottom again, and reflecting back a second time.

Set this high, the unit is sensitive enough *at that moment* to pick up tiny baitfish, weeds, and of course, gamefish.

Why do you have to continue to turn the sensitivity up when you have already found the bottom? Good question.

The signal reflecting back from the bottom is normally the strongest one received by the unit. But, the quality of the receiver is measured not by its ability to gather and display the bottom reading only—any two-bit unit can do that for you—but to go beyond that and detect the *weaker* signals as well.

The signal bouncing off the back of a three-inch perch, for example, is certainly not going to be as dramatic as that bouncing off the bottom. So you must *tune* the receiver, turn it up, make it more sensitive, whatever you want to call it, so that it picks up those weak signals too.

The double bottom echo is the key thing to look for. When you have that, you know that the receiver is tuned for the fishing situation you are in at the moment.

This is the ideal setting to strive for. And don't think this works only with flashers. You need to do the same thing, the same way, with a paper graph, liquid crystal or video sonar.

As you run around the lake, your boat comes over a variety of conditions. You move into deeper or shallower water, over hard rock and then sand and then mucky bottoms, in and out of weedy areas. As you move, you must continue to re-tune the unit for maximum performance under the various conditions.

As conditions change considerably, you have to learn to field tune your sonar unit for those changing conditions. Here, I am reaching in to back off the sensitivity on my paper graph because I'm coming in to shallow water.

As you come into shallower water or over harder bottom, the signal has a much easier time getting down and back, so more sound waves return to the transducer and get displayed by the unit. Consequently, you can usually have the sensitivity, or gain, turned down from where you need it when you are over softer bottom, or in deep water.

This is a very important concept to understand fully. The harder bottom densities reflect back more sound waves. Consequently, the signal being displayed on a flasher unit is much wider, and brighter, than that returning from a lake bottom of softer density, such as mud. Much or most of the sound waves are absorbed by soft, organic type bottoms, giving you a very thin, pale bottom signal display in comparison to that given off by a good, hard bottom.

I hope this helps you understand the need for constantly re-tuning the sonar unit as you go from spot to spot in a day of fishing.

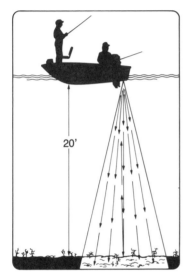 

Figure 14—Over a soft, mucky bottom, or where there is a lot of decayed vegetation, you'll receive a thin, weak signal. Usually, the second echo will fade out. Understanding how these soft bottoms display allows you to quickly find areas of harder bottom, by watching for the second echo to return.

But, are there times when you might want to leave the sensitivity at a constant setting, to check for variations in the lake's underwater structure? You bet.

Using this idea, I often scout a lake, looking for differences in bottom densities as well as key structural things like points, sunken islands, etc.

To do this, go out on a lake and find an area with fairly hard bottom. If the water is clear, it will be a simple matter to locate a 10 foot deep rocky area, for example. When you *know* you are over hard bottom, field tune your sonar unit for the double echo reading.

Now, leave your sonar unit set as it is, and begin motoring at medium speed all over the lake in grid patterns. As you now know, the signal from a flasher shows up brighter and wider when you are over harder bottom, and thinner and weaker over softer, or mucky bottoms.

You will soon become accustomed to seeing your display go brighter and dimmer, thicker and thinner, and know when your boat is over bottom contents of different densities. You will soon teach yourself to locate large areas of sand, huge mud flats, points that drop steeply into mud basins, etc.

Concentrate, while doing this, on finding *exactly* where the bottom densities change. Those *edges*, where two densities meet, such as where sand meets rock or gravel, are very important spots to check out. They often hold concentrations of fish.

Changes in bottom density are structure, just as much as points and stumps are structure. In some lakes, in fact, where the entire basin doesn't have a lot of dramatic changes in depth or a lot of cover, subtle changes in bottom density might be the main pieces of "structure" that fish in that body of water have to relate to.

Now you're using your sonar for more than a "clock!"

(By the way, this is just a brief mention of some of the strategies for putting sonar to proper use. Please carefully study chapter 8, an in-depth look at this very important subject.)

Remember, after you have located a certain area you want to fish, you should forget about the idea of leaving the sonar unit tuned to the same level it was for the 10 foot rock shelf (unless you are on another one). In order to set your unit to a sensitivity level capable of showing you baitfish, weeds, fish and other subtle targets, you need to fine tune. When you were motoring around checking out the lake, you weren't necessarily looking for every little detail, but now you are.

Filtering interference: the good and bad in suppression

"Targets" are not the only things that show up on the display screens of sonar units. Interference, which can come from a variety of sources, also rears its messy head, clogging the screen with markings and blips that make it tough to find the real information.

As I said while discussing field tuning, many people go along for years using their sonar only to tell them the depth of the water. That could be because they freak out at the prospect of all those blips, or an almost-totally black display on their screens. Many sonar users just aren't sure when the amount of information is still "okay" and when it becomes ridiculous.

Interference is actually not that tough to identify. When your flasher lights up like a Mexican omelette, you've probably got interference problems.

When your graph, video or liquid crystal is so clogged with display that you can't decipher anything, you might just have the sensitivity turned up too high (this is especially true when using these type of units in shallow water). But, when there are lines filling the display that look like zillions of little dotted lines, that usually means interference.

(Water conditions are an important variable in how many targets get displayed by your sonar unit. If you go out on a clear lake on a calm day when there isn't much plankton in the water, you will get beautiful, clean displays on any good sonar unit. If, however, you're on a wind-swept reservoir that has seen a huge bloom of algae and there are tons of suspended particles and junk floating around in the water, *with the same sonar unit set the same* you would have so many things displaying on your screen or dial that you might think it was interference. Just be aware of this.)

Before we go any further, let me talk about when you should *expect* interference. If your transducer has been installed properly (pp. 126), you should never need to turn the suppression on at all during a fishing situation. By fishing situation, I mean just drifting along, or moving slowly with an outboard or electric motor.

If you do get a "dial full of signals" in a fishing situation, you probably have an installation or other electrical problem, that better be checked by an expert sonar repair person. On the other hand, during high-speed runs across the water, you might see interference and need to suppress it.

In general, there are two types of interference: water turbulence over the face of the transducer, and electrical interference.

Turbulence is caused by water rushing over ribs, or *keelsons*, and rivets on the bottom of your boat, by the leading edge of the transducer being pointed down, etc. It is simply air bubbles and an uneven flow of water over the face of the transducer. It breaks up the signal and interferes with good sonar performance.

Electrical interference can come from many sources. Your wiring might be sub-standard, someone near you might be running sonar on the same frequency, your livewell aerator could be the culprit, or some other electrical "gremlin" might be working against you.

(By the way, I'm only going to list the probable causes of interference here. For a more complete discussion on how to avoid these problems, see chapter 6 on installing sonar units.)

With flasher units, it is fairly easy to pinpoint where your trouble is coming from. If your dial lights up completely, and the spikes are stationary, it's caused by turbulence over the face of the transducer. If that's the case, check your transducer installation closely. If, however, the red spikes of interference are rotating either direction, the trouble is probably caused by electrical interference and you should have your wiring checked.

Some interference in certain situations is inevitable. The solution is to turn up the suppression feature—the second control knob on all good flashers and found on all good paper graphs and liquid crystals. Your .particular unit should have one, and if you are shopping for electronics, by all means insist on a model that has a variable control for minimizing interference.

The function of a suppressor is to help eliminate unwanted signals. Then, if the world were perfect, you would be left with *exactly* and *only* the signals you wanted to receive: fish, the lake bottom, weeds, etc.

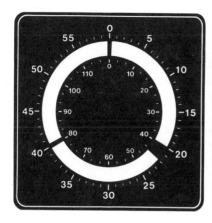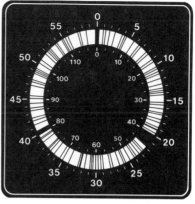

A—WITH SUPPRESSION   B—WITHOUT SUPPRESSION

Figure 15—Sometimes on high-speed runs, a sonar unit will completely clog with interference. In this case, the flasher dial has filled with red spikes. I call this condition "the need for suppression." If you encounter this while moving slowly and fishing, you have some sort of problem that needs to be straightened out.

But, of course, the world ain't perfect, folks.

Sure, suppressors can eliminate many unwanted signals. But they can also have some unwanted effects on your unit's ability to show you accurately what's going on "down there."

Suppression: not always a "positive"

While suppression can be a "positive" by helping you eliminate unwanted electrical or turbulence-caused interference, there is a good reason to use it only when you absolutely have to.

When you turn up the suppression control, you also lengthen the pulse length of your sonar unit. If you've already read the chapter on the History of Sonar, you know that the early, crude sonar units used in the ocean had very long pulse lengths.

So, while these units did an admirable job of showing the rough contours of the bottom, the long pulse lengths did not have good *resolution*, or the ability to discriminate between two or more targets that were close to each other.

In other words, when you turn up the suppressor on your modern sonar, you also might be blending the signal from two 10-pound walleyes holding a foot off the bottom, right into each other and the bottom signal. You might not see anything but the bottom signal.

Let's say you come upon these fish while passing over a rocky point. For whatever reason you have the suppressor turned up. Even though normally these fish would easily display separately, the longer pulse length (created by having the suppressor turned up), causes the fish to blend together, and to blend in with the bottom signal!

It doesn't zap the fish and make them disappear from the lake, of course; you could still catch them. But you won't see them on your sonar.

Please take a good, long look at figure 16. This graphically spells out what I'm talking about. It shows how, when the suppressor is turned up to help eliminate interference, it sort of forces the unit to "lie" to you about what's under your boat.

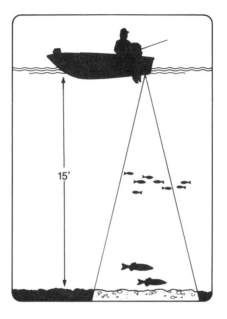

 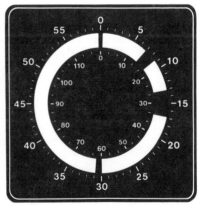

A—PROPER SUPPRESSION   B—TOO MUCH SUPPRESSION

Figure 16—Most suppression systems lengthen the pulse of the sonar signal, cutting the unit's resolution. The unit in (A), using no suppression, clearly distinguishes among the gamefish and baitfish. But, (B), after turning up the suppression and lengthening the pulse, blends the two big fish into the bottom signal, and the baitfish into one blob. Which unit would you like to try to interpret?

So, for anyone who has ever told you that as long as you can turn up the suppressor and dial away unwanted signals you don't need to worry about any interference problems, you now know which guys you will never share your stash of Fuzz-E-Grub jigs with! Or, at the very least, you know which of your fishing buddies you need to re-educate on this concept.

And now you also know my rule for using suppression:

Unless you are forced to use suppression and it should only happen during high speed runs don't turn it on at all. During fishing situations you shouldn't ever have to use it. If you do you have a problem somewhere that should be fixed.

Sophisticated 'noise reduction' systems

The science of eliminating unwanted noise has seen tremendous advancements in recent years, and is worth knowing about, especially if you own a sonar unit with one of the new systems built into it.

Regular suppression controls work on the principle that most noise pulses are much shorter in frequency than wanted sonar pulses. So, when you lengthen the pulse being sent out and received by the unit, you eliminate the shorter pulses—mostly the noise you didn't want to see in the first place.

But, this has that drawback of giving you a sonar unit with less resolution. That is why sonar engineers worked hard to find a better way to cut down on unwanted noise. That is why "plain old suppression" has become an outdated technology.

There is a new system of interference control, that doesn't change the pulse width. Eagle calls this feature *discrimination*. Discrimination works on the theory that the targets we want to see, such as the bottom, fish, weeds, etc. occur with more regularity than noise signals do. In other words, if a signal gets bounced back to the unit enough times, the unit recognizes it as "meaningful" and displays it.

A signal that enters the receiver only once, or not often enough to make it appear "normal," the unit ignores, and doesn't show to you.

How do you know when you have turned up discrimination too high? It's easy. Pay attention to how fish are printing out. With any discrimination on, they will lose their perfect rounded "arch" appearance, and start looking more fuzzy. But, when they get to the point where they start looking "blobby" and indistinct, you should turn the discrimination feature down a bit.

Because discrimination filters unwanted signals through "probablities of being meaningful," it is now the noise reduction system of choice.

Now, that wasn't so bad, was it? Armed with a basic understanding of how sonar works, you can cut through years of trial-and-error learning, and get right down to the business of catching fish.

Chapter 4
Flasher, graph, liquid crystal or video: which is for you?

Frankly, it gives me a headache even thinking about this subject.

Flashers, paper graphs, liquid crystal, video. A huge and growing number of brands. Claims and counter-claims. Fancy simulators. Color vs. black & white. Zillions of depth ranges, alarms, gauges . . . I feel truly sorry for the fisherman out there today, trying to figure out what to buy.

What I'm going to do is systematically lay out the strengths and weaknesses, advantages and disadvantages, of each sonar *mode*. (I won't compare specific brands.) And, I'm going to look at where the future of each mode of display appears to be heading. Then, the buying decision is up to you.

Before we start, let me stress something that's already been said: sonar is sonar. No matter how the machines are set up to *display* the information (on a flasher dial, or one of the picture-type modes), they all work the same.

That doesn't mean that every brand of sonar performs equally well. That is far from the case. There are a lot of sonar units that work well only as living room decorations. Some have fancy simulators that look great in the booth at a sport show, but the performance of the unit falls far short of its promise in actual on-the-water use. And, because of inherent display limitations (ex: a crude liquid crystal), many sonar units can't show you all the details that the unit is capable of gathering.

How do you shop for a sonar unit? If possible, get a demonstration, in a fishing situation, of the ones you are considering. Find friends who have them, and ask to see the display. Assuming the units are properly installed and adjusted, that can be a fair way of comparing, and

deciding which you like best. Also, stick to established sonar companies with a strong service network backing up their products. In many ways, it really is true that a product is only as good as the service people behind it. No matter how good a sonar unit is, there's a chance it is going to break down. Where do you have to go, or send the unit, if that happens?

If possible, get a demonstration, on the water, of each sonar unit you are considering buying. It's a great way to see how well a unit performs, away from the showroom floor and fancy simulators.

Specific brand and model consideration aside, is any *mode* of sonar more durable than others? For instance, if you buy a flasher, will it be likely to break down as often as a liquid crystal, paper graph or video?

Interesting question, according to the experts we talked with (repair technicians at service centers, and officials at sonar companies), but there's no way to predict.

They all have their problems, is the consensus. Good quality sonar today, in fact, rarely breaks down of its own accord. According to a survey of several top warranty repair stations, over half the repair problems are a direct result of user abuse or neglect.

When a sonar unit breaks down, what kind it is *does* affect how complex the repair becomes, and to a degree, the cost of getting it fixed. When comparing costs of similar repairs, flashers are the cheapest to fix, then liquid crystals, paper graphs and finally video units. But again, repair center personnel don't feel that the difference is enough to affect your initial buying decision.

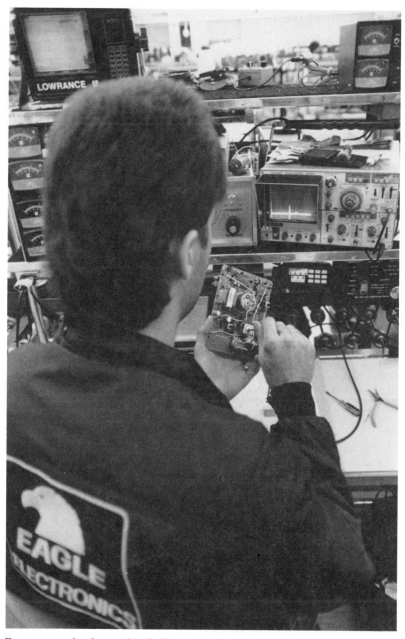

Does any mode of sonar break down more frequently than others? Apparently not enough that it should affect your buying decision, in the opinion of industry experts.

So, the bottom line is, don't let this question of durability clutter your mind as you shop. Sort out which mode of sonar is best for your type of fishing and budget, and make your decision that way.

The lure of the picture

The miniaturization of electronics, particularly tiny microprocessors (computer chips) has given us a new age in complex, small, many-function products. From digital watches that sell for a few dollars, to personal computers and yes, to sonar, we are basking in the research and development efforts of the space program and the computer industry.

Unfortunately, the giant leap forward by mankind has brought with it a few backward steps in the sonar department. As microprocessors became smaller, more reliable and less expensive, sonar makers jumped at the chance to make units with more "bells and whistles."

The advent of liquid crystal technology, and its marriage with touch keypad controls that can do everything but bake bread, is a prime example. To the consumer, a flasher is a plain Jane item, because it is perceived as being difficult to learn to read. To these same people, a liquid crystal screen, *no matter how crude*, is seen as a step *up* from a flasher. "If it gives me a picture of what's below me, rather than just a bunch of blips on a dial," fishermen reason, "it's got to be a better unit than a flasher."

The plain truth is that a good flasher shows you *much more* detail than a crude liquid crystal display. The resolution on a top-notch flasher is incredible. You can spot tiny baitfish, algae, and see fish that are very close to the bottom. With the cruder liquid crystals, you are handicapped by a factor that you wouldn't want to think about if you already own one.

To someone who has never had a sonar before and buys a crude liquid crystal display, it might seem like a wonderful piece of equipment. But to anyone who is even moderately accomplished with a flasher, and who got caught up in the hype surrounding the early liquid crystal units (you know who you are), the ensuing disappointment has been big.

Simply put, beware the lure of the picture-type sonar.

A picture is only as good as the detail in it. Don't spend your money on anything less than today's finest (and I mean finest!) liquid crystal, video or paper graphs. If you do, you have something that will only frustrate you. Fishing with sophisticated sonar should be a fun learning experience.

The flasher, the most maligned and least understood piece of sonar equipment, has also been enhanced with microprocessor technology. It should not be automatically dismissed in your search for the right sonar unit.

Flashers

Here's where sonar started. The earliest units intended for the inland freshwater fisherman were flashers, beginning with Carl Lowrance's red box (which became the green box).

Early flashers, of course, were not microprocessor-driven. They worked on the principle of a physical relationship between two constant speeds: that of the whirling scan disk (the dial), and the measured number of sonar pulses sent out by the transmitter. When a unit was switched from a 30- to a 60-foot scale, the motor driving the scan disk would change speeds. In deeper water, the motor slowed to give the signal time to get down to the bottom and back.

Nowadays, a computer determines the *rep rate* (how often sonar signals are sent from the transmitter) on state-of-the-art flashers. The dial motor speed remains the same all the time. The computer determines how long it is taking for a signal to get to the bottom and back to the unit, handles all the mathematical equations, and adjusts the rep rate.

I realize that's nowhere near a complete explanation for how these things work, but I don't think one is needed. The bottom line is that today's flashers are more accurate and useful than ever before.

Admittedly, flashers are not the latest thing in sonar. They are regarded as difficult to learn to interpret. They are viewed as being less sophisticated than other modes of sonar.

To the first charge, I must admit that it's probably true. Fishermen have an easier time reading the display of a picture-type sonar than a flasher. But to the second, I must raise a hearty objection. Flashers are a mature product, one that has reached a high degree of polish. They are capable of showing you nearly as much information as the finest paper graph, and considerably more than a middle-of-the-road liquid crystal or video unit.

The other major drawback to using a flasher is that it's hard to see the dial in bright sunlight. You constantly have to hold your hat up between the flasher and the sun, or get your body between the unit and the sun. But as you'll see, this problem is not unique to flashers.

I could fill this book with stories of lakes I've pulled onto for the first time in my life, and how in the matter of a few minutes or hours, with the aid of my flasher, got a grip on that watery environment. But I'm afraid that I am of a dying breed that came along with the flasher, is comfortable reading its rotating dial, and knows its virtues. I am afraid that I can't stop its inevitable obsolescence.

But there's nothing to stop me from talking about its advantages. There will be flashers around, at least in small numbers, for many years. You will still be able to get them fixed. Maybe I can keep a minority of informed fishermen using them for the time being.

The flasher does exactly what its name implies: it flashes you instant and very complete updates on what's below. Many folks see the *history* you get with the picture-type sonar (whatever is left on the screen other than what is directly below you) as being a tremendous advantage. I see history on the screen of a sonar unit as more of a convenience. I can easily remember what came a few feet back. I guess I have trained myself to be constantly picturing the lake bottom in my mind. For that reason, I sometimes find the absence of history on a flasher a welcome relief. On the dial, I only see what's "right now," and that's all I'm really interested in at the moment.

Maybe it's just psychological (I can't get sonar engineers to verify it), but it seems a flasher reports things quicker, and more often. At high speeds when sounding a lake, for example, I always go to my flasher. The reading comes up instantaneously, and I can quickly get a good idea of a contour before slowing down to zero in and seriously fish. When I come up on a slight change in bottom density, in the flick of a light I see it on my flasher. For my money, you just don't get that instantaneous reading with liquid crystals, videos or graphs. Eagle and Lowrance engineers agree with me that a flasher has a higher rep rate than a paper graph (three times higher, in fact). But they say that all sonar works so fast that the difference is too small to notice, in reality. I say there is a difference, that I can see it and that's real enough for me.

(A side note of interest: our research staff tried to uncover a standard vehicle of comparison among sonar companies, for this business of how quickly the various brands of units can send and receive signals. Theoretically, the faster one signal goes down and gets back up to the unit, the sooner another can be sent, helping you get that "instantaneous" reading that the flasher has always been favored for. But, we didn't find any standard. You will hear manufacturers speaking of the *rep rate, echoes per second, screen update* and *real time analysis,* among other things.)

I will continue to use flashers for the foreseeable future, because they are capable of so much. You should give some serious thought to doing the same. They are inexpensive, compared with other sonar modes. They are reliable. Their resolution is topped only by the finest paper graphs. You have the information right in this book to help you learn to read one.

In fact, what I would propose to all of you who will choose to buy a liquid crystal, video or paper graph is that a flasher should be in your boat as well. You shouldn't have a liquid crystal by itself, for example. If you really want to do the right job of understanding a lake bottom and quickly finding areas to zero in on, there is still nothing that does it like the flasher. After you find a general area you want to look at closer, that's when you turn off the flasher and turn on the liquid crystal or whatever else you own. Or, when you see something on the flasher you can't identify for sure, turn on the picture-type sonar and see what it is. That way, you can really get good at interpreting all modes of sonar.

If you are going to limit yourself to one purchase, consider this last thought: I don't know of a good fisherman who, if told he could have only one sonar unit in his boat, would pick anything but a flasher. If you approached a whole group of the finest fishermen around and said "boys, you can have your pick of a paper graph, liquid crystal, video or flasher, but you can only have one," they would all pick flashers.

No question about it, at least for now.

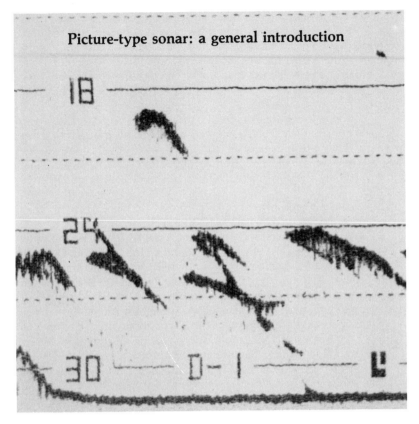

As I started to say, fishing with sonar can be broken down into a two-part sequence. First, you need to take an overall look at a lake, or section of a big lake, to find general areas you want to fish. For that job, I really feel like a flasher is still the top tool for getting the job done.

But, once you begin to settle down and really take a detailed look at a piece of structure or weedline or whatever, the picture-type displays (as long as they provide at least as much definition as a flasher does) have definite advantages.

Ease of interpretation by the operator is a big advantage. The biggest problems with flashers come when fishermen try to use them in serious fishing situations, and try to interpret the signals. They try to find where the weedline is, and they try to see fish on the flasher. They see them, but sometimes don't believe what they've seen.

Blip-blip-blip, a few fish come and go on the screen. The angler was blinking, or just doesn't *believe* they were fish. He doesn't increase his concentration like he would if he were seeing hooks on a picture-type display. Many fish bite softly. If a person is ready to react at the slightest hint of a bite, aided by the fact that he believes what he has seen on the display of his graph, liquid crystal or video, he is a better fisherman than someone who isn't as alert.

Can a sonar unit really do that for you? Yes, it can.

There are some fishermen, many so good that I wouldn't bet a nickel against them in a tournament, who fish with nothing but a flasher. They could have the finest paper graph or any other sonar there is, if they wanted (many have, in the past), but they choose not to.

These anglers feel there is nothing the picture-type sonar can offer them. They realize how much resolution there is in a good flasher, and rely on only a flasher to guide them to fish. While, as I said, I wouldn't bet against them in a tournament, it would indeed be them and their fishing talents I respected, not their electronic artillery. Because there are some situations where a pictorial display of what's under you is more helpful than just blips on a flasher. I'm the first to agree with that contention. My stand in defense of the flasher is based on its overall effectiveness.

Once you settle down to really work an area, you can see more things—especially studying the response of fish to what you do—with a good paper graph than you can with a flasher. Where exactly is that bunch of fish that is riding 3-7 feet off the bottom, in relation to the tip of the point? Move slowly enough and give the graph a chance to pick a spot apart, and it becomes a deadly tool, used in the way it was intended to be used. The finest liquid crystals and videos fit in there also, but to a lesser degree. They simply don't always have the detailed display or the power to show you everything the best paper graphs can.

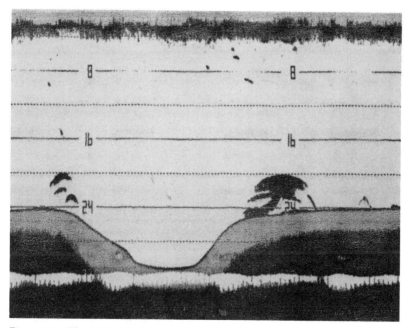

Figure 17—The pictorial display offered by the paper graph is unrivaled for letting you really study a fishing situation. Notice here that the bigger fish are relating to the steeper side of the old creek channel, the depth they are at, and how they are riding up off the bottom. All these things are apparent at a glance.

Let's compare the resolution capabilities of graphs, liquid crystal and video. The finest paper graphs have screens with 1,000 lines of horizontal resolution. The finest liquid crystal has a screen with 192 lines of equivalent horizontal resolution. The finest video screen on a sonar unit today has 256 lines of horizontal resolution. (Yes, there are now television monitors, known as super-fine pitch, with 3,000 lines of resolution, but they are far too expensive to find their way into video sonar in the near future.) In a direct comparison, the winner by a wide margin is the paper graph.

In fact, everything other than a paper graph is being unsuccessfully compared with the paper graph. Every engineer working on liquid crystal and video sonar is trying desparately to come up with a unit that rivals the paper graph! And yet, sales of liquid crystals have gone right into the clouds, and video units are seeing an increase. Sales of paper graphs, on the other hand, are not what they used to be. Paper graphs are far and away the finest units you can buy, for seriously looking at the fish's underwater world, and yet the fishermen of today can't seem to regard them as a serious choice when shopping for sonar.

Why? I believe it's because you have to purchase and change rolls of paper, that graphs are viewed as being big and heavy, and there are a number of moving parts in a graph which require periodic maintenance.

Strengths, drawbacks and the future of the paper graph

Of all the picture-type display modes developed for sonar, the paper graph is the only one which has matured. The resolution on the finest paper graphs are now darn near as fine as they could ever get. Any further improvement, in fact, would fall deeply into what is known as the law of diminishing returns.

Simply put, you probably don't need anything with more resolution capability than today's finest paper graphs. They come with the most sophisticated suppression systems available, and computer-controlled keypads allowing the choice of numerous depth ranges and zooms.

*The apparent drawbacks, as I began discussing, are led by the perception that it is difficult to change rolls of graph paper. It is about as tough as putting a new roll of toilet paper on the roller. It takes me less than 60 seconds to completely change a roll of graph paper. Believe me, the owner's manuals come with detailed photographs showing how to do it. Don't let that deter you from buying a paper graph. If you are capable of writing out a check to buy the graph, changing paper won't be a problem.

Also, fishermen are told horror stories (usually by people trying to sell video or liquid crystal) of how quickly a roll of paper runs out. If you use your graph in conjuction with a flasher as I do, you won't be running the graph non-stop. With my Eagle Z-15 paper graph, I can get over four hours from a single roll, running continuously, with the paper speed on full blast! It takes me numerous outings to pile up four hours of running time on my graph.

I should point out that paper graphs are not the best tool for fishing in water less than 10 feet deep. They are so sensitive and capable of printing so much information, that you often get displays that become quite blackened with printout.

To some, the paper graph is not a logical choice, because they need a unit that can be easily used as a portable, whether on a rental boat, canoe trip, or for ice fishing. To you, I agree that a flasher and/or liquid crystal would be a better pick.

But, if you are a serious fisherman, serious about wanting to understand the fish's world, look closely at the paper graph. It is everything, right now, that the other picture-type sonar modes are trying to become.

Strengths, drawbacks and the future of video sonar

Of all modes of sonar, video is probably perceived as being the fanciest, *the* most hi-tech entry into the increasingly hi-tech sonar arena. To own and use a video is thought of as just about as fancy as it gets.

Once again, beware the lure.

Video is expensive. And, most of today's video units are not worth the high price. And, paying top dollar is no assurance of getting quality. A good video sonar unit cost $600-800 in 1987. But, you could also purchase a $500-600 piece of junk.

Once again, don't misunderstand me. I'm not saying video is bad; there are some very nice video units out there, with pretty fair resolution. But, the best ones have 256 lines of horizontal resolution, about one-fourth as good as a top-notch paper graph. One-fourth the display potential at a higher price.

Video has drawbacks and good points, just like every other sonar mode. A major perceived drawback is the fact that any machine with a cathode ray tube in it is fragile and easily damaged when subjected to abuse like pounding over waves. Video units have picture tubes in them, just like your television set.

As one of my trusted advisors told me, putting a video sonar unit in your boat and going out crashing over the waves is "like taking your TV set and putting it in your kid's wagon and letting him drag it down the street, over chuckholes and everything. Sooner or later, the thing is going to break."

And breakage is not the only trouble that can befall cathode ray tubes subjected to rough treatment. The tubes, especially in color sets, are prone to coming out of alignment and needing adjustment. At least, that is a belief held among many knowledgeable folks.

In reality, from talking with sonar repair experts (people not on the payroll of video manufacturers), this has not yet proven to be the case. The number of video units is very small compared with sales of liquid crystal, flashers or paper graphs, but so far, the top video companies have some of the lowest return rates of any sector of the sonar industry.

The companies have come up with a way to mount the picture tube in a free-floating state, not rigidly connected to the housing. That way, the tube is not nearly as subjected to pounding as it could be. So, once again, I can't say with any certainty that you should be concerned about this if you are considering buying a video unit.

Another problem is that, like the flasher, video units are very tough to see in bright sunlight. Most folks don't recommend them for use in an open boat, suggesting them instead for mounting inside a cabin of a larger boat. Video units come in monochromatic (often amber against a black background) and color.

Video units consume much more power than liquid crystals, and almost as much as paper graphs. Video is not a good choice for someone looking for a unit that can be used as a portable.

But, I think video may go on a hot streak. The word *video* is so hot right now. People perceive video sonar as being the thing, if they can afford it. Yes, the lure of a wide variety of colors is intriguing. And yes, there are some very nice, high-quality video units out there on the market. If you want to pay the price, and you shop very carefully, you can buy a wonderful tool and toy that will help make your fishing fun.

And, after all, that's a big part of fishing.

Liquid crystal: how it works

Despite how I felt about the early, crude liquid crystal display sonar units, I have been predicting that they will one day become our primary mode of sonar. Now, I feel even more confident in making that prediction, because it can hardly be considered a prediction any longer.

Liquid crystal has arrived, at least in the eyes of the public.

The definition on the screens of the finest liquid crystals still can't beat the best paper graphs, but it can now compete somewhat. Advancement is coming quickly, because it is fueled by the demand of consumers. Sonar manufacturers can see the payoff down the road for developing a better liquid crystal display, and they are aided by similar strivings in the television and computer industries.

It's easy to see why the theory behind liquid crystal technology has appealed to scientists and engineers. It takes very little power to produce images that are clear and highly reliable. In reality, the technology is complex and difficult to work with, explaining why it took this long for liquid crystal sonar to develop as far as it has.

The liquid crystal, itself, is a unique organic substance which was discovered way back in 1888. It is a liquid substance, but also has the structure of a crystal, hence the name. Its molecules are long and narrow, and can be manipulated with a variety of forces (magnetic, electrical, surface pressure or mechanical). By aligning the liquid crystal molecules in various ways, they can be made to either pass (thereby appearing white) or reflect (appearing black) polarized light.

In a nutshell, this is how liquid crystal technology is used in sonar:

Two panes of polarized glass, only hundreths of an inch apart, encase a pool of the liquid crystal molecules. Before you turn on your unit, all the molecules are aligned to pass the light right through, so the whole screen looks whitish. But, let's say you are over 20 feet of water, there is a fish at 10 feet and you turn on the unit.

Now, the microprocessor in the unit "knows" where every tiny square division of the display screen (or *pixel*) is. (The more pixels on the screen, the better the resolution, or the more detail the unit can show you.) The sonar signal goes down and bounces off the bottom at 20 feet, and also the fish at 10 feet. Voltage is applied to the pixels which correspond to 20 and 10 feet on the far right-hand side of the display screen, and liquid crystals corresponding to those pixels get moved by the charge, and become aligned to reflect the light coming onto the screen. This causes a double polarizing effect, and they appear black.

(If you have ever taken two pairs of polarized sunglasses and put the lenses together at right angles, you know what I'm describing. Polarizing something twice almost totally blocks all light from passing, and you can't see through the lenses at all.)

Strengths, drawbacks and the future of liquid crystal

Now, back to the importance of pixels. Look at figure 18. The early liquid crystal sonar units did not have enough pixels on the screen to allow a detailed display. Remember how top-of-the-line paper graphs have resolution equal to 1,000 lines? And video screens about 250? Today's finest liquid crystals have resolution less than 200 lines. When liquid crystals first came out, the story was even worse.

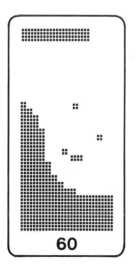 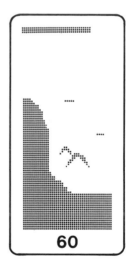

Figure 18—Crude liquid crystal displays, like the one here having only 30 pixels vertically, can seriously handicap your efforts. Notice how the large gamefish and the baitfish display as being exactly the same size on the crude display, while on the more refined screen having 192 vertical pixels, you get a much more realistic rendering of what's beneath you.

Many were as crude as *30* pixels (similar to lines of resolution) vertically, on a 60-foot scale. Do you realize how crude this is? That means that every pixel, or the smallest single square that can be blackened in showing a sonar target, represents *two feet* of water. A fish within two feet of the bottom will display as part of the bottom. A bunch of baitfish or gamefish that are at no point more than two feet away from the next baitfish, gamefish or the bottom, will all display as a black blob on such a unit. The bottom doesn't look like a smooth contour, it looks like a bunch of children's blocks laid on top of each other. And fishermen were actually led to believe that these units were a step *up* from flashers!

Like I said, this entire subject gives me a headache.

You know what the scary part is? There are still some units on the market today, being hyped and sold, with definition as poor as 30 pixels vertically on the screen! And there are a *lot* with only 60 pixels vertically. If you buy such a unit, you are handicapping yourself seriously.

It takes a minimum of 75 pixels vertically on a 4-inch screen to produce a fairly useful sonar tool. And even then, you have something more than 10 times inferior to a paper graph.

Today's finest liquid crystal units are approaching 200 pixels vertically, making them acceptable sonar. Plus, the ability to zoom in a portion of the screen improves the resolution, for taking a close look at a small area.

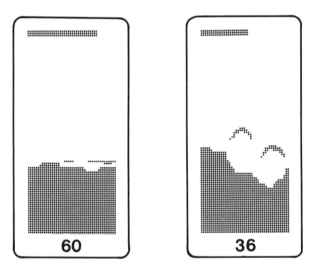

Figure 19—Being able to zoom in on a selected portion of the underwater world with a liquid crystal unit vastly improves the unit's resolution. This also holds true for paper graphs and video units.

But, don't look at the ultimate defintion, achievable only through zooming, as the end-all. Most of the time, you want to be looking at the entire water column, from top to bottom, as you fish. Zooming is only for special situations, usually for going back over something you've already seen and want to look at closer.

Automatic mode: one of the drawing cards

One of the big reasons liquid crystal units have been so popular with beginning sonar users is that they have the automatic modes. I sort of compare them with automatic, autofocus cameras that have made more and more people into somewhat capable photographers.

With many liquid crystals, all you have to do is turn the unit on if that's all you want to do. The computer in the unit does the rest: adjusts the sensitivity, sets the depth range automatically as you go into deeper or shallower water, etc. Is this really the panacea it would seem?

Let's go back to automatic cameras for a second. Do they *always* produce good pictures? Think about it. Many backlit situations, for example, fool the light meter into thinking you want a picture of the trees and the sky, or what's outside the kitchen window. Your aunt Martha comes back with a dark, indistinguishable face. You get mad at the "stupid camera" that is supposed to do everything for you. Also, what is the limit of your photographic creativity? Does putting an automatic camera in your hand make you a good photographer? No. Years of developing an eye for what makes a good composition, along with natural talent, see to that.

There isn't a professional photographer around who would trust an atuomatic camera to do his or her job. Good photographers don't even use the automatic features that come with their cameras—they do everything in the manual mode.

Well, folks, it's the same way with sonar. Yes, automatic mode is convenient. It is nice. But it doesn't always produce the best display. It is also fooled some of the time. The sensitivity doesn't always go up high enough to show you all the little baitfish, or weeds, or whatever. To get the most out of your unit, you should also learn to run it in the manual mode. Don't convince yourself you can simply buy the sonar unit that is the most automatic and let it do everything for you.

Or, let me take that back, at least halfway. If you really aren't that serious about getting the most out of your sonar unit or your fishing, then letting the sonar unit fly on autopilot won't kill you. In fact, if it makes your time on the water free of hassles, and you're happy with it, then maybe it's the direction you should go. After all, "success" in fishing is also measured by how much fun you have.

The hidden price of more pixels

As liquid crystal technology brings us better and better pixel counts, it also gives us a problem most people haven't considered: lack of contrast.

I pointed out that flashers can be hard to read in bright sunlight. Video screens are the same way. One of the sales pitches for liquid crystal is that it is *easier* to read in bright sunlight. That is very true. It is.

But, did you realize that the best liquid crystals, those which have the kind of defintion we are looking for, can be hard to read in *low* light? With smaller and smaller pixels, the distance between the black and white molecules gets less. The effect produces less of a contrasty black-and-white image, and more of a "grayish" image. Especially early in the morning and late in the evening, these screens can be hard to see.

With the latest round of liquid crystal technology, sonar engineers have developed something of an answer to this problem. A new type of display, called *super twist*, gives better contrast and makes it easier to see the screen when you are looking at it at an angle. Several manufacturers have come out with models that display in shades of navy blue. Those screens are a lot easier to see.

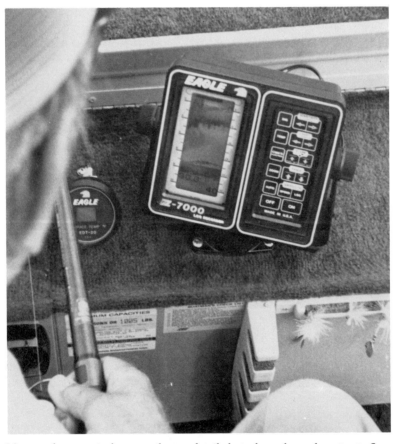

More and more pixels means better detail, but also a loss of contrast. Super twist technology promises a wider viewing angle, but still, liquid crystal units are most easily viewed from straight on.

Another of liquid crystal's strong suits is that there are no moving parts in the unit. Everything is done electronically, with tiny microprocessors. Still, the little liquid crystal display is fragile and expensive to replace, so the unit has to be sealed to prevent water from getting in. This is fine, because most companies do a good job of purging the air from the unit and filling it with nitrogen, which keeps all moisture out.

Some manufacturers, however, seal the unit without purging the air. Whatever the moisture content in the air was at the factory the day they built your unit is thus captured inside forever. That can, and does, cause condensation problems. Ask if the unit you are considering is purged and then filled with nitrogen. If it isn't, buy it at your peril.

The big picture: future sonar

Predictions of the future of sonar technology are hard to make. The field has become increasingly hi-tech, with the introduction of microprocessors and a variety of new display modes. But even for me, an old devoted user of flashers and paper graphs, it is exciting.

The super twist liquid crystal displays will no doubt continue to be refined. Liquid crystal screens will come in higher and higher resolution until they rival or even surpass the finest paper graphs.

There is also something called a dye display, which I don't know much about, but is supposedly a whole new technology being developed, that will produce a beautiful, very detailed image.

Another thing sonar engineers are playing with is the whole concept of the display itself. Until now, we have been given only one dimension, as if a cross-section of the water column were laid out for us. Tomorrow—and it might not be as far away as you think—may bring two-dimensional sonar displays.

But future enhancements are not solely going to be in displaying information. The tools for gathering and receiving information are also being improved and expanded. We already have, for example, transducers that switch easily between two different cone angles. You will be able to buy one transducer and use it at about 20 degrees for average inland fishing, or easily switch it to about 40 degrees for tracking downrigger balls or just getting a wider view of the bottom.

Also on the horizon are scanning sonar units, capable of easily looking at a 360-degree swath. It will be much easier to see where that school of fish went when you lose contact with them.

Because of market forces, you will see changes in sonar units every year. Some will be meaningful, many nothing more than sales hype. Be critical as you shop, and try to see which features and units are really more *useful* than what you already have, or other manufacturers offer.

Do some soul searching also. Be realistic about how serious fishing is to you. I run into countless people every year at sports shows who tell me that they are "really going to get into fishing." They say they are going to invest whatever it takes—time, money, and practice—to learn to catch a bunch of fish. But do they really? Do they end up really doing it after they go home, and the summer comes?

If it is important to you, if fishing is one of your main hobbies or a real passion like it is for me, then spend the little extra it costs to get top-of-the-line equipment. First class only costs ten cents more in the long run.

And remember: sonar is sonar. Just because something displays sonar information to us in a new and interesting way, doesn't mean it has changed the laws of physics. If you are really confused about which sonar unit is best for your type of fishing, go back and read the wise words of Professor Kilohertz in the chapter on the principles of sonar. First, learn how the units work. Then, figuring out what you really need should be a lot easier.

Chapter 5
Reading your sonar display: interpreting the blips and scratches

I don't know how·you feel when the television weatherman flashes his "color weather radar" screen across the set for four seconds and says, "as you can see, a band of highly-precipitous cumulous clouds which formed out to the west of us moved quickly into the region overnight, then were forced out by a band of low-lying high pressure which should keep us in this stalled weather pattern for at least the next couple of days . . ."

What exactly does he mean by "as you can see?"

He can see it, or at least it sounds like he can. But then, he *should* be able to see things by glancing at a radar screen. He has learned to decipher the signals, and to know what different weather patterns look like in the way the machine shows them to him.

The same looks I give the weatherman are often directed at me, while I'm fishing with someone who isn't used to using sonar. It's fun for me to teach people what certain types of weeds look like on a flasher dial, how to tell the difference between a soft and hard bottom density, etc. And, because there are only so many signals that you normally encounter, in no time at all even a rank beginner becomes pretty darn good at signal interpretation.

Really, I think people get overwhelmed for no reason by the prospect of learning to interpret sonar signals. It's really true: there just aren't that many signals you need to learn. In this chapter, we will go over almost everything you will encounter in your fishing life.

Like anything else, the "blips and scratches" will look foreign at first. Take your time; learning anything takes longer than putting it to use will later.

Before we start looking at rocks, weeds and fish, there are several important concepts I want to get across. Number one, you need to get the idea out of your head that what you see on the "picture" type displays (paper graphs, liquid crystal and video) is just like a television screen.

When you see things on the display, where are they? If you think about it, and understand how sonar signals are sent down in the cone angle, you will realize that everything on the screen isn't directly below you, all stacked on top of each other. That's pretty obvious. And yet, many fishermen have the notion that as they look at the display, it's just like a TV, that whatever is in the middle of the screen is exactly below them, whatever is at the far left of the screen is off to their left, and whatever is just coming on to the screen is off to their right.

Take a look at figure 20. It will help you see that fish on your sonar display can be behind you, in front of you, or off to the side—not just directly below the boat. Remember the section on cone angle in Chapter 3? If you aren't clear about how the signal is sent down, review that section.

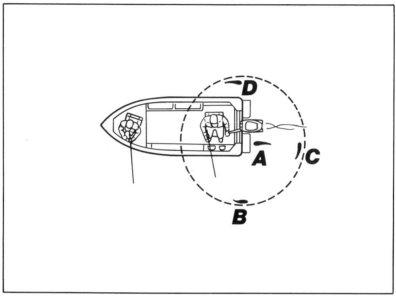

Figure 20—Fish will print as a relatively straight line on picture-type sonar displays when they pass through your cone angle but never directly underneath your boat. In this example, fish (A), because it is passing through the middle of the cone, will wind up printing as the classic "arch" or "hook" sonar users talk about (more on why this occurs later in this chapter). Fish (B), (D) and even (C), if it scoots along the back side of the cone without coming under the boat, will show up as straight lines. The point is, many fish you mark you won't be able to pinpoint. They can be behind you, or more likely to either the right or left sides.

What is most immediate, what is closest to being directly beneath you, is that portion of the display at the right of the screen. As you will see in this chapter, a fish that displays as a nice arched hook is actually directly below you at the instant it is printing as the top of the arch. After that, it is into what is known as the "trailing edge" of the cone angle and in most cases has already left the area of your lure.

All those beautiful fish hooks, and little rock humps, that have moved into the center or left side of your sonar screen are *not* directly beneath you. They are what we call "history," simply for your reference—to help you remember what you've gone over.

(With a flasher, you don't get into this particular problem. Only what is most immediate is shown to you on the dial. That presents a problem in itself, in that you have to constantly watch a flasher so you don't miss anything. But it also points up one of the flasher's strong suits.)

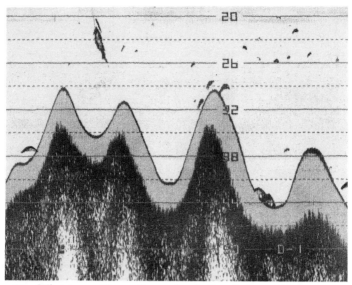

Figure 21—What is most immediate, what is directly beneath your boat, is the portion of the sonar display just coming in at the far right of the screen. Everything to the left of that is what we call "history," simply for your reference. Many beginning sonar users mistakenly think of their unit like a television set, believing whatever is in the middle must be directly under the boat.

Adjusting sensitivity

You also need to realize that there won't be any signals to interpret, or there might be too many to wade through, if you don't have the sensitivity adjusted properly. You need to turn up the sensitivity until you get a good bottom reading, and then continue to turn it up until you get that double bottom reading, or *second echo,* that we went over in Chapter 3 (see *field tuning*).

The reason for this is that it is easy to send out a signal strong enough to get a bottom reading. But, in order to adjust your unit to detect all the little things, like fish, minnows and weeds, you have to continue to turn the signal strength up.

With paper graphs and flashers, you have to know how to adjust sensitivity yourself. On many of the new liquid crystals, sensitivity is adjusted for you, automatically. When run in the automatic mode, these units adjust sensitivity, depth range and other functions as the conditions below you change. Theoretically, they send out stronger signals as the water gets deeper, and as the bottom composition gets softer.

However, in practice there are situations where automatic sensitivity doesn't work that well. With most units, you can bump the sensitivity up without taking the unit out of automatic mode. Learn to do this by reading the owner's manual. I'd suggest turning the sensitivity up until you start to get "too much" information on the screen, and then backing off a bit.

How do you know when you're getting "too much" information? The display will become clogged with so many blackened pixels that you won't be able to see individual fish, for one thing. When the unit is set properly, you should see nice fish arches, specks of baitfish and plankton in the surface area, clouds of baitfish, and cover such as weeds and brush connected to the bottom, if any is present. If you aren't seeing a display that looks "right," chances are it isn't. At that point, turn the sensitivity down until things become less cluttered.

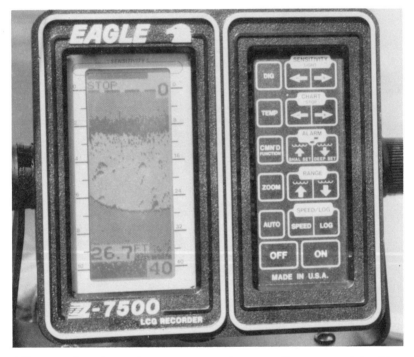

When your liquid crystal unit is set properly, you will see many of the things you see here: larger fish, baitfish, plankton in the surface area, and a defined bottom line.

Realize, however, that in some situations there is going to be "that much stuff" in the water below you. On days of strong algae blooms, or when you are going over huge clouds of baitfish and plankton, or when you are sitting over extremely thick weed beds, the display is going to be cluttered with information. Again, about the only thing you can do is turn the sensitivity down a bit to "dial out" some of the returning signals.

In most cases, sensitivity in a paper graph needs to be set fairly high. For example, with my Eagle Z-15 graph, I keep it turned up to about the 3/4 mark as a normal starting point. With the sensitivity that high, the unit will print fish clearly even when they are in the outside fringes of the cone angle—crucial to getting good hook-shaped markings. By watching the quality of my printout, I can judge whether to turn the sensitivity up or down.

(If it starts getting almost totally black with confusing markings, I turn down the sensitivity; if it looks too "white" I turn it up. This comes with experience. If you aren't getting any "hooks" from fish, you probably don't have the sensitivity high enough.)

Adjusting paper or display speed

Thirdly, you need to know how adjusting paper speed on a graph, or display speed on a liquid crystal or video, affects the way things are shown to you.

(This is not necessary with flashers. With older flashers, the dial always spins at a constant speed, and the motor slows down to pump the signal into deep water. With modern, microprocessor-driven flashers, the rate at which signals are sent into the water is varied automatically by the microprocessor, based on the depth of the water. Either way, it's all done for you.)

With the picture-display modes, you need to adjust how fast that display goes by you on the screen.

The faster the paper or display is moving, the more details it can print for you. Think about it. If the paper is moving faster, your graph can paint more "brush strokes," can spread the scene out farther horizontally, than it can with the paper moving slower.

The result is that you see more details. In other words, you get better *horizontal resolution* as the scene is more spread out by the faster chart or display speed. For that reason, I usually run my paper graph or liquid crystal at a fast speed. Notice I said usually. I slow the display when my boat is barely moving or stationary.

About the only drawback to a faster display speed is that the underwater scene comes and goes off the screen faster. That can make it tough for a beginner to follow the action; it's like putting a movie on fast forward and trying to see everything. But once you get used to quickly reading the signals, you should keep the display speed up high most of the time.

With a faster display speed, fish hooks are going to look longer and bigger, because the display is more stretched out. In fact, depending on how fast your boat is moving, you can actually get the display moving too fast, especially if you have zoomed in to look at a narrow band of depths. See figure 22. By turning the display too fast, a part of a fish can take up the entire display! That can make it difficult to interpret the signals you are receiving.

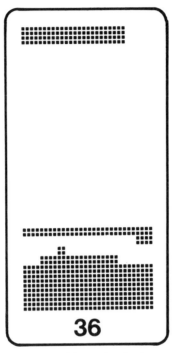

Figure 22—When you zoom in and have the display speed set fast on a liquid crystal or video, you can actually end up with a fish hook that is larger than the display area on the unit! The entire screen can become filled with a portion of a fish's display.

Slow the display or paper speed down and the same scene becomes more compressed, and in some cases, easier to decipher.

How fast you run your display speed is your choice. Just remember this: even at full speed, the display or paper speed of one of the picture-type sonar units is still a bit slower than a flasher. It becomes impossible to give set rules for how fast to have your display or paper speed set. Remember that how fast your boat is traveling affects how fast you need the display to move. As your boat moves faster, you need the display to move faster. As your boat slows, it might make sense to slow the display also.

Teach yourself, by comparing the display you are getting to the ones in the book. If you are getting fish arches, your display speed is probably set about right.

As you can see, there are many variables affecting arch size. Another is boat speed. If your boat is traveling very fast over the fish, for example, the sonar doesn't have as much time to record the information as when you are going slow. A fish will pass in and out of the cone faster if your boat is going faster. That makes the fish appear smaller—and the whole display more compressed, by the way—than if the same fish went through your cone while the boat was just drifting along, or moving at idle speed.

Look at figure 23. The far left side of the tape clearly shows how the underwater scene is compressed, and fish display smaller, when the boat is traveling fast. As I slowed the boat to a trolling speed (middle and right sides of the tape), the whole scene stretched out and looked "normal," or the way we are used to seeing it.

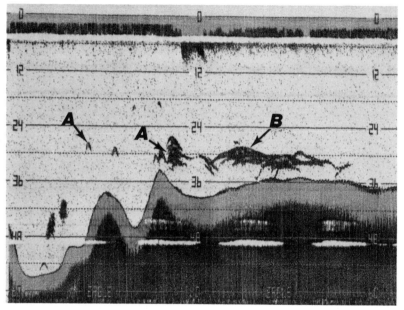

Figure 23—The shape of the arch is determined by several variables such as boat speed, fish movement and paper speed. During the first (left) part of this recording, the boat was moving very fast. Once the arches appeared I slowed the boat. The slower speed caused the tight arches (A) to stretch out into long, gradual arches (B), and I discovered a school of feeding walleyes.

Reading and understanding a flasher

Depending on who you talk to, the day of the flasher is either certainly doomed or almost over already. As far as I'm concerned, it is sad that these rumors are probably true.

We are coming into the picture-mode era of sonar. Liquid crystal, or whatever comes along that will provide even greater display detail, will become the dominant sonar mode within ten years, probably. Does that mean flashers won't be around, and still be used by good numbers of anglers? Heck no.

The flasher, because of its low cost, reliability and high-speed performance, will be with us for years.

Granted, the signals are not as easy to interpret as those of the picture-type displays. But they are not impossible to interpret—far from it. All it takes is practice, and the flasher can easily become your most trusted sonar friend.

Determining bottom density with a flasher

The flasher does a great job of showing you instantly when you have come over a harder or softer lake bottom. It can be critical to your success to be able to find the areas of gravel or rock, and to know where the expanses of mud are, for example.

Simply put, hard bottoms return more sound signals, and from a wider area, than soft bottoms do. Consequently, the harder bottoms show up as a wider, brighter display on the flasher dial. Also, you can have the sensitivity turned down over harder bottom, and you need to turn it up over softer bottom, relatively speaking.

Because I've already treated this topic in Chapter 3 (see "field tuning"), I'm not going to repeat myself here. If you haven't read that section, do so now.

Seeing fish on a flasher

On a flasher unit, fish show up as distinct lines between the top and bottom (or as little bumps right on the bottom, on occasion). They can either "blip" on and off the screen in an instant, or remain on the dial for a long time.

Remember, signals from fish are not as strong as those from the lake bottom. Still, you can get a clue as to which signals are from bigger fish and which from baitfish, for example.

Bigger fish give off a brighter, wider signal than smaller fish. This is simply because more sound pulses are bounced off the bigger fish's back and directed back to the unit.

A school of tiny minnows shows up on a flasher as a whole bunch of little tiny lines, as you can see in the illustration.

Bigger gamefish, as you can see by looking at the same illustration, show up as similar but wider, brighter displays.

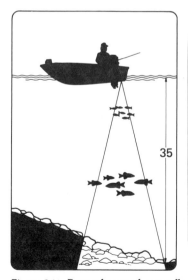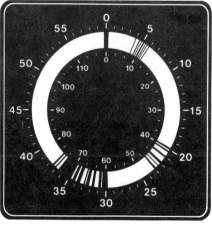

Figure 24—Properly tuned, your flasher can display a wealth of information. In this case, we are positioned over a rocky dropoff, there is a school of gamefish five or six feet off the bottom, underneath a school of baitfish.

One odd situation you might encounter with a flasher unit is shown in figure 25.

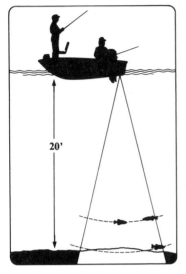 

Figure 25—Fish that are on the outside of the cone angle and right on the bottom can actually display below the bottom! That's because the portion of the signal that reflects off the fish has traveled a longer distance than that showing the bottom depth. Also, even though the two suspended fish are at different depths, they display as being at the same depth. That's because the sound pulses hitting them are traveling the same distance.

If a fish is very near the bottom but on the outside edge of your cone angle coverage, as the illustration shows, the fish can show up on the display but actually be shown *below* the bottom reading.

This is because the sound waves hitting the fish, at the outside edge of the cone, actually travel a longer distance to get to that fish than to the lake bottom directly below the boat.

The factor we are dealing with here, as I said, is the distance the object (or target) is from the transducer.

Is it a weed or a fish?

On a flasher unit, can you always tell a weed from a fish? Well . . . not always.

First, to get a good look at what weeds look like on a flasher, study Figure 26. They either show up as fine, thin lines or a solid band of lighted display, that stretch from the lake bottom to the top of the weeds. (At the end of this chapter, I am going to show you a trick for being able to tell what *kind* of weeds are down there, by the display, whether you are using a flasher or one of the picture-type displays.)

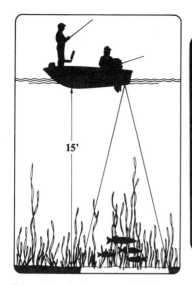

Figure 26—Finding weed beds is often the key to finding fish. This is what weeds look like on a flasher. The bottom is at 15 feet, and the weeds grow up to about nine feet. Notice the weeds go all the way to the bottom; they're not suspended. Sometimes, you can also see stronger signals in the weeds, which are often fish. A lot, however, depends on the type of weeds. If they are thin and grassy, an astute sonar user may be able to pick out fish signals. But, if the weeds are dense like coontail, it is practically impossible to read fish within the weeds.

Notice I said they stretch from *the bottom* up. Weeds are not suspended. That's a clue when you are faced with the question "are those weeds or fish I am looking at?" If they are connected to the bottom and string straight up to a logical ending point, you can normally assume the signals are coming from weeds.

If, on the other hand, you see a group of signals that are suspended between the bottom and the top, chances are those are not weeds. They are probably fish—either gamefish or a big school of baitfish.

Now, you may ask yourself, "but fish are so often right in the weeds, so why don't they show up somehow that is distinguishable?"

Sometimes they do—especially if the fish are in thin, stringy weeds. You'll sometimes see "heavier" signals in among the weed signals, and those can be fish. It takes some experience to be able to discern between the fish and the weeds, but it can sometimes be done.

But, if the weeds are super thick like summer stands of coontail, it is virtually impossible to tell the fish from the weeds.

But, keep this little trick in mind: if you aren't sure whether you are seeing fish in a dense stand of weeds, hold your boat stationary for a while and study the display. Weeds grow up from the bottom and can't swim around. If some of the signals come in and out, those babies are fish down there, right in the weeds!

Another of the best ways to tell weed signals from fish on a flasher is to know the bottom you are over. It is important that you use the business end of your fishing rod, your bait, as an ever-searching scout, probing the bottom and first few feet. Are you constantly having to take weeds off your bait? Or is your jig bouncing merrily along a very solid rocky bottom that doesn't have any weeds on it, or holds very sparse weed growth?

If you are fishing an area you know doesn't have much weed growth, or you're in water deeper than weeds would likely grow, and you see "serious blips" you can be pretty sure they are fish.

When learning to use a flasher, or any time you aren't sure whether you are over weeds (or what type of weeds), use your lure as a scout. By snagging these cabbage weeds, the angler knows what is beneath him, and can now study the flasher dial to really learn what cabbage weeds look like on his unit.

Fishermen have to face the fact that many times, it is going to be impossible to detect the presence of fish in dense weedbeds. Does that mean that the technology behind sonar has somehow failed you? Heck no. And it sure doesn't mean that sonar is an ineffective aid in fishing weedy areas.

As I said before, I am going to go into detail on strategies for using sonar in fishing situations later. Just let me say this for now: many times, you aren't using sonar to help you find fish as much as locations fish are likely to be. Simply finding the weeds—especially weed edges, and the places where weeds occur on inside turns in structure, or along breaks to deep water—is often all the help you need in locating fish.

And we can certainly agree sonar allows us to do that.

You need to learn to use sonar for more than finding fish. Teach yourself to use it to understand the fish's world, and to learn to hunt fish.

Deciphering confusing flasher signals

A type of terrain you will encounter and should learn to decipher is the *broken, rocky bottom*. As you can see in Figure 27, the signal being registered from a broken rocky bottom will be, understandably, broken up.

As you can imagine, the sound waves deflect off the many faces of a rugged rocky bottom at all kinds of weird angles. The signals coming back to the transducer are coming from many different distances, and that explains why you get a display like the one you see in the illustration. It shows up as very bright and very wide, typical of hard bottom, but as a series of broken signals.

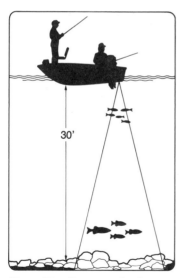
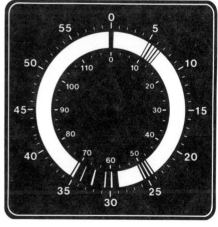

Figure 27—Over a rocky bottom, a flasher signal becomes broken up. In this example, the bottom shows up from 29 to 34 feet, because the sound waves have struck the many boulders and bounced from one to another before being reflected to the surface. You'll notice the fish from five to seven feet and at 24 to 26 feet, appear as thin, bright lines. If the fish were sitting among the rocks, it would be impossible to see them.

One of the tough things about signal interpretation here is that fish holding right in the rocks will be lost in all the various bottom readings. So you can never assume fish aren't here just because you can't see them on the locator. On many days, especially during the middle of a sunny day, fish will tuck right up on the shady side of rocks to get out of the bright sunlight.

Sunken brush piles and trees (Fig. 28) look like electronic interference in a lot of ways.

They look just like it shows in the illustration—tons of little blips on the flasher face. And, as in the case of weeds, fish that are right in among the branches won't show up distinctly. That's just the way it is.

To look closely at underwater brush for fish, try to hold your boat stationary right over the top like you did in the earlier weed bed example. The signals that remain stationary are the branches and trunk of the brush, and if the fish are moving about at all, you will see their signals come and go.

Remember, fish holding in brush many times will just sit tight, so don't give up on a spot just because you don't see fish.

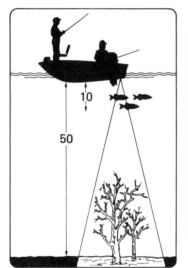

Figure 28—Sunken brush piles and trees can be super "fish magnets." As with weeds, the signals will appear attached to the bottom rather than suspended.

Rocky bluffs (Fig. 29) can really be a wild experience for a sonar user trying to get a grip on things! The whole dial can light up, again maybe making you think you are getting interference.

Study this diagram closely, because I am trying to show you two things at once. Number one, get a good feel for what a bluff bank looks like, especially you folks who fish canyon reservoirs and deep Canadian lakes a lot. But also notice something that might confuse you at first: even though the scale on this particular unit only goes to 60 feet, it can read bottom in water much, much deeper than that. It simply "wraps the signal around" the face and keeps on going.

This figure is an example of this *wrap around*. The shallowest portion of the bluff bank is at 15 feet, and it goes all the way down to 65 feet, five feet past the "end" of the scale. When you see this, don't let it fool or worry you. There is nothing wrong with your unit.

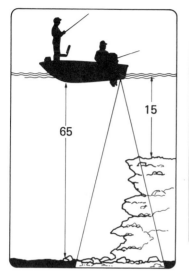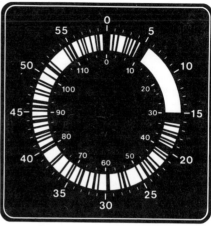

Figure 29—A bluff or ledge can really confuse a new sonar user! Here, the shallowest portion of the ledge is at 15 feet, and the bottom of it at 65 feet, which is deeper than the scale of the flasher dial, making for a potentially confusing situation.

Yet another situation that can be tough to interpret is a *sloping bottom* with a fairly steep but smooth contour. As you can see in figure 30, this type of slope yields a series of wide bands that make it impossible to spot individual fish. No matter what you do, you won't be able to see fish with a flasher along this type of contour. Well, almost never: if you come out of the deep water and up onto this contour, and fish are sitting down at the deep edge of the slope, you might catch a glimpse of them before the signal blends together as you climb up the slope.

But, despite their relatively few drawbacks, for my money I still firmly believe that a flasher is the number one unit a person should consider buying when first looking at sonar. And yes, I realize that I'm probably one of the last of a dying breed who feels this way. The age of liquid crystal is coming fast. But, unless I change my attitude on the usefulness of flashers, I'll continue to use and recommend them until they stop manufacturing them.

A flasher, especially because of its responsiveness that gives you a "right below the boat" reading even at very high speeds, will allow you to understand the fish's world faster than anything else.

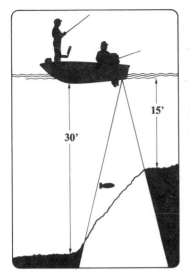

Figure 30—On a sharp, sloping bottom, a fish may get lost in the signal. The bottom reading simply comes from too many angles and distances for the flasher to show you anything but a wide, bright area on the dial.

You can come on to a strange lake and start running at fairly high speeds, and immediately find points, drop offs, weeds, the weedline, where fish are, hard- and soft-bottom areas, rock piles, muck basins, etc.

Flashers simply allow you to get a good grip on the total environment the fish in that lake live in. You can find the logical places—food shelves, holding spots—that those fish should be drawn to.

The "picture-type" displays

But, as I've said for a number of years, once you've got a good overall look at the lake, and begin zeroing in to fish a smaller area, the graph becomes the king. Here, with the way the graph can draw you a cross-section of the bottom and show you in easily-understood symbols what is down there, it becomes a deadly tool for the serious business of fishing.

And I now *am* including the very top-of-the-line liquid crystals and video units when I say graph, because they have begun to approach the good paper graphs in terms of detail of display.

Here's, basically, how I use my sonar system for attacking a fishing situation: first, I use my flasher to run around and really understand the environment in that lake. Then, after settling on an area to work, I turn off the flasher and turn on the paper graph to really "zero in" and take a look. What I'm checking for, among other things, are the structures-within-a-structure (what I call "mini" structures, such as smaller rock humps on a big rock hump), the apparent response of fish to my boat, where the fish are in relation to any nearby deep water, etc.

I sort of view my separate units as part of a team, a kind of detective squad, each good at certain aspects of the job, each contributing to my success as a fisherman.

They are, really, my "eyes" for peering into the fish's world.

Here' I'm pointing to a school of salmon and the printout of my downrigger balls. Because I knew the depth of the fish and my lure, I was able to run the bait right through the school and trigger a strike. This is a perfect illustration of how the graph can be used to really zero in on fish.

Using picture display sonar

So, what can the paper graph, liquid crystal and video sonar modes show you?

Basically, everything that's under your boat, as long as interference doesn't ruin your display. The fact is, the human brain can only track a few variables at a time. So, while you must be constantly looking at the display of a flasher in order to catch all the signals, and have to interpret a series of blips, the task is much easier with a graph, liquid crystal or video unit.

With this type of display, you get that nice picture drawn out, and it stays on the screen for a time before disappearing. If, for example, you are using a graph and decide to look back to watch a group of ducks fly over, you won't miss a fish that slides through your cone angle for a second. The signal will remain on the screen, allowing you the chance to notice it as long as you get your gaze back on the unit in a reasonable length of time.

It's like the old saying, "a picture is worth a thousand words." A graph, liquid crystal or video sonar can show you what's going on under your boat, without asking you to interpret the signals as much as you need to with a flasher. Therefore, many of the potentially confusing signals (like broken rocky bottoms, steep dropoffs, etc.) that we went over in the flasher section are easy to read on the picture-type displays. A steep dropoff, as long as you're not running parallel with it, looks like a steep dropoff.

From that picture can come a true understanding of the mysterious world we can't see with our own eyes. But remember: the picture-type sonar modes are not quite as well suited to high-speed sounding of a lake, or even to dead-still or barely moving situations. They operate best when your boat is moving at a slow trolling speed.

Picture-type sonar will not only draw out a picture of the bottom, but also fish, hard vs. soft bottom, weeds, trees, and all kinds of things. Let's take a look at how the fish's world displays on these units.

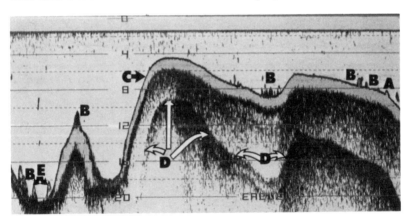

0 - 20 FT. SCALE

ROCKS, STUMPS AND BOTTOM CHANGES
CLEARLY DEFINED

A ROCKS
B STUMPS
C BOTTOM
D SECOND ECHO
E FISH

Figure 31—Picture-type display units, like the example here from a paper graph, show you an actual cross-section drawing of the bottom. They reveal depth, rocks, stumps, weeds, structures, and most importantly, fish.

It's a simple matter to tell where areas of softer and harder bottom are with picture sonar. Simply put, harder lake bottoms reflect more sonar signals, so more signals get returned and displayed on the screen. A harder bottom shows a wider "bottom black area" below the bottom line than a softer bottom does. Look at figure 32. Often, it is also true that the harder bottom will produce a sharper, more defined bottom line than a softer bottom.

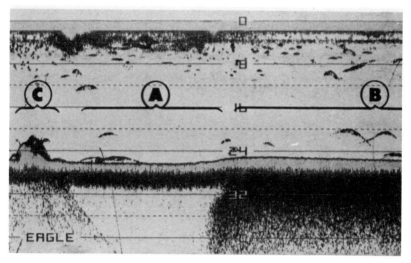

A SOFT BOTTOM	NARROW GRAY LINE AND NARROW BOTTOM BLACK AREA ARE DUE TO SIGNALS BEING ABSORBED INTO NON-REFLECTIVE SOFT MATERIAL.
B HARD BOTTOM	WIDER GRAY LINE AND WIDE BLACK AREA ARE DUE TO SIGNALS RETURNING FROM WIDER, HARDER OR MORE REFLECTIVE AREA.
C ROCK PILE	NOTE SOME BRUSH AND FISH.

Figure 32—With picture sonar, it's easy to tell hard from soft lake bottoms. Rock, sand, clay or gravel reflect more signals than softer substrates do, producing a wider black bottom area on graphs, and a wider grayline area on all picture-type modes. Here, notice the harder bottom under the hump (C). It's only slightly harder than the rest, while the area shown by (B) is much harder.

In the case of liquid crystals being used in the fully automatic mode, another trick is to watch the indicator that tells you how much power is being sent out by the unit. If the LCD is having to pump out a relatively strong signal to get a good bottom reading, you can assume that much of the signal is being absorbed, and you must be over a soft bottom.

This sounds tricky, and it is at first. Only after using your LCD for a time will you learn how much signal strength is "normal," say, for a 20-foot depth and a fairly hard bottom. Then, if you watch the signal strength, you can learn to notice when it goes up or down, indicating differences in bottom density.

The *grayline* or similar function (some call it *whiteline*, for example) will also give a clue to the bottom density. A hard bottom gives a relatively wider grayline area than a softer bottom. In other words, if you set the grayline control and leave it, you might be able to see a difference in the width of the grayline that will help you determine how hard the bottom is.

(Grayline controls do more than that, too. Another main value they have is in showing you details in what would otherwise be a clogged up bottom reading. Look at figure 33. Because the blanking circuit in the grayline control gives you a fine, thin bottom reading, you can better see what markings are above the bottom, and might be fish and cover. Without it, a large dense display might leave you bewildered.)

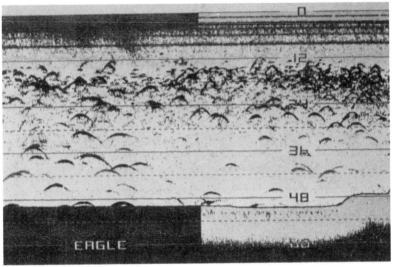

GRAY LINE OFF   GRAY LINE ON
LARGER FISH BELOW SCHOOL FISH

Figure 33—The grayline control in picture sonar is a circuit that blanks out everything below the strongest returning signal for a short interval, resulting in the grayish or whiteish appearance below the lake bottom, and even below big fish if the feature is turned up quite high.

Weeds and brush

Underwater cover such as weeds and brush are also a piece of cake to identify. Such cover prints out as objects connected to the bottom and growing up to a certain depth. You can even pick out pockets in weedbeds.

Look at figures 34 and 35. With just a little bit of practice, identifying cover will be second nature.

94

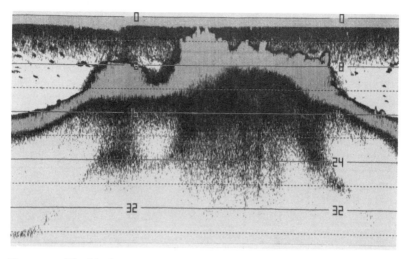

Figure 34—Weed beds are easy to identify on paper graphs. In some cases, such as you can see here, you can even spot pockets within the weeds.

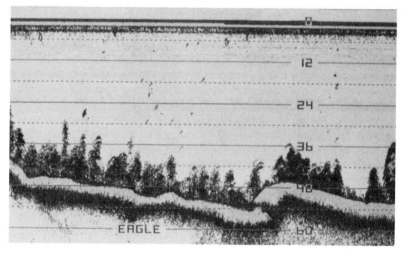

Figure 35—Here we have trees on the bottom of a reservoir. Picture-type sonar actually lets you see different trees, and even fish among them.

Seeing fish on a picture display

During what many people think must be the "off" season for me, the winter months, I travel across North America giving seminars on fishing techniques, answering questions on radio and television, and just plain talking to what seems to be a never-ending stream of fellow fishermen. They are all hungry for information that will help them become a better fisherman, and I am very grateful for that. That is my business.

I get asked just about everything you can imagine. A lot of questions from the more advanced anglers concern the finer points of sonar interpretation, and I never get tired of helping folks with this subject.

I get tons of questions regarding the location of fish that show up on their graphs or liquid crystals. "Where are those fish?" "Are they directly below my boat, or off to the side?" "How can I know?"

It's very important to be able to tell whether a fish is directly beneath you or not. Because of the width of the cone angle, there is some distance to both sides where fish can be detected, and yet many anglers think everything they see on their sonar unit is right under them. Is there a way for you to know whether you are putting your bait right in front of a fish, or whether that fish might be 15 feet to the side?

Yes, there is. Here's how.

If you look at figure 36, you will get a real education on how a fish forms the classic "arch" that sonar users talk about.

We are going to use a paper graph in this example, but the principle is the same for liquid crystal, video and even flasher units (although it takes a *very* trained eye to catch it on a flasher).

As your boat approaches a fish, or as a fish swims through the cone angle while your boat sits stationary, there is what we call the *leading* and *trailing* edge of the cone. When the fish first comes into contact with sound waves from the cone (the leading edge), the graph begins to record that fish. Because it is at the outside edge of the cone, the fish is being hit by sound waves that are traveling a longer distance than those going directly to the bottom, so the unit begins marking the fish as *deeper* than it actually is. I know, that is a complicated idea. Just take a deep breath and read that sentence again.

As your boat comes directly over the fish, or as the fish swims directly into the middle of the cone, the unit continues to mark it. But now, the sound waves hitting the fish are traveling a shorter distance, so the mark being made seems to rise, and the fish seems to be shallower than before.

Right at that instant, the fish is directly beneath your boat. As the fish is marked by the trailing edge of the cone, the sound waves are again traveling a longer distance, making the last marks appear deeper than the middle ones. As all these phases are strung together, the classic arch is formed. Is this information important to you as a fisherman?

Do smallmouth bass fight hard?

When your sonar unit displays these arches, you know the fish *was* right under your boat (during the phase shown by letter B in the diagram). If you were backing up, such as when you are backtrolling for walleyes, you know that the spot where that fish was is now directly in front of you, on the path you just followed. That doesn't mean the fish is still there, because fish often move, sometimes scooting to the side, when a boat goes directly over them. But at least it gives you a clue that can help you try to stay on top of the fish.

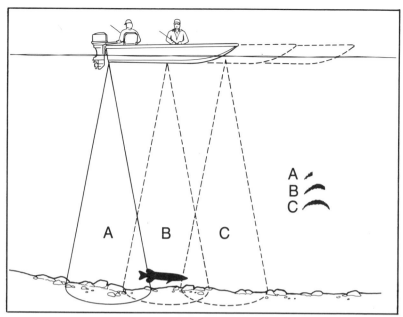

Figure 36—Fish that pass directly under your boat display on picture sonar as arches, or hooks. When the fish enters the cone (A), the sound pulses hitting it are traveling a longer distance than when the fish is directly beneath you (B). Then, as the fish leaves the cone (C), the pulses hitting it are again traveling a longer distance. This effect makes the fish display as if it rose, then went down again, causing the hook-shaped mark.

Now, we know what a mark looks like that indicates the fish was directly under the boat. But how does a fish that is off to the left or right show up on the display?

If a fish stays to the outside edge of the cone the whole time we pass over it, the sound waves striking it are traveling about the same distance the entire time.

Because of that fact, you don't see the arch like you do when a fish is directly beneath you. You get a more-or-less straight line that can be very short or quite long, depending on how long the fish stays in the cone. When you see those straight line markings, you know the fish was off to the side.

But you don't know *which* side. It could be the right or the left. To try to zero in on such a fish, first make another loop over to the left. If you get no more marks, try moving to the right. You may find the fish over there. Of course, while you're searching you may encounter other fish and not necessarily the one you "lost." Who cares, as long as you are finding fish!

Now, like I said, this example was written for the paper graph, but it works exactly the same way for a liquid crystal or video. When I go to use my Eagle Z-7500, I don't suddenly have to learn a whole new set of rules. The principle is identical, so it works no matter what picture-type sonar you are using.

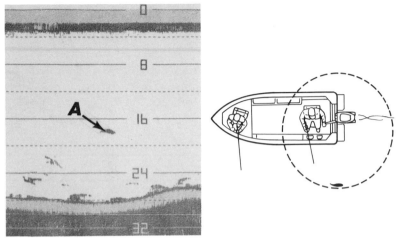

Figure 37—Fish off the sides of the cone angle display as small marks or lines rather than hooks (A). In these cases, a large fish can make an extrememly small mark on your sonar display. But, by understanding that the fish was to the side of the boat, you have the opportunity to turn around and try for a better look at the fish.

How big is that fish down there?

Can you make a guess as to the size of a fish by the size of the mark it makes on your sonar unit? Yes and no.

Let's say your graph shows you two arches, side by side at the same depth and both symmetrical, indicating the fish are directly under your boat. In this case, if one is bigger, you can safely assume the bigger arch is made by a bigger fish.

How deep a fish is makes a big difference in how big or small it looks on your sonar. Did you realize that? Think about it for a second and it will make sense.

Look at figure 38. The closer a fish is to your transducer (or in other words, the shallower it is), the less time it will be in the cone while being marked by the sonar unit. (The distance from edge to edge of the cone is shorter in shallower water.)

Consequently, it will show up as a relatively small mark, compared to the same size fish in deeper water. The exact same fish, 10 or 20 feet deeper, will be inside the cone longer while being marked. The deeper fish will *appear* to be considerably bigger than the shallow fish.

But, you need to also realize that this only pertains to fish that mark in the classic "arch" indicating the fish was directly under the boat.

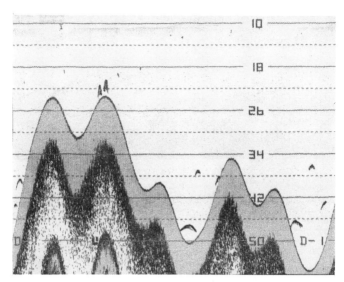

Figure 38—Here's a graphic look at an important sonar concept. Fish in shallow water spend less time in the cone angle than fish in deep water, because the cone is narrower (hasn't spread out) in shallow water. Therefore, fish naturally display relatively smaller when in shallower water. Keep this in mind when you are using picture sonar. Don't automatically assume that the small markings you see in shallow water are from small fish! Or, that the large markings in deep water are from huge fish.

Let's say a 10 pound walleye down in 25 feet of water passes through only the edge of your cone angle, and is out of the cone after just a second or so. That fish will mark as a short straight line, which certainly doesn't give away its size. At that same time, you might be passing over a 2-pound walleye in 20 feet of water that is right under your boat. The small fish would appear larger than the big fish, if you look only at the mark on your sonar unit!

With fish on the edge of your cone, it is difficult to guess size. Even a huge fish, which would mark with a deep, lengthy arch if you passed right over it—some even "grayline" out—might show up as a dinky little streak if you pass by it on the edge of your coverage. Don't give up on marks like this; try other passes to both sides.

You may have come over the very edge of a huge school, in fact. Take a look at figure 39. On this day, I was trolling over what I thought was a large flat. I came upon a few fish off to the side of the cone. If I hadn't known what those straight-line marks mean, I wouldn't have thought of taking another pass slightly off to the side.

On the first try, I guessed right and came over a good-sized school of walleyes. One more pass to the side and I found a hump that wasn't on the map. All because I noticed those fish had been off to the side of the cone angle! Oh, and how did I know they were walleyes? It was easy to tell when we caught some.

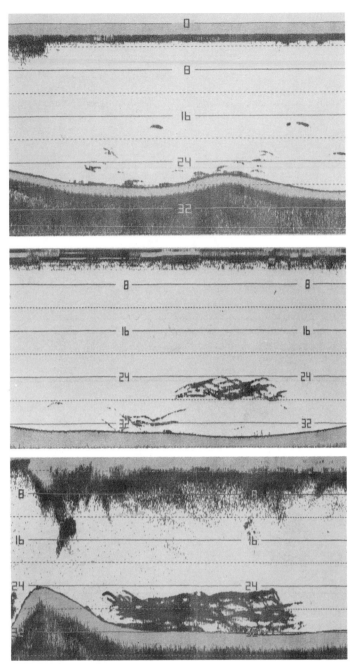

Figure 39—By knowing that the first scratchings I marked while trolling what I thought was a large flat (1), indicated that some fish were off to the side of my cone angle, I turned (2) and got a better look at a huge school of walleyes. One more pass (3) and I found a sharp hump that the fish were relating to. We caught a sock full of these fish!

Minnows and other small fish (even heavy concentrations of plankton) show up on a picture-type sonar display as a blob, or little tiny specks. That's the best way I can think of to describe them. A school of perch, for example, normally shows up as a dark blob. Individual small fish, which you will often see in the upper portion of the display, can mark as little tiny flecks.

Look at figure 40. You can clearly see what a school of baitfish looks like on a paper graph. It would mark the same on a liquid crystal or video sonar.

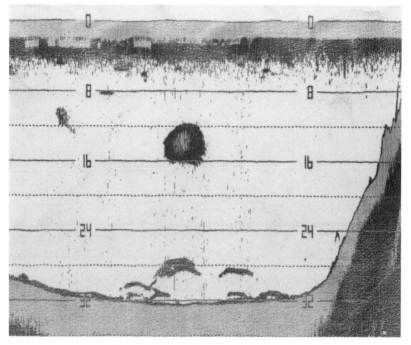

Figure 40—When you find baitfish, you'll usually find predatory gamefish. This is a school of ciscoes suspending at 12 feet (A). Directly below them is a school of walleyes (B). Even though the walleyes were semi-inactive, they were still staying with the baitfish. Some of these fish were catchable.

Taking a closer look

As you scan over expanses of water looking for the right combination of elements that will hold active, feeding fish, you are going to see plenty of things that confuse you. And you are going to see plenty of fish.

In many cases, you are going to want to "go in for a closer look." With modern picture-type sonar, it's no sweat. You simply use the zoom function found on *all* good units today.

I'm not going to go into detail on how to use any specific zoom features on any specific units, because that will change from year to year anyway. It's enough to know that you can do this, and it will really help you decide "what the heck that was" that you saw on the first pass over an area. Zooming also improves the screen resolution of liquid crystals a ton. Imagine: if you go from being on a 0-60' scale on a liquid crystal and zoom in to a ten-foot window (now having a 0-10' scale on the same screen), you have given yourself a unit with six times the detail!

Look at figure 41. It will show you a bit about the value of zooms.

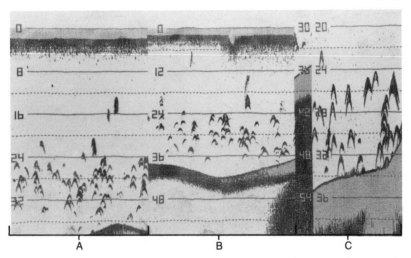

Figure 41—Zoom features allow you to take a closer look at something worth investigating. Here a school of fish was located in 24 to 36 feet (A). By switching to the 60-foot scale (B), you get a better picture of the fish and what they are relating to, a series of rolling humps. Zooming even tighter (C), you get an excellent closeup of the fish.

Beyond perfect arches

Keep in mind that so far, I have only talked about two situations, really. We've only encountered fish that were right under the boat, which printed as neat arches; or off to one side or the other which printed as more-or-less straight lines.

In actual fishing situations, a lot of other things happen. Many times, as you approach fish with a boat they go off to the side, or up or down. Sometimes, fish are actively feeding and their movements are recorded. These moving fish display as erratic arches, or long, stringy markings, or just about anything you can imagine.

Only by studying actual graph tapes, or liquid crystal or video screens made out in the field, can you get good at interpreting these signals. And it's not enough to get good at identifying the signals you want to see, like fish and weeds and bottom structure. You need to learn what the unwanted signals and confusing signals look like, so you don't waste your fishing time trying to figure out what they are.

Let's take a look at a series of on-the-water tapes made by me and members of my Research Team, that will go a long ways toward making you proficient at reading a graph, liquid crystal or video sonar display.

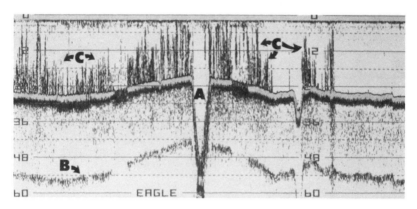

A RIVER CHANNEL
B SECOND ECHO SHOWING
C TREES

Figure 42—Through today's technology, most high quality paper graphs can read bottom structure at high boat speeds. This is an important bonus when scouting a new lake, as I was here when I found the old river channel in a brush-filled southern reservoir.

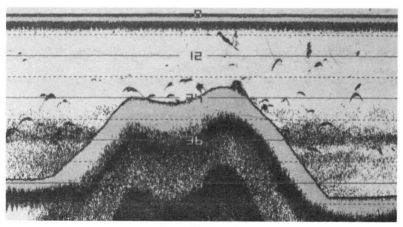

THERMOCLINE AT 36 FT.

Figure 43—Plankton and other particles often build up enough in the thermocline so your picture sonar can display it as a band of pepper-like specks. The thermocline can be important in determining fish location in summer, because there is often not enough oxygen below it to support fish life. Also, the small plankton gathered in it attract minnows and in turn pull in gamefish.

103

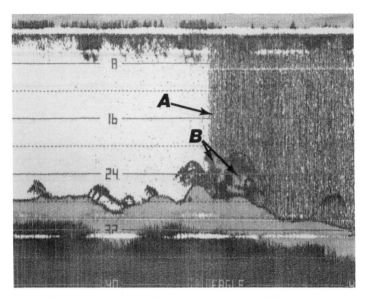

Figure 44—Graph malfunction? No, this is interference (A) from a nearby sonar unit that operates at about the same frequency. Yet, notice how the big fish grayline and reverse out (B) from the interference.

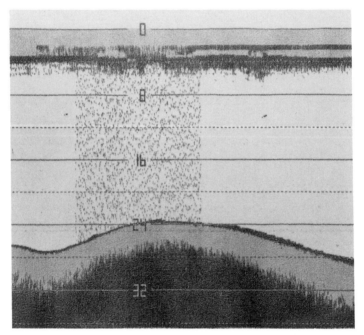

Figure 45—This is also interference, but in this case, it was caused by my aerator. Simply learn to identify interference, and you can do things to alleviate it. This kind of thing can be corrected by re-routing the wiring, or insulating the wires with rubber tubing.

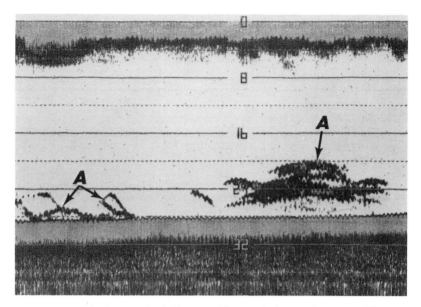

Figure 46—While this may look like a problem with the graph, it's not. The rise and fall of the transducer in waves gives everything a zig-zag appearance as shown. The things identified by (A) are fish.

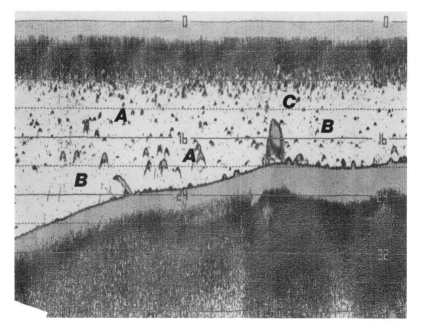

Figure 47—This is a mass of various fish species. The symmetrical arches (A) tell us the fish were directly under the boat. You'll also notice how the bigger fish grayline (B), while the smaller fish don't. The grayline was actually turned up a bit too high in this case, because the school of baitfish (C) also graylined.

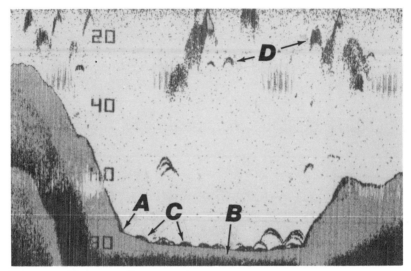

Figure 48—This is a valley in an oligotrophic lake that has filled in with silt. Notice how the rock walls return a strong, thick signal (A), while the silt on the bottom (B) absorbs more sound waves and produces a thinner grayline by comparison. Over the silt are a number of fish (C), probably negative lake trout. Up above them are other fish actively working (D), probably lake trout feeding on ciscoes. I can't tell these things solely from this graph tape; they are educated guesses based on the lake, time of year, etc.

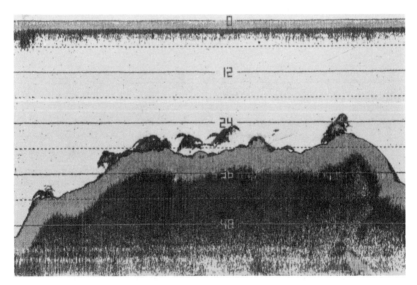

Figure 49—Here is a great example of a situation where picture sonar is more helpful than a flasher, when zeroing in and seriously fishing a spot. We have a large rock pile, but notice the two mini structures within the structure indicated by (A) and (B). These are the kind of tiny spots-within-the-spot that the big fish relate to, while the rest of the fish work the entire structure. Even though these would have displayed on a flasher, you probably wouldn't have noticed them.

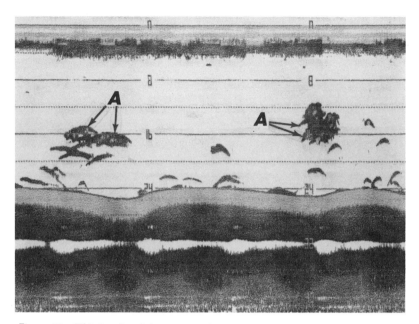

Figure 50—This is what fishermen are looking for: big fish feeding on clouds of baitfish. You can actually see the fish, undoubtedly gorging themselves, mixed in with the baitfish schools.

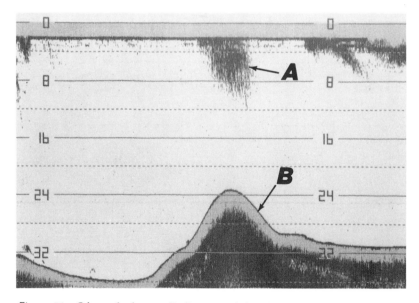

Figure 51—Often, the key to finding gamefish is locating what they eat. This school of baitfish (A), though at the surface, is still relating to the sunken island in 23 feet (B). I would come back to a spot like this and check it later, for the presence of gamefish.

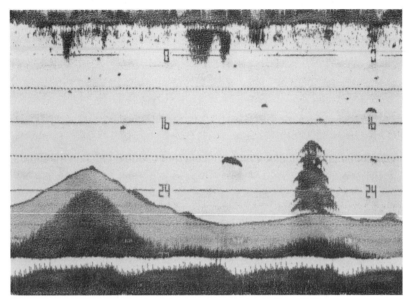

Figure 52—For some reason, fish, especially crappies, often stack up in what we call "Christmas tree" fashion. A school of fish like this is almost always negative and hard to catch.

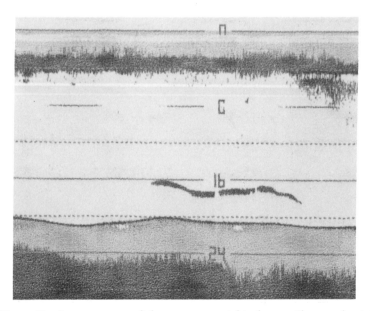

Figure 53—In some cases, fish may move right along with your boat (A), stringing the signal out very long and "snakey" looking. Many times, this indicates a fish that is curious, active, and catchable.

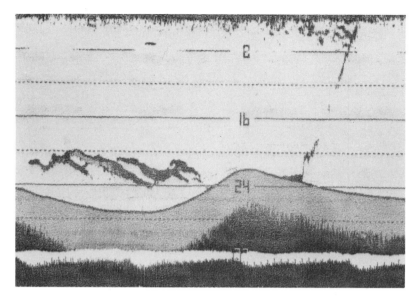

Figure 54—The most basic use of a picture sonar is to find structures and fish. The walleyes shown here (A) are relating to the hump (B) in 22 feet of water. On the right side of the hump was a fish (C) lying on the bottom, that grabbed my jig. You can actually see the fish struggle as it is pulled to the surface (D).

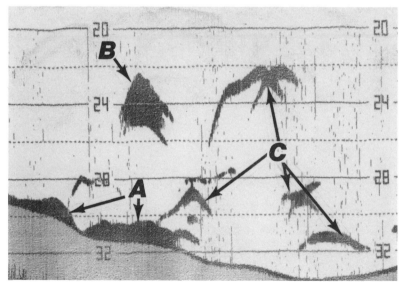

Figure 55—Here is the spot that every walleye angler dreams about. A school of big fish is shown close up, in the 20-40 foot zoom mode. Notice the school of baitfish on the bottom (A), and the school of baitfish off the bottom with gamefish feeding on them (B). The other walleyes (C) are moving and active also. If you can't catch these fish, you're doing something wrong! (The little specks are interference from my aerator.)

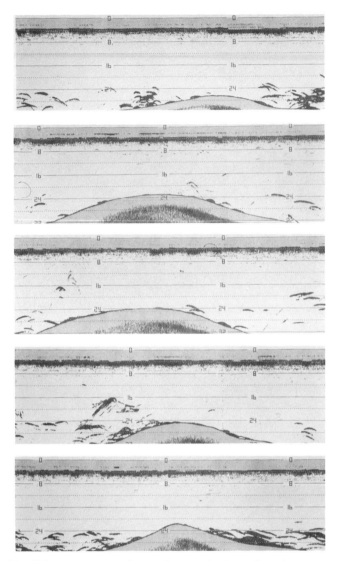

Figure 56—This sequence reveals a stark example of a walleye feeding spree. On the first pass (1), the school of fish is moving from 32 feet of water to the structure at 27 feet. On the second pass (2), the walleyes are approaching the crest and beginning to feed. In (3), the walleyes have become "kings of the hill!" They are chasing baitfish up as shallow as 16 feet. By the time the boat circles for another pass (4), the fish are thinning out, but those that remain are still feeding. Eventually (5) the main school left the structure. By the way, it was fun! The feeding activity lasted nearly 45 minutes.

This sequence explodes the myth that walleyes are strictly low-key bottom feeders, and tells a lot about how walleyes feed and relate to structures and baitfish. Also, how about what it tells us concerning returning to a good-looking spot several times in a day to check—with our sonar—for signs of such a "here now, gone later" feeding binge?

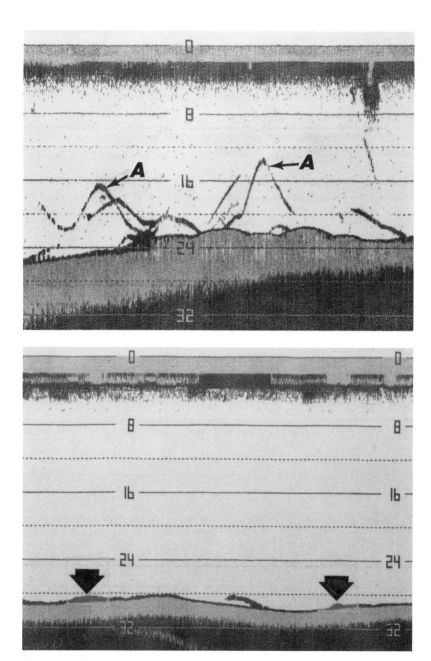

Figure 57—Picture sonar can tell you a lot about the activity level of gamefish. On the top section of graph paper you see a small school of big fish chasing baitfish. Fish that display like this (A) are almost always catchable. On the other hand, the bottom section of graph paper tells a different story. This is the same school of fish, after it became extremely negative and laid flat on the bottom. Notice the arrows, which indicate what a fish looks like when laying directly on the bottom. Normally, these fish are tough to catch.

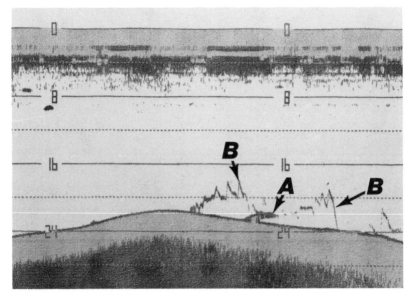

Figure 58—One fall, I discovered a pattern that produced several large fish on an otherwise fruitless day. Occassionally I'd find a single fish belly-to-the-bottom (A), which usually indicates a negative fish. By watching my jig on the graph (B), I could drop it right on the fish's nose. About half of these walleyes could be tempted if I put the bait directly in front of their noses long enough. This was shortly after the passage of a cold front and the fish had turned basically negative.

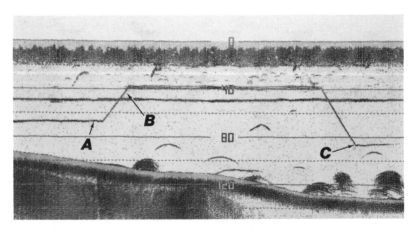

Figure 59—Picture-type sonar has completely changed downrigger fishing from a guessing game to a precise fish catching system. Transducers that shoot a 45-degree cone angle allow you to see the exact depth of the downrigger balls and run the lure right by the fish. Here, you can see one weight running at 60 feet (A), then brought up to 40 feet (B), and back down to about 85 feet (C).

But picture-type sonar makes it easy to raise and lower the weights along with the changing depths, allowing the lure to hug fish-attracting structures, and yet remain free of trouble.

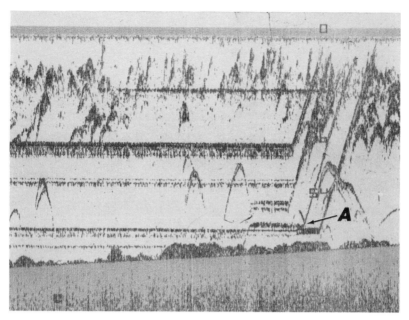

Figure 60—*The end result of correct downrigger placement, aided by sonar. Fish (A) on! Notice that the downriggers are set to cover a variety of depths.*

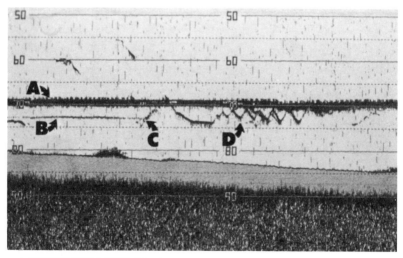

A DOWNRIGGER CANNON BALL 69 FT.
B 4 INCH LURE 73 FT.
C "FISH ON"
D SMALL FISH FIGHTING RELEASE ON DOWNRIGGER. RELEASE SET TOO
TIGHT. CAUGHT 2 LB. LAKE TROUT.

Figure 61—*Here's a fish actually hitting the bait, but the fish wasn't big enough to trip the release. Great Lakes fishermen call these small fish "shakers."*

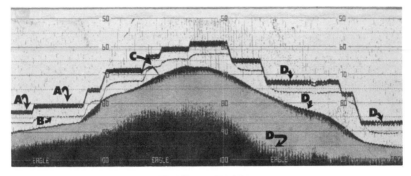

50 FT. TO 100 FT. SCALE

A DOWNRIGGER BALL STAIR STEPS UP FROM 83 FT TO 58 FT AND
DOWN TO 87 FT.
B 4 INCH LURE FOLLOWS ALONG
C FISH TOOK A LOOK, BUT DIDN'T TAKE IT
D SAW TOOTH EFFECT FROM SURFACE WAVES MOVING BOAT UP
AND DOWN

Figure 62—Snagging downrigger weights on the bottom used to be a nightmare (and a very expensive one) for trollers. But picture-type sonar makes it easy to raise and lower the weights along with the changing depths, allowing the lure to hug fish-attracting structures, and yet remain free of trouble.

Let's now take a close look at a variety of actual liquid crystal displays shot on the water. These are not done using a simulator. Notice as we go through these examples that everything looks identical to the way it displays on a paper graph, and the only difference is that the liquid crystal displays are not quite as detailed; the lines not quite as smooth. That is because they *are* exactly the same thing. Liquid crystal, just like video, is simply another mode of displaying the exact same information as that seen on a paper graph or flasher.

Also, as you look through these displays, realize that a video screen would look much the same if used to record the identical scene. Once you learn to decipher picture-type sonar signals, you can do it regardless of the mode of display.

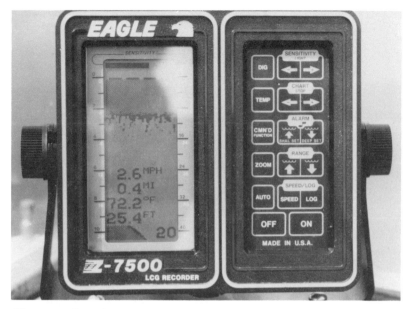

Figure 63—Top-of-the-line liquid crystal units offer a variety of digital readouts that previously were available only by adding separate instruments. Here, we are able to track boat speed, distance traveled since we turned on the unit, surface water temperature and depth to one-tenth foot increments!

Figure 64—This is what a liquid crystal display looks like with the sensitivity turned down too low. It would look very similar on a video display. The faint specks on the display are probably gamefish or baitfish that aren't being completely recorded by the unit.

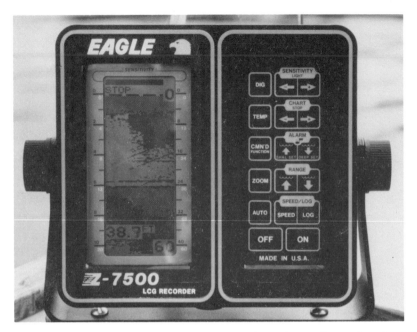

Figure 65—Concentrate your attention here on how the grayline widens from left to right on the screen. The wider grayline on the right indicates that you have come over a harder bottom composition.

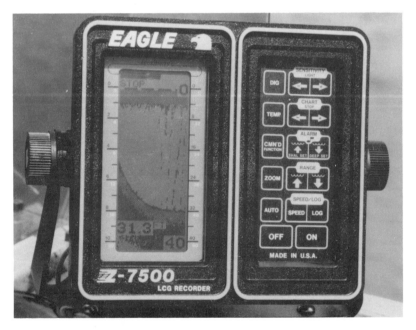

Figure 66—Here is what interference looks like on a liquid crystal display. Notice that it is almost identical to what it looks like on a paper graph.

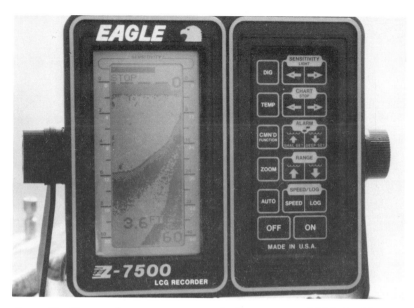

Figure 67—Here, we have run up a steep-sloping structure of fairly hard bottom (note the nice wide grayline and second bottom echo). It was in the fall, and I was looking for walleyes or bass or big northern pike holding here. We are looking for fish, but none are obvious, at least over the path we traveled. If we look over this area closely and don't find any fish, we might move on to another spot.

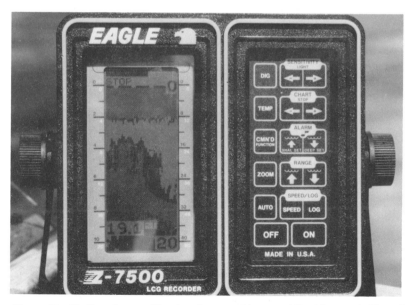

Figure 68—Finding the weedline is a breeze with a good liquid crystal. Here, I can see a good growth of weeds down to about 14 feet, where they end rather abruptly. Following and fishing that weedline can produce fish of all species!

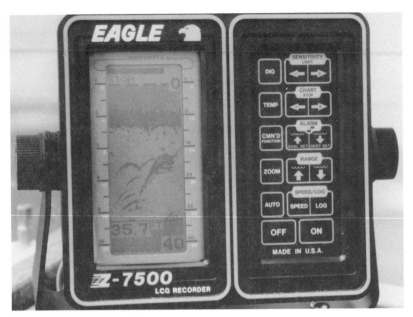

Figure 69—Just like with a paper graph, a liquid crystal of sufficient detail can be used to find active gamefish and baitfish. Here, we have a bunch of good-sized fish riding high off the bottom (often a sign of active, feeding fish), right under a bunch of baitfish. You better believe I would stop and fish this situation!

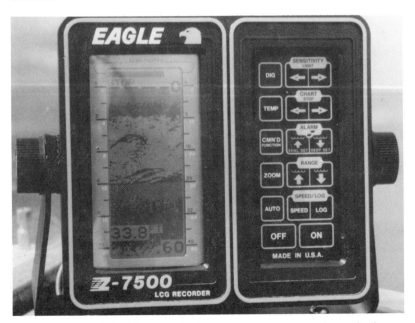

Figure 70—The fish riding up off the bottom in this example are feeding on smaller fish. The smaller specks are baitfish.

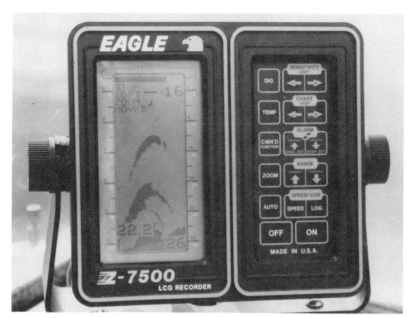

Figure 71—This illustrates the kind of detailed display you can get on a good liquid crystal by zooming in. Here, we are taking a closer look at a couple of big fish sitting off the edge of a steep dropoff. There's nothing crude about this screen!

An advanced weed interpretation seminar

Let's take a step beyond basic signal interpretation. I think you're ready for it!

How would you like to be able to look at your sonar display and not only tell there are weeds down there, but to also be pretty sure what *kind* of weeds they are? I knew you would.

It's not some magic act, and it's not a pile of baloney. There is a core of advanced anglers who have been doing this for a number of years now, and it really helps them catch fish.

"Big John" Christianson, a close friend and business associate, is one of the finest fishermen you will ever come across. Through years of sonar experience, in casual fishing and competitive tournaments, he has developed as good a feel for weed types as anyone I know. I'm going to let him talk on this subject.

John Christianson:

"It seems amazing to some people, but I'll be running over a weedline in a tournament, and turn to my partner and say 'well, we've got cabbage here,' and he will look at me like I'm nuts. I'll tell you how I've learned to do this. I've seen each type of weed display at least 10,000 times. In the early days, I used to study the display, and then cast out a jig or crankbait and hook some of the weeds and bring them in the boat to look at. Over the years, I've learned what the different types of weeds look like on the sonar. I use a flasher exclusively now, and I have no trouble identifying weed types."

The weeds don't necessarily display the way you think they should! Cabbage, which you think would be so thick it would completely clog up a flasher or picture-type display, actually is less dense than a stand of coontail or similar weed.

Cabbage shows up on a flasher as definite lines that have at least minute separations between them. On a picture-type display, cabbage shows up as characteristic stalks of weed that, again, show some separation between the plants.

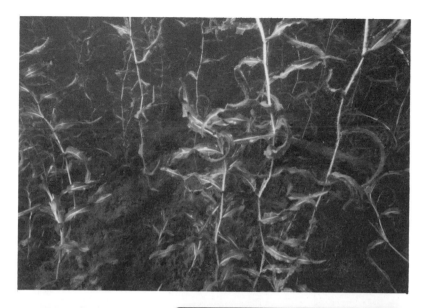

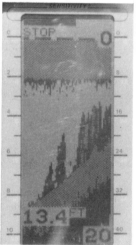
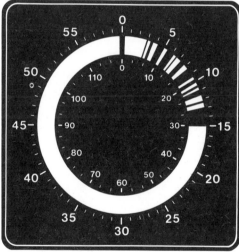

Figure 72—Cabbage weeds, or any similar weed of definite stalks and leaves, will show up on sonar like this. Notice the flasher display shows minute separations between the blips, and the picture-type displays show the characteristic long, individual stalks of the plants.

Coontail, or other similar weeds, are actually denser by comparison. They show up on all types of sonar as one continous "blob" of display. A flasher displays coontail as a solid band of light. Picture-type displays show coontail as a continous blob of marking.

Figure 73—Coontail, or any other regional weed of similar thickness, grows in very dense bunches. Unlike the cabbage weeds, notice how this type of weed displays as one continous "blob" regardless of sonar mode.

Thin weed growth that only covers the bottom, such as sandgrass, is not known as particularly good fish-holding habitat. You can also become good enough with your sonar unit to identify sandgrass on the bottom.

It will take practice, but you can learn to see it easily on a flasher. If the bottom reading simply looks "fuzzy and moving" you are probably over sandgrass or some similar bottom cover. This is very difficult to show with an illustration, so you'll just have to learn to see it by looking for it.

A plain old soft lake bottom without weeds on it shows up simply as a thin, pale display on the flasher. The weed cover causes the display to move up and down ever-so-slightly. It's a subtle difference, but very much there.

This has been a fairly exhaustive look at reading sonar displays. Take some time to go back through it, or refer to the various sections occasionally as a review.

But don't get hung up on studying this, or any other book on sonar, to try to really learn to use sonar in your fishing. Now, get the heck out on the water and spend some hours using your own sonar unit. Now you know a bit about what certain displays are showing you, but you still need your own experiences to back this up.

It takes practice to get good at using sonar. We can talk about it and talk about it, but it still takes time, using a sonar unit on the water, for you to really understand all the things it can do for you.

Right now, there is a very small minority of fishermen who are getting much at all out of their sonar units, compared to what the units can deliver. I say let's change that; let's make it a minority who aren't getting the *most* out of their sonar.

Chapter 6
Out of the box and into your boat: installing and caring for sonar

You know, as I think back on the short history of fishing sonar, I realize how few years we have been taking advantage of a technology that every previous generation of fishermen would have considered "Star Wars" fantasy. The pioneering efforts of people like Carl Lowrance, the man who brought sonar to the average angler, are still fresh memories to some of us.

And yet, it has only taken fishermen, and I include myself, a few years to take these amazing machines for granted. I guess that's human nature. Sonar units have become so much a part of our fishing gear that many anglers don't give enough thought to how important proper installation can be. Also, sonar units don't get treated like the sophisticated, fairly delicate instruments they are.

Sure, mounted in place they can withstand a lot of pounding, as your boat rides through heavy waves. And sure, most units can be left out in the rain and heavy splashing.

Still, there are things you should know, and things you should do, to ensure that your sonar unit works well from day one, and serves you for a number of trouble-free years, before you buy one of the new units that continually come from advancing technology.

One of the most important recommendations I can make is that you read your owner's manual, *before all else fails*. These books are a wealth of solid, useful information. I know, because I have sat with the writers of the manuals at the Eagle Electronics factory in Tulsa, OK. Just for fun, we have run down a list of the most common problems people have when trying to install and use sonar. You know what? They are all covered in owner's manuals!

Some folks are so frantic to get things done and get out there on the water, that they don't take a couple hours in the evening to read the instructions. Please, be one of the few who do.

It might be age-old advice, but almost every common problem encountered by people trying to install or use sonar can be solved by reading the owner's manual.

Proper transducer installation

Many people think of their sonar unit as only the housing with the display screen on it. But in order for the sonar display to light up with information, it has to send signals into the water, and receive some back.

The lifeline between the unit and the underwater world, the device that sends and receives signals, is the *transducer*. For a discussion of how to pick the right transducer for your type of fishing, see Chapter 3.

I don't want to belabor the point, but I do want to make sure you realize the importance of having the right transducer, and installing it for maximum performance. It doesn't make any sense to buy a quality unit and then do a half-baked job of putting the transducer in position.

It's such a critical matter for getting performance from your unit, in fact, that you shouldn't feel embarrased about having it done professionally if you're not sure about how to do it yourself.

The fishermen from north-central Minnesota have been fortunate since the dawn of sonar technology to have a guy named Jim Wentworth around. Now, I don't want to give you the impression that I have any special arrangement going with Jim. The reason I want to tell you about him, and have him walk us through much of this discussion on installing and caring for sonar, is that he is simply the best there is.

It's been more than 20 years since Marv Koep, another household name in my neck of the woods because of his fine Nisswa Bait & Tackle store, began a side business offering sonar repair—mainly to keep his famed Nisswa Guides in operational sonar. Jim Wentworth was there even in the beginning, working part time as a repair technician.

Here's sonar repair expert Jim Wentworth at work in his Nisswa, Minnesota Fish Lectronics shop. Jim has been deeply involved in sonar technology since its beginnings, and his contributions to this chapter make it a must-read for all sonar users!

Wentworth had his introduction to sonar technology in the Navy, but has really blossomed into a top-flight pro in the years since. He hasn't slowed down in the 20-plus years he's been operating Fish Lectronics, and recently purchased the business. As sonar has progressed, Jim has moved step-by-step with it. He has long since lost count of the number of units he has repaired or customized. If it involves sonar, or has happened to a sonar unit, Jim has seen it first hand and can speak about it from experience. There aren't many guys like that in the sonar world.

That's why I go to Jim Wentworth with my sonar questions, and that's why he is qualified to help you, too.

As I started to say, getting your transducer mounted properly is a real key to sonar performance. It is also a step that confuses many fishermen. If you want to install your unit yourself, fine. But before you decide which method of installation to go with, think about it carefully. The type of boat hull you have (fiberglass, aluminum, wood, kevlar, or whatever) makes a tremendous difference in how you should install the transducer. Let's go over each type of installation, so you'll have them all to compare.

What's a high speed transducer?

Before we get into any specific type of mounting, let's look at the question of "high speed" transducers. You hear this term kicked around from boat ramps to the floors of sports shows all the time.

Basically, all a high speed transducer is, is one that is permanently mounted in place, in a proper way so that it yields a good sonar reading even at medium and high speeds. Jim Wentworth has been around transducers as long as anybody except maybe Carl Lowrance, and here's what he has to say about this:

"The one that I can think of that really isn't high speed," Wentworth said, "is the suction cup-type mount that often comes with specifically portable units. But, I could take that suction cup transducer and mount it permanently and it would run perfectly at high speed. The physics of these transducers is all the same; the only differences are in how they are mounted. I can take one of those wedge-shaped transducers that has the one pointed end, and do a poor job of installing it and it won't give me anything for a high-speed reading. How they're mounted to the boat, and the kind of housing around them, are the only differences among transducers. Rounded transducers are most commonly used in through-hull mountings, and the wedge-shaped ones for mounting outside the hull, but they really can all be considered high speed transducers if they are mounted permanently and properly."

Through-hull mounting

Commonly referred to as "shoot through the hull" mounting, this method involves actually embedding (and normally gluing) the transducer into a small depression made in the hull, usually near the stern (back) of the boat.

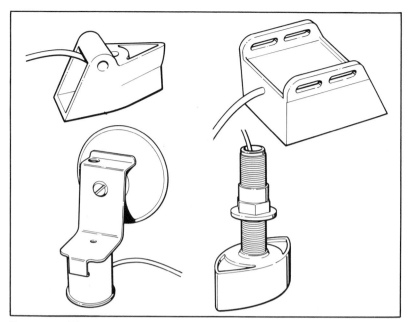

Figure 74—There are a variety of transducer styles made, essentially geared toward differing installation techniques. It's important to know that any transducer, regardless of the shape of the housing, can be used as a "high speed" transducer if it's mounted permanently. Pod-type fixed to a suction cup is most common for portable units, and that shape is commonly used for mounting through-the-hull on fiberglass boats. Wedge-shaped transducers are often used for mounting outside on the transom of any boat. Block styles are common on large ocean and Great Lakes boats.

If done properly, this method gives a beautiful high-speed sonar reading, and works perfectly at slower fishing speeds. The obvious advantage is that the transducer is protected from damage when putting the boat into the water on shallow ramps, and when running up on shallow water obstructions such as rocks or stumps.

Be aware that this method doesn't work well with some hull types. It is primarily used on fiberglass hulls. Historically, some anglers have mounted their transducers inside the hull on aluminum boats, but aluminum kills up to half the sonar signals. My advice is "don't" if you are thinking of mounting through the hull on an aluminum boat.

The main disadvantage to through-hull mounting is that, should the transducer go bad or require any attention, it is a pain to get at it. Normally, the transducer is epoxied into place very carefully. Taking it out of its mounting position is no small job.

Another drawback, in some experts' eyes, is the fact that, once the transducer is in position, its operational angle can't be changed. Jim Wentworth feels that the ability to play with the "angle of attack" on the transducer can be critical to getting the right-looking "hook" markings (signals from fish), with picture-type sonar. With flashers, it isn't as critical.

In my years of using picture-type sonar with through-hull mounted transducers, I have never had a problem generating beautiful looking hooks on the screen. Still, it might be something to watch out for in your own situation. If your unit isn't printing fish the way you want it to, that could be the problem.

Despite the drawbacks, this seems to be the mounting style of choice when the opportunity affords it.

This installation allows the transducer to send and receive signals from in front of the spot where the outboard motor is churning up that turbulence-producing wake. Therefore, the water making contact with the bottom of the boat at the transducer is usually smooth. That is crucial to good sonar performance.

One thing that makes this installation tricky is the chance that your boat has some wood framing or false-floor construction under the sump area. You *cannot* shoot signals through thick wood; it simply can't be done. So, before you install your transducer in this way, make sure whoever is doing the job knows what's between the sump area and the surface of the lake!

Normally, according to Jim Wentworth, it's a good bet to put the transducer right in the middle of the sump area, in front of the drain hole.

"Most of the time," Wentworth says, "you'll be safe right there. In some cases, you may have some wood blocking that area, though. You can call your boat dealer or manufacturer, to find out for sure where there is a pure fiberglass area on the hull that will make for good transducer mounting."

You will sometimes hear that the type of transducer is critical in this type of mounting, but not so, says Wentworth.

"That's a bunch of baloney," he said. "It doesn't make any difference what kind of transducer you use, as long as it's mounted in a pure fiberglass spot—although the round puck-type transducer is by far the most commonly used for this. In fact, you can even take one of those suction cup transducers used with portable units. Just take the suction cup off and slap that thing in there and away you go."

The actual mounting procedure

First and foremost, make sure it's at least 70 degrees F. when doing the job. The first step is to sand down the hull where the transducer will go. Take the paint off and get down to bare fiberglass. Then, Wentworth says, actually lightly sand the face of the transducer so you get a good connection while gluing. "I've seen a lot of transducers pop out of there because they didn't sand like this," he said.

As far as adhesives go, Wentworth said, any good epoxy—be it five-minute or the slower-curing type, will work fine.

To install a transducer in a fiberglass boat, first form a tinkers dam out of caulking compound to trap the epoxy in a pool. Then, mix two-part epoxy and pour into the dam.

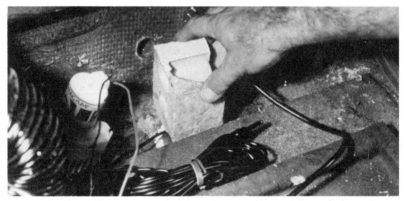

Press the transducer into the epoxy and move it around, to force out any trapped air. It's recommended to put a half brick on the transducer to hold it still while the epoxy cures. Otherwise, the transducer might tip and allow air to be trapped between it and the hull.

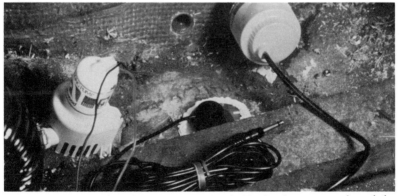

The transducer after the epoxy has hardened. The brick is removed, and the wire is ready to be attached to the sonar unit.

There is no problem with mounting multiple transducers in the same area, to be used with two or three sonar units on the same boat. They can be fairly close together; just make sure all transducers are mounted over a pure fiberglass portion of the hull.

If you own two or more sonar units—say, a flasher and a graph—but won't run more than one at once, it's okay to mount just one transducer and run two or three units off it. But, they normally have to be the same brand and run off the same frequency.

(With Eagle sonar units, the ones I use, all the transducers are interchangeable to all units, except those operating at the lower frequency of 50 KHz.)

The disadvantages of going with one transducer for multiple units are:

● If something goes wrong with your transducer, you have no backup.

● Every time you want to change from one unit to the next, you have to unplug the transducer cord from one and plug it into the unit you want to use. That takes time, and introduces the possiblity of damaging the cord from handling it so much.

(One final clarification: notice that I am saying this method allows the signal to be shot *through the hull*. It is not the same thing as actually drilling a hole through the hull and mounting the transducer flush with the bottom of the boat, as is sometimes done in special saltwater applications. Here, we are simply talking about gluing the transducer flush to the inside of the hull.)

Outside (transom) mounting

Another way of mounting the transducer is on the transom (back panel), on the outside of the boat. And while this does expose the transducer to being more easily damaged, many experts recommend this style.

"I know I normally prefer an outside mount to an inside mount," Jim Wentworth says. "Sometimes it's a disadvantage to mount them inside the hull, because some boats create a lot of cavitation in those areas, and those bubbles can screw up your sonar reading. Some boats just suck a lot of air right in the area you want to mount the transducer, so you have to mount them on the outside."

The other big advantage to this mounting style is the ease of getting at the transducer to fix it if something goes wrong.

Mounting a transducer to the outside of the hull is a fairly simple operation, but the location of the mount is the critical aspect for getting good sonar performance.

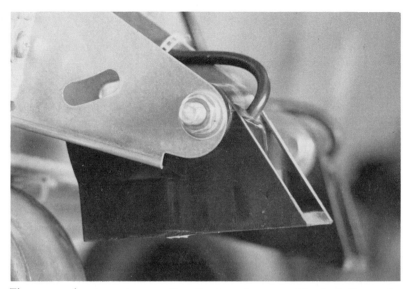

There are advantages to mounting the transducer outside the hull, on the transom. This installation makes it easy to adjust the angle of the transducer, and to get at it for any needed repairs.

I can't stress strongly enough either having an expert install it for you, or getting out on the water to determine where the transducer should be, before installing it. Finding the turbulence-free areas is easy—it just takes time to get out and do it.

Look at figure 75. It shows how to check for this area. Get off by yourself in an area free of reefs and other shallow water. Then, motor around, watching where you are going but spending most of your time facing backwards, studying the water flowing off the back of the boat. Vary your speed, from trolling speed to half throttle or even faster. Find the areas of blue, turbulence-free water coming off the back. Whitish water means cavitation. Find a spot fairly close to the middle of the boat, and mark it so you can find it exactly while mounting the transducer.

Normally, on an aluminum boat, this will be an area between the ribs (or keelsons). But there's more to it. Let's let an expert take over again.

Jim Wentworth:

"Really, the best transducers for transom mounting are those high-speed jobs with one flat and one pointed end. Some manufacturers are still making that square, blocky-looking transducer, that can only be mounted parallel to the base of the hull. If you mount those beneath the hull, you get too much cavitation to get a good reading, especially at higher speeds. That design is old, outdated, and crazy!

"So, anyways, you should pick one of those transducers with the pointed end. They should be mounted point forward and underneath the hull, maybe half an inch. A lot of guys try to mount their transducers flush with the bottom of the boat, and I'm telling you, that's trouble city. Sometimes, you can't even get a reading that way.

"You also want to set up the transducer so that, when the boat is sitting in the water, the transducer is aiming pretty much straight down. That means setting up the transducer so it has a 3-6 degree forward angle."

If your aluminum boat has a back end particularly full of rivets, there is another neat trick you can do to cut down on the amount of turbulence they cause. Take silicone caulking and smooth the rivets over, concentrating on the area where you will mount the transducer. With your fingers, you should be able to get them glass-smooth.

With fiberglass hulls, the process is much the same, except the hull will have much smoother water coming over it due to the lack of rivets. Simply run the boat to locate the smoothest water coming off the back. In fact, with fiberglass hulls, you can sometimes mount the transducer flush with the hull and still get a good reading.

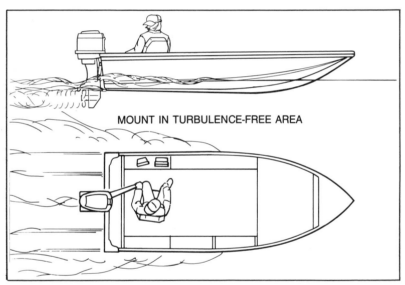

MOUNT IN TURBULENCE-FREE AREA

Figure 75—Run your boat before mounting the transducer, so you can find the area where the least turbulence is created by the hull. Water turbulence across the face of the transducer will ruin your sonar performance.

Adjusting the angle of the transducer

After you have the bracket attached to the hull, put the transducer in place but leave the bolt loose. (Before you screw or bolt it in place, make sure the transducer sticks down $3/8$-$1/2$ inch below the bottom of the hull.) Work with the angle of the transducer until you have it tipped forward somewhere in that 3-6 degree area. That way, when the water comes off the hull it will wash across the face of the transducer smooth and free. Also, that slight forward angle ensures that the signal you send down is going straight down.

As I already mentioned, Wentworth believes strongly that it is critical to be able to adjust the angle of the transducer, for paper graphs, videos and liquid crystals.

When you initially install a transom mount transducer, set the forward angle somewhere in that 3-6 degree area. Then, go fishing! Pay attention to the types of hooks you are getting on your sonar screen from fish. If you are happy with them, leave the transducer the way it is. If you aren't happy, you can adjust the angle until you are.

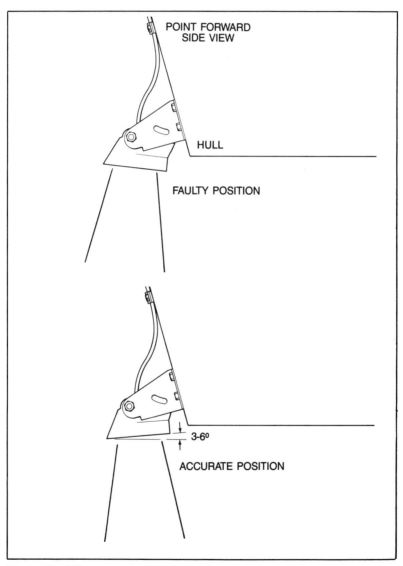

Figure 76—When mounting your transducer on the transom, set it up point forward and a bit under the hull. Make sure it is positioned at a 3-6 degree angle forward, not pointing backward.

Attaching the bracket to the hull

Regardless what type of bracket you have, there are some keys to follow to make sure your transducer is on to stay:

● Use stainless steel fasteners. Whether screws or bolts, it's the only way to go. (Incidentally, don't worry about what kind of metal your hull is made of, or any reinforcing plate you might be using in the installation. There won't be any reaction of significance between the transducer crystal and the screws, bolts or hull plates. *Galvanic action* of this sort is very slow, and no problem for everyday sonar performance.)

● Use a good sealer in and around the fastener holes. The best of these is silicone. Within reason, it's hard to get too much silicone in there.

● Make sure your transducer cords are fastened somehow to the hull, but leave 6-10 inches of slack directly above the transducer. The slack is insurance, in the event you hit something. If your wires are tightly bound to the hull, and the transducer gets knocked off, the wires will probably get ripped right out of the crystal.

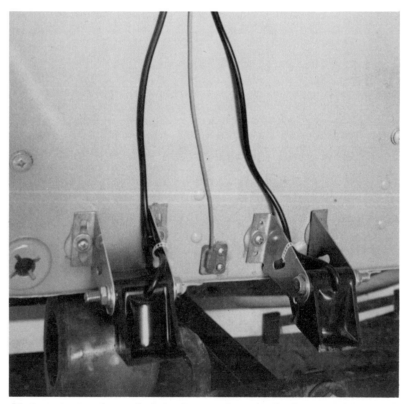

It's important to leave slack in the transducer cord when mounting on the transom. The slack is insurance, in the event you hit something in the water and the transducer gets dislodged from its mount. With no slack in the cord, the transducer crystal could be ripped free from the housing.

136

A separate sonar in the bow

For many fishermen, and I certainly include myself, it would be hard if not impossible to fish seriously out of a boat with only one sonar unit! The main unit always goes in the back, from where you run the outboard motor. Then, when you walk up to the front of the boat to run the bow electric trolling motor and cast, what do you do about sonar? Show me somebody with good enough eyes to read the face of a sonar unit 16 feet away!

The answer, of course, is to install a separate sonar unit in the bow, for the time you spend fishing there. Another matter is where the transducer goes for that unit. Should you simply run a longer cord from the transducer you use for the main sonar unit? You can, but then the bow sonar unit is reading a signal coming from the back of the boat—which is a long ways away and can be radically different from the depth and terrain directly under the bow in many cases.

What do I suggest? Mounting the transducer directly to the housing of the bow electric trolling motor. That way, your sonar unit is reading a signal going directly down from where you are.

One method for installing a transducer this way is shown in figure 77 . A special *pod*-type transducer, with a slotted mounting brace built right into it, is available from many manufacturers.

Mounting it is a simple operation. You can get a big hose clamp at any hardware or automotive supply store, and it will fit right into the slots on the housing of the transducer. Slide the whole works over the motor housing, and tighten it down with the transducer facing down.

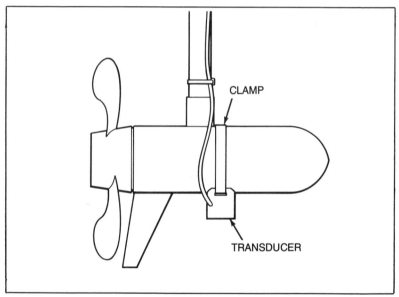

CLAMP

TRANSDUCER

Figure 77—The standard way of mounting a transducer onto bow trolling motors is to fasten it directly to the motor housing using an ordinary hose clamp. A special pod-style transducer, with a slot designed to accept the hose clamp, makes the job easy.

Although this type of transducer is far and away the most common in this situation, it isn't the only one that will work. As Wentworth says, "if you can mount it on the motor, it will work." In fact, there is a wonderful product that will allow you to mount about any transducer to the bow trolling motor.

Johnny Ray Sports of Gadsden, AL, makes a mounting bracket that securely holds the transducer off to the side of the motor shaft, where it's less susceptible to being damaged or encountering interference from electric motor operation. Mounted with the hose clamp, the transducer is actually underneath the motor housing, where it might get damaged if you run the motor hard into the lake bottom or a stump.

The Johnny Ray bow mount allows you to install the transducer away from electric motor cavitation, and in a safer spot than below the motor housing, as in the traditional hose clamp mounting method.

Use electrical tape to fasten the transducer cable right to the shaft of the trolling motor. But, go about the taping job slowly and think it through. If you simply tape it tightly to the shaft, you don't allow yourself any slack for adjusting the length of the motor shaft while fishing.

(On windy days, for example, you want more of the motor in the water, because waves will be pulling the prop out of the water constantly if it is only submerged a few inches. On calm days in very shallow or weedy water, on the other hand, you will want to put only the prop of the motor in the water so you don't clog it up or hit something.)

Determine where that "adjustment area" is, by changing the length of the shaft a few times. Leave sufficient slack in the transducer cable for full adjustment.

Another caution: because the cable is tied right to the motor shaft, the cable is susceptible to being bent severely or even cut when putting the motor in and out of its bracket. But, this doesn't have to happen. Before taping the cable down, raise and lower the motor several times, as if you are putting it in and out of the water. Study how the motor shaft positions itself as it goes in and out of the bracket. Now, tape the cable one portion at a time, keeping it free from being pinched at any point by the bracket. Voila! You're ready to go.

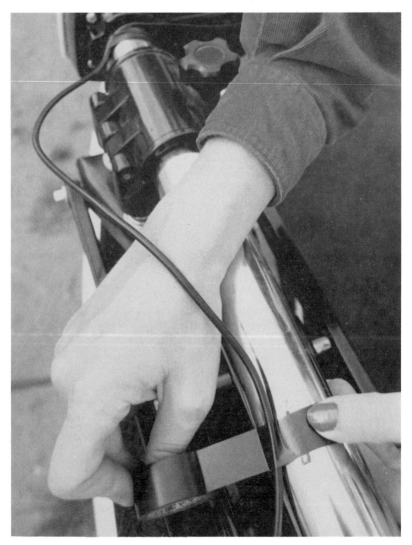

When taping the transducer cable to the bow trolling motor, leave sufficient slack in the "adjustment area" of the motor shaft. Also, study how the motor sits in its mounting bracket, and secure the cable so it won't be bent or cut by the bracket.

Mounting transducers for portable units

If a person fishes a lot from rental boats, or takes fly-in trips, or does a lot of ice fishing with a sonar unit, it makes great sense to own a portable unit.

If you plan to use your sonar unit in rental boats or for ice fishing, it makes sense to consider a portable.

Mounting the transducer with a portable involves special considerations, especially recognizing limitations. Most portables come with a transducer that can be attached to the boat with a suction cup affair. Well, let me tell you, there are more transducers ground up in outboard props because of suction cups that give way than I care to think about.

If you are going to use this suction cup device, do it the right way. There is normally a lanyard that can be tied to the boat to limit how far the transducer can go, should the suction cup free itself. Use it. Tie it down securely, and tight enough so that if the transducer does come free, it can't swing into the teeth of the prop.

Or better yet, Lindy-Little Joe makes a portable transducer bracket (figure 78) that really works slick. It allows you to tilt the transducer up or down, and gives you a solid seating of the transducer in operation. Still, it's not a good idea to leave a portable transducer in the water while running at high speeds in powerful boats. That's why the ability to tip the bracket quickly out of the water is such a nice feature (it also is a lifesaver when you come up onto shallow water and are about to ding the transducer on a rock or something).

141

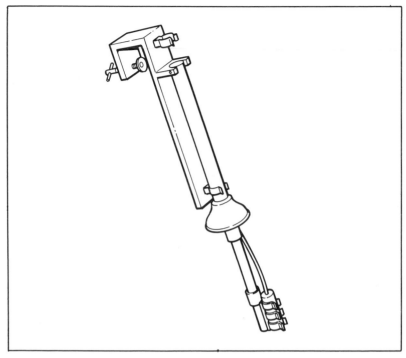

Figure 78—The Lindy-Little Joe portable transducer bracket makes using portable sonar even more convenient.

If you invest a few bucks in this bracket, you will get better medium-speed readings from your portable sonar unit, and you can concentrate on fishing rather than worrying about whether the transducer is still sticking to the side of the boat.

And for mounting the portable sonar unit in place while fishing, I haven't seen anything slicker than the oar-lock mounting bracket manufactured by Goldeneye Products of Minneapolis, MN. Look for it at your local sporting goods dealer, or ask them to order one for you.

Adding swivel to your sonar

Of all the accessories available for making your sonar installation more complete, there is one that stands out. In fact, in my mind, Johnny Ray swivel brackets should be standard equipment on all permanent mount sonar. Just about all good sporting goods and marine dealers carry these little devices, which allow you to swivel the face of the unit so no matter where you sit, as long as you're in the vicinity of the unit, you can get a straight-on look at the sonar screen.

They are well-made and come in a variety of sizes to fit different units. And they provide an added bonus: the bracket pops out easily, so you can take your sonar units off the boat without having to unscrew the gimbal bracket. This is a great feature for many situations, such as when you pull up to a restaurant at the end of a hard day of fishing and want to stash the sonar units in the truck before going inside.

Before figuring the cost of your complete sonar investment, include the price of Johnny Ray swivel mounts.

Because you can never be sure where in the boat you'll be sitting or standing from minute to minute, a good swivel bracket like the Johnny Ray should be standard equipment.

Picking a power supply: the marine battery

Supplying power to your sonar unit is only one consideration today, when picking power supplies for the modern fishing boat. Battery power is the heart of your boat's electronics system. It powers your trolling motor, starts your engine, and runs all the other gadgetry that's in there.

It's hard for me to believe, but I've seen people skimp on boat batteries. It's a very big mistake. You spend $400-500 for a top-of-the-line graph, $150 for a good flasher, more money on temperature guages and other things, so don't try to get by with an old used car battery. It's just simply not made to handle the use a boat battery gets.

In general, sonar units don't draw much power. Paper graphs draw the most, up to about two amps per hour. Considering that batteries most commonly used in fully-rigged boats have either 80 or 105 amp-hour ratings, it would take a long time of continous running to discharge a big battery from sonar use alone.

All sonar units run on 12-volt systems. As Wentworth put it, "as long as it's 12 volts, it doesn't matter what kind of battery you want to use. You can run your unit off a motorcycle battery, an electric fence battery, two dry cells, a car battery or a marine battery. It simply doesn't make any difference as long as it's 12 volts."

However, from an overall performance standpoint, if you are fishing from a permanent or semi-permanent setup, you should purchase good marine batteries to do the job.

If you have a large engine with electric start, you will likely have a marine starting battery like my GNB *Super Crank*. This battery is designed to provide large, short bursts of power for turning over the engine. Then, the engine, if equipped with an alternator, continually recharges the battery as you run.

Because sonar is such a small drain on power, most boat riggers will simply attach the sonar units to the cranking battery. So, it does double duty, starting the motor and running your sonar.

If you don't use such a battery for starting your motor, but still want long, continous use from your sonar, I would suggest powering it with a *deep cycle* battery, such as a *Stowaway* or *Action Pack*. These batteries are built to withstand repeated deep cycling, the act of running down and then recharging the battery. (By comparison, cranking batteries, whether made for starting boats or cars, will lose much of their capacity after about 50 such discharge-recharge cycles.)

Although we aren't concerning ourselves with the total electronic picture in your boat, it is important that you know the difference between batteries made for marine use and those that aren't. Marine batteries have denser, thicker plates, reinforced with special separators that reduce vibration damage and loss of active plate material from pounding over waves. An old car battery is not a good choice for use in your boat, regardless of the application.

In the case of portable sonar, many run off two small six-volt lantern batteries that combined provide 12 volts. If you are fishing where it's no problem to carry a heavier battery to the boat, it can be a good idea to "power up" a bit for longer life, by temporarily running the portable with a marine or motorcycle battery.

The heart of your electrical system is the battery (or batteries). Specialized marine batteries like these, whether cranking or deep-cycle, are made for the rugged use boat batteries get.

Battery maintenance

Batteries, of course, don't last forever. Even the best, most powerful marine battery will wear out after a few years, or after a large number of discharge-recharge cycles.

There are a few common-sense things you can do to ensure that your batteries die of old age rather than from abuse, however.

Number one, use only a trickle charger on your marine battery. I've seen so many guys fry batteries trying to quick charge them I can't tell you. Just get in the habit of using the batteries all day, and leaving them plugged into a charger all night. It's the only way to go, unless you are on a wilderness or camping trip with no electricity. In those cases, you can carry an extra battery or two and charge all of them when you get back to civilization. Or, better yet, do what we do when we go on the road: take a portable generator. I have a little John Deere generator that runs very quietly, and on a tank of gas can keep a trickle charger doing its thing for hours. By next morning, the generator has run out of gas and shut off, and my boat battery is ready for another day.

If you think you are saving time by putting your boat batteries on any kind of a boost charger, or any faster charging cycle, you better guess again. All that will do is shorten the life of the battery dramatically. The fast charges just burn out the battery, and that can get to be an expensive proposition.

Number two, make sure you check the water levels every time or every couple times you charge the battery.

There are a few obvious points, such as keeping the batteries clean and the contacts free of corrosion to ensure good contacts. Keep the battery tied down securely in the boat, and keep grease on the terminals to prevent corrosion buildup.

And, if you live in the North country like I do, where people put their boats away for the winter, don't just come off the water for the last time in the fall and leave the batteries in the boat. Take them out, charge them up and store them properly. There is a preferred storing temperature range for today's batteries, in the range of about 30-60 degrees F. At room temperature, the self-discharge increases and the ultimate life of the battery can be shortened. But, if you leave your batteries subjected to below-zero temperatures, the electrolyte can actually freeze.

A cool spot, then, like an insulated but unheated garage, or a cool closet, or similar location, is the best place for your batteries if you want multiple seasons out of them.

There is an old wive's tale that the folks at GNB Batteries clarified for me, concerning what surface is acceptable to store you batteries on. For years, we've all heard that you should never leave batteries on concrete floors, because that accelerates the self-discharge. The experts say that's hogwash! The temperature, not the surface on which the battery rests, is the critical factor.

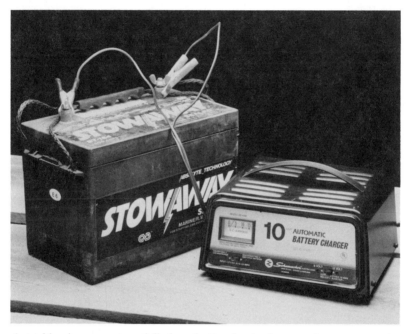

A trickle charger puts a full, long-lasting load of power into your marine battery. By trying to save time with a quick-charging method, you will shorten the life of your battery.

Wires and wiring

Now, don't get panicky at this point. Yes, you need to do some wiring if you install your own sonar unit. But it's not open-heart surgery we're talking about here.

Once again, your owner's manual is the single source you should look to for basic information. If you follow the recommendations in the manual, there is nothing magical about hooking up the wires.

There are, however, some general rules and fine points for overcoming potential problems:

● When you hook up any sonar, make sure the positive line is fused. It can be an in-line fuse, or attached to the fuse panel.

● Quick-connect devices are handy and help prevent passive electricity draw (anytime you leave the cables connected to your unit and the battery, there is some voltage in the line, which can cause corrosion in time). If you do a lot of connnecting and disconnecting of the actual sonar plugs, you can easily wreck one with a wrong twist.

● While you are wiring your boat, and forever after while using the sonar unit, take care not to sharply bend or twist the wires. If you do, in time you will have broken wires and a repair problem.

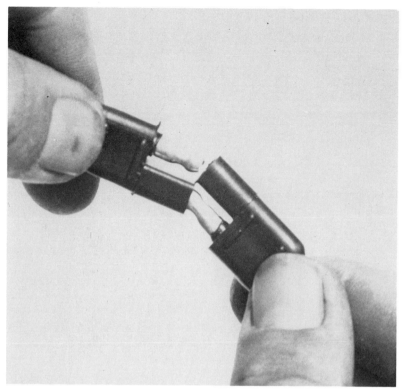

A quick-connect device like this can be installed on your sonar power cords, allowing you to easily disconnect power to the unit when not fishing. Whenever your power cords are hooked up, there is a passive electricity draw from your battery.

Avoiding sources of electrical interference

It's tough enough to identify and interpret the signals you want to receive, much less deal with a lot of nonsense signals caused by interference. And yet, as Wentworth put it "there are a lot of monsters out there in your boat, and you've got to be aware of them to be able to correct them."

Interference can come from a variety of sources. *Mechanical* interference can be caused by physical vibration of the hull (even something as seemingly benign as a loose screw can cause noise on the dial of your flasher).

Cavitation, as we've already discussed, is caused by air bubbles racing over the face of the transducer.

Radio frequency interference can come from outboard motors, CB radios, and many other electrical devices. Anything that causes radio frequency interference at a similar frequency to your sonar can show up on the display.

The suppression controls on your sonar will knock much of this interference out. But, remember what we said about suppression? Don't use it unless it's absolutely necessary, because in most cases it affects the ability of your sonar to show you details such as fish and subtle bottom contours. Any problem caused by improper transducer installation should be fixed by re-installing the transducer and doing it right.

To prevent electrical interference from ruining your experience of fishing with sonar, isolate the wire going from the sonar unit to your transducer. Get it completely separated from all other wires in the boat. One good way is to put the sonar wire into a plastic tube, away from all the other wires. But, if you try this and your electrical problems persist, you better have an electrician or somebody who's very good with electrical problems in boats look at your whole wiring arrangement. There may be another problem somewhere, and the sonar unit is picking up on it.

Another source of potential trouble is pulse-width modulators, used to get longer use from your electric trolling motor on one battery charge.

Actually, more was made of this when the pulse-width modulators first came out than the situation actually warrants. I have used Minn Kota's *Maximizer* since day one, and haven't had a bit of interference problems with my sonar. Why? Because I trusted Jim Wentworth with installing the system, and he knew exactly what to do.

Jim Wentworth

"The pulse-width modulators are mostly a problem with front trolling motor mounts, where you are putting the transducer right onto the housing of the motor. If your motor has a pulse-width modulator (PWM), you can't hook up the sonar unit to the same battery that the trolling motor runs off. It's usually as simple as that. If you hook up a motor with a PWM to the same battery as your sonar, you will pick up interference, especially when the sensitivity is turned up high on the sonar. But if you wire to a separate power source, you shouldn't have any problem.

"You may have heard that this sort of interference can wreck your sonar unit. It can blow out a flasher, but on a paper graph it will normally just throw the stylus into saturation (meaning it marks totally black from top to bottom, as if you had pressed the 'marker' button) and it burns paper. With liquid crystal and video, all that happens is the dial lights up funny, but it doesn't hurt anything."

There. Maybe we can lay to rest a controversy that has been burning, high and low, since these pulse-width modulators came onto the marketplace.

You cut your cable in half: now what?

It happens for a lot of reasons, but cutting a transducer cable out on the water doesn't have to be a panic situation. It's easy and quick to repair the coaxial cable of a sonar unit.

Always carry electrical tape, and something sharp to trim the cable, in case this ever happens to you.

The cable is easy to understand. Look at the diagram. You can see the outer section of wire, or the ground wire, and the transfer wire in the middle. They are kept separate by insulation.

To begin the field repair, peel away the plastic from the broken ends of the cable. Next, wrap the two center wires together and cover that junction with electrical tape. Then, do the same thing with the two broken outside wires. Seal over the entire thing with electrical tape, and you should be back in business. (When you get home, the wires should be soldered back together. If you don't know how, take it to someone who does.)

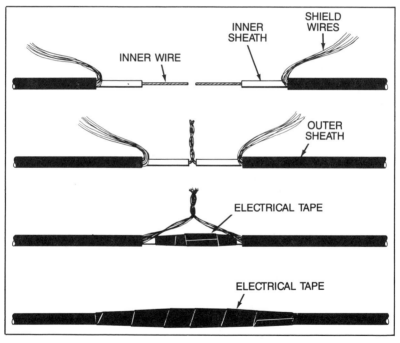

Figure 79—To make an emergency splice on a coaxial transducer cable, all you need is something to cut with and electrical tape. First, peel back the plastic shielding and twist the two inner wires together. Fold this splice back and wrap it down with tape. Then, wrap the outer wires together and fold them back. Wrap the entire splice with electrical tape so no water can get in.

Any time you want to add length to a sonar power cord, simply splice in an appropriate length of 14-16 guage wire. Just try to limit any changes in wire length.

Be careful not to shorten the transducer cable any more than necessary. If you take an inch or two out of it, that won't affect the calibration of your unit. But if you take four feet it probably will, and you'll have to have the unit re-calibrated by a professional sonar repair person. Now, according to Wentworth, this is a complex subject. He said that any time you change the length of the transducer cord you affect the unit, but that with more powerful units, the affect might not be as drastic and might not show up after taking away a few feet or adding a few feet. But how do you know ahead of time, when it comes to your unit?

An ounce of prevention: avoiding problems before they start

If you know anything about human nature, this next item won't surprise you a bit: a majority of the problems and breakdowns fishermen have with sonar units, they cause themselves. It probably wouldn't matter what bullet-proof material manufacturers made their sonar from, we would find a way to bash right through it and damage the unit.

I see guys come off the lake, unpack their boat, grab their sonar units along with a huge armful of rods, drop the sonar unit three times on the way to the car, toss it in the trunk like it's a football helmet, and leave it there, parked in the sun, for a week until they go fishing again.

This is just one example of the kinds of abuses that occur. It's often a matter of carelessness; with a little effort and common sense, the problems that this treatment causes can be avoided.

That, as a matter of fact, *is* the first rule of sonar care: treat it like the most valuable fishing partner you have and it will last and perform for many years. If your sonar isn't working, can any of your human friends take over for it?

Many problems you can encounter with sonar are just too tricky to try to fix. I run into things that I don't even consider touching. For these situations, turn to an an expert. I have been living by a guideline Jim Wentworth set out a number of years back, and it has worked well.

"If you don't understand it," he always says, "don't mess with it. Most people can work with power cords and clean their units, but after that, they should at least call us or get them in to a shop, and we'll take care of them."

How do you know who you can trust to do the job right? Well, if you send your ailing unit to a factory authorized repair center, the workers should be well qualified.

But, if you don't know who to turn to, package your sonar unit and ship it to Jim Wentworth. His address is Fish Lectronics, Box 577, 303 Smiley Rd, Nisswa, MN 56468.

Don't be afraid to ship your unit away, but be thorough in preparing it for the trip:

● Put at least four inches of packing around the perimeter of the unit.

● Send the transducer along (unless it's sealed in a through-hull mount, for example, and inaccesible).

● Include a note of explanation, detailing what is wrong.

● If it is a portable unit, *don't* ship batteries with it. Heavy batteries can cause a lot of damage in the shipping process.

By following the steps outlined, you need not worry about shipping your sonar unit away for repairs.

There are a number of things you can do to minimize the chances of damaging your unit, including:

● Take good care of the wires. Damage to the wires is the most common reason a piece of sonar equipment has to go into a repair shop. Be careful when plugging and unplugging all connections, and make sure your system is fused properly.

Jim Wentworth

"One of the most common problems people have is that the display goes out on their unit, or they can't get a good high-speed reading. Most of them have smashed their transducer cords, or broken the little plug that connects the cord to the back of the unit. I would venture that most of these cases are caused by abuse of the wires. People just aren't careful. They take the plug in and out by just grabbing and pulling, and a broken wire eventually happens. Also, a lot of people don't put a fuse in their lines, and they burn the cords out."

● Handle the transducer with care. It might look like a hockey puck, but it's not meant to get banged around. One of the most important things you can do is make sure you don't put any pressure on the point where the wire joins the transducer. If that junction gets damaged, you've got problems. Having to replace a transducer, in fact, is the single most costly thing that can go wrong. An average transducer in 1987 cost $40-50 to replace.

● Take steps to prevent condensation. Condensation causes problems with sonar—not as much as it did in the days of flasher units with exposed electronics, but it remains a problem to watch for. A morning that sees everything covered with dew, a big temperature change and you can have problems. Before storing your unit—even for just a few days—make sure there isn't any water buildup inside it. Don't get me wrong, with most good sonar units these days, it is very rare for any water to actually get inside the unit. But condensation can get inside anything.

Believe it or not, a major cause of sonar problems is leaving a unit in the "dry storage" compartments of modern fishing boats. Dry storage is not usually dry—water can get in when it rains, and from waves. If you store your sonar unit in "dry storage" that has water in it, your unit can become full of water. Then, you take it out of the storage, hook it up, turn it on and *pooof!* the unit shorts out and you have a repair problem.

With the old, exposed guts units like the Lowrance green box, a hand-held hair dryer, car heater, or temporary exposure to direct sunlight can quickly dry out excess water. But if you see condensation on the face of a nitrogen sealed unit, such as a liquid crystal or video, and it doesn't go away in about 24 hours, get it in to a repair shop as soon as you can. A sonar repair person can dry it out with minimal damage to the internal components, and then re-seal the unit. Don't wait a week, or you could have major problems.

Never store sonar units more than a few hours in your trunk, especially if your car is parked in the hot sun. Keep the units clean, dry and cool and they will last much longer.

With all sonar units, it's a good idea to store them inside the house during winter.

Transducer care

In normal use, simply be careful of the transducer and try to avoid hitting it sharply against anything. Remember, a sonar unit is *calibrated*, so that the transducer and the sending/receiving device work in concert to show you accurate depth readings, minute details like fish and cover, etc.

Over time, even with proper care, a transducer can change frequencies, according to Wentworth, and require re-calibration. "And another reason to have your sonar unit checked every few years," he said, "is that transducers can lose up to 40-50 percent of their ability to transmit signals without you knowing it. People don't realize the natural degredation that occurs with their units. Transducers really do change frequencies, and really do go bad, and then we have to fix or replace them."

One thing you can do in the short term is keep the face of the transducer clean. If you get oil or stubborn dirt on the transducer, or even algae growth from leaving a boat in the water all summer, it can really cut down signal reception. Clean them with a brillo pad if they get really dirty, or simply use a household cleaner like Formula 409 for periodic touchups.

Specific care

Let's look for a minute at proper maintenance and care of specific types of sonar units, beginning with paper graphs.

A problem that plagues users of paper graph recorders (it is, in fact, often cited as the reason people buy liquid crystals over paper graphs) is the buildup of carbon inside the unit. Jim Wentworth tipped me off to a great way to clean it out. First, blow out the bulk of the carbon with compressed air. Then, clean a bit more thoroughly with some alcohol (although this is not necessary). Then, blow the entire unit clean with something called a "tuner degreaser" that you can buy from some television repair and sonar repair shops. (Tuner degreaser comes in an aerosol can.) Then, put a little light weight oil on the paper transport gears and your graph should be printing out cleanly again.

If you don't think carbon buildup can become a major problem, listen again to Jim Wentworth:

"Sometimes, when I get graphs in my shop with this problem, I have to tear down the whole machine and de-carbon it, and then repack the transport gears. I've seen them come in clogged up so bad with carbon that the stylus belt would hardly move. And the guy will actually wonder why his graph doesn't work anymore. It's a very good idea to clean out the carbon every once in a while."

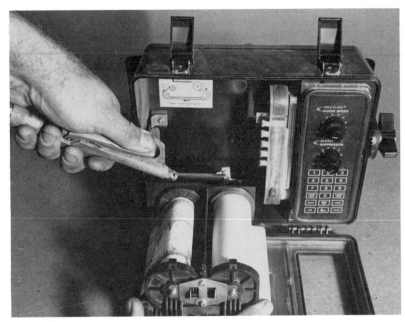

To clean carbon buildup out of a paper graph unit, open it up and blow the bulk of the carbon out with compressed air. (Then, you may clean more thoroughly with alchohol and tuner degreaser, although this isn't absolutely necessary.)

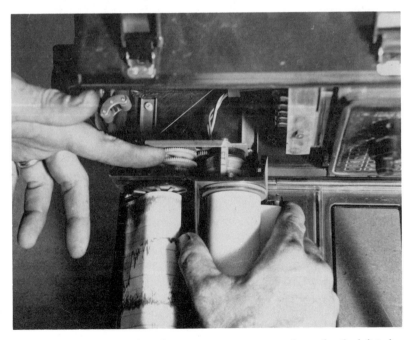

Lastly, put a little light oil on the paper transport gears, shown by the left index finger in the photo.

Periodic professional maintenance, Wentworth says, will often keep big problems from showing up down the road. "People should take their paper graph units in to a shop every two years, on the average, to have them completely cleaned and re-calibrated," he said.

Another common problem for graph users is a band across their paper that "doesn't seem to be printing" even though the rest of the area is printing fine. This normally shows up as a white band through the black areas that are printing correctly.

If you suspect you might be having this trouble, here's how to test it. If you have a "marker" switch or button on your graph, hold it down and run out about a half-inch of paper. This should give you a totally black printout. If there are any blank spots in your printout, they will be obvious.

When you get one or more white bands across your paper graph display like this, it is known as "skip printing." It's caused by either insufficient stylus pressure on the paper, or a worn stylus belt. First try bending the stylus to create more pressure on the paper. If that doesn't solve the problem, have a sonar repair person check your stylus belt.

Jim Wentworth:

"The most common reason for this sort of trouble is the stylus pressure. With a lot of popular brands, a new stylus comes with every new roll of paper. The way the new stylus comes in the package, it is flattened out. When you put them in your unit, you have to bend down the right and left sections. When you bend down the right section, you are providing good contact with a high-voltage bar. When you bend down the left section, you provide good pressure on the paper.

"So, anytime you see that 'skip print' on your graph readout, it's caused by not enough stylus pressure in that area, or your stylus belt has worn out so much that it's stretched to the point that the belt is actually flying away from the face of the graph as it comes around. If that's the case, you need a new belt."

Actually, it's a good idea to replace the stylus belt every year or so, unless you rarely use the graph. Change the stylus every two or three rolls of paper, to keep a source of clean printing contact working for you.

This next point applies to all picture-type sonar for sure, and it isn't a bad rule to follow for flashers as well: keep the faceplate as clean as possible, and don't trailer your boat, open, down the road with the graphs installed! You can't believe what the road grit does to the face of all sonar units over just a short time.

Liquid crystal care

Liquid crystals are small, light weight and fairly tough sonar units. But they do require good care. The front lens (screen) gets scratched very easily, even while cleaning. So, while it's important to keep the screen clean, use a soft rag or even lens tissue you buy for your glasses or camera lenses. For a lot of dirt buildup, use a light cleaner like Windex.

Do not rub or even touch the screen with your hands any more than necessary (and none should be necessary). Your hands will scratch the screen easily.

Now, about bug spray. I'll let Jim Wentworth tell you about bug spray. "A lot of guys are spraying bug spray on their arms and it gets right on the face of a liquid crystal," he said, "and this is also a very big problem with graphs or video. That bug spray etches right into the screen and you can't clean it off sometimes. It can completely fog out your unit's face."

When your display goes away

Sometimes, no matter how careful you are, you are going to have sonar trouble. Let's say you turn your sonar unit on to start fishing and don't get a signal, or are out fishing and your signal goes out.

Wentworth says that this can be caused by two different things:

"Number one," he said, "you can be having a transducer failure. In that case, you will get no depth reading at all. Let's say you're running a flasher. All you will get is your zero light (showing the surface of the lake) and no bottom signals at all. To test for this, turn the sensitivity full up and leave the suppression all the way off. Now, rub the bottom of the transducer with your hand. There should be signals firing up all around the dial if the transducer is still good. If you don't get any signals while doing this, it either means the transmitter or receiver is out, or it could be the transducer.

"If you have access to another similar transducer, plug it in and see if you can get any depth readings to come on, or if the hand-rubbing test gives you any signals. If you still can't get any signals, you better get the unit in for repairs."

"This test works exactly the same for other types of sonar. With liquid crystal and video, you'll see a vertical bar of display moving up and down, or even completely covering the screen, as you move your hand around on the transducer. With a paper graph, you'll also see a vertical bar of print as you check. Also, with high power units (those with 200 watts RMS or more), you can actually hear the transducer 'clicking' if you listen carefully, if it is working properly."

It's a sad fact that not enough guys take proper care of their sonar equipment. It's a big investment, and it's your window on the fish's world. Keep that window clean, and functioning strong. It has earned a place in your boat, and it deserves a little TLC to keep it working the way it can.

Chapter 7
What else is there?

Sonar is what this book is about. But there are a number of devices that complement its use that I want to quickly mention. They help me find fish, avoid getting lost on new lakes, and just plain increase my fishing enjoyment.

My fishing boats (I maintain several at all times for different types of fishing) have been compared to cockpits, full of little gadgets, gauges, wires, and machines. To me, they are a floating laboratory I can take on the water to help me study fish.

I use about every device known to man (somebody has to test all that stuff) during the course of the year. And yet, I try hard not to get caught up in using electronic fishing aids just for the sake of using them. Under situations where they will truly help me, I use them.

I urge you to take a similar position on these accessories. Don't feel that you have to own one of everything we're about to talk about. If, however, something fits into your fishing style, put it on your boat.

There are a lot worse ways to spend your money.

LORAN-C: a great navigational aid

LORAN navigation, once known only to the military, ocean-going ships and some Great Lakes charter captains, is becoming a hot topic in all fishing circles these days, and for good reason. It works great, and helps people find and return to fishing spots on unfamiliar or big waters.

But its value to fishermen goes far beyond guiding us to fishing spots. If you know the panicky feeling of being caught out on the water in a heavy fog or upcoming storm, you have felt the need to get back to shore quickly, even though you can't see any landmarks.

Loran navigation was introduced to freshwater sportfishing in the Great Lakes, but its use has spread to other sprawling inland lakes.

The word LORAN (from now on, I won't capitilize the whole word, but that's the proper way to do it) stands for LOng RAnge Navigation. It is a highly refined system that operates off am radio waves. A series of shore-based towers takes Loran to boaters the world over, although there are some "dead areas" that we will talk about in a minute.

There actually was Loran navigation before Loran-C, called Loran-A. During World War II, the Coast Guard developed it to help ships and aircraft navigate over large expanses of water. (To this day, Loran towers operate non-stop, and are effectively used for navigation over water, land or air.)

Loran-C is more accurate, and useable over much greater distances, than Loran-A. It operates off a series, or *chain*, of radio towers. Each group has a master station and two-four secondary stations. The master and secondary stations each broadcast signals at precise intervals. The signals overlap each other at many points, and these intersections (known as *waypoints*) are the basis of Loran navigation.

By receiving the signals sent out by these master and secondary stations, a Loran unit "knows" the position of your boat, and can tell you how to get to any other destination (waypoint) you program into it. It tells you how fast your boat is traveling, the course you should steer, the course you are steering, and even how long it will take to get to your destination at the speed you are moving! Many Lorans also have a "course correction" feature. Sometimes, even though you are steering at the precise heading the Loran gives you, wind and currents can carry you off course. This feature allows you to correct for this *drift* and head straight for your destination.

Let's say you catch a nice bunch of salmon on one of the Great Lakes, at a spot you found by accident while wandering around ten miles off shore. It's a sunken ship, not the biggest thing in the world, and there are no land markings anywhere. Next summer, when you come back here, you'd like to be able to return to this spot without spending the first half of your only week of vacation looking for the blasted thing.

With a Loran-C, you can store the coordinates of your location the first time you find it. Then, the next day, next month or three years later return to within a few feet of that spot, by simply re-entering the coordinates and letting the Loran tell you where to go! They really are amazing.

Darrell Lowrance and I caught these beautiful salmon at an offshore location on one of the Great Lakes. It's been a few years now since I've been there, but I could locate this spot in minutes with the use of a Loran navigator!

But Loran-C isn't just for the Great Lakes. There are plenty of big natural lakes in this world, and huge sprawling reservoirs with miles and miles of shoreline and mazes of islands. Think about this scenario: You run up a reservoir you've never fished before, and 12 miles from the landing you find a neat spot where an old road bed meets the edge of a deeper creek channel. It's a real deep-water honey hole, and you have two more days of vacation. If you're equipped with Loran, simply punch in the coordinates, and the next day, you can zip right to it, or close to it.

Then, zero in with your sonar and some shore markings you took the day before. What a fishing tool!

(One thing I haven't mentioned is that, even with the deadly accuracy of Loran technology, you still normally only get to within about 50 feet of your intended target. But, it is assumed that if the machine can get you that close, you can poke around on your own and find the exact spot.)

As I said, the system blankets the entire world. But, there are some small inland areas that don't receive good Loran reception (normally, because of physical impediments like moutain ranges). Unfortunately for fishermen in areas around the Rocky Mountains and the south-central United States, these are two of the areas so affected.

There is promising news about this, though, with the Federal Aviation Administration considering building a chain of Loran stations for this midsection of the country.

I could go into considerable detail on how to operate a Loran unit, but there are so many different models and brands, and they all have their features and methods of operation. Instead, let's consider the basic things to look for as you shop for a Loran.

● Ease of operation: The various Loran units have tons of options, and they vary in the amount of information that can be seen on the screen at once. Some machines show a lot of things continously. That can be a big advantage, especially if you become familiar enough with the units to pick out the information you need at a glance. But some people find a display full of numbers confusing. The units that display fewer functions at once, though, require more user programming to get at all the other functions. Decide which type would be best for you, as long as it fits your price range.

Find out how *user friendly* each machine is. How many keys do you have to press, how many sequences do you have to remember, to get the Loran to do basic things? If it's complicated to run, and you don't use it more than a few weekends a year, it might become another source of frustration, in a world with too many already.

● Quality of the filtering system: All Lorans should have some sort of filtering system, to cut out unwanted radio interference (coming from nearby am radio broadcasts, among other sources). Don't look so much at the number of filters as the quality of the system as a whole. Ask a salesman who handles a lot of units for an opinion, and then ask two or three others the same thing. In general, the brand names you recognize, those companies that have been around a long time, make units you can trust to be quality.

There is a variety of Loran brands available, each with its own features and methods of operation. As long as you know which features are important for your style of fishing, you'll be able to shop intelligently for one.

● Memory capacity: Units vary widely in the number of waypoints they can store in memory. As long as you have a written log of the destinations you have saved, it doesn't matter much if you don't mind manually entering coordinates into the machine. But, being able to simply punch up a destination by asking for "waypoint 53" can be convenient and reduce the chance for human error. (By the way, it's a cardinal sin to only enter a prized fishing spot into the Loran's memory and neglect to write it into a permanent log. Like any other little computer, the memory on the Loran can go out and leave you with nothing but your own, vague memories.)

● Get a good antenna: People who buy a $500-1,000 Loran unit and then equip it with a dime-store antenna are the same ones (I'm convinced) who spend $2,000 flying into Alaska and fish with four-year-old monofilmanent line. Line is your only connection with the fish, so it doesn't make sense to skimp on it. A Loran antenna is your only connection with tower reception, and thereby good performance. The world's greatest Loran unit, with a bad antenna, becomes an expensive piece of junk that doesn't work. *Don't skimp on an antenna.* The finest one you can buy costs about $80. They are made of metal, so they are practically indestructible. Get a good one.

● Installation is critical: Unless you really know what you are doing, I recommend you have a professional install your Loran. The antenna positioning, relative to any other marine radio you have on board, not to mention your other electronics like sonar, can be the deciding factor in how well the Loran works.

Temperature gauges

One unit I use an awful lot during certain seasons is the temperature gauge. I mount Eagle surface temperature gauges in the front and back of all my boats. And early.in the year, when the lakes are just coming out of the ice-out phase, I rely on them to help me find fish.

Most of our freshwater fish—bass, walleyes, northern pike, muskies, panfish, etc. spawn in spring. Water temperature, along with other factors like day length, trigger the spawning movements of the different species at different points during the spring. Each species tends to spawn in characteristic locations, which vary from water to water depending on what is available to the fish. By studying the various fish and then checking the temperature of the water, it is fairly easy to key in on the likely areas for them to be at this time of year.

Walleyes, for example, like to spawn on rock/rubble areas along windswept shorelines, up major rivers, and even along large shallow reefs. If I know that the water temperature is still too cold for spawning, I look for walleyes in good pre-spawn haunts. If the water temperature is right in the spawning range for the latitude I'm in, I will more than likely go find another lake where the walleyes aren't right in the middle of the spawn. During spawning, walleyes can be tough to catch. If the water temperature indicates spawning is probably over, I look for walleyes in likely post-spawn locations.

The same is true for any fish you can name. This isn't the time to get into detail on seasonal locations of various fish, though. That's what I wrote the other books in this *Comprehensive Guide* series for. In any case, finding warmer water in the spring of the year can be the key to finding fish—at least active fish.

Another phenomenon that occurs all the time is that wind can stack up warm surface waters on the windward side of the lake. If you get a good hard wind out of the same direction for a solid day or more, check the temperature of the water at the end of the lake where the waves have been piling into. It can be significantly warmer!

Then, look for good cover or structure in the zone of warmer water and you have probably located active, feeding fish.

You can see why I rely on temperature gauges early in the season. They allow me to find these areas of warmer water quickly, without having to drag a thermometer over the side of the boat and pick it up to read it. Could you imagine doing that? Me either.

In the heat of summer, northern pike are famous for hanging around spring holes. With a good surface temperature gauge, you can find the cooler water bubbling up from the springs, or trickling into the lake from a cold-water feeder stream, even at moderate boat speeds.

In this case, finding the cooler water is as important as finding the warmer water in springtime. And the surface temperature gauge is the most reliable way I know of to quickly locate the cooler water.

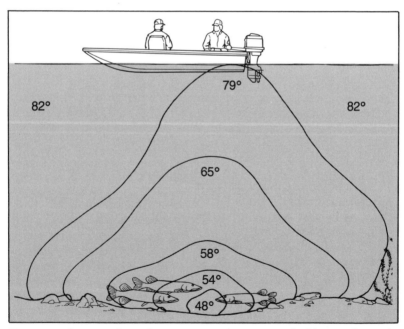

Figure 81—One use of a surface temperature gauge is to find big northern pike during hot, calm summer days. Pike prefer cool to cold water, and will stack up in pockets of spring water. With a quality gauge, you can run the lake and quickly pinpoint any cool water areas.

(Note: on many of today's top-of-the-line liquid crystal and video units, surface temperature probes, as well as speedometers, are built in.)

I also use a *temperature probe* on some occasions, for certain types of fish. The probe, as opposed to the surface temperature gauge, allows you to take temperature readings in deeper water.

The one I use, the Eagle Temperature Depth Probe, gives me 75 feet of cable with a probe on the end of it. I simply lower the probe, reading temperature on the dial and watching the marked cable to know how deep I've gone.

That way, it's easy to locate the preferred temperature range of fish like lake trout and salmon, and get your lures down to that depth. Also, there are temperature probes that mount right to the cannon ball of a downrigger system, enabling the big-water angler to monitor the water temperature as he fishes.

A temperature probe allows you to quickly learn water temperatures from the surface down to 75 feet and deeper. Knowing this can be critical to locating temperature-sensitive species like lake trout and salmon, and is a sure way of finding thermoclines.

Trolling speed indicators

There are certain times, such as when I'm speed trolling for walleyes or northerns, that a definite depth and speed will really trigger the fish. I find this to be particularly true in mid to late summer.

With a trolling speed indicator, you can return to exactly the same speed after you catch a fish. There's no guesswork, and that's what modern fishing is all about. Especially in Great Lakes fishing, the speed your lures are running is often a critical factor. And it's also very true that certain lures, particularly light-weight spoons, have good action only at specific speeds.

167

Combination devices

More and more units are coming on the market, that attach to a downrigger ball, that tell you water temperature at the ball, trolling speed, and other information. These can be great gadgets for serious anglers!

Marine radio

If you thought there were a lot of brands, and models, and features when it comes to Loran-C, wait until you look into marine radios. I'm not going to get into functions. I just want to say that these units can be useful, fun and a life-saver. They give you direct contact with weatherband radio, the Coast Guard, and other boats in the case of emergencies.

Also, it's fun to trade fishing information with nearby boats that have radios. Just remember, when evaluating the odds of the other guy's story being true, that he is a fisherman, just like you!

Even moreso than with sonar and Loran units, there is a wide variety of brands and models of marine radios available. Buy one that will perform at the longest range you can afford (this is also dependent on quality of antenna), and a radio might one day save your life in an emergency.

What have we forgotten?

Well, there are some other things. A good marine *compass* is nice to have, especially if you don't have a Loran or a particularly good sense of direction. Out on a new lake, you can line up a lake map exactly as it should be, by holding it over the compass. It helps you find points and mid-lake structures.

A good fisherman we know, who spends a lot of time on sprawling Mille Lacs Lake in Minnesota fishing walleyes, came up with an innovative way to combine a compass with the *trip log* feature on an Eagle Z-7000 liquid crystal sonar unit.

The trip log gives you an accurate measurement of the distance you have traveled since you turned on the sonar unit. When he hits a new walleye spot way the heck out in the middle of Mille Lacs, he nails down where it is by shutting off the sonar unit, turning it back on, and heading on a straight compass heading for his dock, or anywhere else he happens to be near. He makes a note of the compass heading he used and the distance it took to get somewhere he can easily return to.

Then, next time he wants to find that spot, he goes to the starting point, turns on the Z-7000 and heads on the opposite compass heading he used when returning from the spot. It gets him back into the ballpark, and he uses the sonar unit to find the exact spot.

The poor man's Loran-C!

A quality marine compass has many uses for the average angler.

Spotlights are also useful fishing tools. You can quickly run expanses of shoreline at night, shining to note presence or absence of fish, and the relative size of fish. They are also good safety tools, for landing and navigating at night.

And don't neglect your *legal responsibilities* as a licensed boater. Know the laws regarding use of exterior boat lights, and turn them on when you should.

Portable generators can be a saving grace on trips to remote areas. We have a little John Deere generator we take with us on filming trips, and use it a lot to run our trickle battery chargers, for both the boat and video camera batteries. Once you own one, you come up with uses for it, and soon wonder what you did without it!

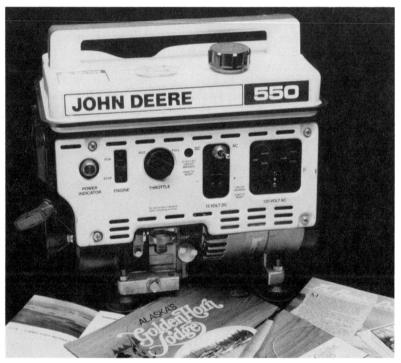

Portable generators can provide electricity for remote fishing camps. Besides giving you light and power for other uses, they can power a charger for your marine batteries.

Could there possibly be anything else? Yes, there is other stuff. But it's mostly for serious big-water boaters and ocean-going ships. Things like *autopilots* that interface between your boat's steering wheel and the Loran-C, to run the boat while you do something else! And there are *map plotters*, that use paper maps, and some that plot courses on a video screen. There is *color radar* available for your boat that the local television station would love to have. There are *facsimile receiver/ recorders* that can give you near-photographic quality printouts from transmitting stations of present and forecasted weather conditions (including details on high- and low-pressure systems with speed and direction of movement), an analysis of ocean currents and waves, sea conditions including wave heights, and, get this, even fishing charts and news printouts, where available!

Maybe, someday, a sonar unit that can bake bread.

Chapter 8
Learning and fishing a new lake

Imagine we are standing on top of a hill that overlooks your favorite lake. You have fished this lake for years, and have heard all the stories about people catching big fish from it, but you sure can't catch one.

While we watch people fish, you suddenly realize you can see down into the water! Frantically, you look all over, as fast as you can, wanting to see as much as possible before this "dream" is over.

You look at all the places people have told you are hotspots, but your eyes keep getting drawn to movement off to your left, down along a shoreline where nobody ever fishes. There, right before your eyes, along that out-of-the-way little shoreline stretch, at the edge of where a lush growth of cabbage weeds ends, is a little rock pile. Nobody ever told you about that spot, and it's not on the map.

In and out, along that edge and on that rock pile, move four of the biggest bass in the lake. Just off its deep edge, a school of huge walleyes fins lazily.

Imagine, for a moment, that you *have* that ability. You can see through water, even stained water, no matter how deep. And not just during the day, either; you can do this at night as well. With this incredible edge over other fishermen, you could run your boat around any lake and see exactly how some of the shoreline tapered slowly, some dropped off sharply, some of it had weedgrowth and some didn't. You would see details that other anglers never will, like the edges where rocky points meet a sand or mud bottom, and where weed growth is thickest. You could see mid-lake humps and sunken islands, and easily note the expanses of deep and shallow water. You could even see fish, and which way they moved when your boat approached.

You would be able to see what you have always wanted to see, and fishing would be so much easier.

How much would you be willing to pay for this power?

This is not a dream, folks. You can do everything I just described, with today's modern sonar units. What if I told you that a lot of good fishermen are already doing it, every time they go out on the water?

It is being done. I do it all the time, and have for years. Granted, it takes a lot of practice to see *everything* I described, but with a high quality sonar unit and even a little bit of information, you can start seeing the whole picture. If you've read the rest of the book, you already have various pieces of the puzzle, like how weeds, fish, rocks, baitfish, etc. display on the various modes of sonar.

But now, we're going to put it all together. We're going to take sonar use to a level where it really belongs. We're going to give you a system for fishing a lake you've never seen before, or finally learning the lake you've had a cabin on for 25 years.

Using fishing sonar to its potential is one of the main things separating good fishermen from average fishermen. Good fishermen "use" more of the lake than casual fishermen. They move around. They seek fish. They *hunt* fish.

Here is where, finally, you join your mind with your depth finder.

Seeing a lake "with the water drained out"

There are few people who can get the big picture like "Big John" Christianson. A very successful tournament bass fisherman, John can slide onto a lake he's never seen before and in a few hours know it well enough to draw you a complete map of it, including structure, bottom composition, weed types, and locations of schols of fish.

How does he do it? Let him tell you.

John Christianson

"After running the drop off or weedline all the way around a lake, I have a good idea of what kind of lake it is. Am I dealing with slow-tapering mud aprons, or fast-breaking rock shorelines? Where are the weeds? After I look the lake over, running fairly fast with my flasher, I can shut my eyes and see that whole lake, as if the water had been drained out of it. That's what people need to be able to do. It's one thing to be able to tell what's right under you, in the cone angle at the moment, but can you also picture how that fits in next to what you have gone over so far?"

Boy, is that a good point! I toiled a few years, in fact, with my early flasher unit, before I understood this. Learning to get this complete mental picture of the lake, *as if all the water had been drained out*, is what you have to strive for.

Even if you have to spend some time learning to do this, and not fishing at all, it will do you a tremendous amount of good in the long run.

You should aspire to become a complete fisherman like "Big John" Christianson. His ability to study a lake with his sonar, and soon be catching fish, has made him a name in tournament circles.

First things first: gathering information

Let's take a complete look at the process of learning about a lake. There is much you can do before you even push your boat off the trailer.

In fact, there is some homework you can do while winter has the lake covered in ice. Natural resources agencies in your state will send you survey information on the lake you are considering fishing.

Reading and understanding lake surveys

Probably every outdoor writer who has written an article entitled *How to fish a strange lake* has included the now trite phrase: "and be sure to write your local department of natural resources to get information on the lake."

Then, they stop there. I know, because I have done it too.

Compared to reading and interpreting a sonar signal, a lake survey report can be like deciphering hieroglyphics. Research biologists gather fish population estimates with a variety of nets and traps, which tend to catch different types and sizes of fish; they do their sampling at different times of year; they make guesses as to what causes water color. It takes knowledge of how they gather information, to understand what it all means.

Just what information is included on a lake survey? How is the information gathered? Of all the things included, what is useful to the average fisherman?

Glad you asked.

I'll speak about the particulars of the reports issued by my home state Minnesota, but it's similar in other states. There are different reports available, depending on whether you want them sent by mail or can go to the area Fisheries Headquarters to pick them up.

Surveys, reports and assessments done by natural resources agencies can be valuable to anglers, but only if they understand how the information was gathered, and how much of it is useful.

A *Lake Survey Report* is a lengthy, detailed description of the water and the fish population. It is done every ten years in Minnesota. Five years after the Lake Survey is done, a *Population Assessment* is done, which is essentially the same thing. A report from either can be as long as 20 pages, so officials understandably don't like to send them in the mail.

A *Lake Information Report* is a condensed version of the Lake Survey or Population Assessment, usually only one or two pages.

A *Stream Population Assessment* is a detailed survey done on a particular stretch of river or stream, and includes much the same information.

Here's what to look for on the various reports, and how they can help you decide which of several lakes to fish, where on the lake to fish, and other things:

● Water quality—much information is given here. A secchi disc reading, in feet, comes first. This is a measure of clarity, and can help you make a guess as to approximately how deep the weeds will grow in the lake, and how deep you might expect to fish for various species.

To get this reading, a biologist lowers a disc from the shaded side of a boat into the water until it disappears from view. He then measures how far down the disc can still be seen. The average of three readings is taken, giving you a relative idea how clear the water is, at the time of year the reading is taken. (Time of year is important to know.)

Let's attempt to standardize things from a fishing point of view, for the entire United States and Canada. Roughly speaking, a secchi reading of 0-4 feet means the lake has fairly dark water; 5-8 feet moderately clear; more than 8 feet would be considered clear water. For comparison, parts of Lake Superior, a super clear body of water, have secchi readings of 30 feet and more. Some lakes that we might call "gin clear" would have secchi readings approaching 20 feet.

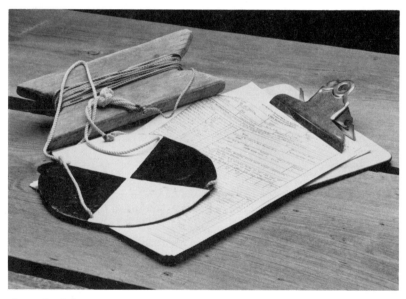

A secchi disk is an instrument used by biologists to measure water clarity. Looking at secchi readings on survey reports can give you an idea how well weeds might grow in the lake, what time of day the lake might give up the most fish, etc.

Also given are water *color* and the estimated *cause* of the color. There are no standard terms for different water colors, because you have different people in different parts of the country making the color determinations. You just get "light green" or "brown" or something like that.

But the cause, now that's a different story. Look closely at this description, and the date the survey was taken. If the lake was surveyed on July 17, for example, and the cause of the color is given as "algae bloom," that is evidence that earlier in the spring or summer, and again in fall, the water in that lake is probably far clearer than it was when the survey was performed.

If, however, the survey was done June 5 and the cause of the color is "bog stain," you might guess that water will stay about the same clarity all summer. Still, that lake might experience a midsummer algae bloom, and a quick phone call to a resort or bait shop near the lake would probably provide an answer.

The point is, water clarity—and therefore sunlight penetration—can change radically from season to season, so you should be aware of that.

Okay, now you know something about the relative clarity of the water, and what causes it. So what? What does that tell you, from a fishing standpoint? Plenty.

There are exceptions to every rule, but a good rule of thumb is that the darker water lakes have shallower fish, the clearer lakes deeper fish. It stands to reason: in darker lakes, sunlight cannot penetrate to the depths it can in clearer waters. So, darker lakes don't have weed growth in deep water.

Darker-water lakes also don't have good visibility for sight feeders like largemouth bass. In them, more life goes on in shallow water—so that's where you should begin your search for fish.

In clearer water lakes, by contrast, you will have good "fish" weeds like cabbage and coontail growing to depths like 10 or 12 feet and even deeper in some cases. The sunlight will usually be "too much" for most big gamefish in the shallows during the day. More baitfish and gamefish activity will take place along the deep weedline and even deeper than that.

Let me make one thing clear: you cannot look at the secchi disc reading and consistently guess how deep the weedline is likely to be. There are simply too many factors involved. The only way to learn for sure where the weedline is on any given lake is to find it with your sonar unit.

More on this topic in a minute, when we actually go onto the water and start learning a new lake.

(Also realize that in many flood-control reservoirs, the water levels fluctuate so drastically that there may not be any weed growth to speak of.)

● Lake classification—this reveals a lot about what *type* of lake it is. The biologist will list what fish species are naturally suited to this lake (such as "walleye" or "walleye-centrarchid" (centrarchid is a fancy word for fish like sunfish and bass) or "roughfish" (carp and suckers are roughfish).

Then, they list what species of fish the lake is *managed* for. This usually means that the fish indicated are stocked in the lake, and their populations closely monitored to ensure a satisfactory fishery for the public. Typical indications here are "warm-water gamefish," "walleye-centrarchid," "centrarchid," etc.

● Depth indicators—there are several on a good lake survey report. Look at the maximum depth and median (average) depth. Realize that a lake with a deep maximum depth can also have expanses of shallow water. Often, the best lakes are those with areas of deep water *and* extensive shallow (food shelf) areas for fish to come up and feed on.

Also, some surveys include a measurement of "percent littoral zone." To a scientist the "littoral" area of a lake is the water less than 15 feet deep. If a lake has a deep maximum depth and a fairly high percentage of littoral area, it certainly has the ingredients, at least on paper, to hold a good population of fish.

(Yes, you guessed it: a lake map is a better indicator of *where* the shallow water areas sit in relation to the deeper water. Use a lake survey and a map hand-in-hand, and you have strong information tools on your side!)

● Population estimates and creel surveys—here is a real can of worms.

Can you tell whether a lake has a good population of your favorite species by reading the results of the test netting information?

Maybe.

The reports will give you figures for the number and size of the fish taken in the sampling, by the various methods. Biologists use gill nets, trap nets, seines and electroshocking techniques to get their data. Each method "selects" for certain species better than others, and for certain size fish of each species.

When evaluating test netting data in survey reports, make sure you know what type of netting was done and at what time of year. Various netting procedures tend to yield different species, and different size fish.

Gill nets, for example, are typically set out in water from 15-30 feet deep, in locations a biologist feels will hold a lot of fish at the time. Because of their locations, gill nets tend to catch fish like northern pike, walleyes, perch and some adult bass, rather than fish that spend more time in shallower areas.

Trap nets are set in shallower water, and so they select for fish like crappies, sunfish, and younger, smaller individuals of many species.

Seining, depending on the length of the seine, depth it was used, time of year, etc., can select for a variety of species. The standard seine is 50 feet long, 6 feet "high" or deep, and is used in less than 4 feet of water. Biologists will also use seines of 200 or even 400 feet long, up to 12 feet in height, to sample water as deep as 6, 8, or even 10 feet. Most seines, regardless of length and height, use 1/4-inch mesh.

Seines are used in what are known as *natural reproduction checks*. In midsummer, field workers will run a seine through shallow water to check for the presence of tiny, young-of-the-year (YOY on the reports) fish such as bass, northerns, walleyes, muskies, etc. They are checking whether the lake was host to a good hatch of baby fish that year. If not, they might be tempted to stock more heavily, or regard the lake as a poor producer of a certain species.

Biologists use a variety of nets to sample fish populations. Knowing which netting technique was used, and the fish it tends to select for, can help you analyze survey report data.

Ice out surveys done in northern lakes are just what they say: biologists will sample shallow-water areas with trap nets and seines immediately after the ice melts, checking for a variety of species. Because so many large gamefish are in the shallow, warming water, it is one of the only times the biologist's nets catch good numbers of large fish. Because of this, ice-out survey population data are good indicators of how many big, catchable fish are in a certain body of water.

Electroshocking is done mostly in rivers. It involves sending an electrical field into the water, which can temporarily stun fish that are hit by it, causing their muscles to tighten up. Workers net fish as they rise to the surface, for tagging, measuring, and/or use as brood stock.

Biologists readily admit that some fish species are not easily sampled using any of these methods. Largemouth and smallmouth bass are two that are particularly elusive; not easily caught by gill nets, many times not vulnerable to trap nets, and often too fast for seiners.

Biologists also admit that several factors can affect how accurate the netting results are. Don Pereira, area fisheries manager in Glenwood, Minnesota, points out two biggies that might throw off netting figures:

"For one thing," Pereira said, "the time of year nets are put out seems to affect the number of fish caught. Test netting done before a lake thermoclines appears to yield fewer fish per net than when it's done after the thermocline sets up. After a lake thermoclines is when fish locations tend to be more stable and predictable.

"Also, particularly in the case of gill net catches, results have appeared to vary dramatically from day-to-day, based on weather changes. (This, and his thermocline observation above, he carefully points out are 'casual' observations, not yet proven.) It's something to be cautious about when you are looking at test netting data. Always look at the time of year the netting was done, and be careful when comparing one lake to another.

"If you notice that one lake has 15 walleyes per gill net, and another has three, you can probably assume the one with 15 has more walleyes in it. But you sure can't say anything like that if one lake has 15 walleyes per net and another has eight. There are just too many factors involved that can mess up the validity of the results."

I can really see the possibilities that Don's weather idea has merit. Fishermen have for a long time known that weather affects how many fish we catch. On some days, fish seem to be active; on other days (particularly after cold fronts pass through), they seem to be sitting on the bottom in a stupor. It makes sense that a biologist won't catch as many fish in the nets if the fish aren't active.

Creel census information can reveal a lot about how "fishable" a lake is. But because it is expensive to have a field worker stationed at a public launching site or resort, to check how many and what size fish get caught, creel census data are not available all that often. But when it is, take a good close look at it.

With a creel census, you can see the size and number of fish of each species that is typically caught by other fishermen, and also see at what time of year most people catch their walleyes, or their big muskies, or bass, or whatever you are interested in.

Getting and reading a lake map: another big step

Before the days of lake maps, how did serious fishermen get a good "feel" for a lake before they launched their boat? They didn't, and that should help us step back and appreciate what lake maps allow us to do.

Every time I get ready to fish a lake I haven't seen—and even when I'm returning to a lake I haven't been to for a while—I spend a few minutes studying a topographic map of it.

Before fishing a new lake, get ahold of a lake map and study it. Call friends who have fished the lake, and learn as much as you can from them. That way, you can have a plan by the time you arrive at the landing.

(In the event you haven't used one before, a topographic map is made up of a series of depth lines, or *contours*, which reveal the structure of the lake bottom. It takes practice to be able to read a map and visualize the bottom of the lake, but once you do, the map becomes a valuable tool.)

Who has and sells lake and river maps? In most states, the natural resources agency (such as the Minnesota Department of Natural Resources) has them available. Also, there are a growing number of private companies manufacturing and marketing maps. (We have a company in Minnesota, for example, which produces and sells a product known as *Lakemaps*, on waterproof plastic, that is a beautiful and trusted map series.)

If you are fishing flood-control impoundments (reservoirs), you will get your maps from the Army Corps of Engineers. For example, if you live in the East or Midwest, you can get a complete list of reservoir maps by writing District Engineer, U.S. Army Corps of Engineer District, Box 1027, Detroit, MI 48231.

Become familiar with various sources for lake maps in your area. Normally, they are available from both public agencies and private companies. In the Upper Midwest, anglers rely on a product called Lakemaps, a laminated plastic map series that covers most of the best fishing waters.

How are lake maps made, and why aren't they perfect?

Before I say the first word about the natural limitations of lake maps, let me say this: besides a good sonar unit, a lake map is the most wonderful thing a fisherman can have for learning a body of water. Without them, we would have to patiently map each lake we wanted to fish, from scratch! How many of you would have the time or energy to do that?

Still, I think it's important to realize lake maps aren't all that perfect. Once again, I'll give you the example of my home state, Minnesota. The situation will be much the same for natural lakes in other states.

First of all, lake maps aren't made for fishing. They are made to aid scientific study and management. The Department of Natural Resources, for example, likes to know how much shallow water is in a lake (remember the "percent littoral zone" figures given in the survey reports?). That helps them guess how good oxygen levels will be in the summer, for example, when evaluating the stocking potential of a lake. Also, by knowing the total water volume in a lake, they can effectively dose out chemicals and poisons for controlling plants, undesireable fish species, etc.

The mapping is done on a priority basis, from recommendations given by area fisheries managers and biologists. To date, about 4,000 lakes in Minnesota have been mapped by the DNR.

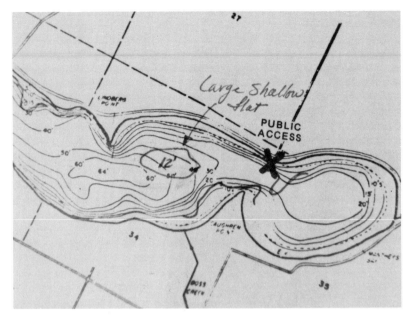

It's important to remember that lake maps are not made for fishing purposes, and structural elements don't usually appear on the map exactly as they are. Sometimes, as this example shows, large structural elements can even be missing altogether!

The actual mapping process goes like this: DNR *cartographers* (mapmakers) blow up an aerial photograph of the selected lake with a device known as a pantograph. The enlarged photo is used to plot an accurate outline of the shoreline. Then, at the lake, mappers run north-south and east-west *transects* (straight lines) from shore to shore, at a constant boat speed, sounding the bottom with a paper graph.

The graph tapes are laid onto the enlarged aerial photo, giving a fairly detailed picture of the lake bottom. The key word is *fairly*. DNR officials admit they don't have time or money to build into the maps the incredible detail fishermen would like.

Before the advent of sonar, some lake mapping was done in winter by the Civilian Conservation Corps (CCC). Beginning in the late 1930s, CCC workers would cut holes in the ice along selected transects and then record the depth, which was measured using weighted lines. It was a slow process, and as you can imagine, they didn't run as many transects as they do today. In 1949, the Minnesota DNR began using flasher units to map lakes in the summer, and graphs in 1955.

So, you can see, for the purposes they are made, lake maps are as detailed as they need to be. But, they don't have all the little details— every little point, and inside turn on every little point. Sometimes, fairly large structural elements aren't even on the map. So, what does that mean to you?

It means you must take a close look at each structural element with your own sonar unit, and even look for ones that aren't on the map.

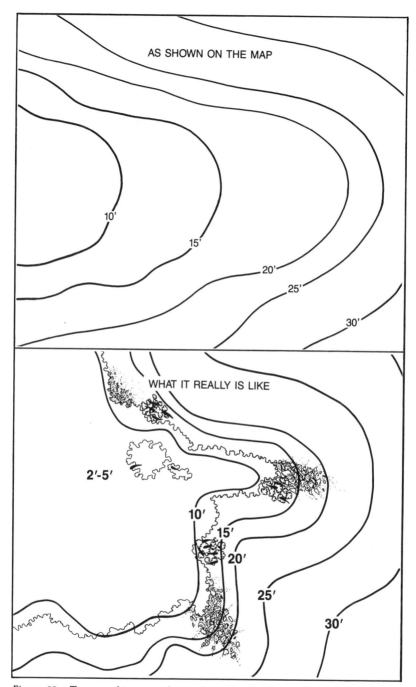

AS SHOWN ON THE MAP

10'

15'

20'

25'

30'

WHAT IT REALLY IS LIKE

2'-5'

10'

15'

20'

25'

30'

Figure 82—Topographic maps don't often show the exact detail of a structure. Only with the use of sonar can you get a precise picture, in the kind of detail you need for fishing, of the structure and any "mini-structure" that may hold fish.

185

(Reservoir maps are often more accurate than maps of natural lakes. They are usually made on dry ground, before the river is dammed.)

When you get the map in front of you, what do you look for? This is going to change radically at different seasons of the year, and depending on what species of fish you are after.

Finding the longest tapering point in the lake that feeds into 65 feet of water would do you a lot of good in the middle of summer when you're looking for walleyes. But how important is it when you're after springtime crappies in shallow bays? Not very.

I think you get the idea. Before heading onto the water, have a game plan. Study the seasonal movements and basic nature of the fish you are after. Know where the fish are likely to be, and concentrate on finding those types of areas. (I have written other volumes in this *Comprehensive Guide* series that go into detail on specific fish, like largemouth and smallmouth bass, walleyes, northern pike, crappies, and others. They will help you understand the nature of these species.)

Spend time studying the map before you go out on the water. You can quickly see where the large areas of shallow and deep water are, for example. This is a great headstart. I call this "getting a feel for the basins." Many fish, like bass, walleyes, northerns and even panfish, at many times of the year will be in areas containing good shallow feeding areas *and* the sanctuary of deep water nearby.

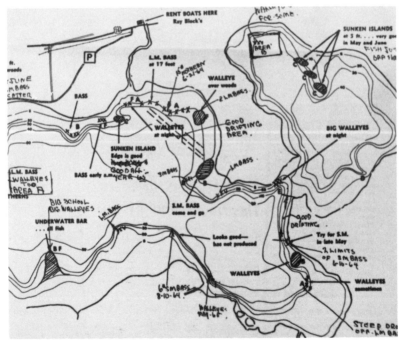

Studying a lake map can give you a "feel for the basins" of a lake. In other words, you can quickly see where the expanses of shallow and deep water are. Other markings, such as notes on where fish have been caught in the past, can help you narrow your search of new waters.

186

If you know, before you go out on the lake, that the entire north end has a maximum depth of only 15 feet, while the south end has expanses of deep water and some good-looking shelf areas, where would you spend most of your fishing time? Again, it depends on the time of year and the species you're after, but there is an awful lot of useful information contained on a lake map.

Talking to others

It's time to get our noses out from under the lake surveys and maps, and make some human contact.

One of the first things you should consider doing as you research lakes is contacting the people who write up the Lake Survey Reports: the area fisheries managers. Although these folks are very busy, part of their job is to answer questions from the angling public, and that means you.

According to Jim Lilienthal, another Minnesota area fisheries manager, there is much you can learn from professional fisheries biologists.

"One of the best things you can do," Lilienthal said, "is identify which fish species you are most interested in. Then, he (the fisheries biologist) should be able to give you some information as to the size of the fish, and the size of the populations, in area lakes. Many of them can also help you with general areas on each lake to fish, based on the season of the year.

"The average fisheries biologist has a wealth of practical information that might not be included in their lake reports. Go ahead and call them up, but just understand if they are in a busy field season or something, and have to return your call later."

And how many of you try to learn something about a given lake by talking to other fishermen? It's a great way to get information, even if it is second-hand. If you know you want to give Lake XYZ a try this weekend, call a friend who fishes that lake a lot. Trade him or her a future favor for some inside information.

After you arrive at the area, stop in at as many local bait shops as you can. I often buy a dozen minnows from three or four shops, just to spend a few minutes picking the brain of the owner or manager.

Ask the right questions: what live baits do most people catch their fish on? (Local anglers will buy a certain size or type of minnow, or mostly leeches, for a reason.) Ask them about peak times of year. Are walleyes only caught in the first two weeks of the season? Maybe there's a reason for that. If that's the case, ask what depth, types of areas and methods people try for the rest of the summer that are so unsuccessful. Maybe local fishermen don't catch walleyes in the summer because they are doing the wrong things. How has the weather been the past week or so? How have fishermen been doing?

Talk with as many people as possible about a new lake. When you go into the bait shop, pick up some ideas on where the fish are biting along with your minnows.

Also, local anglers are a good source of information.

Many good fishermen are willing to share information on general things like the types of spots they are fishing, the depths, how they are working their baits, etc. Don't expect them to take you by the hand and lead you to their secret spots; just ask general questions. (Remember: you are becoming a fisherman who *hunts* fish. With your knowledge of fish habits, types of spots fish are likely to be in, and your growing ability to use sonar, you can find plenty of spots by yourself.)

By comparing notes with other anglers, you can also compare relative results and both learn something.

Good fishermen sort of become "detectives" when they arrive at the scene of a new lake. Let's listen to Big John Christianson again, on how he digs up answers before launching his boat.

John Christianson:

"You have to know the right questions to ask. When I arrive at a lake that I want to fish seriously, or am fishing for a tournament, I always ask people at the docks and bait shops things like, 'what's the biggest bass you know of that's come out of this lake?' If I hear a lot of people saying three or four pounds, I don't usually count on the lake to produce a trophy for me. 'Do people staying at the resorts catch a lot of bass?' If everyone says 'yes,' I assume there is a pile of fish in the lake. 'Do they catch walleyes?' 'How do they catch them?'

"And another of my biggies that I always ask is, 'Do you know about any hidden, secret sunken islands?' They always seem to, and they are usually proud to show me that they know exactly where it is."

But caution: don't allow yourself to get blocked into local biases such as "we never catch anything off Bluff Point." Not always, but sometimes, the locals will have a string of bad days, or even an entire bad year, fishing a certain spot, and completely write it off for life. If it looks good on the map, or to your eyes, check it out. Fish can change locations from month to month and year to year. Let the fish tell you if a spot is no good.

After fishing a few hours, pull up to other nearby boats and compare notes. Don't expect anglers to give you their secret spots, but most people will offer general information, such as how deep they're fishing, and what lure they're using. Use that information to help you find your own hotspots.

Another source of possible information is large fishing contests. Results of weekly contests are often printed in newspapers. By following results, you can see that certain bodies of water give up a lot of big smallmouth bass, or walleyes, or largemouths, or muskies. And, you can see at what time of year they tend to give up the most big fish.

Be aware that some fishermen will register their catches in a lake other than the one they actually catch the fish from, to keep other anglers from finding out about "their" lake. But, contest results can still provide a lot of information.

Hiring a guide before you're in trouble

If you are going to a new area and plan to fish for at least a few days, consider hiring a good guide for the first day. Most people go about hiring guides for the wrong reasons. They first flail away at the waters of a new lake for four days, then panic and hire a guide on the last day, trying to salvage the trip. Do the opposite; hire a guide on the *first* day, and let him or her teach you about the lake, show you spots, local techniques, lures and live baits, and help you avoid getting lost.

Then, the rest of the trip, you can expand on what the guide taught you. Go off on your own with confidence, and find spots that are similar to the ones the guide showed you. Go back and fish the guide's spots, and really look them over with your sonar. Find out *why* they are good spots. You might end up offering the guide some information, such as "did you know that Eddie's reef has a long point that sticks way out off the south end?"

If you teach the guide something, you have made a friend for life, who will share information with you every time you hit town.

Step by step: learning a lake

Approaching a new lake—or even taking a new look at waters you've had a cabin on for 25 years—can be fun, systematic and eye-opening.

Step 1: observing water clarity

The first thing you should do, as the boat glides away from the landing, is put your polarized sunglasses on and take a good long look at the clarity of the water. A few minutes checking this out can give you a tremendous amount of information.

Studying the clarity of the water is the first thing you should do on a new lake. It will give you a general idea of how deep to look for fish, how deep weeds might be expected to grow, etc.

Generally speaking, clear-water lakes have the potential to have numbers of fish in deep water; darker-water lakes usually have more fish in shallow water. The weeds will grow to greater depths in lakes with clearer water.

Wayne Ekelund, a tremendous fisherman and member of my Advisory Staff, has some good comments on the importance of water clarity.

Wayne Ekelund

"Looking at the clarity tells me where I'm going to start fishing. If I drop my spinnerbait down into the water six inches and I can't see it any more, I know I'm going to be dealing with a lot of shallow fish, especially bass. In a lake like that, there probably aren't any weeds deeper than about three feet, so it's a waste of time looking for a deep weedline. The fish are going to be tucked right up tight into shallow water, along shoreline objects.

Wayne Ekelund is an educated fisherman who knows how to assemble all the information at his disposal and quickly find fish in new waters. He caught these crappies in spring in a Minnesota lake.

"But, if I'm pulling away from the landing and in 6, 8 or 10 feet of water I can still see the rocks on the bottom of the lake, I know I'm probably dealing with a lake that has a good deep weedline, and a lot of fish will be using it, assuming it's midsummer and the weedline is developed."

As you look for yourself at the clarity and color of the water, you will be able to evaluate what is causing the color. If it is muddy from runoff, for example, the amount of sunlight penetration will be almost nil. But if the color is more of a bog stain, it might surprise you how far down you can still see your jig or spinnerbait! In some lakes that look to be quite dark, sunlight can penetrate to surprising depths.

Wayne has a story he likes to tell about fishing a new lake in a bass tournament a few years back, that really drives home this concept of water clarity and possible fish location.

"It was right in the heat of the summer," Wayne said, "and the first thing I looked at was the color of the water, like usual. The water was very dark, so I didn't expect to be finding bass down deep. I spent the entire first day working shallow areas and caught only a couple small fish. I mean, I was within a few *feet* of the shore a lot of the time.

"The second day, I talked with a few people who were sitting down on their docks. I started hearing stories about people killing fish with their lawnmowers while they were cutting grass that bordered the water! I wasn't fishing shallow enough! So I began finding the heaviest cover right up against the banks, and I started to catch nice bass. It was a real learning experience, one that I tucked into my reserves for when I run up against similar situations."

Step 2: finding and checking the weedline

The next thing you want to do, in the case of a natural lake, is slide on out into deeper water and find the *weedline*, the depth that the deep water weed growth—usually cabbage and coontail in our northern part of the country—stops.

Here is an underwater photo of what a weedline looks like. Notice how the coontail grows out to a certain depth and then stops abruptly. You can really see why fish select these places as holding spots from which to ambush prey, and escape bright sunlight.

John Christianson, a master at fishing lakes that are new to him, has some thoughts on the importance of finding and checking out the weedline:

"One of the most basic things there is in fishing a strange lake," he says, "is finding the level that the good, fish-holding weeds like cabbage and coontail grow to. You can't find that without using your locator, and you can't find it if you don't know what you're looking at on the face of your locator."

Earlier I said that there's no way to predict exactly what depth the weedline will be by looking at the clarity of the water. I stand by that statement, but just to throw out some food for thought, here are some rough estimations that we came up with:

- Dirty water (your lure disappears from view within 6" or so)—

weeds grow down to 2 1/2-4 feet, maximum. Many fish are normally very shallow, even in midsummer.

- "Dark" water (not dirty, but not clear)—

These lakes can be deceiving. Often, the cause of the color is more important than the clarity. Some can have weedlines down to 10 or 11 feet. If such a lake has a deeper weedline, by all means fish it!

- Medium-clear water (very clear in spring and fall, some color in summmer)—

Weedline typically grows down to about 15-17 feet.

- Very clear water—

Weedline will be very deep, sometimes down to 25-27 feet.

Depth and thickness of weedlines can be tough to predict for quite a few reasons, some of which don't have much to do with the clarity of the water. Climatic factors can play a big role, according to Biologist Lielenthal. During years of severe winters, where we get thick ice cover and accompanying heavy snowfalls, places that used to have lush weedgrowth might not.

"And on the other hand," he said, "during years of low snowfall, there tends to be less runoff for initial water turbidity. That seems to give the weeds a chance at a headstart in the spring, and contributes to thicker, and maybe even deeper, weed growth."

Many factors, such as the length and severity of winter, affect the summer weedgrowth in lakes.

The bottom composition, of course, can affect weed growth. Weeds don't grow as deep or thick on sand as on more organic-based "soil" type bottoms. And along areas that are predominantly rock, there will normally be only scattered clumps of weeds, on areas where organic-based bottom sits among the rocks.

Biologists and fishermen also agree that the depth and thickness of the weedline can change dramatically during the course of the summer. During cool summers when we get less of an algae bloom, the water stays clearer through the summer, promoting better and deeper weed growth. But, when the opposite happens, during a hot summer, algae blooms can go crazy—severely cutting light penetration—and cut out weeds.

On some lakes, the phenomenon we might call the "disappearing weedline" is pretty common.

Wayne Ekelund:

"One lake I fish all the time in central Minnesota, normally has a beautiful weedline set up in about 8-10 feet by early June. But if you go to that same lake at the end of July, there is no weedline at all any more. That lake sees such an algae bloom that the light penetration is cut off to even the mid-range depths, and the weeds die. The fish that might earlier in the summer be holding on the weedline are no longer in those spots, obviously, because those spots aren't there any more. That's why you have to see for yourself, with your sonar, where the weedline is, and even *if* the weedline exists. I've seen this same thing happen on other lakes, so I know this is not an isolated occurence."

But let's get back on the water. Assume we find the weedline at 15 feet. Now, I'll take that 15 foot depth, where the deep weeds stop growing, and stay right on it, running all the way around the entire lake. Or, if it's a really big lake, I'll take a section of it at a time.

I'll run at a fairly high speed, maybe half-throttle on my 45-horse Mariner outboard, using my flasher. I still consider the flasher to be the best tool available for this job.

Make your run on sort of a zig-zag course, so you don't miss spots where little points and inside turns come in. When my sonar reading starts getting deeper, I steer in toward shore until I come back to the weeds again. If it gets shallower, I steer outward, as far as I have to go to stay on the weedline.

Do this slowly at first! Don't go any faster than your sonar skills can keep up with. Learn it slow, and you'll get good enough to speed up in a few years. It won't take you long to realize that the weedline isn't perfectly straight all the way around the lake. You will be finding spots that aren't obvious from the shoreline contours, and many spots that aren't on the map.

What I'm looking for are irregularities in the weedline: any inside turns, any points, any bottom density changes, etc. I'm looking also for places where the weed growth suddenly stops and then starts again—a sign that I just missed an inside turn that is caused by differences in bottom composition.

I also want to know if there is a large area of rock or gravel coming right up against the weedline—those are fish magnets that will concentrate groups of fish.

Simply put, I'm looking for the "something different" in the contour, shape, and makeup of the fish's environment. Spence Petros, a good friend and managing editor of *Fishing Facts* magazine, says that he looks for spots that have "character." We are talking about the same thing: a combination of fishy-looking ingredients. Your sonar unit has to become your eyes in this deeper water. With some serious practice, you can find these irregularities, these gathering spots for food and predator fish, just as well as I or any other fisherman can.

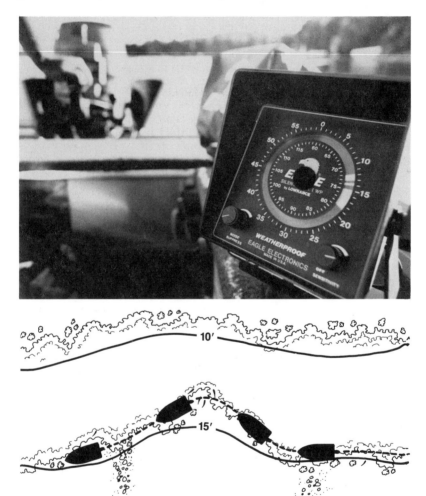

Weedlines are one thing that don't show up on any map, but indentations, points and inside turns in them are important fish locations in midsummer. Find the weedline with your sonar, then make a quick run along it to find these irregularities, before beginning to fish seriously.

As you do this, on many lakes you will notice that fairly shallow "shoreline" depths of less than 15 feet will stick out quite a ways in some areas. This is what we call the *flats*. Especially if they are covered with good weedgrowth, they can be important fish locations a large part of the season.

The key to this whole thing is making yourself more independent and successful as an angler. When you get good at studying a lake, you won't have to spend the rest of your life counting on other people to show you good fishing spots. Even on a lake you've never seen before, in a couple hours you can pinpoint some areas you want to concentrate on.

Once you've made your run at the weedline, you will have found some areas you want to check out closer. Let's say you've found three or four points. Now, go back and look really closely at those points. Study them. Here is where a paper graph, or any other good picture-type sonar unit, really shines.

Comb that piece of structure until you know everything on it that might hold fish. It might sound like a lot of work, but to me it's all part of the fun of fishing.

What am I looking for? I ask myself the following types of questions:

Are there deep-water breaks to one side of a point, and slower tapers to the other side? On the "spine" of the point (the top, or shallow portion), what is the bottom composition—rock, sand, gravel? Does it seem to stay the same off to the sides? Until it gets how deep? Is there nice hard bottom even down to 20 feet and deeper, or does it change to soft bottom a little ways from the spine?

What about other little irregularities? Look for anything: short fingers that stick out off the point, little pockets, places where the weeds seem to be a little thicker than in other places (clumps of weeds often hold the biggest fish, folks). Look for the big things, too, like inside and outside turns in the edges of the point. Take a good look at the illustration to get a better feel for what I am talking about.

You've got to look closely at these spots, and ask yourself these kinds of questions. It's the only way you'll begin to understand what types of spots are holding fish on the day you are on the water, and why one point produces more fish than another, even though they look so similar.

There are reasons that fish group up, or use, some spots and not others. The more you know, the more details you consider, the more you will understand why, and the more strides you will have taken toward becoming a good fisherman.

"Mapping" a spot: a field exercise

I want to suggest an exercise for you to do, at least the first time you run closely over a complex point and try to really understand every nook and cranny on it. Take along a good number of marker buoys, say about 10 of them. Find a point, and follow the contours of it, steering right or left to track little arms and corners. If it's a gradually-tapering point, just pick an intermediate depth and choose that as your breakline.

Drop a buoy every so often, so that you "outline" the entire point. Now, motor back away from the spot and take a good look. The exact shape of that point will be drawn out for you when you play "connect the dots" in your mind. Compare the actual shape of the point to what it looks like on the map.

Take a few seconds and fix the map. Draw in the way the point really sits, for future reference.

Are we having fun yet?

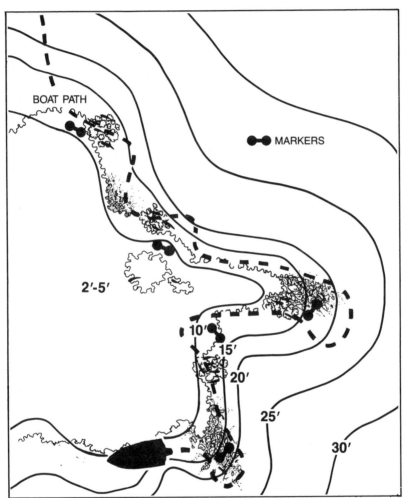

Figure 85—A good exercise for learning to scout and visualize structures is to run a selected depth and plot the contour with marker buoys. Here, we have run along the 12-foot weedline of a point, turning in when the depthfinder tells us we're too deep, and out when we're too shallow. The correct way to drop the buoys is to wait until you go too deep or shallow, then when you turn back and re-contact the structure, place a marker. When you've run all the way around the structure, back off and play "connect the dots" in your mind. Note the complexities of the structure on your lake map, for future reference.

It might take extra concentration to find these little "mini structures" as I call them, but it can pay off big. Listen again to a success story from John Christianson:

"I was fishing a tournament," John said, "and motored around a group of boats that were fishing a weedline. I was moving along, checking it out, watching the cabbage weeds on the flasher, when all of a sudden I hit a stretch of about 20 feet where the weeds disappeared from the flasher reading. The bottom was flat as a table top, but something created that area where the weeds stopped. I went around the area and studied it, moving with the electric motor. I found that the weeds just dipped in about 30 feet and continued again. It was a classic point-inside turn combination, not made from depth changes but strictly from weed growth. Nobody else found it, and I sat there within sight of them, and pulled bass after bass after bass from that spot. It was unreal."

Knowing Christianson, you probably could have been within 10 feet of him while he had a 5-pound bass on and you wouldn't have known it, either. The guy is a great fisherman, and you know why? He pays attention to little details like where the weed growth stops and then picks up again. He takes time to go back and check it out, to find out why.

There is also a *lot* to be said for being thorough in checking out the weedline. Gary Lake, another successful tournament bass fisherman, spends more time fishing the weedline than would seem necessary when he's on a lake for the first time.

He backs his boat off the trailer, starts up the big motor, and runs only out to the edge of the deep weedline. There, he shuts off the big motor and doesn't turn it on again until he has fished the entire weedline, or it gets dark! If he has to do it for two days, he simply takes up where he left off the day before. Can you believe that? In pre-fishing for a tournament, it sometimes takes him up to three days to do this, moving around with only his electric motor. But by the time he has taken his "lap," he knows where every little *anything* is on that weedline. Talking to this guy after a tournament, he sounds like somebody's old uncle who grew up on the place! (You also know that by the time he gets around the lake, he knows where a few bunches of bass are, too.)

This guy does very well on the tournament circuit, by the way. Is there any wonder why? Admittedly, he has more time to pre-fish than most people have to fish, but it shows what you can accomplish when you're methodical.

Only after he has completely hunted the weedline does he start up the big motor again and start criss-crossing the lake, looking for mid-lake humps and sunken islands. When he finds them, he again methodically fishes the whole thing, looking for any little spots-within-the-spot that might hold concentrations of fish.

Which brings me to my next topic.

While I'm still scouting the lake, after locating shoreline points, inside turns and the flats, I'll go looking for mid-lake structures.

Mid-lake structures can be a variety of things. I'm looking for sunken islands, little humps, and even just plain bottom density changes on an otherwise fairly uniform bottom.

To find these areas, you are going to have to do something very similar to what cartographers do while making a lake map. Just simply criss-cross the lake, waffle pattern (figure 86), making runs both up-and-down and side-to-side. Try your best to keep on a straight line, although I realize this is not always the easiest thing to do, especially on fairly large bodies of water.

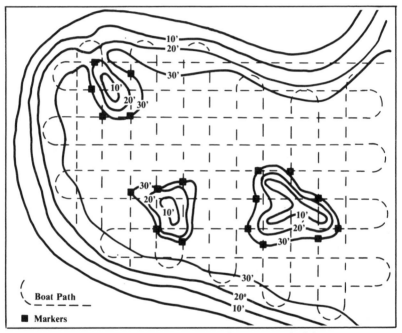

Figure 86—You can find mid-lake structures by running the lake in a criss-cross pattern, marking sharp depth changes as you go. Use lots of marker buoys to give you an accurate idea of how the mid-lake structures are shaped.

Look for changes in depth and bottom density. Let's say you are running along in 25 feet of water and all of a sudden your sonar reading indicates the bottom got harder for a few feet before going back to a soft bottom again. What does that tell you? Maybe nothing more than there is a density change there—but that in itself might be enough to hold fish if there isn't a lot of other structure in the lake.

But it might signal the very edge of a sunken island. Drop a marker buoy and take a look around to all sides. Does the depth climb up to one side? Bingo. You've found yourself a sunken island, partner. This really is starting to get fun!

If you do find a good hump or sunken island, take a few minutes and run around it, just like you first did with the shoreline points. Throw out markers that outline the structure for you. Then, back off and take a look at it, in proper perspective. Take a few minutes and draw yourself a map. Note harder and softer bottom in your notes.

Also, take shoreline sightings, so you can easily return to this spot, and even know whether you are on the north or south side of the structure. Here's how to take shoreline sightings:

Get situated over the spot, and look around. Find two things that line up in a straight line, but are as far apart as possible. (Usually, I try to find one thing right on the shore of the lake, such as a boathouse, and then a more distant object like a tree on a high hill.) Then, turn 90 degrees to either side and find another shoreline marker, such as a peculiar tree, a big white rock, a boat landing, etc. In the future, whenever you line up your two straight-line objects, then come into line with your object that sits off to 90 degrees, you should be right back in the same place.

(By the way, this same process is excellent for quickly returning to shoreline points and inside turns, or a certain section of a big flat. It sounds like a lot of work, but it becomes second nature. I find that when I hit a good spot, I quickly scramble around for shore sightings the way you would naturally grab for the side of the boat if you were falling overboard.)

When taking shore sightings to help you pinpoint exact spots, find two things that line up and are as far from each other as possible. Here, I have lined up the white house with the tower in the distance. At this same time, I found another set of sightings on another shoreline, and noted both sets on my map. By positioning my boat at the intersection of the two lines made by these two sets of sightings, I can return to this spot with ease.

Once you have shore markings, it's a good idea to note them on your map. I have sometimes failed to do this, and when I return to that lake two years later, I can't remember if I lined up the pine tree with the pink boathouse, or the dog kennel with the state highway sign, or . . .

Fishing rivers: a whole new ballgame

Judging from the volume of mail I get on this, there are a lot of you river fishermen out there!

Believe me, I'm a river fisherman too, so let's look at some of the big differences between rivers and lakes.

You can certainly use your sonar to help you fish big rivers. Humps, shallow sand bars, deep holes and the like can be found only with your sonar in most cases. But much more so than in lake fishing, an ability to "read the water" is necessary for successful river fishing.

In a river, current is as much a piece of structure as a point is in a lake. Yes, lakes will have currents running through them that are important, too. But in rivers, current is often the overriding factor determining fish location.

Eddies

Recognizing *eddies* is critical to success. An eddie is a current break, a place where the heavy flow of the main current breaks around something and creates an area of lesser current. Many fish will hold just on the edge of the slack water, waiting for food to get washed by in the faster current. The easiest way to find eddies is closely study the current flow; on the inside of an eddie, the current actually flows "upstream!"

Most eddies are found fairly close to shore, and are cause primarily by underwater obstructions like wing dams, rocks, brush piles, etc. They can also be found on the downstream side of above-water points that stick out into the river.

An eddy is a current break in a river. They are easier to see in smaller rivers, but they are a key to fish location in any river. Look for fish to hold just inside the slower current on the inside of the eddy, waiting for food to be washed to them.

Wing dams

Wing dams, man-made rock structures, tend to hold fish primarily from late spring into early fall. Walleyes, saugers and smallmouth bass are especially drawn to these areas. Surprisingly, the current is often slack right at the front (upstream) face of the wing dam, where you might expect it to be very strong. Fish right at the front of wing dams from time to time.

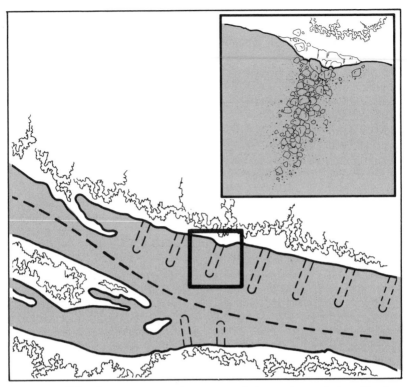

Figure 87—Wingdams are manmade structures in larger rivers, designed to slow the natural current flow. They are real fish "magnets" at certain times of the year.

Backwaters

In larger rivers, there will be extensive *backwater* areas that are sort of bays off the main river channel. Many fish species, such as panfish, largemouth bass and northern pike seem to prefer these areas out of the current. Early in the year, the water in these areas warms much quicker than that in the main channel (and, of course, stays warmer in most cases through the summer).

Generally speaking, river fish move more than lake fish do. If possible, spend time learning long stretches of a favorite river, finding good fish-holding areas at many points. The fish will move as often as every day, especially during changing seasons and periods of unstable weather.

Another general rule that might help: during periods when the river level is rising, or anytime it is high and the current flow in the main channel is fast, fish tend to move toward the shore and the wing dams. During periods of falling or lower water levels, fish tend to scatter below the wing dams and out into the deeper holes, if the current isn't too strong for them.

Larger rivers have many backwaters areas that have little or no current. Here, thick weedgrowth usually occurs, and there is normally abundant cover for baitfish and larger fish. These areas are excellent spots to look for largemouth bass and northern pike, among other species.

I believe this must be some sort of survival response by the fish. Think about it this way and it'll be easy to remember: when the water starts drying up on them (levels are falling), fish swim out into deeper water, maybe to avoid being trapped on dry ground; when it is rising, they move into shallow areas to avoid the hard work of swimming in the heavy current flow, and also probably to cash in on flooded cover and abundant food found in it. (By the way, I have noticed this same thing in lake fishing. During years of little rainfall and low lake levels, fishing tends to be better on deeper spots. During years of high lake levels and lots of rain, we seem to catch more fish in shallow water.)

Some final thoughts

Join the crowd

In your search for fishing spots, don't neglect the really obvious, such as looking around to see where groups of boats are fishing. In many cases, groups of fishermen know in general that a certain area is good, that it gives up nice bass at a certain time of year, for example. But rarely, very rarely, do those same people have any idea *why* a spot is so good. By finding groups of boats, and slowly working around and through them with your sonar (be careful not to interfere with their fishing), you can find out *what* it is they are fishing. Maybe there is a long weed finger that sticks out to the side of where they are fishing, that they only drift over by accident once in a while.

Wayne Ekelund has some excellent comments on this subject:

"Heading right for a big group of boats might seem like the last thing you should do, especially if you don't like to fish in crowds," Wayne said, "but that's exactly what I do all the time. I'm not going out there to join them, but to see what type of spot they are on. Then, I go find something similar somewhere else on the lake. If there's a bunch of boats on a long shoreline point with cabbage weeds, I'll go find another shoreline point with cabbage weeds, if there is one. If you've looked the whole shoreline over good, you should know where they are."

It might seem foolish, but joining in for a few minutes with a big group of boats can give you an idea what type of spot they are fishing. Then, you can go off by yourself and find similar spots using your sonar.

"Usually, I have that spot to myself, and the fishing is better because the fish aren't being bothered by 50 boats, motors and lures all day long. Most people don't know how to go find a spot by themselves, so they just follow the crowd. There are so many 'spot fishermen' out there, that being able to find your own spots is a sure ticket to being able to fish good spots all by yourself."

The "community spot" syndrome

One thing to consider when fishing a good-looking spot, is that every other decent fisherman probably knows about it and fishes it, too. Sometimes, the most obvious spot, like the only long, tapering point in the lake, gets pounded day after day by everybody and both of his brothers. These we call "community spots," and sometimes they just get plain burned off.

Too much pressure on a spot can cause the fish to get fished down, and even driven off to other areas. Think about this possibility if you find a spot that seems to have all the right ingredients, and fish it hard at different times of day, at different times of year, and yet it just doesn't seem to produce.

As you can see, there is a lot more to using sonar to catch fish than turning it on and seeing how deep the water is! I try to use sonar for all it can be, and yet I'm constantly discovering new ways that it can help me understand, locate and catch fish.

It takes an open mind and adventurous heart to become good at working with sonar, but it can really be a lot of fun. Leave your mind open, too, to fishing for species other than the one you came looking for.

If you have your heart set on walleyes and the lake doesn't turn out to be a good walleye producer, don't spend even one whole day banging your head against the wall. Find out about bass opportunities, or panfish, or northerns, or catfish, or whatever. Maybe it's just me, but I'd much rather catch a bunch of nice crappies than no walleyes.

Glossary of sonar terms

sonar—an abbreviation derived from SOund, NAvigation and Ranging. Originally developed for tracking enemy submarines during World War II, it has become one of the most important technologies allowing modern fishermen to understand the underwater world of fish.

cone angle—the theoretical shape taken by sonar signals as they disperse while traveling through water. Although thought of as being cone-shaped, the signals actually take on more of a "suspended balloon" shape.

leading and *trailing edges* of cone—refers to the first and last sonar signals, within the coverage of the cone, to bounce off any underwater object, such as a fish. For instance, your moving boat may come over a stationary fish. Your sonar signals pick it up at the outside (leading) edge of the cone, continue to display the fish as it goes through the center of the cone, and finish displaying the fish as it passes through the other (trailing) edge of the cone. Because the sonar signals at the outside of the cone have to travel farther to reach the bottom, the fish will display deeper at both edges, even if the fish remains at the same depth while the boat passes over. This explains why you see *arch*-shaped markings (*hooks*) when a fish passes directly under your boat.

sensitivity—measure of how high a sonar signal is "turned up" or amplified. A control on sonar units which adjusts the power of the signal being sent into the water. Similar to the volume control on a radio. Some manufacturers call this feature *gain*.

total sonar performance—means that every component making up a given sonar unit (transmitter, transducer, receiver, display screen or dial) is of high quality and operates well in an on-the-water situation. Some sonar units lack quality in one or more areas, making them poor tools for the fisherman.

interference—anything that causes your sonar unit to display unwanted signals, or prevents desired signals from being displayed. Interference, sometimes called *noise*, is usually displayed as random dots, lines or images. Most interference comes from *electrical* (often caused by sparks or radio waves) or *cavitational* (air bubbles washing across the face of the transducer) sources.

suppression—used in the general sense, means any feature built into the sonar unit to prevent interference from being displayed to you. Early technology works on the principle of blocking shorter pulse width signals and displaying longer ones. This, unfortunately, decreases the unit's ability to distinguish between objects that are close together. Recent advancements in suppression features (called *discrimination*, among other things) don't change the pulse width of the unit in order to block out unwanted interference.

grayline—sometimes referred to as *whiteline*, is a blanking circuit in picture-type sonar which makes it easier to see fish and other objects that are close to the bottom, and even can "reverse out" big fish among a cloud of baitfish. This term often refers to the area below the exact bottom reading, which appears gray in varying amounts when the grayline feature is turned on. The size of this grayish area is an indicator of bottom density. Hard bottoms, like rock, sand and gravel cause a relatively wide grayline area to appear on the display. Soft bottoms such as mud or silt absorb more sonar signals and display a very narrow grayline, if any at all.

target—literally, anything denser than water which reflects enough sonar signals to be received and displayed by the sonar unit. Can be weeds, boulders, trees and stumps, dense concentrations of algae in the thermocline, baitfish and of course, fish. Although the lake bottom would seem to fit the definition, it is not normally considered a *target*.

transducer—sonar component which converts electrical impulses from the transmitter into sound waves, sends them into the water, receives returning sound waves and converts them back into electrical impulses, and feeds them back to the unit.

high-speed transducer—any transducer, regardless of shape (including those sold as part of portable sonar packages), which is mounted permanently by means of a *gimbal* bracket, and gives good sonar readings at faster boat speeds.

picture-type sonar—a general term describing all sonar units which display information pictorially, including paper graphs, liquid crystal and video.

resolution and *definition*—are confusing terms which, strictly defined, mean different things. Because they are so similar, however, the two terms are used interchangably by the sonar industry. Strictly defined, *resolution* means the ability of a sonar display to show you fine details (early, crude liquid crystal displays had poor resolution). *Definition* refers to the ability of the sonar unit to gather that detail in the first place (in other words, how close sonar targets can be to each other and still be recognized as separate by the unit).

rep rate—(repetition rate) refers to how often a sonar signal is sent by the transmitter. (Sonar signals are sent one at a time, bounce off the lake bottom and any targets in between, and return to the unit before another is sent.) The average repetition rate for all sonar modes is about 10 times per second! Some manufacturers term this "real-time analysis," "echoes per second," etc.

fish hook or *arch*—the way a picture-type display sonar unit shows you fish. If a fish was directly beneath you at some point while it was being displayed, it will show up as an arch-shaped signal on your screen.

Kilohertz (KHz)—a measurement of the frequency a sonar unit operates at. One KHz is equal to 1,000 cycles per second. Early sonar units operated at 28-50 KHz, making them good for use in very deep water, but poor at showing schools of fish or individual fish. Most modern-day sonar used in inland freshwater fishing operates at about 200 KHz.

ost modern-day sonar used in inland freshwater fishing operates at about 200 KHz.

The "Facts of Fishing" Video Library

The **Facts of Fishing Video Library** is the only video tape series that teaches a *complete system* for catching fish. Each fantastic tape outlines a specific area of fishing and features a complete understanding of the methods and techniques for successful angling. 18 Unique and exciting titles to choose from. $39.95 each

VT01—**Walleye I**—Waging War on Weed Walleyes, Suspended Walleye of Lake Erie, Beaver House Walleye, Deadliest Method for Trophy Walleye, Minnow Madness for Walleye, Trophy Walleye of Lake Sakakawea

VT02—**Largemouth Bass I**—Cattail Bass, Bullrush Bassin' Tactics, Coping with Cold Fronts, The Fall Bonanza, Lily Pad Bucketmouths, Understanding Weedline Bass

VT03—**Great Lakes Salmon and Trout**—Kings of the Great Lakes, Chinook Stocking Builds Fishery, Early Season Lake Trout Secrets, Ski for Steelhead and Lake Trout, Fall Run Pink Salmon

VT04—**Smallmouth Bass I**—Early Season Tactics, Cranking Summer Smallies, Fall Run River Smallmouth, Autumn's Bronze Bombshells, Smallmouth Bassin—Great Lakes Style

VT05—**Walleye II**—Bill Binkelman—A Fishing Legend, The Great Lakes Walleye Breakthrough, Creating a Walleye Bonanza, Dr. Loren Hill—pH & the Walleye, A Unique Pattern for Big "Weed Walleyes," Porkin' Out Walleyes—A Totally New System, Walleye Secrets from Around the World

VT06—**Largemouth Bass II**—Bass & Rice—A Unique Combination, Dr. Loren Hill On pH & Bass Fishing, Bustin' Bass Off the "Flats," Flippin for Timber Bass, Boat Dock Bassin', Frog Run Bassin', Jig & Pig Bassin'

VT07—**Panfish I**—White Bass—The Silver Scrapper, EZ Summer Crappies, Whitefish...Panfish of the North, Small Pond Panfish, Deep Water Slab Crappies, ABCs of Ice Fishing

VT08—**Northern Pike I**—Fight'n Pike of Manitoba, Trophy Pike Tackle, Monster Northerns of Recluse Lake, Reindeer Lake—BIG Water, BIG Pike

VT19—**Jig Fishing**—Jigs—The All-Around Lure, Jigs & Walleyes...a Natural, Jiggin' Leeches, Jigs...Crappie Magic, Quiver Jigs & Smallmouth Bass, Jigs & Crawlers for Walleyes

VT20—**Northern Pike II**—Bucktail Spinnerbait Secrets, Jerkbait Pike Trolling Tactics, Trophy Lake—Trophy Pike

VT21—**Smallmouth Bass II**—Jig & Leech Smallies, Smallmouth Gold, Minnowbait Tactics, St. Clair Smallmouth, Spinnerbait Smallmouth

VT22—**Live Bait Rigging**—Back to Bobbers, Floater Rigs, One Deadly System, The Crawler "Hauler"?, Time Tested—The Lindy Rig

VT23—**The Basics of Fishing**—A Beginners Guide To..., How to Get Started, Basic Tackle, Basic Skills, Fish and Their World, Babe's Pattern Fishing Principles

VT24—**Fishing—The Electronic Age**—In the Beginning, Sonar...Which One For You, Big Water Electronics, Battery Maintenance, Electronic Accessories, Future Electronics

VT25—**Atlantic Salmon: A New Brunswick Angling Tradition**—In the Canadian province of New Brunswick, there is an angling tradition so important it borders on religious. Fly-fishing for the acrobatic, immense atlantic salmon is a sport handed down to today's anglers by the fanatic, gentlemen casters of the past.

VT26—**Canoe Country Fishing: Angling in the Quetico-Boundary Waters**—Come fish a place where there are no motors, no sounds except those made by animals and the wind. The experience of wilderness is the same as it was when this expansive natural garden served as the water highways for the rugged voyagers.
   Babe Winkelman gives you everything you need to know to make such a trip yourself. Through leading authorities, you learn: how to plan; why it is best (and less expensive) to work through an outfitter; how to paddle and portage a canoe; how to select a camp site; and, of course, Babe himself teaches you how to fish the scrappy smallmouth bass and abundant walleye.

VT27—**Fishing Ontario: It's Incredible!**—Ontario! The name alone conjures up images. Lakes, crystal clear and rimmed with rock and pine. Fish as long as your arm. The lonely cry of the loon. Join Babe Winkelman as he catches fish from one of his favorite places on earth. He feels the pulse of this world, capable of giving up numbers of huge fish. It is a fragile yet bountiful environment and this is a tape you will love. Species featured are walleye, lake trout, northern pike, and brook trout.

VT28—**Understanding Walleye**—The name is simple, but the subject a constant source of fascination and frustration for anglers throughout North America. Learn the complete story of this fish from the man who built an international reputation for catching them! Babe Winkelman lays a foundation of knowledge that is a basis for future walleye videos to come. This is the angler's encyclopedia of walleye information from seasonal movements and the basic biology of the species to, most of all, tips and secrets for catching them under all conditions. If you only have one walleye video, this is the one to have!

Babe Winkelman's "Fishing Secrets"

   Babe introduces a sizzling new video series titled, *Fishing Secrets*. Each action-packed video is crammed with facts, tips and fishing's best-kept secrets. *Fishing Secrets*, at a very affordable price, contains the type of "inside" information anglers are looking for from a man they know they can trust...except with their secrets! Approx. 50 min. each. $19.95

VT100—**Land of the Midnight Sun: Saskatchewan Fly-In Fishing**—The rugged beauty of a wilderness land untamed by man comes to life as Babe Winkelman offers a special journey into the heart of fishing's dream land. Explosive and awe-inspiring segments on northern pike, arctic grayling, and lake trout.

VT101—**Water Wolves of the North: A Northern Pike Spectacular**—Babe Winkelman entertains and teaches viewers everywhere to catch savage northern pike. Contains thrilling non-stop action footage of some of the largest pike ever captured on video.

VT102—**Wilderness Walleyes: The Lure of Ontario**—In a home video destined to be a scenic and educational classic, Babe Winkelman teaches four separate modern approaches to finding and catching the fish he built his reputation on: the walleye. Spectacular underwater footage.

VT103—**"Summer Heat" Bass: No Sweat!**—Most fishermen have trouble catching bass in midsummer. Babe Winkelman teaches his time-tested methods for catching big bass, in a variety of locations, during the scorching days of summer.

VT104—**The Great Lake Erie: A Fishing Success Story**—Babe Winkelman shows you more than one way to catch walleye and smallmouth bass from Lake Erie and tells the amazing story of the lake's comeback from environmental disaster.

VT105—**Trophy Time: Fall Fishing Bonanza**—The crisp weather of fall stirs the biggest lunkers into action and Babe Winkelman shows how to be in the right place at the right time. Take this personally guided hunt for those rod-busting brutes of autumn! Features walleye, bass, and crappie.

VT106—**Land of 100,000 Lakes: Manitoba Magic**—Come fish the land where legends are born, with legendary fisherman Babe Winkelman. Yes, Manitoba is a huge land of huge fish. If you love fishing, or ever plan to visit the *Land of 100,000 Lakes,* let Babe show you what the legends are all about.

VT107—**Cold Water — Hot Action: Ice Fishing Fever**—Ice fishing has undergone a recent revolution in techniques and knowledge unlike anything in the history of the sport. Today's winter fisherman is more mobile and scientific in his approach. Get the inside scoop on today's tactics for catching fish through the ice from Babe Winkelman, a true northern son.

VT108—**Fishing the Canadian Shield: The Ultimate Experience**—Babe Winkelman has long been considered *the* expert on fishing the bountiful yet fragile lakes of the Canadian Shield. Join Babe as he experiences a fishing smorgasbord in the rugged, pristine waters of Ontario. Catch smallmouth bass and stop for shore lunch, and then watch as one of Babe's fishing partners hooks a big surprise he didn't quite bargain for!

VT109—**Bronzebacks of the North: Smallmouth Spectacular**—Built like a bullet and muscled like a prize fighter, the smallmouth bass is everything you are looking for in a gamefish. Join Babe Winkelman on a tour of the scenic, unspoiled waters "smallies" inhabit. He will share a complete system for catching these bronzed acrobats.

VT110—**Spring Fishing: The Cure For Cabin Fever**—After a winter of dreaming, the first day spent fishing on open water is a time to savor. Join Babe Winkelman in a celebration of spring in the north country. Unleash a winter of pent-up energy with this entertaining and fact-filled video guaranteed to cure your cabin fever at any time of the year!

VT111—**Big Water Bounty: Great Lakes Fishing Made Easy**—The huge, sprawling Great Lakes are home to a breed of fish that is used to its freedom. These fish wage a battle they don't intend to lose, in some of the most spectacular fight scenes ever! Babe Winkelman, the man everyone seeks for angling advice, shows you there is fantastic Big Water fishing within easy reach of the average angler.

VT112—**Family Fishing Fun: Sharing the Good Times**—This tape will help the entire family learn about fishing together. Babe Winkelman, despite his busy schedule as a professional fishing educator, knows the value of quality time with his wife and four daughters. Join the Winkelman family on a houseboat trip where they find a renewed appreciation for the traditional values that make fishing the most universal and endearing lifetime sport of all.

VT113—**Fishing the Flow: Wonders of the River**—The flowing peacefulness of a river draws the heart and soul of a fisherman deeply into its grasp. Babe Winkelman is at home in the ever-changing world of river fishing. In the style that has drawn him an enormous following, Babe shares his secrets for catching fish from the river's currents.

VT114—**Great Plains Reservoirs: Fishing Midwestern Impoundments**—Some of the most fabled names in fishing history belong to a group of relative newcomers: the flood-control reservoirs. Let Babe Winkelman unravel the secrets to catching walleye and bass in a world where river fish have become lake fish. Or have they?

THE LIBRARY OF FISHING KNOWLEDGE
COMPREHENSIVE GUIDE SERIES

Babe Winkelman, America's most renown fishing educator, brings you the highly acclaimed **Comprehensive Guide Series**. These are without question the most authoritative books on freshwater fishing ever produced.

Each book contains concise, detailed information put together into a total system for understanding, finding, and catching more and bigger fish...a system that's guaranteed to improve anyone's fishing results! $11.95 each.

Largemouth Bass Patterns—Not just another "ho-hum" bass book. Babe uses detailed diagrams and photos to explain his "pattern system" and revolutionary approaches to bass fishing. Absolutely the last word on largemouth bass! 256 pages.　　　BK04

Jig and Live Bait Fishing Secrets—The basic fundamentals of jig fishing and live bait rigging are covered in Babe's easy-to-understand style. But this book goes well beyond, into the tips and secrets that can help you become a master fisherman. 268 pages.　　　BK06

The Strictly Fish Cookbook—Not just another cookbook—this book includes illustrated "how-to's" on cleaning, filleting, and preparing. Includes smoking, pickling, canning, grilling, and other unconventional cooking methods. 256 pages.　　　BK05

Walleye Patterns—This finicky, highly prized critter is Babe's specialty. His unusual methods and patterns are explained in detail. Includes valuable material never before in print. 304 pages of solid walleye knowledge.　　　BK02

Fishing Canada—The angler's roadmap that unlocks the mysteries of the vast Canadian wilderness. Babe shares his secrets and information on all major species. This book is a MUST if you're planning to fish "God's Country." 230 pages.　　　BK01

COMPREHENSIVE GUIDE SERIES GIFT PACK

A new six-volume set of the entire **Comprehensive Guide Series**. $71.70 retail. Sixpk

"Good Fishing" Audio Cassette Series—Four 1-hour tapes feature Babe answering some tough questions about catching panfish, bass, walleye, northerns and muskies. Babe explains how his "pattern method" works throughout the seasons. This one-of-a-kind item is the perfect companion at home, in the car, or even on the water. $24.95.   CT01

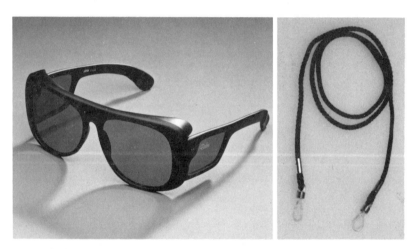

BABE WINKELMAN'S "FISHERMAN'S FAVORITE" POLARIZED SUNGLASSES

See what you've been missing with Babe's **"Fisherman's Favorite"** polarized sunglasses, now in two sizes: large (regular) and new medium size for ladies or smaller men. Both styles feature high quality *glass* lenses in two colors, gray and amber. Floatable case included. $19.95

SG01-A: regular size, amber   SG03-A: medium size, amber
SG01-G: regular size, gray   SG03-G: medium size, gray

Keep sunglasses handy and secure with Babe's new **Sunglass Lanyard**, worn comfortably around the neck. Nylon 24" cord with plastic retainers slide directly on bow of glasses and cinch down tight. $1.49 retail.   SG05

"Good Fishing" Team Hat

Comes with patch sewn on. Black front with silver mesh back. Quality hats made in U.S.A. Adjustable size fits all. $5.95

Patch

"Good Fishing" embroidered patch. $1.50

Decal

Fade-resistant "Good Fishing" Research Team emblem printed black on silver polyester. Water-resistant adhesive. 5½" high x 5" wide. $1.00

Tankard

12 oz. capacity insulated tankard with wide non-tip base. Handsome black trim with "research team" emblem printed in silver. Each $3.95
Set of 6 $19.95

For complete details and ordering information, for all of Babe's products, send for a free catalog:

Babe Winkelman Productions, Inc.
P.O. Box 407
Brainerd, MN 56401
or call: (218) 829-1144

THE MODERN LIBRAR

OF THE WORLD'S BEST BOOK

THE TRIAL

THE TRIAL

by

Franz Kafka

DEFINITIVE EDITION
TRANSLATED FROM THE GERMAN BY
Willa and Edwin Muir

REVISED,
AND WITH ADDITIONAL
MATERIALS TRANSLATED BY
E. M. Butler

The Modern Library
NEW YORK

Random House IS THE PUBLISHER OF The Modern Library
BENNETT CERF · DONALD S. KLOPFER
Manufactured in the United States of America

CONTENTS

CONTENTS

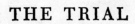

THE TRIAL

CHAPTER ONE

The Arrest / Conversation with Frau Grubach Then Fräulein Bürstner

SOMEONE must have traduced Joseph K., for without having done anything wrong he was arrested one fine morning. His landlady's cook, who always brought him his breakfast at eight o'clock, failed to appear on this occasion. That had never happened before. K. waited for a little while longer, watching from his pillow the old lady opposite, who seemed to be peering at him with a curiosity unusual even for her, but then, feeling both put out and hungry, he rang the bell. At once there was a knock at the door and a man entered whom he had never seen before in the house. He was slim and yet well knit, he wore a closely fitting black suit, which was furnished with all sorts of pleats, pockets, buckles, and buttons, as well as a belt, like a tourist's outfit, and in consequence looked eminently practical, though one could not quite tell what actual purpose it served. "Who are you?" asked K., half raising himself in bed. But the man ignored the question, as though his appearance needed no explanation, and merely said: "Did you ring?" "Anna is to bring me my breakfast," said K., and then studied the fellow, silently and carefully, trying to make out who he could be. The man did not submit to this scrutiny for very long, but turned to the door and opened it slightly so as to report to someone who was evidently standing just behind it: "He says Anna is to bring him his breakfast." A short guffaw from the next room came in answer; and it rather sounded as if several people had joined in. Although the strange man could not have learned anything from it that he did not know already, he now said to K., as if passing on a statement: "It can't be done." "This is news indeed," cried K., springing out of bed and quickly pulling on his trousers. "I must see what people these are next door, and how Frau Grubach can account to me for such behavior." Yet it occurred to him at once that he should not have said this aloud and that by doing so he had in a way admitted the stranger's right to superintend his actions; still, that did not seem important to him at the moment. The stranger, however, took his words in some such sense, for he asked: "Hadn't you better stay here?" "I shall neither stay here nor let you address me until you have introduced yourself." "I meant well enough," said the stranger, and then of his own accord threw the door open. In the next room, which K. entered more slowly than he had intended, everything looked at first glance almost as it had the evening before. It was Frau Grubach's living room; perhaps among all the furniture, rugs, china, and photographs with which it was crammed there was a little more free space than usual, yet one did not perceive that at first, especially as the main change consisted in the presence of a man who was sitting at the open window reading a book, from which he now glanced up. "You should have stayed in your room! Didn't Franz tell you that?" "Yes, but what are you doing here?" asked K., looking from his new acquaintance to the man called Franz, who was still standing by the door, and then back again. Through the open window he had another glimpse of the old woman, who with truly senile inquisitiveness had moved along to the window exactly opposite, in order to go on seeing all that could be seen. "I'd better get Frau Grubach—" said K., as if wrenching himself away from the two men (though they were standing at quite a distance from him) and making as if to go out. "No," said the man at the window, flinging the book down on the table and getting up. "You can't go out, you are arrested." "So it seems," said K. "But what for?" he added. "We are not authorized to tell you that. Go to your room and wait there. Proceedings have been instituted against you, and you will be informed of everything in due course. I am exceeding my instructions in speaking freely to you like this. But I hope nobody hears me except Franz, and he himself has been too free with you, against his express instructions. If you continue to have as good luck as you have had in the choice of your warders, then you can be confident of the final result." K. felt he must sit down, but now he saw that there was no seat in the whole room except the chair beside the window. "You'll soon discover that we're telling you the truth," said Franz, advancing toward him simultaneously with the other man. The latter overtopped K. enormously and kept clapping him on the shoulder. They both examined his nightshirt and said that he would have to wear a less fancy shirt now, but that they would take charge of this one and the rest of his underwear and, if his case turned out well, restore them to him later. "Much better give these things to us than hand them over to the depot," they said, "for in the depot there's lots of thieving, and besides they sell everything there after a certain length of time, no matter whether your case is settled or not. And you never know how long these cases will last, especially these days. Of course you would get the money out of the depot in the long run, but in the first place the prices they pay you are always wretched, for they sell your things to the best briber, not the best bidder, and anyhow it's well known that money dwindles a lot if it passes from hand to hand from one year to another." K. paid hardly any attention to this advice. Any right to dispose of his own things which he might possess he did not prize very highly; far more important to him was the necessity to understand his situation clearly; but with these people beside him he could not even think. The belly of the second warder— for they could only be warders—kept butting against him in an almost friendly way, yet if he looked up he caught sight of a face which did not in the least suit that fat body, a dry, bony face with a great nose, twisted to one side, which seemed to be consulting over his head with the other warder. Who could these men be? What were they talking about? What authority could they represent? K. lived in a country with a legal constitution, there was universal peace, all the laws were in force; who dared seize him in his own dwelling? He had always been inclined to take things easily, to believe in the worst only when the worst happened, to take no care for the morrow even when the outlook was threatening. But that struck him as not being the right policy here, one could certainly regard the whole thing as a joke, a rude joke which his colleagues in the Bank had concocted for some unknown reason, perhaps because this was his thirtieth birthday, that was of course possible, perhaps he had only to laugh knowingly in these men's faces and they would laugh with him, perhaps they were merely porters from the street corner—they looked very like it—nevertheless his very first glance at the man Franz had decided him for the time being not to give away any advantage that he might possess over these people. There was a slight risk that later on his friends might possibly say he could not take a joke, but he had in mind—though it was not usual with him to learn from experience—several occasions, of no importance in themselves, when against all his friends' advice he had behaved with deliberate recklessness and without the slightest regard for possible consequences, and had had in the end to pay dearly for it. That must not happen again, at least not this time; if this was a comedy he would insist on playing it to the end.

But he was still free. "Allow me," he said, passing quickly between the warders to his room. "He seems to have some sense," he heard one of them saying behind him. When he reached his room he at once pulled out the drawer of his desk. Everything lay there in perfect order, but in his agitation he could not find at first the identification papers for which he was looking. At last he found his bicycle license and was about to start off with it to the warders, but then it seemed too trivial a thing, and he searched again until he found his birth certificate. As he was re-entering the next room the opposite door opened and Frau Grubach showed herself. He saw her only for an instant, for no sooner did she recognize him than she was obviously overcome by embarrassment, apologized for intruding, vanished, and shut the door again with the utmost care. "Come in, do," he would just have had time to say. But he merely stood holding his papers in the middle of the room, looking at the door, which did not open again, and was only recalled to attention by a shout from the warders, who were sitting at a table by the open window and, as he now saw, devouring his breakfast. "Why didn't she come in?" he asked. "She isn't allowed to," said the tall warder, "since you're under arrest." "But how can I be under arrest? And particularly in such a ridiculous fashion?" "So now you're beginning it all over again?" said the warder, dipping a slice of bread and butter into the honey-pot. "We don't answer such questions." "You'll have to answer them," said K. "Here are my papers, now show me yours, and first of all your warrant for arresting me." "Oh, good Lord," said the warder. "If you would only realize your position, and if you wouldn't insist on uselessly annoying us two, who probably mean better by you and stand closer to you than any other people in the world." "That's so, you can believe that," said Franz, not raising to his lips the coffee-cup he held in his hand, but instead giving K. a long, apparently significant, yet incomprehensible look. Without wishing it K. found himself decoyed into an exchange of speaking looks with Franz, none the less he tapped his papers and repeated: "Here are my identification papers." "What are your papers to us?" cried the tall warder. "You're behaving worse than a child. What are you after? Do you think you'll bring this fine case of yours to a speedier end by wrangling with us, your warders, over papers and warrants? We are humble subordinates who can scarcely find our way through a legal document and have nothing to do with your case except to stand guard over you for ten hours a day and draw our pay for it. That's all we are, but we're quite capable of grasping the fact that the high authorities we serve, before they would order such an arrest as this, must be quite well informed about the reasons for the arrest and the person of the prisoner. There can be no mistake about that. Our officials, so far as I know them, and I know only the lowest grades among them, never go hunting for crime in the populace, but, as the Law decrees, are drawn toward the guilty and must then send out us warders. That is the Law. How could there be a mistake in that?" "I don't know this Law," said K. "All the worse for you," replied the warder. "And it probably exists nowhere but in your own head," said K.; he wanted in some way to enter into the thoughts of the warders and twist them to his own advantage or else try to acclimatize himself to them. But the warder merely said in a discouraging voice: "You'll come up against it yet." Franz interrupted: "See, Willem, he admits that he doesn't know the Law and yet he claims he's innocent." "You're quite right, but you'll never make a man like that see reason," replied the other. K. gave no further answer; "Must I," he thought, "let myself be confused still worse by the gabble of those wretched hirelings?— they admit themselves that's all they are. They're talking of things, in any case, which they don't understand. Plain stupidity is the only thing that can give them such assurance. A few words with a man on my own level of intelligence would make everything far clearer than hours of talk with these two." He walked up and down a few times in the free part of the room; at the other side of the street he could still see the old woman, who had now dragged to the window an even older man, whom she was holding round the waist. K. felt he must put an end to this farce. "Take me to your superior officer," he said. "When he orders me, not before," retorted the warder called Willem. "And now I advise you," he went on, "to go to your room, stay quietly there, and wait for what may be decided about you. Our advice to you is not to let yourself be distracted by vain thoughts, but to collect yourself, for great demands will be made upon you. You haven't treated us as our kind advances to you deserved, you have forgotten that we, no matter who we may be, are at least free men compared to you; that is no small advantage. All the same, we are prepared, if you have any money, to bring you a little breakfast from the coffee-house across the street."

Without replying to this offer K. remained standing where he was for a moment. If he were to open the door of the next room or even the door leading to the hall, perhaps the two of them would not dare to hinder him, perhaps that would be the simplest solution of the whole business, to bring it to a head. But perhaps they might seize him after all, and if he were once down, all the superiority would be lost which in a certain sense he still retained. Accordingly, instead of a quick solution he chose that certainty which the natural course of things would be bound to bring, and went back to his room without another word having been said by him or by the warders.

He flung himself on his bed and took from the wash-stand a fine apple which he had laid out the night before for his breakfast. Now it was all the breakfast he would have, but in any case, as the first few bites assured him, much better than the breakfast from the filthy night café would have been, which the grace of his warders might have secured him. He felt fit and confident, he would miss his work in the Bank that morning, it was true, but that would be easily overlooked, considering the comparatively high post he held there. Should he give the real reason for his absence? He considered doing so. If they did not believe him, which in the circumstances would be under-standable, he could produce Frau Grubach as a witness, or even the two odd creatures over the way, who were now probably meandering back again to the window opposite his room. K. was surprised, at least he was surprised con-sidering the warders' point of view, that they had sent him to his room and left him alone there, where he had abundant opportunities to take his life. Though at the same time he also asked himself, looking at it from his own point of view, what possible ground he could have to do so. Because two warders were sitting next door and had inter-cepted his breakfast? To take his life would be such a senseless act that, even if he wished, he could not bring himself to do it because of its very senselessness. If the intellectual poverty of the warders were not so manifest, he might almost assume that they too saw no danger in leaving him alone, for the very same reason. They were quite at liberty to watch him now while he went to a wall-cupboard where he kept a bottle of good brandy, while he filled a glass and drank it down to make up for his breakfast, and then drank a second to give him courage, the last one only as a precaution, for the improbable contingency that it might be needed.

Then a shout came from the next room which made him start so violently that his teeth rattled against the glass. "The Inspector wants you," was its tenor. It was merely the tone of it that startled him, a curt, military bark with which we would never have credited the warder Franz. The command itself was actually welcome to him. "At last," he shouted back, closing the cupboard and hurrying at once into the next room. There the two warders were standing, and, as if that were a matter of course, immediately drove him back into his room again. "What are you thinking of?" they cried. "Do you imagine you can appear before the Inspector in your shirt? He'll have you well thrashed, and us too." "Let me alone, damn you," cried K., who by now had been forced back to his wardrobe. "If you grab me out of bed, you can't expect to find me all dressed up in my best suit." "That can't be helped," said the warders, who as soon as K. raised his voice always grew quite calm, indeed almost melancholy, and thus contrived either to confuse him or to some extent bring him to his senses. "Silly formalities!" he growled, but immediately lifted a coat from a chair and held it up for a little while in both hands, as if displaying it to the warders for their approval. They shook their heads. "It must be a black coat," they said. Thereupon K. flung the coat on the floor and said—he did not himself know in what sense he meant the words—"But this isn't the capital charge yet." The warders smiled, but stuck to their: "It must be a black coat." "If it's to dispatch my case any quicker, I don't mind," replied K., opening the wardrobe, where he searched for a long time among his many suits, chose his best black one, a lounge suit which had caused almost a sensation among his acquaintances because of its elegance, then selected another shirt and began to dress with great care. In his secret heart he thought he had managed after all to speed up the proceedings, for the warders had forgotten to make him take a bath. He kept an eye on them to see if they would remember the ducking, but of course it never occurred to them, yet on the other hand Willem did not forget to send Franz to the Inspector with the information that K. was dressing.

When he was fully dressed he had to walk, with Willem treading on his heels, through the next room, which was now empty, into the adjoining one, whose double doors were flung open. This room, as K. knew quite well, had recently been taken by a Fräulein Bürstner, a typist, who went very early to work, came home late, and with whom he had exchanged little more than a few words in passing. Now the night table beside her bed had been pushed into the middle of the floor to serve as a desk, and the Inspector was sitting behind it. He had crossed his legs, and one arm was resting on the back of the chair.*

In a corner of the room three young men were standing

looking at Fräulein Bürstner's photographs, which were
stuck into a mat hanging on the wall. A white blouse
dangled from the latch of the open window. In the window
over the way the two old creatures were again stationed,
but they had enlarged their party, for behind them,
towering head and shoulders above them, stood a man
with a shirt open at the neck and a reddish, pointed beard,
which he kept pinching and twisting with his fingers.
"Joseph K.?" asked the Inspector, perhaps merely to
draw K.'s roving glance upon himself. K. nodded. "You
are presumably very much surprised at the events of this
morning?" asked the Inspector, with both hands rear-
ranging the few things that lay on the night table, a
candle and a matchbox, a book and a pincushion, as if
they were objects which he required for his interrogation.
"Certainly," said K., and he was filled with pleasure at
having encountered a sensible man at last, with whom he
could discuss the matter. "Certainly, I am surprised, but
I am by no means very much surprised." "Not very much
surprised?" asked the Inspector, setting the candle in the
middle of the table and then grouping the other things
round it. "Perhaps you misunderstand me," K. hastened
to add. "I mean"—here K. stopped and looked round him
for a chair. "I suppose I may sit down?" he asked. "It's
not usual," answered the Inspector. "I mean," said K.
without further parley, "that I am very much surprised,
of course, but when one has lived for thirty years in this
world and had to fight one's way through it, as I have had
to do, one becomes hardened to surprises and doesn't take

them too seriously. Particularly the one this morning."*
"Why particularly the one this morning?" "I won't say
that I regard the whole thing as a joke, for the preparations that have been made seem too elaborate for that.
The whole staff of the boarding-house would have to be
involved, as well as all you people, and that would be past
a joke. So I don't say that it's a joke." "Quite right,"
said the Inspector, looking to see how many matches there
were in the matchbox. "But on the other hand," K. went
on, turning to everybody there—he wanted to bring in the
three young men standing beside the photographs as well
—"on the other hand, it can't be an affair of any great
importance either. I argue this from the fact that though
I am accused of something, I cannot recall the slightest
offense that might be charged against me. But that even
is of minor importance, the real question is, who accuses
me? What authority is conducting these proceedings?
Are you officers of the law? None of you has a uniform,
unless your suit"—here he turned to Franz—"is to be
considered a uniform, but it's more like a tourist's outfit.
I demand a clear answer to these questions, and I feel sure
that after an explanation we shall be able to part from
each other on the best of terms." The Inspector flung the
matchbox down on the table. "You are laboring under a
great delusion," he said. "These gentlemen here and myself have no standing whatever in this affair of yours, indeed we know hardly anything about it. We might wear
the most official uniforms and your case would not be a
penny the worse. I can't even confirm that you are charged

with an offense, or rather I don't know whether you are. You are under arrest, certainly, more than that I do not know. Perhaps the warders have given you a different impression, but they are only irresponsible gossips.* However, if I can't answer your questions, I can at least give you a piece of advice; think less about us and of what is going to happen to you, think more about yourself instead. And don't make such an outcry about your feeling innocent, it spoils the not unfavorable impression you make in other respects. Also you should be far more reticent, nearly everything you have just said could have been implied in your behavior with the help of a word here and there, and in any case does not redound particularly to your credit."

K. stared at the Inspector. Was he to be taught lessons in manners by a man probably younger than himself? To be punished for his frankness by a rebuke? And about the cause of his arrest and about its instigator was he to learn nothing?

He was thrown into a certain agitation, and began to walk up and down—nobody hindered him—pushed back his cuffs, fingered his shirt-front, ruffled his hair, and as he passed the three young men said: "This is sheer nonsense!" Whereupon they turned toward him and regarded him sympathetically but gravely; at last he came to a stand before the Inspector's table. "Hasterer, the lawyer, is a personal friend of mine," he said. "May I telephone to him?" "Certainly," replied the Inspector, "but I don't see what sense there would be in that, unless you have

some private business of your own to consult him about."
"What sense would there be in that?" cried K., more in
amazement than exasperation. "What kind of man are
you, then? You ask me to be sensible and you carry on in
the most senseless way imaginable yourself! It's enough
to sicken the dogs. People first fall upon me in my own
house and then lounge about the room and put me through
my paces for your benefit. What sense would there be in
telephoning to a lawyer when I'm supposed to be under
arrest? All right, I won't telephone." "But do telephone
if you want to," replied the Inspector, waving an arm
toward the entrance hall, where the telephone was, "please
do telephone." "No, I don't want to now," said K., going
over to the window. Across the street the party of three
was still on the watch, and their enjoyment of the spectacle received its first slight check when K. appeared at the
window. The two old people moved as if to get up, but
the man at the back pacified them. "Here's a fine crowd
of spectators!" cried K. in a loud voice to the Inspector,
pointing at them with his finger. "Go away," he shouted
across. The three of them immediately retreated a few
steps, the two ancients actually took cover behind the
younger man, who shielded them with his massive body
and to judge from the movements of his lips was saying
something which, owing to the distance, could not be
distinguished. Yet they did not remove themselves altogether, but seemed to be waiting for the chance to return
to the window again unobserved. "Officious, inconsiderate wretches!" said K. as he turned back to the room

again. The Inspector was possibly of the same mind, K. fancied, as far as he could tell from a hasty side-glance. But it was equally possible that the Inspector had not even been listening, for he had pressed one hand firmly on the table and seemed to be comparing the length of his fingers. The two warders sat on a chest draped with an embroidered cloth, rubbing their knees. The three young men were looking aimlessly round them with their hands on their hips. It was as quiet as in some deserted office. "Come, gentlemen," cried K.—it seemed to him for the moment as if he were responsible for all of them— "from the look of you this affair of mine seems to be settled. In my opinion the best thing now would be to bother no more about the justice or injustice of your behavior and settle the matter amicably by shaking hands on it. If you are of the same opinion, why, then—" and he stepped over to the Inspector's table and held out his hand. The Inspector raised his eyes, bit his lips, and looked at K.'s hand stretched out to him; K. still believed he was going to close with the offer. But instead he got up, seized a hard round hat lying on Fräulein Bürstner's bed, and with both hands put it carefully on his head, as if he were trying it on for the first time. "How simple it all seems to you!" he said to K. as he did so. "You think we should settle the matter amicably, do you? No, no, that really can't be done. On the other hand I don't mean to suggest that you should give up hope. Why should you? You are only under arrest, nothing more. I was requested to inform you of this. I have done so, and I have also observed your reactions. That's enough for today, and we can say good-by, though only for the time being, naturally. You'll be going to the Bank now, I suppose?" "To the Bank?" asked K. "I thought I was under arrest?" K. asked the question with a certain defiance, for though his offer to shake hands had been ignored, he felt more and more independent of all these people, especially now that the Inspector had risen to his feet. He was playing with them. He considered the idea of running after them to the front door as they left and challenging them to take him prisoner. So he said again: "How can I go to the Bank, if I am under arrest?" "Ah, I see," said the Inspector, who had already reached the door. "You have misunderstood me. You are under arrest, certainly, but that need not hinder you from going about your business. Nor will you be prevented from leading your ordinary life." "Then being arrested isn't so very bad," said K., going up to the Inspector. "I never suggested that it was," said the Inspector. "But in that case it would seem there was no particular necessity to tell me about it," said K., moving still closer. The others had drawn near too. They were all gathered now in a little space beside the door. "It was my duty," said the Inspector. "A stupid duty," said K. inflexibly. "That may be," replied the Inspector, "but we needn't waste our time with such arguments. I was assuming that you would want to go to the Bank. As you are such a quibbler over words, let me add that I am not forcing you to go to the Bank, I was merely assuming that you would want to go. And to facilitate that, and render your arrival at the Bank as unobtrusive as possible, I have detained these three gentlemen here, who are colleagues of yours, to be at your disposal." "What?" cried K., gaping at the three of them. These insignificant anemic young men, whom he had observed only as a group standing beside the photographs, were actually clerks in the Bank, not colleagues of his—that was putting it too strongly and indicated a gap in the omniscience of the Inspector—but they were subordinate employees of the Bank all the same. How could he have failed to notice that? He must have been very much taken up with the Inspector and the warders not to recognize these three young men. The stiff Rabensteiner swinging his arms, the fair Kullich with the deep-set eyes, and Kaminer with his insupportable smile, caused by a chronic muscular twitch. "Good morning!" said K. after a pause, holding out his hand to the three politely bowing figures. "I didn't recognize you. Well, shall we go to our work now, eh?" The young men nodded, smilingly and eagerly, as if they had been waiting all the time merely for this, but when K. turned to get his hat, which he had left in his room, they all fled one after the other to fetch it, which seemed to indicate a certain embarrassment. K. stood still and watched them through the two open doors; the languid Rabensteiner, naturally, brought up the rear, for he merely minced along at an elegant trot. Kaminer handed over the hat and K. had to tell himself expressly, as indeed he had often to do in the Bank, that Kaminer's smile was not intentional, that the man could not smile intentionally if he tried. Then Frau Grubach, who did not appear to be particularly conscious of any guilt, opened the front door to let the whole company out, and K. glanced down, as so often before, at her apron-string, which made such an unreasonably deep cut in her massive body. Down below he decided, his watch in his hand, to take a taxi so as to save any further delay in reaching the Bank, for he was already half an hour late. Kaminer ran to the corner to get a taxi, the other two were obviously doing their best to distract K., when suddenly Kullich pointed to the opposite house door, where the tall man with the reddish, pointed beard was emerging into sight, and immediately, a little embarrassed at showing himself in his full height, retreated against the wall and leaned there. The old couple must be still coming down the stairs. K. was annoyed at Kullich for drawing his attention to the man, whom he had already identified, indeed whom he had actually expected to see. "Don't look across," he said hurriedly, without noticing how strange it must seem to speak in that fashion to grown-up men. But no explanation proved necessary, for at that moment the taxi arrived, they took their seats and drove off. Then K. remembered that he had not noticed the Inspector and the warders leaving, the Inspector had usurped his attention so that he did not recognize the three clerks, and the clerks in turn had made him oblivious of the Inspector. That did not show much presence of mind, and K. resolved to be more careful in this respect. Yet in spite of himself he turned round and craned from the back of the car to see if he could perhaps catch sight of the Inspector and the warders. But he immediately turned away again and leaned back comfortably in the corner without even having attempted to distinguish one of them. Unlikely as it might seem, this was just the moment when he would have welcomed a few words from his companions, but the others seemed to be suddenly tired: Rabensteiner gazed out to the right, Kullich to the left, and only Kaminer faced him with his nervous grin, which, unfortunately, on grounds of humanity could not be made a subject of conversation.

That spring K. had been accustomed to pass his evenings in this way: after work whenever possible—he was usually in his office until nine—he would take a short walk, alone or with some of his colleagues, and then go to a beer hall, where until eleven he sat at a table patronized mostly by elderly men. But there were exceptions to this routine, when, for instance, the Manager of the Bank, who highly valued his diligence and reliability, invited him for a drive or for dinner at his villa. And once a week K. visited a girl called Elsa, who was on duty all night till early morning as a waitress in a cabaret and during the day received her visitors in bed.

But on this evening—the day had passed quickly, filled with pressing work and many flattering and friendly birthday wishes—K. resolved to go straight home. During every brief pause in the day's work he had kept this resolve in mind; without his quite knowing why, it seemed to him that the whole household of Frau Grubach had been thrown into great disorder by the events of the morning and that it was his task alone to put it right again. Once order was restored, every trace of these events would be obliterated and things would resume their old course. From the three clerks themselves nothing was to be feared, they had been absorbed once more in the great hierarchy of the Bank, no change was to be re-marked in them. K. had several times called them singly and collectively to his room, with no other purpose than to observe them: each time he had dismissed them again with a quiet mind.*

When at half past nine he arrived at the house where he lived he found a young lad in the street doorway, standing with his legs wide apart and smoking a pipe. "Who are you?" K. asked at once, bringing his face close to the lad's—one could not see very well in the darkness of the entrance. "I'm the house-porter's son, sir," said the lad, taking the pipe from his mouth and stepping aside. "The house-porter's son?" asked K., tapping his stick impatiently on the ground. "Do you want anything, sir? Shall I fetch my father?" "No, no," said K., and his voice had a reassuring note, as if the lad had done something wrong but was to be forgiven. "It's all right," he said and went on, yet before he climbed the stair he turned round for another look.

He had intended to go straight to his room, but as he wanted to speak to Frau Grubach he stopped instead to knock at her door. She was sitting darning at a table, on which lay a heap of old stockings. K. excused himself awkwardly for knocking so late, but Frau Grubach was most cordial and would hear of no apology, she was always

, his head sunk on his breast. "I only wan
e to her for having borrowed her room toda
ite unnecessary, Herr K., you are too scrup
ein Bürstner knows nothing about it, she has
ince early this morning, everything has be
 its place again too, see for yourself." A
 the door of Fräulein Bürstner's roo
 believe you," said K., but went in throug
r all the same. The moon shone softly into th
er. As far as one could see everything wa
proper place, and the blouse was no longe
m the latch of the window. The pillows o
d strangely high, they were lying partly in
t. "She often comes home late," said K.
au Grubach as if she were to blame for it
le are like that," said Frau Grubach apolo-
rtainly, certainly," said K., "but it can go
at it can," said Frau Grubach, "how right
K.! In this case especially, perhaps. I have
ak ill of Fräulein Bürstner, she is a dear,
, decent, punctual, industrious, I admire all
 in her, but one thing is undeniable, she
re pride, should keep herself more to her-
month I have met her twice already on out-
nd each time with a different gentleman.
and as sure as I stand here, Herr K., I
ybody but you, but I'm afraid there's no
hall have to talk to Fräulein Bürstner
 Besides, it isn't the only thing that has
ous of her." "You're quite on the wrong

glad to have a talk with him, he knew very well that he was her best and most valued boarder. K. looked round the room; it had reverted completely to its old state, the breakfast dishes which had stood that morning on the table by the window had apparently been cleared away. Women's hands are quietly effective, he thought. He himself might have smashed the dishes on the spot, but he certainly could never have quietly carried them away. He gazed at Frau Grubach with a certain gratitude. "Why are you still working at this late hour?" he asked. They were both sitting at the table now, and from time to time K. buried one hand in the pile of stockings. "There's a lot to do," she said; "during the day my time belongs to my boarders; for keeping my own things in order I have only the evenings." "I'm afraid I've been responsible for giving you extra work today." "How is that?" she asked, becoming more intent, the work resting in her lap. "I mean the men who were here this morning." "Oh, that," she said, resuming her composure, "that didn't give me much to do." K. looked on in silence while she took up her darning again. ("She seems surprised that I mentioned it," he thought, "she seems to think it not quite right that I should mention it. All the more need for me to do so. I couldn't mention it to anyone but this old woman.") "It must certainly have made more work," he said at last, "but it won't happen again." "No, that can't happen again," she said reassuringly, with an almost sorrowful smile. "Do you really mean it?" asked K. "Yes," she said softly, "and above all you mustn't take it too much to heart. Lots of things happen in this world! As you've spoken so frankly to me, Herr K., I may as well admit to you that I listened for a little behind the door and that the two warders told me a few things too. It's a matter of your happiness, and I really have that at heart, more perhaps than I should, for I am only your landlady. Well, then, I heard a few things, but I can't say that they were particularly bad. No. You are under arrest, certainly, but not as a thief is under arrest. If one's arrested as a thief, that's a bad business, but as for this arrest— It gives me the feeling of something very learned, forgive me if what I say is stupid, it gives me the feeling of something learned which I don't understand, but which there is no need to understand."

"What you've just said is by no means stupid, Frau Grubach, at least I'm partly of the same opinion, except that I judge the whole thing still more severely. There's nothing learned about it. It's completely null and void. I was taken by surprise, that was all. If immediately on wakening I had got up without troubling my head about Anna's absence and had come to you without regarding anyone who tried to bar my way, I could have breakfasted in the kitchen for a change and could have got you to bring me my clothes from my room; in short, if I had behaved sensibly, nothing further would have happened, all this would have been nipped in the bud. But one is so unprepared. In the Bank, for instance, I am always prepared, nothing of that kind could possibly happen to me there, I have my own attendant, the general telephone and the office telephone stand before me on my

desk, people keep coming in t
and above all, my mind is alw
on the alert, it would be an
situation like that cropped
past history now and I didn't
it again, only I wanted to he
ment of a sensible woman, a
agreement. But now you mu
agreement such as this mu
shake."

"Will she take my han
it," he thought, gazing at
critical eye. She stood up
was a little embarrassed,
that he had said. And be
said something which sl
which was, moreover, ra
so much to heart, Herr
voice, forgetting, natur
idea that I was taking
tired and seeing how li
with him or not.

At the door he as
"No," replied Frau
piece of information
sympathy. "She's at
something? Shall I
wanted a word or tw
when she will be ba
usually late." "It's

to the doo
to apologiz
"That's qu
lous, Fräul
been back
put back i
she opened
"Thanks, I
the open doo
dark chamb
really in its
dangling fr
the bed looke
the moonligh
looking at F
"Young peop
getically. "C
too far." "Th
you are, Herr
no wish to spe
good girl, kind
these qualities
should have m
self. This very
lying streets, a
It worries me,
haven't told an
help for it, I
herself about it.
made me suspici

track," said K., with a sudden fury which he was scarcely able to hide, "and you have obviously misunderstood my remark about Fräulein Bürstner, it wasn't meant in that way. In fact I frankly warn you against saying anything to her; you're quite mistaken, I know Fräulein Bürstner very well, there isn't a word of truth in what you say. But perhaps I'm going too far myself. I don't want to interfere, you can say what you like to her. Good night." "Good night, Herr K.," said Frau Grubach imploringly, hurrying after him to his door, which he had already opened, "I don't really mean to say anything to her yet, of course I'll wait to see what happens before I do anything, you're the only one I've spoken to, in confidence. After all it must be to the interest of all my boarders that I try to keep my house respectable, and that is all I'm anxious about in this case." "Respectable!" cried K., through the chink of the door; "if you want to keep your house respectable you'll have to begin by giving me notice." Then he shut the door and paid no attention to the faint knocking that ensued.

On the other hand, as he felt no desire to sleep, he resolved to stay awake and take the opportunity of noting at what hour Fräulein Bürstner returned. Perhaps when she did so it might still be possible, unsuitable though the hour was, to have a few words with her. As he lounged by the window and shut his tired eyes, he actually considered for a moment paying Frau Grubach out by persuading Fräulein Bürstner to give notice along with him. Yet he saw at once that this was an excessive reaction, and he began to suspect himself of wishing to change his lodgings because of that morning's events. Nothing could be more senseless, not to say pointless and contemptible.*

When he became weary of gazing out into the empty street he lay down on the sofa, after having slightly opened the door to the entrance hall, so that from where he was lying he might see at once anyone who came in. Until about eleven he lay quietly on the sofa smoking a cigar. But then he could not endure lying there any longer and took a step or two into the entrance hall, as if that would make Fräulein Bürstner come all the sooner. He felt no special desire to see her, he could not even remember exactly how she looked, but he wanted to talk to her now, and he was exasperated that her being so late should further disturb and derange the end of such a day. She was to blame, too, for the fact that he had not eaten any supper and that he had put off the visit to Elsa he had proposed making that evening. He could remedy both omissions still, it was true, by going straight to the wine restaurant where Elsa worked. He would do that later, he decided, after his talk with Fräulein Bürstner.

It was a little after half past eleven when he heard somebody on the stairs. Absorbed in his thoughts, he had been marching up and down the entrance hall for some time as if it were his own room, and now he fled behind his bedroom door. It was Fräulein Bürstner coming in. As she locked the front door she shivered and drew her silk shawl round her slim shoulders. In a minute she would be going into her room, where K. certainly could glad to have a talk with him, he knew very well that he was her best and most valued boarder. K. looked round the room; it had reverted completely to its old state, the breakfast dishes which had stood that morning on the table by the window had apparently been cleared away. Women's hands are quietly effective, he thought. He himself might have smashed the dishes on the spot, but he certainly could never have quietly carried them away. He gazed at Frau Grubach with a certain gratitude. "Why are you still working at this late hour?" he asked. They were both sitting at the table now, and from time to time K. buried one hand in the pile of stockings. "There's a lot to do," she said; "during the day my time belongs to my boarders; for keeping my own things in order I have only the evenings." "I'm afraid I've been responsible for giving you extra work today." "How is that?" she asked, becoming more intent, the work resting in her lap. "I mean the men who were here this morning." "Oh, that," she said, resuming her composure, "that didn't give me much to do." K. looked on in silence while she took up her darning again. ("She seems surprised that I mentioned it," he thought, "she seems to think it not quite right that I should mention it. All the more need for me to do so. I couldn't mention it to anyone but this old woman.") "It must certainly have made more work," he said at last, "but it won't happen again." "No, that can't happen again," she said reassuringly, with an almost sorrowful smile. "Do you really mean it?" asked K. "Yes," she said softly, "and above all you mustn't take it too much to heart. Lots of things happen in this world! As you've spoken so frankly to me, Herr K., I may as well admit to you that I listened for a little behind the door and that the two warders told me a few things too. It's a matter of your happiness, and I really have that at heart, more perhaps than I should, for I am only your landlady. Well, then, I heard a few things, but I can't say that they were particularly bad. No. You are under arrest, certainly, but not as a thief is under arrest. If one's arrested as a thief, that's a bad business, but as for this arrest— It gives me the feeling of something very learned, forgive me if what I say is stupid, it gives me the feeling of something learned which I don't understand, but which there is no need to understand."

"What you've just said is by no means stupid, Frau Grubach, at least I'm partly of the same opinion, except that I judge the whole thing still more severely. There's nothing learned about it. It's completely null and void. I was taken by surprise, that was all. If immediately on wakening I had got up without troubling my head about Anna's absence and had come to you without regarding anyone who tried to bar my way, I could have breakfasted in the kitchen for a change and could have got you to bring me my clothes from my room; in short, if I had behaved sensibly, nothing further would have happened, all this would have been nipped in the bud. But one is so unprepared. In the Bank, for instance, I am always prepared, nothing of that kind could possibly happen to me there, I have my own attendant, the general telephone and the office telephone stand before me on my desk, people keep coming in to see me, clients and clerks, and above all, my mind is always on my work and so kept on the alert, it would be an actual pleasure to me if a situation like that cropped up in the Bank. Well, it's past history now and I didn't really intend to speak about it again, only I wanted to hear your judgment, the judgment of a sensible woman, and I am very glad we are in agreement. But now you must give me your hand on it, an agreement such as this must be confirmed with a handshake."

"Will she take my hand? The Inspector wouldn't do it," he thought, gazing at the woman with a different, a critical eye. She stood up because he had stood up, she was a little embarrassed, for she had not understood all that he had said. And because of her embarrassment she said something which she had not intended to say and which was, moreover, rather out of place. "Don't take it so much to heart, Herr K.," she said with tears in her voice, forgetting, naturally, to shake his hand. "I had no idea that I was taking it to heart," said K., suddenly tired and seeing how little it mattered whether she agreed with him or not.

At the door he asked: "Is Fräulein Bürstner in?" "No," replied Frau Grubach, and in giving this dry piece of information she smiled with honest if belated sympathy. "She's at the theater. Do you want to ask her something? Shall I give her a message?" "Oh, I just wanted a word or two with her." "I'm afraid I don't know when she will be back; when she goes to the theater she's usually late." "It's of no consequence," said K., turning to the door, his head sunk on his breast. "I only wanted to apologize to her for having borrowed her room today." "That's quite unnecessary, Herr K., you are too scrupulous, Fräulein Bürstner knows nothing about it, she hasn't been back since early this morning, everything has been put back in its place again too, see for yourself." And she opened the door of Fräulein Bürstner's room. "Thanks, I believe you," said K., but went in through the open door all the same. The moon shone softly into the dark chamber. As far as one could see everything was really in its proper place, and the blouse was no longer dangling from the latch of the window. The pillows on the bed looked strangely high, they were lying partly in the moonlight. "She often comes home late," said K., looking at Frau Grubach as if she were to blame for it. "Young people are like that," said Frau Grubach apologetically. "Certainly, certainly," said K., "but it can go too far." "That it can," said Frau Grubach, "how right you are, Herr K.! In this case especially, perhaps. I have no wish to speak ill of Fräulein Bürstner, she is a dear, good girl, kind, decent, punctual, industrious, I admire all these qualities in her, but one thing is undeniable, she should have more pride, should keep herself more to herself. This very month I have met her twice already on outlying streets, and each time with a different gentleman. It worries me, and as sure as I stand here, Herr K., I haven't told anybody but you, but I'm afraid there's no help for it, I shall have to talk to Fräulein Bürstner herself about it. Besides, it isn't the only thing that has made me suspicious of her." "You're quite on the wrong track," said K., with a sudden fury which he was scarcely able to hide, "and you have obviously misunderstood my remark about Fräulein Bürstner, it wasn't meant in that way. In fact I frankly warn you against saying anything to her; you're quite mistaken, I know Fräulein Bürstner very well, there isn't a word of truth in what you say. But perhaps I'm going too far myself. I don't want to interfere, you can say what you like to her. Good night." "Good night, Herr K.," said Frau Grubach imploringly, hurrying after him to his door, which he had already opened, "I don't really mean to say anything to her yet, of course I'll wait to see what happens before I do anything, you're the only one I've spoken to, in confidence. After all it must be to the interest of all my boarders that I try to keep my house respectable, and that is all I'm anxious about in this case." "Respectable!" cried K., through the chink of the door; "if you want to keep your house respectable you'll have to begin by giving me notice." Then he shut the door and paid no attention to the faint knocking that ensued.

On the other hand, as he felt no desire to sleep, he resolved to stay awake and take the opportunity of noting at what hour Fräulein Bürstner returned. Perhaps when she did so it might still be possible, unsuitable though the hour was, to have a few words with her. As he lounged by the window and shut his tired eyes, he actually considered for a moment paying Frau Grubach out by persuading Fräulein Bürstner to give notice along with him. Yet he saw at once that this was an excessive reaction, and he began to suspect himself of wishing to change his lodgings because of that morning's events. Nothing could be more senseless, not to say pointless and contemptible.*

When he became weary of gazing out into the empty street he lay down on the sofa, after having slightly opened the door to the entrance hall, so that from where he was lying he might see at once anyone who came in. Until about eleven he lay quietly on the sofa smoking a cigar. But then he could not endure lying there any longer and took a step or two into the entrance hall, as if that would make Fräulein Bürstner come all the sooner. He felt no special desire to see her, he could not even remember exactly how she looked, but he wanted to talk to her now, and he was exasperated that her being so late should further disturb and derange the end of such a day. She was to blame, too, for the fact that he had not eaten any supper and that he had put off the visit to Elsa he had proposed making that evening. He could remedy both omissions still, it was true, by going straight to the wine restaurant where Elsa worked. He would do that later, he decided, after his talk with Fräulein Bürstner.

It was a little after half past eleven when he heard somebody on the stairs. Absorbed in his thoughts, he had been marching up and down the entrance hall for some time as if it were his own room, and now he fled behind his bedroom door. It was Fräulein Bürstner coming in. As she locked the front door she shivered and drew her silk shawl round her slim shoulders. In a minute she would be going into her room, where K. certainly could not intrude at such an hour; he would therefore have to speak to her now, but unfortunately he had forgotten to switch on the light in his room, so that if he were to emerge out of the darkness it would look as if he were waylaying her and at least must be somewhat alarming. No time was to be lost, so in his confusion he whispered through the chink of the door: "Fräulein Bürstner." It sounded like a prayer, not like a summons. "Is anyone there?" asked Fräulein Bürstner, looking round with wide-open eyes. "It's I," said K., stepping forward. "Oh, Herr K.!" said Fräulein Bürstner, smiling. "Good evening," and she held out her hand to him. "I should like to have a word or two with you, will you allow me to do so now?" "Now?" asked Fräulein Bürstner. "Must it be now? A little unusual, isn't it?" "I've been waiting for you ever since nine." "Well, I was at the theater, you know, I had no idea you were waiting." "What I want to talk to you about didn't happen till today." "Oh, well, I have no serious objection, except that I am so tired I can scarcely stand on my feet. So come for a few minutes to my room. We can't possibly talk here, we should waken everybody, and I should dislike that for our own sakes even more than for theirs. Wait here till I have turned on the light in my room, and then you can switch off the light here." K. did so, but waited until Fräulein Bürstner from her room again invited him, in a whisper, to come in. "Take a seat," she said, pointing to the sofa; she herself stood leaning against the foot of the bed in spite of her confessed weariness; she did not even take off her small but lavishly flower-bedecked hat. "Well, what is it?

I am really curious." She crossed her ankles. "Perhaps you will say," began K., "that there was no urgent need to speak about it now, but—" "I never listen to preambles," said Fräulein Bürstner. "That makes it easier for me," said K. "This morning your room was thrown into some slight confusion and the fault was mine in a certain sense, it was done by strange people against my will, and yet as I have said the fault was mine; I want to beg your pardon for this." "My room?" asked Fräulein Bürstner, and she cast a critical eye round the room instead of looking at him. "That is so," said K., and now they gazed into each other's eyes for the first time. "The actual manner in which it happened isn't worth mentioning." "But surely that is the really interesting part," said Fräulein Bürstner. "No," said K. "Well," said Fräulein Bürstner, "I don't want to pry into secrets; if you insist that it is uninteresting, I shall not argue the point. You have begged my pardon and I herewith freely grant it, particularly as I can find no trace of disturbance." With her open palms pressed to her hips, she made a tour of the room. Beside the mat where the photographs were stuck she stopped. "Look here," she cried, "my photographs are all mixed up! That is really odious. So someone has actually been in my room who had no right to come in." K. nodded and silently cursed the clerk Kaminer, who could never control his stupid, meaningless fidgeting. "It is curious," said Fräulein Bürstner, "that I should be compelled now to forbid you to do something which you ought to forbid yourself to do, that is to enter my room in my absence." "But I have explained to you, Fräulein," said K., going over to the photographs, "that it was not I who interfered with these photographs; still, as you won't believe me, I have to confess that the Court of Inquiry brought three Bank clerks here, one of whom, and I shall have him dismissed at the first opportunity, must have meddled with your photographs." In answer to the Fräulein's inquiring look he added: "Yes, there was a Court of Inquiry here today." "On your account?" asked the Fräulein. "Yes," replied K. "No!" cried the girl, laughing. "Yes, it was," said K. "Why, do you think I must be innocent?" "Well, innocent," said Fräulein Bürstner, "I don't want to commit myself, at a moment's notice, to a verdict with so many possible implications, besides, I don't really know you; all the same, it must be a serious crime that would bring a Court of Inquiry down on a man. Yet as you are still at large—at least I gather from the look of you that you haven't just escaped from prison—you couldn't really have committed a serious crime." "Yes," said K., "but the Court of Inquiry might have discovered, not that I was innocent, but that I was not so guilty as they had assumed." "Certainly, that is possible," said Fräulein Bürstner, very much on the alert. "You see," said K., "you haven't much experience in legal matters." "No, I haven't," said Fräulein Bürstner, "and I have often regretted it, for I would like to know everything there is to know, and law courts interest me particularly. A court of law has a curious attraction, hasn't it? But I'll soon remedy my ignorance in that respect, for next month I am joining the clerical staff of a lawyer's office." "That's excellent," said K. "Then you'll be able to help me a little with my case." "That may well be," said Fräulein Bürstner, "why not? I like to make good use of my knowledge." "But I mean it seriously," said K., "or at least half-seriously, as you yourself mean it. The case is too trifling to need a lawyer, but I could do very well with an adviser." "Yes, but if I am to be an adviser I must know what it's all about," said Fräulein Bürstner. "That's just the trouble," said K. "I don't know that myself." "Then you've simply been making fun of me," said Fräulein Bürstner, extravagantly disappointed, "it was surely unnecessary to choose this late hour for doing so." And she walked away from the photographs, where they had been standing together for a long time. "But, Fräulein," said K., "I'm not making fun of you. Why won't you believe me? I have already told you all I know. In fact more than I know, for it was not a real Court of Inquiry. I called it that because I didn't know what else to call it. There was no interrogation at all, I was merely arrested, but it was done by a Commission." Fräulein Bürstner sat down on the sofa and laughed again.* "What was it like, then?" she asked. "Horrible," said K., but he was no longer thinking of what he was saying, for he was completely taken up in staring at Fräulein Bürstner, who was leaning her head on one hand—her elbow was resting on the sofa cushions—while with the other she slowly caressed her hip. "That's too general," she said. "What's too general?" asked K. Then he came to himself and asked: "Shall I let you see how it happened?" He wanted to move about and yet he did not want to leave.

"I'm tired," said Fräulein Bürstner. "You came home so late," said K. "So you've gone the length of reproaching me, and I deserve it, too, for I should never have let you in. And there was no need for it, either, that's evident." "There was a need for it. I'll make you see that in a minute," said K. "May I shift this night table from beside your bed?" "What an idea!" cried Fräulein Bürstner. "Of course not!" "Then I can't show you how it happened," said K. in agitation, as if some immeasurable wrong had been inflicted upon him. "Oh, if you need it for your performance, shift the table by all means," said Fräulein Bürstner, and after a pause added in a smaller voice: "I'm so tired that I'm letting you take too many liberties." K. stationed the table in the middle of the room and sat down behind it. "You must picture to yourself exactly where the various people are, it's very interesting. I am the Inspector, over there on the chest two warders are sitting, beside the photographs three young men are standing. At the latch of the window— just to mention it in passing—a white blouse is dangling. And now we can begin. Oh, I've forgotten about myself, the most important person; well, I'm standing here in front of the table. The Inspector is lounging at his ease with his legs crossed, his arm hanging over the back of the chair like this, an absolute boor. And now we can really begin. The Inspector shouts as if he had to waken me out of my sleep, he actually bawls; I'm afraid, if I am to make you understand, I'll have to bawl too, but he only bawls my name." Fräulein Bürstner, who was listening with amusement, put her finger to her lips to keep K. from shouting, but it was too late, K. was too absorbed in his role, he gave a long-drawn shout: "Joseph K.," less loud indeed than he had threatened, but with such explosive force that it hung in the air a moment before gradually spreading through the room.

Then there was a knocking at the door of the adjoining room, a loud, sharp regular tattoo. Fräulein Bürstner turned pale and put her hand to her heart. K. was violently startled, it took him a moment or so to withdraw his thoughts from the events of the morning and the girl before whom he was acting them. No sooner had he come to himself than he rushed over to Fräulein Bürstner and seized her hand. "Don't be afraid," he whispered, "I'll put everything right. But who can it be? There's only the living room next door, nobody sleeps there." "No," Fräulein Bürstner whispered in his ear, "since yesterday a nephew of Frau Grubach has been sleeping there, a Captain. There was no other room he could have. I forgot all about it. Why did you have to shout like that? I'm all upset." "There's no need for that," said K., and as she sank back on the cushions he kissed her on the brow. "Away with you, away with you," she said, hastily sitting up again, "do go away, do go now, what are you thinking about, he's listening at the door, he hears everything. How you torment me!" "I won't go," said K., "until you are a little calmer. Come to the far corner of the room, he can't hear us there." She let herself be led there. "You forget," he said, "that though this may mean unpleasantness for you, it is not at all serious. You know how Frau Grubach, who has the decisive voice in this matter, particularly as the Captain is her nephew, you know how she almost venerates me and believes absolutely everything I say. She is also dependent on me, I may say, for she has borrowed a fair sum of money from me. I shall confirm any explanation of our being together here that you like to invent, if it is in the least practicable, and I pledge myself to make Frau Grubach not only publicly accept it but also really and honestly believe it. You needn't consider me at all. If you want to have it announced that I assaulted you, then Frau Grubach will be informed accordingly and she will believe it without losing her confidence in me, she's so devoted to me." Fräulein Bürstner, silent and somewhat limp, stared at the floor. "Why shouldn't Frau Grubach believe that I assaulted you?" K. added. He was gazing at her hair: it was reddish hair, parted in the middle and fastened with a bun at the back, and very neatly dressed. He expected her to look up at him, but she said without changing her posture: "Forgive me, I was terrified at the sudden knocking rather than at any consequence of the Captain's being there. It was so still after you shouted and then there came these knocks, that was why I was so terrified, I was sitting quite near the door, too, the knocking seemed to be just beside me. I thank you for your offer, but I'm not going to accept it. I can bear the responsibility for anything that happens in my room, no matter who questions it. I'm surprised you don't see the insult to me that is implied in your suggestion, together with your good intentions, of course, which I do appreciate. But now go, leave me to myself, I need more than ever to be left in peace. The few minutes you begged for have stretched to half an hour and more." K. clasped her hand and then her wrist. "But you aren't angry with me?" he asked. She shook his hand off and answered: "No, no, I'm never angry with anybody." He felt for her wrist again, she let him take it this time and so led him to the door. He was firmly resolved to leave. But at the door he stopped as if he had not expected to find a door there; Fräulein Bürstner seized this moment to free herself, open the door, and slip into the entrance hall, where she whispered: "Now, please do come! Look"—she pointed to the Captain's door, underneath which showed a strip of light—"he has turned on his light and is amusing himself at our expense." "I'm just coming," K. said, rushed out, seized her, and kissed her first on the lips, then all over the face, like some thirsty animal lapping greedily at a spring of long-sought fresh water. Finally he kissed her on the neck, right on the throat, and kept his lips there for a long time. A slight noise from the Captain's room made him look up. "I'm going now," he said; he wanted to call Fräulein Bürstner by her first name, but he did not know what it was. She nodded wearily, resigned her hand for him to kiss, half turning away as if she were unaware of what she did, and went into her room with down-bent head. Shortly afterwards K. was in his bed. He fell asleep almost at once, but before doing so he thought for a little about his behavior, he was pleased with it, yet surprised that he was not still more pleased; he was seriously concerned for Fräulein Bürstner because of the Captain.

CHAPTER TWO

First Interrogation

K. WAS informed by telephone that next Sunday a short inquiry into his case would take place. His attention was drawn to the fact that these inquiries would now follow each other regularly, perhaps not every week, but at more frequent intervals as time went on. It was in the general interest, on the one hand, that the case should be quickly concluded, but on the other hand the interrogations must be thorough in every respect, although, because of the strain involved, they must never last too long. For this reason the expedient of these rapidly succeeding but short interrogations had been chosen. Sunday had been selected as the day of inquiry so that K. might not be disturbed in his professional work. It was assumed that he would agree to this arrangement, but if he preferred some other day they would meet his wishes to the best of their ability. For instance, it would be possible to hold the inquiries during the night, although then K. would probably not be fresh enough. At any rate they would expect him on Sunday, if K. had no objection. It was, of course, understood that he must appear without fail, he did not need to be reminded of that. He was given the number of the house where he had to go, it was a house in an outlying suburban street where he had never been before.

On receiving this message K. replaced the receiver without answering; his mind was made up to keep the appointment on Sunday, it was absolutely essential, the case was getting under way and he must fight it; this first interrogation must also be the last. He was still standing thoughtfully beside the telephone when he heard behind him the voice of the Assistant Manager, who wanted to telephone and found K. barring his way. "Bad news?" asked the Assistant Manager casually, not really wanting to know but merely eager to get K. away from the telephone. "No, no," said K., stepping aside but without going away. The Assistant Manager lifted the receiver and said, speaking round it while he waited to be connected: "Oh, a word with you, Herr K. Would you do me the favor of joining a party on my yacht on Sunday morning? There will be quite a large party, doubtless some of your friends will be among them. Herr Hasterer, the lawyer, among others. Will you come? Do come!" K. made an effort to attend to what the Assistant Manager was saying. It was of no slight importance to him, for this invitation from a man with whom he had never got on very well was a sort of friendly overture and showed how important K. had become to the Bank and how valuable his friendship or at least his neutrality had become to its second highest official. The Assistant Manager had definitely humbled himself in giving this invitation, even though he had merely dropped it casually while waiting at the telephone to get a connection. Yet K. had to humble the man a second time, for he said: "Thanks very much. But I'm sorry I have no time on Sunday, I have a previous engagement." "A pity," said the Assistant Manager, turning to speak into the telephone, which had just been connected. It was not a short conversation, but in his confusion K. remained standing the whole time beside the instrument. Not till the Assistant Manager had rung off did he start out of his reverie in some alarm and say, to excuse his aimless loitering: "I have just been rung up and asked to go somewhere, but they forgot to tell me at what time." "Well, you can ring up and ask," said the

Assistant Manager. "It isn't so important as all that," said K., though in saying so he crippled still further his first lame excuse. The Assistant Manager, turning to go, went on making remarks about other topics. K. forced himself to answer, but what he was really thinking was that it would be best to go to the address at nine o'clock on Sunday morning, since that was the hour at which all the law courts started their business on weekdays.

Sunday was dull. K. was tired, for he had stayed late at his restaurant the night before because of a celebration; he had nearly overslept. In a great hurry, without taking time to think or co-ordinate the plans which he had drawn up during the week, he dressed and rushed off, without his breakfast, to the suburb which had been mentioned to him. Strangely enough, though he had little time to study passers-by, he caught sight of the three clerks already involved in his case: Rabensteiner, Kullich, and Kaminer. The first two were journeying in a streetcar which crossed in front of him, but Kaminer was sitting on the terrace of a café and bent inquisitively over the railing just as K. passed. All three were probably staring after him and wondering where their chief was rushing off to; a sort of defiance had kept K. from taking a vehicle to his destination, he loathed the thought of chartering anyone, even the most casual stranger, to help him along in this case of his, also he did not want to be beholden to anyone or to initiate anyone even remotely in his affairs, and last of all he had no desire to belittle himself before the Court of Inquiry by a too scrupulous punctuality.

Nevertheless he was hurrying fast, so as to arrive by nine o'clock if possible, although he had not even been required to appear at any specified time.

He had thought that the house would be recognizable even at a distance by some sign which his imagination left unspecified, or by some unusual commotion before the door. But Juliusstrasse, where the house was said to be and at whose end he stopped for a moment, displayed on both sides houses almost exactly alike, high gray tenements inhabited by poor people. This being Sunday morning, most of the windows were occupied, men in shirt-sleeves were leaning there smoking or holding small children cautiously and tenderly on the window-ledges. Other windows were piled high with bedding, above which the disheveled head of a woman would appear for a moment. People were shouting to one another across the street; one shout just above K.'s head caused great laughter. Down the whole length of the street at regular intervals, below the level of the pavement, there were little general grocery shops, to which short flights of steps led down. Women were thronging into and out of these shops or gossiping on the steps outside. A fruit hawker who was crying his wares to the people in the windows above, progressing almost as inattentively as K. himself, almost knocked K. down with his pushcart. A phonograph which had seen long service in a better quarter of the town began stridently to murder a tune.

K. penetrated deeper into the street, slowly, as if he had now abundant time, or as if the Examining Magistrate might be leaning from one of the windows with every opportunity of observing that he was on the way. It was a little after nine o'clock. The house was quite far along the street, it was of unusual extent, the main entrance was particularly high and wide. It was clearly a service entrance for trucks, the locked doors of various warehouses surrounded the courtyard and displayed the names of firms some of which were known to K. from the Bank ledgers. Against his usual habit, he studied these external appearances with close attention and remained standing for a little while in the entrance to the courtyard. Near him a barefooted man was sitting on a crate reading a newspaper. Two lads were see-sawing on a hand-barrow. A sickly young girl was standing at a pump in her dressing-jacket and gazing at K. while the water poured into her bucket. In one corner of the courtyard a line was stretched between two windows, where washing was already being hung up to dry. A man stood below superintending the work with an occasional shout.

K. turned toward the stairs to make his way up to the Court of Inquiry, but then came to a standstill again, for in addition to this staircase he could see in the courtyard three other separate flights of stairs and besides these a little passage at the other end which seemed to lead into a second courtyard. He was annoyed that he had not been given more definite information about the room, these people showed a strange negligence or indifference in their treatment of him, he intended to tell them so very positively and clearly. Finally, however, he climbed the first stairs and his mind played in retrospect with the saying of the warder Willem that an attraction existed between the Law and guilt, from which it should really follow that the Court of Inquiry must abut on the particular flight of stairs which K. happened to choose.

On his way up he disturbed many children who were playing on the stairs and looked at him angrily as he strode through their ranks. "If I ever come here again," he told himself, "I must either bring sweets to cajole them with or else a stick to beat them." Just before he reached the first floor he had actually to wait for a moment until a marble came to rest, two children with the lined, pinched faces of adult rogues holding him meanwhile by his trousers; if he had shaken them off he must have hurt them, and he feared their outcries.

His real search began on the first floor. As he could not inquire for the Court of Inquiry he invented a joiner called Lanz—the name came into his mind because Frau Grubach's nephew, the Captain, was called Lanz—and so he began to inquire at all the doors if a joiner called Lanz lived there, so as to get a chance to look into the rooms. It turned out, however, that that was quite possible without further ado, for almost all the doors stood open, with children running out and in. Most of the flats, too, consisted of one small single-windowed room in which cooking was going on. Many of the women were holding babies in one arm and working over the stove with the arm that was left free. Half-grown girls who seemed to be dressed in nothing but an apron kept busily rushing about. In all the rooms the beds were still occupied, sick people were lying in them, or men who had not wakened yet, or others who were resting there in their clothes. At the doors which were shut K. knocked and asked if a joiner called Lanz lived there. Generally a woman opened, listened to his question, and then turned to someone in the room, who thereupon rose from the bed. "The gentleman's asking if a joiner called Lanz lives here." "A joiner called Lanz?" asked the man from the bed. "Yes," said K., though it was beyond question that the Court of Inquiry did not sit here and his inquiry was therefore superfluous. Many seemed convinced that it was highly important for K. to find the joiner Lanz, they took a long time to think it over, suggested some joiner who, however, was not called Lanz, or a name which had some quite distant resemblance to Lanz, or inquired of their neighbors, or escorted K. to a door some considerable distance away, where they fancied such a man might be living as a lodger, or where there was someone who could give better information than they could. In the end K. scarcely needed to ask at all, for in this way he was conducted over the whole floor. He now regretted his plan, which at first had seemed so practical. As he was approaching the fifth floor he decided to give up the search, said good-by to a friendly young workman who wanted to conduct him farther, and descended again. But then the uselessness of the whole expedition filled him with exasperation, he went up the stairs once more and knocked at the first door he came to on the fifth story. The first thing he saw in the little room was a great pendulum clock which already pointed to ten. "Does a joiner called Lanz live here?" he asked. "Please go through," said a young woman with sparkling black eyes, who was washing children's clothes in a tub, and she pointed with her damp hand to the open door of the next room.

K. felt as though he were entering a meeting-hall. A crowd of the most variegated people—nobody troubled about the newcomer—filled a medium-sized two-windowed room, which just below the roof was surrounded by a gallery, also quite packed, where the people were able to stand only in a bent posture with their heads and backs knocking against the ceiling. K., feeling the air too thick for him, stepped out again and said to the young woman, who seemed to have misunderstood him: "I asked for a joiner, a man called Lanz." "I know," said the woman, "just go right in." K. might not have obeyed if she had not come up to him, grasped the handle of the door, and said: "I must shut this door after you, nobody else must come in." "Very sensible," said K., "but the room is surely too full already." However, he went in again.

Between two men who were talking together just inside the door—the one was making with both outstretched hands a gesture as if paying out money while the other was looking him sharply in the eye—a hand reached out and seized K. It belonged to a little red-cheeked lad. "Come along, come along," he said. K. let himself be led off, it seemed that in the confused, swarming crowd a slender path was kept free after all, possibly separating two different factions; in favor of this supposition was the fact that immediately to right and left of him K. saw scarcely one face looking his way, but only the backs of people who were addressing their words and gestures to the members of their own party. Most of them were dressed in black, in old, long, and loosely hanging Sunday coats. These clothes were the only thing that baffled K., otherwise he would have taken the gathering for a local political meeting.*

At the other end of the hall, toward which K. was being led, there stood on a low and somewhat crowded platform a little table, set at a slant, and behind it, near the very edge of the platform, sat a fat little wheezing man who was talking with much merriment to a man sprawling just behind him with his elbow on the back of the chair and his legs crossed. The fat little man now and then flung his arms into the air, as if he were caricaturing someone. The lad who was escorting K. found it difficult to announce his presence. Twice he stood on tiptoe and tried to say something, without being noticed by the man up above. Not till one of the people on the platform pointed out the lad did the man turn to him and bend down to hear his faltered words. Then he drew out his watch and with a quick glance at K., "You should have been here an hour and five minutes ago," he said. K. was about to answer, but had no time to do so, for scarcely had the man spoken when a general growl of disapproval followed in the right half of the hall. "You should have been here an hour and five minutes ago," repeated the man in a raised voice, casting another quick glance into the body of the hall. Immediately the muttering grew stronger and took some time to subside, even though the man said nothing more. Then it became much quieter in the hall than at K.'s entrance. Only the people in the gallery still kept up their comments. As far as one could make out in the dimness, dust, and reek, they seemed to be worse dressed than the people below. Some had brought cushions with them, which they put between their heads and the ceiling, to keep their heads from getting bruised.

K. made up his mind to observe rather than speak, consequently he offered no defense of his alleged lateness in arriving and merely said: "Whether I am late or not, I am here now." A burst of applause followed, once more from the right side of the hall. "These people are easy to win over," thought K., disturbed only by the silence in the left half of the room, which lay just behind him and from which only one or two isolated handclaps had come. He considered what he should say to win over the whole of the audience once and for all, or if that were not possible, at least to win over most of them for the time being.

"Yes," said the man, "but I am no longer obliged to hear you now"—once more the muttering arose, this time unmistakable in its import, for, silencing the audience with a wave of the hand, the man went on: "yet I shall make an exception for once on this occasion. But such a

delay must not occur again. And now step forward."
Someone jumped down from the platform to make room
for K., who climbed on to it. He stood crushed against
the table, the crowd behind him was so great that he had
to brace himself to keep from knocking the Examining
Magistrate's table and perhaps the Examining Magistrate himself off the platform.

But the Examining Magistrate did not seem to worry,
he sat quite comfortably in his chair and after a few final
words to the man behind him took up a small notebook,
the only object lying on the table. It was like an ancient
school exercise-book, grown dog-eared from much
thumbing. "Well, then," said the Examining Magistrate,
turning over the leaves and addressing K. with an air of
authority, "you are a house painter?" "No," said K.,
"I'm the chief clerk of a large Bank." This answer evoked
such a hearty outburst of laughter from the Right party
that K. had to laugh too. People doubled up with their
hands on their knees and shook as if in spasms of
coughing. There were even a few guffaws from the gallery.
The Examining Magistrate, now indignant, and having
apparently no authority to control the people in the body
of the hall, proceeded to vent his displeasure on those in
the gallery, springing up and scowling at them till his
eyebrows, hitherto inconspicuous, contracted in great
black bushes above his eyes.

The Left half of the hall, however, was still as quiet as
ever, the people there stood in rows facing the platform
and listened unmoved to what was going on up there as

well as to the noise in the rest of the hall, indeed they actually suffered some of their members to initiate conversations with the other faction. These people of the Left party, who were not so numerous as the others, might in reality be just as unimportant, but the composure of their bearing made them appear of more consequence. As K. began his speech he was convinced that he was actually representing their point of view.

"This question of yours, Sir, about my being a house painter—or rather, not a question, you simply made a statement—is typical of the whole character of this trial that is being foisted on me. You may object that it is not a trial at all; you are quite right, for it is only a trial if I recognize it as such. But for the moment I do recognize it, on grounds of compassion, as it were. One can't regard it except with compassion, if one is to regard it at all. I do not say that your procedure is contemptible, but I should like to present that epithet to you for your private consumption." K. stopped and looked down into the hall. He had spoken sharply, more sharply than he had intended, but with every justification. His words should have merited applause of some kind, yet all was still, the audience were clearly waiting intently for what was to follow; perhaps in that silence an outbreak was preparing which would put an end to the whole thing. K. was annoyed when the door at the end of the hall opened at that moment, admitting the young washerwoman, who seemed to have finished her work; she distracted some of the audience in spite of all the caution with which she entered.

But the Examining Magistrate himself rejoiced K.'s heart, for he seemed to be quite dismayed by the speech. Until now he had been on his feet, for he had been surprised by K.'s speech as he got up to rebuke the gallery. In this pause he resumed his seat, very slowly, as if he wished his action to escape remark. Presumably to calm his spirit, he turned over the notebook again.

"That won't help you much," K. continued, "your very notebook, Sir, confirms what I say." Emboldened by the mere sound of his own cool words in that strange assembly, K. simply snatched the notebook from the Examining Magistrate and held it up with the tips of his fingers, as if it might soil his hands, by one of the middle pages, so that the closely written, blotted, yellow-edged leaves hung down on either side. "These are the Examining Magistrate's records," he said, letting it fall on the table again. "You can continue reading it at your ease, Herr Examining Magistrate, I really don't fear this ledger of yours though it is a closed book to me, for I would not touch it except with my finger tips and cannot even take it in my hand." It could only be a sign of deep humiliation, or must at least be interpreted as such, that the Examining Magistrate now took up the notebook where it had fallen on the table, tried to put it to rights again, and once more began to read it.

The eyes of the people in the first row were so tensely fixed upon K. that for a while he stood silently looking down at them. They were without exception elderly men, some of them with white beards. Could they possibly be the influential men, the men who would carry the whole assembly with them, and did they refuse to be shocked out of the impassivity into which they had sunk ever since he began his speech, even although he had publicly humiliated the Examining Magistrate?

"What has happened to me," K. went on, rather more quietly than before, trying at the same time to read the faces in the first row, which gave his speech a somewhat disconnected effect, "what has happened to me is only a single instance and as such of no great importance, especially as I do not take it very seriously, but it is representative of a misguided policy which is being directed against many other people as well. It is for these that I take up my stand here, not for myself."

He had involuntarily raised his voice. Someone in the audience clapped his hands high in the air and shouted: "Bravo! Why not? Bravo! And bravo again!" A few men in the first row pulled at their beards, but none turned round at this interruption. K., too, did not attach any importance to it, yet felt cheered nevertheless; he no longer considered it necessary to get applause from everyone, he would be quite pleased if he could make the audience start thinking about the question and win a man here and there through conviction.

"I have no wish to shine as an orator," said K., having come to this conclusion, "nor could I if I wished. The Examining Magistrate, no doubt, is much the better speaker, it is part of his vocation. All I desire is the public ventilation of a public grievance. Listen to me.

Some ten days ago I was arrested, in a manner that seems ridiculous even to myself, though that is immaterial at the moment. I was seized in bed before I could get up, perhaps—it is not unlikely, considering the Examining Magistrate's statement—perhaps they had orders to arrest some house painter who is just as innocent as I am, only they hit on me. The room next to mine was requisitioned by two coarse warders. If I had been a dangerous bandit they could not have taken more careful precautions. These warders, moreover, were degenerate ruffians, they deafened my ears with their gabble, they tried to induce me to bribe them, they attempted to get my clothes and underclothes from me under dishonest pretexts, they asked me to give them money ostensibly to bring me some breakfast after they had brazenly eaten my own breakfast under my eyes. But that was not all. I was led into a third room to confront the Inspector. It was the room of a lady whom I deeply respect, and I had to look on while this room was polluted, yes, polluted, on my account but not by any fault of mine, through the presence of these warders and this Inspector. It was not easy for me to remain calm. I succeeded, however, and I asked the Inspector with the utmost calm—if he were here, he would have to substantiate that—why I had been arrested. And what was the answer of this Inspector, whom I can see before me now as he lounged in a chair belonging to the lady I have mentioned, like an embodiment of crass arrogance? Gentlemen, he answered in effect nothing at all, perhaps he really knew nothing; he had arrested me and that was enough. But that is not all, he had brought three minor employees of my Bank into the lady's room, who amused themselves by fingering and disarranging certain photographs, the property of the lady. The presence of these employees had another object as well, of course, they were expected, like my landlady and her maid, to spread the news of my arrest, damage my public reputation, and in particular shake my position in the Bank. Well, this expectation has entirely failed of its success, even my landlady, a quite simple person—I pronounce her name in all honor, she is called Frau Grubach—even Frau Grubach has been intelligent enough to recognize that an arrest such as this is no more worth taking seriously than some wild prank committed by stray urchins at the street corners. I repeat, the whole matter has caused me nothing but some unpleasantness and passing annoyance, but might it not have had worse consequences?"

When K. stopped at this point and glanced at the silent Examining Magistrate, he thought he could see him catching someone's eye in the audience, as if giving a sign. K. smiled and said: "The Examining Magistrate sitting here beside me has just given one of you a secret sign. So there are some among you who take your instructions from up here. I do not know whether the sign was meant to evoke applause or hissing, and now that I have divulged the matter prematurely I deliberately give up all hope of ever learning its real significance. It is a matter of complete indifference to me, and I publicly empower the

Examining Magistrate to address his hired agents in so many words, instead of making secret signs to them, to say at the proper moment: Hiss now, or alternatively: Clap now."

The Examining Magistrate kept fidgeting on his chair with embarrassment or impatience. The man behind him to whom he had been talking bent over him again, either to encourage him or to give him some particular counsel. Down below, the people in the audience were talking in low voices but with animation. The two factions who had seemed previously to be irreconcilable, were now drifting together, some individuals were pointing their fingers at K., others at the Examining Magistrate. The fuggy atmosphere in the room was unbearable, it actually prevented one from seeing the people at the other end. It must have been particularly inconvenient for the spectators in the gallery, who were forced to question the members of the audience in a low voice, with fearful sideglances at the Examining Magistrate, to find out what was happening. The answers were given as furtively, the informant generally putting his hand to his mouth to muffle his words.

"I have nearly finished," said K., striking the table with his fist, since there was no bell. At the shock of the impact the heads of the Examining Magistrate and his adviser started away from each other for a moment. "I am quite detached from this affair, I can therefore judge it calmly, and you, that is to say if you take this alleged court of justice at all seriously, will find it to your great advantage to listen to me. But I beg you to postpone until later any comments you may wish to exchange on what I have to say, for I am pressed for time and must leave very soon."

At once there was silence, so completely did K. already dominate the meeting. The audience no longer shouted confusedly as at the beginning, they did not even applaud, they seemed already convinced or on the verge of being convinced.

"There can be no doubt—" said K., quite softly, for he was elated by the breathless attention of the meeting; in that stillness a subdued hum was audible which was more exciting than the wildest applause—"there can be no doubt that behind all the actions of this court of justice, that is to say in my case, behind my arrest and today's interrogation, there is a great organization at work. An organization which not only employs corrupt warders, oafish Inspectors, and Examining Magistrates of whom the best that can be said is that they recognize their own limitations, but also has at its disposal a judicial hierarchy of high, indeed of the highest rank, with an indispensable and numerous retinue of servants, clerks, police, and other assistants, perhaps even hangmen, I do not shrink from that word. And the significance of this great organization, gentlemen? It consists in this, that innocent persons are accused of guilt, and senseless proceedings are put in motion against them, mostly without effect, it is true, as in my own case. But considering the senselessness of the whole, how is it possible for the higher ranks to prevent gross corruption in their agents? It is impossible. Even the highest Judge in this organization cannot resist it. So the warders try to steal the clothes off the bodies of the people they arrest, the Inspectors break into strange houses, and innocent men, instead of being fairly examined, are humiliated in the presence of public assemblies. The warders mentioned certain depots where the property of prisoners is kept; I should like to see these depots where the hard-earned property of arrested men is left to rot, or at least what remains of it after thieving officials have helped themselves."

Here K. was interrupted by a shriek from the end of the hall; he peered from beneath his hand to see what was happening, for the reek of the room and the dim light together made a whitish dazzle of fog. It was the washerwoman, whom K. had recognized as a potential cause of disturbance from the moment of her entrance. Whether she was at fault now or not, one could not tell. All K. could see was that a man had drawn her into a corner by the door and was clasping her in his arms.* Yet it was not she who had uttered the shriek but the man; his mouth was wide open and he was gazing up at the ceiling. A little circle had formed round them, the gallery spectators near by seemed to be delighted that the seriousness which K. had introduced into the proceedings should be dispelled in this manner. K.'s first impulse was to rush across the room, he naturally imagined that everybody would be anxious to have order restored and the offending couple at least ejected from the meeting, but the first rows of the audience remained quite impassive, no one stirred and no one would let him through. On the contrary they actually obstructed him, someone's hand—he had no time to turn round—seized him from behind by the collar, old men stretched out their arms to bar his way, and by this time K. was no longer thinking about the couple, it seemed to him as if his freedom were being threatened, as if he were being arrested in earnest, and he sprang recklessly down from the platform. Now he stood eye to eye with the crowd. Had he been mistaken in these people? Had he overestimated the effectiveness of his speech? Had they been disguising their real opinions while he spoke, and now that he had come to the conclusion of his speech were they weary at last of pretense? What faces these were around him! Their little black eyes darted furtively from side to side, their beards were stiff and brittle, and to take hold of them would be like clutching bunches of claws rather than beards. But under the beards—and this was K.'s real discovery—badges of various sizes and colors gleamed on their coat-collars. They all wore these badges, so far as he could see. They were all colleagues, these ostensible parties of the Right and the Left, and as he turned round suddenly he saw the same badges on the coat-collar of the Examining Magistrate, who was sitting quietly watching the scene with his hands on his knees. "So!" cried K., flinging his arms in the air, his sudden enlightenment had to break out, "every man jack of you is an official, I see, you are yourselves the corrupt agents of whom I have been speaking, you've all come rushing here to listen and nose out what you can about me, making a pretense of party divisions, and half of you applauded merely to lead me on, you wanted some practice in fooling an innocent man. Well, much good I hope it's done you, for either you have merely gathered some amusement from the fact that I expected you to defend the innocent, or else—keep off or I'll strike you," cried K. to a trembling old man who had pushed quite close to him—"or else you have really learned a thing or two. And I wish you joy of your trade." He hastily seized his hat, which lay near the edge of the table, and amid universal silence, the silence of complete stupefaction, if nothing else, pushed his way to the door. But the Examining Magistrate seemed to have been still quicker than K., for he was waiting at the door. "A moment," he said. K. paused but kept his eyes on the door, not on the Examining Magistrate; his hand was already on the latch. "I merely wanted to point out," said the Examining Magistrate, "that today—you may not yet have become aware of the fact—today you have flung away with your own hand all the advantages which an interrogation invariably confers on an accused man." K. laughed, still looking at the door. "You scoundrels, I'll spare you future interrogations," he shouted, opened the door, and hurried down the stairs. Behind him rose the buzz of animated discussion, the audience had apparently come to life again and were analyzing the situation like expert students.

CHAPTER THREE

In the Empty Courtroom
The Student / The Offices

DURING the next week K. waited day after day for a
new summons, he would not believe that his refusal to be
interrogated had been taken literally, and when no appointment was made by Saturday evening, he assumed
that he was tacitly expected to report himself again at the

same address and at the same time. So he betook himself there on Sunday morning, and this time went straight up through the passages and stairways; a few people who remembered him greeted him from their doors, but he no longer needed to inquire of anybody and soon came to the right door. It opened at once to his knock, and without even turning his head to look at the woman, who remained standing beside the door, he made straight for the adjoining room. "There's no sitting today," said the woman. "Why is there no sitting?" he asked; he could not believe it. But the woman convinced him by herself opening the door of the next room. It was really empty and in its emptiness looked even more sordid than on the previous Sunday. On the table, which still stood on the platform as before, several books were lying. "May I glance at the books?" asked K., not out of any particular curiosity, but merely that his visit here might not be quite pointless. "No," said the woman, shutting the door again, "that isn't allowed. The books belong to the Examining Magistrate." "I see," said K., nodding, "these books are probably law books, and it is an essential part of the justice dispensed here that you should be condemned not only in innocence but also in ignorance." "That must be it," said the woman, who had not quite understood him. "Well, in that case I had better go again," said K. "Shall I give the Examining Magistrate a message?" asked the woman. "Do you know him?" asked K. "Of course," replied the woman, "my husband is an usher, you see." Only then did K. notice that the anteroom, which had contained nothing but a washtub last Sunday, now formed a fully furnished living room. The woman remarked his surprise and said: "Yes, we have free house-room here, but we must clear the room on the days when the Court is sitting. My husband's post has many disadvantages." "I'm not so much surprised at the room," said K., looking at her severely, "as at the fact that you're married." "Perhaps you're hinting at what happened during the last sitting, when I caused a disturbance while you were speaking," said the woman. "Of course I am," said K. "It's an old story by this time, and almost forgotten, but at the moment it made me quite furious. And now you say yourself that you're a married woman." "It didn't do you any harm to have your speech interrupted; what you said made a bad enough impression, to judge from the discussion afterwards." "That may be," said K., evading that issue, "but it does not excuse you." "I stand excused in the eyes of everyone who knows me," said the woman. "The man you saw embracing me has been persecuting me for a long time. I may not be a temptation to most men, but I am to him. There's no way of keeping him off, even my husband has grown reconciled to it now; if he isn't to lose his job he must put up with it, for that man you saw is one of the students and will probably rise to great power yet. He's always after me, he was here today, just before you came." "It is all on a par," said K., "it doesn't surprise me." "You are anxious to improve things here, I think," said the woman slowly and watchfully, as if she were saying something which was risky both to her and to K., "I guessed that from your speech, which personally I liked very much. Though, of course, I only heard part of it, I missed the beginning and I was down on the floor with the student while you were finishing. It's so horrible here," she said after a pause, taking K.'s hand. "Do you think you'll manage to improve things?" K. smiled and caressed her soft hands. "Actually," he said, "it isn't my place to improve things here, as you put it, and if you were to tell the Examining Magistrate so, let us say, he would either laugh at you or have you punished. As a matter of fact, I should never have dreamed of interfering of my own free will, and shouldn't have lost an hour's sleep over the need for re-forming the machinery of justice here. But the fact that I am supposed to be under arrest forces me to intervene—I am under arrest, you know—to protect my own interests. But if I can help you in any way at the same time, I shall be very glad, of course. And not out of pure altruism, either, for you in turn might be able to help me." "How could I do that?" asked the woman. "By letting me look at the books on the table there, for instance." "But of course!" cried the woman, dragging him hastily after her. They were old dog-eared volumes, the cover of one was almost completely split down the middle, the two halves were held together by mere threads. "How dirty everything is here!" said K., shaking his head, and the woman had to wipe away the worst of the dust with her apron before K. would put out his hand to touch the books. He opened the first of them and found an indecent picture. A man and a woman were sitting naked on a sofa, the obscene intention of the draftsman was evident enough, yet his skill was so small that nothing emerged from the picture save the all-too-solid figures of a man and a woman sitting rigidly upright, and because of the bad perspective, apparently finding the utmost difficulty even in turning toward each other. K. did not look at any of the other pages, but merely glanced at the title page of the second book, it was a novel entitled: *How Grete Was Plagued by Her Husband Hans*. "These are the law books that are studied here," said K. "These are the men who are supposed to sit in judgment on me." "I'll help you," said the woman. "Would you like me to?" "Could you really do that without getting yourself into trouble? You told me a moment ago that your husband is quite at the mercy of the higher officials." "I want to help you, all the same," said the woman. "Come, let us talk it over. Don't bother about the danger to me. I only fear danger when I want to fear it. Come." She settled herself on the edge of the platform and made room for him beside her. "You have lovely dark eyes," she said, after they had sat down, looking up into K.'s face, "I've been told that I have lovely eyes too, but yours are far lovelier. I was greatly struck by you as soon as I saw you, the first time you came here. And it was because of you that I slipped later into the courtroom, a thing I never do otherwise and which, in a manner of speaking, I am actually forbidden to do." "So this is all it amounts to," thought K., "she's offering herself to me, she's corrupt like the rest of them, she's tired of the officials here, which is understandable enough, and accosts any stranger who takes her fancy with compliments about his eyes." And K. rose to his feet as if he had uttered his thoughts aloud and sufficiently explained his position. "I don't think that could help me," he said; "to help me effectively one would need connections with the higher officials. But I'm sure you know only the petty subordinates that swarm round here. You must know them quite well and could get them to do a lot, I don't doubt, but the utmost that they could do would have no effect whatever on the final result of the case. And you would simply have alienated some of your friends. I don't want that. Keep your friendship with these people, for it seems to me that you need it. I say this with regret, since to make some return for your compliment, I must confess that I like you too, especially when you gaze at me with such sorrowful eyes, as you are doing now, though I assure you there's no reason whatever for it. Your place is among the people I have to fight, but you're quite at home there, you love this student, no doubt, or if you don't love him at least you prefer him to your husband. It's easy to tell that from what you say." "No," she cried without getting up but merely catching hold of K.'s hand, which he did not withdraw quickly enough. "You mustn't go away yet, you mustn't go with mistaken ideas about me. Could you really bring yourself to go away like that? Am I really of so little account in your eyes that you won't even do me the kindness of staying for a little longer?" "You misunderstand me," said

K., sitting down, "if you really want me to stay I'll stay with pleasure, I have time enough; I came here expecting to find the Court in session. All that I meant was merely to beg you not to do anything for me in this case of mine. But that needn't offend you when you consider that I don't care at all what the outcome of the case is, and that I would only laugh at it if I were sentenced. Assuming, that is, that the case will ever come to a proper conclusion, which I very much doubt. Indeed, I fancy that it has probably been dropped already or will soon be dropped, through the laziness or the forgetfulness or it may be even through the fears of those who are responsible for it. Of course it's possible that they will make a show of carrying it on, in the hope of getting money out of me, but they needn't bother, I can tell you now, for I shall never bribe anyone. That's something you could really do for me, however; you could inform the Examining Magistrate, or anyone who could be depended on to spread the news, that nothing will induce me to bribe these officials, not even any of the artifices in which they are doubtless so ingenious. The attempt would be quite hopeless, you can tell them that frankly. But perhaps they have come to that conclusion already, and even if they haven't, I don't much mind whether they get the information or not. It would merely save them some trouble and me, of course, some unpleasantness, but I should gladly endure any unpleasantness that meant a setback for them. And I shall take good care to see that it does. By the way, do you really know the Examining Magistrate?" "Of course," said the woman. "He was the first one I thought of when I offered you my help. I didn't know that he was only a petty official, but as you say so it must naturally be true. All the same, I fancy that the reports he sends up to the higher officials have some influence. And he writes out so many reports. You say that the officials are lazy, but that certainly doesn't apply to all of them, particularly to the Examining Magistrate, he's always writing. Last Sunday, for instance, the session lasted till late in the evening. All the others left, but the Examining Magistrate stayed on in the courtroom, I had to bring a lamp for him, I only had a small kitchen lamp, but that was all he needed and he began to write straight away. In the meantime my husband came home, he was off duty on that particular Sunday, we carried back our furniture, set our room to rights again, then some neighbors arrived, we talked on by candlelight, to tell the truth we simply forgot the Examining Magistrate and went to bed. Suddenly, in the middle of the night, it must have been far into the night by then, I woke up, the Examining Magistrate was standing beside our bed shielding the lamp with his hand to keep the light from falling on my husband, a needless precaution, for my husband sleeps so soundly that not even the light would have wakened him. I was so startled that I almost cried out, but the Examining Magistrate was very kind, warned me to be careful, whispered to me that he had been writing till then, that he had come to return the lamp, and that he would never forget the picture I had made lying asleep in bed. I only tell you this to show that the Examining Magistrate is kept really busy writing reports, especially about you, for your interrogation was certainly one of the main items in the two days' session. Such long reports as that surely can't be quite unimportant. But besides that you can guess from what happened that the Examining Magistrate is beginning to take an interest in me, and that at this early stage— for he must have noticed me then for the first time—I could have great influence with him. And by this time I have other proofs that he is anxious to win my favor. Yesterday he sent me a pair of silk stockings through the student, who works with him and whom he is very friendly with, making out that it was a reward for cleaning the courtroom, but that was only an excuse, for to do that is only my duty and my husband is supposed to be paid for it. They're beautiful stockings, look"—she stretched out her legs, pulled her skirts above her knees, and herself contemplated the stockings—"they're beautiful stockings, but too fine, all the same, and not suitable for a woman like me."

Suddenly she broke off, laid her hand on K.'s hand as if to reassure him, and said: "Hush, Bertold is watching us." K. slowly raised his eyes. In the door of the courtroom a young man was standing; he was small, his legs were slightly bowed, and he strove to add dignity to his appearance by wearing a short, straggling reddish beard, which he was always fingering. K. stared at him with interest, this was the first student of the mysterious jurisprudence whom he had encountered, as it were, on human terms, a man, too, who would presumably attain to one of the higher official positions some day. The student, however, seemed to take not the slightest notice of K., he merely made a sign to the woman with one finger, which he withdrew for a moment from his beard, and went over to the window. The woman bent over K. and whispered: "Don't be angry with me, please don't think badly of me, I must go to him now, and he's a dreadful-looking creature, just see what bandy legs he has. But I'll come back in a minute and then I'll go with you if you'll take me with you, I'll go with you wherever you like, you can do with me what you please, I'll be glad if I can only get out of here for a long time, and I wish it could be forever." She gave K.'s hand a last caress, jumped up, and ran to the window. Despite himself K.'s hand reached out after hers in the empty air. The woman really attracted him, and after mature reflection he could find no valid reason why he should not yield to that attraction. He dismissed without difficulty the fleeting suspicion that she might be trying to lay a trap for him on the instructions of the Court. In what way could she entrap him? Wasn't he still free enough to flout the authority of this Court once and for all, at least as far as it concerned him? Could he not trust himself to this trifling extent? And her offer of help had sounded sincere and was probably not worthless. And probably there could be no more fitting revenge on the Examining Magistrate and his henchmen than to wrest this woman from them and take her himself. Then some night the Examining Magistrate, after long and arduous labor on his lying reports about K., might come to the woman's bed and find it empty. Empty because she had gone off with K., because the woman now standing in the window, that supple, voluptuous warm body under the coarse heavy, dark dress, belonged to K. and to K. alone.

After arguing himself in this way out of his suspicions, he began to feel that the whispered conversation in the window was going on too long, and started knocking on the table with his knuckles and then with his fist. The student glanced briefly at K. across the woman's shoulder, but did not let himself be put out, indeed moved closer to her and put his arms around her. She drooped her head as if attentively listening to him, and as she did so he kissed her loudly on the throat without at all interrupting his remarks. In this action K. saw confirmed the tyranny which the student exercised over the woman, as she had complained, and he sprang to his feet and began to pace up and down the room. With occasional sideglances at the student he meditated how to get rid of him as quickly as possible, and so it was not unwelcome to him when the fellow, obviously annoyed by his walking up and down, which had turned by now into an angry trampling, said: "If you're so impatient, you can go away. There was nothing to hinder your going long ago, nobody would have missed you. In fact, it was your duty to go away, and as soon as I came in too, and as fast as your legs could carry you." There was intense rage in these words, but there was also the insolence of a future official of the Court addressing a displeasing prisoner. K. stepped up quite close to the student and said with a smile: "I am impatient, that is true, but the easiest way to relieve my impatience would be for you to leave us. Yet if by any chance you have come here to study—I hear that you're a student—I'll gladly vacate the room and go away with this woman. I fancy you've a long way to go yet in your studies before you can become a Judge. I admit I'm not very well versed in the niceties of your legal training, but I assume that it doesn't consist exclusively in learning to make rude remarks, at which you seem to have attained a shameless proficiency." "He shouldn't have been allowed to run around at large," said the student, as if seeking to explain K.'s insulting words to the woman. "It was a mistake, I told the Examining Magistrate that. He should at least have been confined to his room between the interrogations. There are times when I simply don't understand the Examining Magistrate." * "What's the use of talking?" said K., stretching out his hand to the woman. "Come along." "Ah, that's it," said the student, "no, no, you don't get her," and with a strength which one would not have believed him capable of he lifted her in one arm and, gazing up at her tenderly, ran, stooping a little beneath his burden, to the door. A certain fear of K. was unmistakable in this action, and yet he risked infuriating K. further by caressing and clasping the woman's arm with his free hand. K. ran a few steps after him, ready to seize and if necessary to throttle him, when the woman said: "It's no use, the Examining Magistrate has sent for me, I daren't go with you; this little monster," she patted the student's face, "this little monster won't let me go." "And you don't want to be set free," cried K., laying his hand on the shoulder of the student, who snapped at it with his teeth. "No," cried the woman, pushing K. away with both hands. "No, no, you mustn't do that, what are you thinking of? It would be the ruin of me. Let him alone, oh, please let him alone! He's only obeying the orders of the Examining Magistrate and carrying me to him." "Then let him go, and as for you, I never want to see you again," said K., furious with disappointment, and he gave the student a punch in the back that made him stumble for a moment, only to spring off more nimbly than ever out of relief that he had not fallen. K. slowly walked after them, he recognized that this was the first unequivocal defeat that he had received from these people. There was no reason, of course, for him to worry about that, he had received the defeat only because he had insisted on giving battle. While he stayed quietly at home and went about his ordinary vocations he remained superior to all these people and could kick any of them out of his path. And he pictured to himself the highly comic situation which would arise if, for instance, this wretched student, this puffed-up whippersnapper, this bandy-legged beaver, had to kneel by Elsa's bed some day wringing his hands and begging for favors. This picture pleased K. so much that he decided, if ever the opportunity came, to take the student along to visit Elsa.

Out of curiosity K. hurried to the door, he wanted to see where the woman was being carried off to, for the student could scarcely bear her in his arms across the street. But the journey was much shorter than that. Immediately opposite the door a flight of narrow wooden stairs led, as it seemed, to a garret, it had a turning so that one could not see the other end. The student was now carrying the woman up this stairway, very slowly, puffing and groaning, for he was beginning to be exhausted. The woman waved her hand to K. as he stood below, and shrugged her shoulders to suggest that she was not to blame for this abduction, but very little regret could be read into that dumb show. K. looked at her expressionlessly, as if she were a stranger, he was resolved not to betray to her either that he was disappointed or even that he could easily get over any disappointment he felt.

The two had already vanished, yet K. still stood in the doorway. He was forced to the conclusion that the woman not only had betrayed him, but also had lied in saying that she was being carried to the Examining Magistrate. The Examining Magistrate surely could not be sitting waiting in a garret. The little wooden stairway did not reveal anything, no matter how long one regarded it. But K. noticed a small card pinned up beside it, and crossing over he read in childish, unpracticed handwriting: "Law Court Offices upstairs." So the Law Court offices were up in the attics of this tenement? That was not an arrangement likely to inspire much respect, and for an accused man it was reassuring to reckon how little money this Court could have at its disposal when it housed its offices in a part of the building where the tenants, who themselves belonged to the poorest of the poor, flung their useless lumber. Though, of course, the possibility was not to be ignored that the money was abundant enough, but that the officials pocketed it before it could be used for the purposes of justice. To judge from K.'s experience hitherto, that was indeed extremely probable, yet if it were so, such disreputable practices, while certainly humiliating to an accused man, suggested more hope for him than a merely pauperized condition of the Law Courts. Now K. could understand too why in the beginning they had been ashamed to summon him into their attics and had chosen instead to molest him in his lodgings. And how well-off K. was compared with the Magistrate, who had to sit in a garret, while K. had a large room in the Bank with a waiting-room attached to it and could watch the busy life of the city through his enormous plate-glass window. True, he drew no secondary income from bribes or peculation and could not order his attendant to pick up a woman and carry her to his room. But K. was perfectly willing to renounce these advantages, at least in this life.

K. was still standing beside the card when a man came up from below, looked into the room through the open door, from which he could also see the courtroom, and then asked K. if he had seen a woman about anywhere. "You are the usher, aren't you?" asked K. "Yes," said the man. "Oh, you're the defendant K., now I recognize you, you're welcome." And he held out his hand to K., who had not expected that. "But no sitting was announced for today," the usher went on, as K. remained silent. "I know," said K., gazing at the man's civilian clothes, which displayed on the jacket, as the sole emblem of his office, two gilt buttons in addition to the ordinary ones, gilt buttons that looked as if they had been stripped from an old army coat. "I was speaking to your wife a moment ago. She's not here now. The student has carried her up to the Examining Magistrate." "There you are," said the usher, "they're always carrying her away from me. Today is Sunday too, I'm not supposed to do any work, but simply to get me away from the place they sent me out on a useless errand. And they took care not to send me too far away, so that I had some hopes of being able to get back in time if I hurried. And there was I running as fast as I could, shouting the message through the half-open door of the office I was sent to, nearly breathless so that they could hardly make me out, and back again at top speed, and yet the student was here before me, he hadn't so far to come, of course, he had only to cut down that short wooden staircase from the attics. If my job were not at stake, I would have squashed that student flat against the wall here long ago. Just beside this card. It's a daily dream of mine. I see him squashed flat here, just a little above the floor, his arms wide, his fingers spread, his bandy legs writhing in a circle, and splashes of blood all round. But so far it's only been a dream." "Is there no other remedy?" asked K., smiling. "Not that I know of," said the usher. "And now it's getting worse than ever, up till now he has been carrying her off for his own pleasure, but now, as I've been expecting for a long time, I may say, he's carrying her to the Examining Magistrate as well." "But isn't your wife to blame too?" asked K.; he had to keep a grip of himself while asking this, he still felt so jealous. "But of course," said the usher, "she's actually most to blame of all. She simply flung herself at him. As for him, he runs after every woman he sees. In this building alone he's already been thrown out of five flats he managed to insinuate himself into. And my wife is the best-looking woman in the whole tenement, and I'm in a position where I can't defend myself." "If that's how things stand, then there's no help, it seems," said K. "And why not?" asked the usher. "If he only got a good thrashing some time when he was after my wife—he's a coward, anyway—he would never dare to do it again. But I can't thrash him, and nobody else will oblige me by doing it, for they're all afraid of him, he's too influential. Only a man like you could do it." "But why a man like me?" asked K., in astonishment. "You're under arrest, aren't you?" said the usher. "Yes," said K., "and that means I have all the more reason to fear him, for though he may not be able to influence the outcome of the case, he can probably influence the preliminary interrogations." "Yes, that's so," said the usher, as if K.'s view of the matter were as self-evident as his own. "Yet as a rule all our cases are foregone conclusions." "I am not of that opinion," said K., "but that needn't prevent me from taking the student in hand." "I should be very grateful to you," said the usher rather formally; he did not appear really to believe that his heart's desire could be fulfilled. "It may be," K. went on, "that some more of your officials, probably all of them, deserve the same treatment." "Oh, yes," said the usher, as if he were assenting to a commonplace. Then he gave K. a confidential look, such as he had not yet ventured in spite of all his friendliness, and added: "Everyone is always rebellious." But the conversation seemed to have made him uneasy, all the same, for he broke it off by saying: "I

must report upstairs now. Would you like to come too?"
"I have no business there," said K. "You can have a look
at the offices. Nobody will pay any attention to you."
"Why, are they worth seeing?" asked K. hesitatingly,
but suddenly feeling a great desire to go. "Well," said
the usher, "I thought it might interest you." "Good," said
K. at last, "I'll come with you." And he ran up the stairs
even more quickly than the usher.

On entering he almost stumbled, for behind the door
there was an extra step. "They don't show much consideration for the public," he said. "They show no consideration of any kind," replied the usher. "Just look at this
waiting-room." It was a long passage, a lobby communi-
cating by ill-fitting doors with the different offices on the
floor. Although there was no window to admit light, it
was not entirely dark, for some of the offices were not
properly boarded off from the passage but had an open
frontage of wooden rails, reaching, however, to the roof,
through which a little light penetrated and through which
one could see a few officials as well, some writing at their
desks, and some standing close to the rails peering
through the interstices at the people in the lobby. There
were only a few people in the lobby, probably because it
was Sunday. They made a very modest showing. At almost regular intervals they were sitting singly along a
row of wooden benches fixed to either side of the passage.
All of them were carelessly dressed, though to judge from
the expression of their faces, their bearing, the cut of
their beards, and many almost imperceptible little details, they obviously belonged to the upper classes. As

there was no hat-rack in the passage, they had placed their hats under the benches, in this probably following each other's example. When those who were sitting nearest the door caught sight of K. and the usher, they rose politely, followed in turn by their neighbors, who also seemed to think it necessary to rise, so that everyone stood as the two men passed. They did not stand quite erect, their backs remained bowed, their knees bent, they stood like street beggars. K. waited for the usher, who kept slightly behind him, and said: "How humbled they must be!" "Yes," said the usher, "these are the accused men, all of them are defendants." "Indeed!" said K. "Then they're colleagues of mine." And he turned to the nearest, a tall, slender, almost gray-haired man. "What are you waiting here for?" asked K. courteously. But this unexpected question confused the man, which was the more deeply embarrassing as he was obviously a man of the world who would have known how to comport himself anywhere else and would not lightly have renounced his natural superiority. Yet in this place he did not know even how to reply to a simple question and gazed at the others as if it were their duty to help him, as if no one could expect him to answer should help not be forthcoming. Then the usher stepped up and said, to reassure the man and encourage him: "This gentleman merely asked what you are waiting for. Come, give him an answer." The familiar voice of the usher had its effect: "I'm waiting—" the man started to say, but could get out no more. He had obviously begun by intending to make an exact reply to the question, but did not know how to go on. Some of the other clients had drifted up and now clustered round, and the usher said to them: "Off with you, keep the passage clear." They drew back a little, but not to their former places. Meanwhile the man had collected himself and actually replied with a faint smile: "A month ago I handed in several affidavits concerning my case and I am waiting for the result." "You seem to put yourself to a great deal of trouble," said K. "Yes," said the man, "for it is my case." "Everyone doesn't think as you do," said K. "For example, I am under arrest too, but as sure as I stand here I have neither put in any affidavit nor attempted anything whatever of the kind. Do you consider such things necessary, then?" "I can't exactly say," replied the man, once more deprived of all assurance; he evidently thought that K. was making fun of him, and appeared to be on the point of repeating his first answer all over again for fear of making a new mistake, but under K.'s impatient eye he merely said: "Anyhow, I have handed in my affidavits." "Perhaps you don't believe that I am under arrest?" asked K. "Oh, yes, certainly," said the man, stepping somewhat aside, but there was no belief in his answer, merely apprehension. "So you don't really believe me?" asked K. and, provoked without knowing it by the man's humility, he seized him by the arm as if to compel him to believe. He had no wish to hurt him, and besides had grasped him quite loosely, yet the man cried out as if K. had gripped him with glowing pincers instead of with two fingers. That ridiculous outcry was too much for K.; if the man would not believe that he was under arrest, so much the better; perhaps he actually took him for a Judge. As a parting gesture he gripped the man with real force, flung him back on the bench, and went on his way. "Most of these accused men are so sensitive," said the usher. Behind them almost all the clients were now gathered round the man, whose cries had already ceased, and they seemed to be eagerly asking him about the incident. A guard came up to K., he was mainly recognizable by his sword, whose sheath, at least to judge from its color, was of aluminum. K. gaped at it and actually put out his hand to feel it. The guard, who had come to inquire into the commotion, asked what had happened. The usher tried to put him off with a few words, but the guard declared that he must look into this matter himself, saluted, and strutted on with hasty but very short steps, probably resulting from gout.

K. did not trouble his head for long over him and the people in the lobby, particularly as, when he had walked halfway down the lobby, he saw a turning leading to the right through an opening which had no door. He inquired of the usher if this was the right way, the usher nodded, and K. then turned into it. It troubled him that he had always to walk one or two paces ahead of the usher, in a place like this it might look as if he were a prisoner under escort. Accordingly he paused several times to wait for the usher, but the man always dropped behind again. At last K. said, to put an end to his discomfort: "I've seen the place now, and I think I'll go." "You haven't seen everything yet," said the usher innocently. "I don't want to see everything," said K., who by now felt really tired. "I want to get away, how does one reach the outside door?" "You surely haven't lost your way already?" asked the usher in surprise. "You just go along here to the corner and then turn to the right along the lobby straight to the door." "You come too," said K. "Show me the way, there are so many lobbies here, I'll never find the way." "There's only the one way," said the usher reproachfully. "I can't go back with you, I must deliver my message and I've lost a great deal of time through you already." "Come with me," said K. still more sharply, as if he had at last caught the usher in a falsehood. "Don't shout like that," whispered the usher, "there are offices everywhere hereabouts. If you don't want to go back by yourself, then come a little farther with me, or wait here until I've delivered my message, then I'll be glad to take you back." "No, no," said K., "I won't wait and you must come with me now." K. had not yet even glanced round the place where he was, and only when one of the many wooden doors opened did he turn his head. A girl whose attention must have been caught by K.'s raised voice appeared and asked: "What does the gentleman want?" A good way behind her he could also see a male figure approaching in the half-light. K. looked at the usher. The man had said that nobody would pay any attention to him, and now two people were already after him, it wouldn't take much to bring all the officials down on him, demanding an explanation of his presence. The only comprehensible and acceptable one was that he was an accused man and wished to know the date of his next interrogation, but that explanation he did not wish to give, especially as it was not even in accordance with the truth, for he had come only out of curiosity or, what was still more impossible as an explanation of his presence, out of a desire to assure himself that the inside of this legal system was just as loathsome as its external aspect. And it seemed, indeed, that he had been right in that assumption, he did not want to make any further investigation, he was dejected enough by what he had already seen, he was not at that moment in a fit state to confront any higher official such as might appear from behind one of these doors, he wanted to quit the place with the usher, or, if need be, alone.

But his dumb immobility must make him conspicuous, and the girl and the usher were actually gazing at him as if they expected some great transformation to happen to him the next moment, a transformation which they did not want to miss. And at the end of the passage now stood the man whom K. had noticed before in the distance; he was holding on to the lintel of the low doorway and rocking lightly on his toes, like an eager spectator. But the girl was the first to see that K.'s behavior was really caused by a slight feeling of faintness; she produced a chair and asked: "Won't you sit down?" K. sat down at once and leaned his elbows on the arms of the chair so as to support himself still more securely. "You feel a little dizzy, don't you?" she asked. Her face was close to him now, it had that severe look which the faces of many women have in the first flower of their youth. "Don't worry," she said. "That's nothing out of the common here, almost everybody has an attack of that kind the first time they come here. This is your first visit? Well, then, it's nothing to be surprised at. The sun beats on the roof here and the hot roof-beams make the air stuffy and heavy. That makes this place not particularly suitable for offices, in spite of the other great advantages it has. But the air, well, on days when there's a great number of clients to be attended to, and that's almost every day, it's hardly breathable. When you consider, too, that washing of all sorts is hung up here to dry—you can't wholly prohibit the tenants from washing their dirty linen—you won't find it surprising that you should feel a little faint. But in the end one gets quite used to it. By the time you've come back once or twice you'll hardly notice how oppressive it is here. Do you really feel better now?" K. did not answer, he realized too painfully the shame of being delivered into the hands of these people by his sudden weakness; besides, even now that he knew the cause of the faintness, it did not get any better but grew somewhat worse instead. The girl noticed this at once, and to help K. seized a bar with a hook at the end that leaned against the wall and opened with it a little skylight just above K. to let in the fresh air. Yet so much soot fell in that she had to close the skylight again at once and wipe K.'s hands clean with her handkerchief, since K. was too far gone to attend to himself. He would have preferred to sit quietly there until he recovered enough strength to walk away, yet the less he was bothered by these people the sooner he would recover. But now the girl said: "You can't stay here, we're causing an obstruction here"—K. glanced round inquiringly to see what he could be obstructing—"if you like, I'll take you to the sick-room.

Please give me a hand," she said to the man standing in the door, who at once came over. But K. had no wish to go to the sick-room, he particularly wanted to avoid being taken any farther, the farther he went the worse it must be for him. "I'm quite able to go away now," he said and got up from his comfortable seat, which had relaxed him so that he trembled as he stood. But he could not hold himself upright. "I can't manage it after all," he said, shaking his head, and with a sigh sat down again. He thought of the usher, who could easily get him out of the place in spite of his weakness, but he seemed to have vanished long ago. K. peered between the girl and the man standing before him, but could see no sign of the usher.

"I fancy," said the man, who was stylishly dressed and was wearing a conspicuously smart gray waistcoat ending in two long sharp points, "that the gentleman's faintness is due to the atmosphere here, and the best thing to do— and what he would like best—is not to take him to the sick-room at all, but out of these offices altogether." "That's it!" cried K., so delighted that he almost broke into the man's words, "I should feel better at once, I'm sure of it, I'm not so terribly weak either, I only need a little support under my arms, I won't give you much trouble, it isn't very far after all, just take me to the door, then I'll sit for a little on the stairs and recover in no time, for I don't usually suffer from these attacks, I was surprised myself by this one. I am an official too and accustomed to office air, but this is really more than one can bear, you said so yourselves. Will you have the goodness, then, to let me lean upon you a little, for I feel dizzy and my head goes round when I try to stand up by myself." And he lifted his shoulders to make it easier for the two of them to take him under the arms.

Yet the man did not respond to his request but kept his hands quietly in his pockets and laughed. "You see," he said to the girl. "I hit the nail on the head. It's only here that this gentleman feels upset, not in other places." The girl smiled too, but tapped the man lightly on the arm with her finger tips, as if he had gone too far in jesting like that with K. "But dear me," said the man, still laughing, "I'll show the gentleman to the door, of course I will!" "Then that's all right," said the girl, inclining her elegant head for a moment. "Don't take his laughter too much to heart," she said to K., who had sunk again into vacant melancholy and apparently expected no explanation. "This gentleman——may I introduce you?" (the gentleman waved his hand to indicate permission) "this gentleman, then, represents our Information Bureau. He gives clients all the information they need, and as our procedure is not very well known among the populace, a great deal of information is asked for. He has an answer to every question, if you ever feel like it you can try him out. But that isn't his only claim to distinction, he has another, the smartness of his clothes. We——that's to say the staff——made up our minds that the Clerk of Inquiries, since he's always dealing with clients and is the first to see them, must be smartly dressed so as to create a good first impression. The rest of us, as you must have noticed at once from myself, are very badly and old-fashionedly dressed, I'm sorry to say; there isn't much sense anyhow in spending money on clothes, for we're hardly ever out of these offices, we even sleep here. But, as I say, we considered that in his case good clothes were needed. And as the management, which in this respect is somewhat peculiar, refused to provide these clothes, we opened a subscription—some of the clients contributed too—and we bought him this fine suit and some others as well. Nothing more would be needed now to produce a good impression, but he spoils it all again by his laughter which puts people off." "That's how it is," said the gentleman ironically, "yet I don't understand, Fräulein, why you should tell this gentleman all our intimate secrets, or rather thrust them on him, for he doesn't want to hear them at all. Just look at him, he's obviously much too busy with his own thoughts." K. felt no inclination even to make a retort, the girl's intentions were no doubt good, probably she merely wanted to distract him or give him a chance to pull himself together, but she had not gone the right way about it. "Well, I needed to explain your laughter to him," the girl said. "It sounded insulting." "I fancy he would overlook much worse insults if I would only take him out of here." K. said nothing, he did not even look up, he suffered the two of them to discuss him as if he were an inanimate object, indeed he actually preferred that. Then suddenly he felt the man's hand under one arm and the girl's hand under the other. "Up you get, you feeble fellow," said the man. "Many thanks to both of you," said K., joyfully surprised, and he got up slowly and himself moved these strangers' hands to the places where he felt most in need of support. "It must seem to you," said the girl softly in K.'s ear as they neared the passage, "as if I were greatly concerned to show the Clerk of Inquiries in a good light, but you can believe me, I only wanted to speak the truth about him. He isn't a hardhearted man. He isn't obliged to help sick people out of here, and yet he does so, as you can see. Perhaps none of us is haidhearted, we should be glad to help everybody, yet as Law Court officials we easily take on the appearance of being hardhearted and of not wishing to help. That really worries me." "Wouldn't you like to sit down here for a little?" asked the Clerk of Inquiries; they were out in the main lobby now and just opposite the client to whom K. had first spoken. K. felt almost ashamed before the man, he had stood so erect before him the first time; now it took a couple of people to hold him up, the Clerk of Inquiries was balancing his hat on the tips of his fingers, his hair was in disorder and hung down over his sweat-drenched forehead. But the client seemed to see nothing of all this, he stood up humbly before the Clerk of Inquiries (who stared through him) and merely sought to excuse his presence. "I know," he said, "that the decision on my affidavits cannot be expected today. But I came all the same, I thought that I might as well wait here, it is Sunday, I have lots of time and here I disturb nobody." "You needn't be so apologetic," replied the Clerk of Inquiries. "Your solicitude is entirely to be commended; you're taking up extra room, here, I admit, but so long as you don't inconvenience me, I shan't hinder you at all from following the progress of your case as closely as you please. When one sees so many people who scandalously neglect their duty, one learns to have patience with men like you. You may sit down." "How well he knows how to talk to clients!" whispered the girl. K. nodded, but immediately gave a violent start when the Clerk of Inquiries asked again: "Wouldn't you like to sit down here?" "No," said K. "I don't want a rest." He said this with the utmost possible decision, though in reality he would have been very glad to sit down. He felt as if he were seasick. He felt he was on a ship rolling in heavy seas. It was as if the waters were dashing against the wooden walls, as if the roaring of breaking waves came from the end of the passage, as if the passage itself pitched and rolled and the waiting clients on either side rose and fell with it. All the more incomprehensible, therefore, was the composure of the girl and the man who were escorting him. He was delivered into their hands, if they let him go he must fall like a block of wood. They kept glancing around with their sharp little eyes, K. was aware of their regular advance without himself taking part in it, for he was now being almost carried from step to step. At last he noticed that they were talking to him, but he could not make out what they were saying, he heard nothing but the din that filled the whole place, through which a shrill unchanging note like that of a siren seemed to ring. "Louder," he whispered with bowed head, and he was ashamed, for he knew that they were speaking loudly enough, though he could not make out what they said. Then, as if the wall in front of him had been split in two, a current of fresh air was at last wafted toward him, and he heard a voice near him saying: "First he wants to go, then you tell him a hundred times that the door is in front of him and he makes no move to go." K. saw that he was standing before the outside door, which the girl had opened. It was as if all his energies returned at one bound, to get a foretaste of freedom he set his feet at once on a step of the staircase and from there said good-by to his conductors, who bent their heads down to hear him. "Many thanks," he said several times, then shook hands with them again and again and only left off when he thought he saw that they, accustomed as they were to the office air, felt ill in the relatively fresh air that came up the stairway. They could scarcely answer him and the girl might have fallen if K. had not shut the door with the utmost haste. K. stood still for a moment, put his hair to rights with the help of his pocket mirror, lifted up his hat, which lay on the step below him—the Clerk of Inquiries must have thrown it there—and then leapt down the stairs so buoyantly and with such long strides that he became almost afraid of his own reaction. His usually sound constitution had never provided him with such surprises before. Could his body possibly be meditating a revolution and preparing a new trial for him, since he was withstanding the old one with such ease? He did not entirely reject the idea of going to consult a doctor at the first opportunity, in any case he had made up his mind—and there he could advise himself—to spend all his Sunday mornings in future to better purpose.

CHAPTER FOUR

Fräulein Bürstner's Friend

IN THE next few days K. found it impossible to exchange even a word with Fräulein Bürstner. He tried to
get hold of her by every means he could think of, but she
always managed to elude him. He went straight home
from his office and sat on the sofa in his room, with the

light out and the door open, concentrating his attention on the entrance hall. If the maid on her way past shut the door of his apparently empty room, he would get up after a while and open it again. He rose every morning an hour earlier than usual on the chance of catching Fräulein Bürstner alone, before she went to her work. But none of these stratagems succeeded. Then he wrote a letter to her, sending it both to her office and to her house address, in which he once more tried to justify his behavior, offered to make any reparation required, promised never to overstep the bounds that she should prescribe for him, and begged her to give him an opportunity of merely speaking to her, more especially as he could arrange nothing with Frau Grubach until he had first consulted with her, concluding with the information that next Sunday he would wait in his room all day for some sign that she was prepared either to grant his request or at least to explain why, even although he was pledging his word to defer to her in everything, she would not grant it. His letters were not returned, but neither were they answered. On Sunday, however, he was given a sign whose meaning was sufficiently clear. In the early morning K. observed through the keyhole of his door an unusual commotion in the entrance hall, which soon explained itself. A teacher of French, she was a German girl called Montag, a sickly, pale girl with a slight limp who till now had occupied a room of her own, was apparently moving into Fräulein Bürstner's room. For hours she kept on trailing through the entrance hall. She seemed to be always

forgetting some article of underwear or a scrap of dra-
pery or a book that necessitated a special journey to
carry it into the new apartment.

When Frau Grubach brought in his breakfast—ever
since she had angered K. she had devoted herself to per-
forming even the most trifling services for him—K. could
not help breaking the silence between them for the first
time. "Why is there such a row in the entrance hall today?" he asked as he poured out his coffee. "Couldn't
it be put off to some other time? Must the place be spring-
cleaned on a Sunday?" Although K. did not glance up at
Frau Grubach, he could observe that she heaved a sigh of
relief. These questions, though stern, she construed as
forgiveness or as an approach toward forgiveness. "The
place is not being spring-cleaned, Herr K.," she said.
"Fräulein Montag is moving in with Fräulein Bürstner
and shifting her things across." She said no more, waiting
first to see how K. would take it and if he would allow her
to go on. But K. kept her on the rack, reflectively stirring
his coffee and remaining silent. Then he looked up at
her and said: "Have you given up your previous suspicions of Fräulein Bürstner?" "Herr K.," cried Frau
Grubach, who had been merely waiting for this question
and now stretched out her clasped hands toward him,
"you took a casual remark of mine far too seriously. It
never entered my head to offend you or anyone else. You
have surely known me long enough, Herr K., to be certain of that. You have no idea how I have suffered during
these last few days! I to speak ill of my boarders! And

you, Herr K., believed it! And said I should give you notice! Give you notice!" The last ejaculation was already stifled in her sobs, she raised her apron to her face and wept aloud.

"Please don't cry, Frau Grubach," said K., looking out through the window, he was really thinking of Fräulein Bürstner and of the fact that she had taken a strange girl into her room. "Please don't cry," he said again as he turned back to the room and found Frau Grubach still weeping. "I didn't mean what I said so terribly seriously either. We misunderstood each other. That can happen occasionally even between old friends." Frau Grubach took her apron from her eyes to see whether K. were really appeased. "Come now, that's all there was to it," said K., and then ventured to add, since to judge from Frau Grubach's expression her nephew the Captain could not have divulged anything: "Do you really believe that I would turn against you because of a strange girl?" "That's just it, Herr K.," said Frau Grubach, it was her misfortune that as soon as she felt relieved in her mind she immediately said something tactless, "I kept asking myself: Why should Herr K. bother himself so much about Fräulein Bürstner? Why should he quarrel with me because of her, though he knows that every cross word from him makes me lose my sleep? And I said nothing about the girl that I hadn't seen with my own eyes." K. made no reply to this, he should have sent her from the room at the very first word, and he did not want to do that. He contented himself with drinking his coffee and leaving

Frau Grubach to feel that her presence was burdensome. Outside he could hear again the trailing step of Fräulein Montag as she limped from end to end of the entrance hall. "Do you hear that?" asked K., indicating the door. "Yes," said Frau Grubach, sighing, "I offered to help her and to order the maid to help too, but she's self-willed, she insists on moving everything herself. I'm surprised at Fräulein Bürstner. I often regret having Fräulein Montag as a boarder, but now Fräulein Bürstner is actually taking her into her own room." "You mustn't worry about that," said K., crushing with the spoon the sugar left at the bottom of his cup. "Does it mean any loss to you?" "No," said Frau Grubach, "in itself it's quite welcome to me, I am left with an extra room, and I can put my nephew, the Captain, there. I've been bothered in case he might have disturbed you these last few days, for I had to let him occupy the living room next door. He's not very considerate." "What an idea!" said K., getting up. "There's no question of that. You really seem to think I'm hypersensitive because I can't stand Fräulein Montag's trailings to and fro—there she goes again, coming back this time." Frau Grubach felt quite helpless. "Shall I tell her, Herr K., to put off moving the rest of her things until later? If you like I'll do so at once." "But she's got to move into Fräulein Bürstner's room!" cried K. "Yes," said Frau Grubach, she could not quite make out what K. meant. "Well then," said K., "she must surely be allowed to shift her things there." Frau Grubach simply nodded. Her dumb helplessness, which outwardly had the look of simple obstinacy, exasperated K. still more. He began to walk up and down from the window to the door and back again, and by doing that he hindered Frau Grubach from being able to slip out of the room, which she would probably have done.

K. had just reached the door again when there was a knock. It was the maid, who announced that Fräulein Montag would like a word or two with Herr K. and that she accordingly begged him to come to the dining room, where she was waiting for him. K. listened pensively to the message, then he turned an almost mocking eye on the startled Frau Grubach. His look seemed to say that he had long foreseen this invitation of Fräulein Montag's, and that it accorded very well with all the persecution he had had to endure that Sunday morning from Frau Grubach's boarders. He sent the maid back with the information that he would come at once, then went to his wardrobe to change his coat, and in answer to Frau Grubach, who was softly lamenting over the behavior of the importunate Fräulein Montag, had nothing to say but to request her to remove his breakfast tray. "Why, you've scarcely touched anything," said Frau Grubach. "Oh, do take it away," cried K., it seemed to him as if Fräulein Montag were somehow mixed up with the food and made it nauseating.

As he crossed the entrance hall he glanced at the closed door of Fräulein Bürstner's room. Still, he had not been invited there, but to the dining room, where he flung open the door without knocking.

It was a very long narrow room with one large window. There was only enough space in it to wedge two cupboards at an angle on either side of the door, the rest of the room was completely taken up by the long dining-table, which began near the door and reached to the very window, making it almost inaccessible. The table was already laid, and for many people too, since on Sunday almost all the boarders had their midday dinner in the house.

When K. entered, Fräulein Montag advanced from the window along one side of the table to meet him. They greeted each other in silence. Then Fräulein Montag said, holding her head very erect as usual: "I don't know if you know who I am." K. stared at her with contracted brows. "Of course I do," he said, "you've been staying quite a long time with Frau Grubach, haven't you?" "But you don't take much interest in the boarders, I fancy," said Fräulein Montag. "No," said K. "Won't you take a seat?" asked Fräulein Montag. In silence they pulled out two chairs at the very end of the table and sat down opposite each other. But Fräulein Montag immediately stood up again, for she had left her little handbag lying on the window sill and now went to fetch it; she trailed for it along the whole length of the room. As she came back, swinging the bag lightly in her hand, she said: "I've been asked by my friend to say something to you, that's all. She wanted to come herself, but she is feeling a little unwell today. She asks you to excuse her and listen to me instead. She would not have said anything more to you, in any case, than I am going to say.

On the contrary, I fancy that I can actually tell you more, as I am relatively impartial. Don't you think so too?"

"Well, what is there to say?" replied K., who was weary of seeing Fräulein Montag staring so fixedly at his lips. Her stare was already trying to dominate any words he might utter. "Fräulein Bürstner evidently refuses to grant me the personal interview I asked for."

"That is so," said Fräulein Montag, "or rather that isn't it at all, you put it much too harshly. Surely, in general, interviews are neither deliberately accepted nor refused. But it may happen that one sees no point in an interview, and that is the case here. After that last remark of yours I can speak frankly, I take it. You have begged my friend to communicate with you by letter or by word of mouth. Now, my friend, at least that is what I must assume, knows what this conversation would be about, and is therefore convinced, for reasons of which I am ignorant, that it would be to nobody's benefit if it actually took place. To tell the truth, she did not mention the matter to me until yesterday and only in passing, she said among other things that you could not attach very much importance to this interview either, for it could only have been by accident that you hit on the idea, and that even without a specific explanation you would soon come to see how silly the whole affair was, if indeed you didn't see that already. I told her that that might be quite true, but that I considered it advisable, if the matter were to be completely cleared up, that you should receive an explicit answer. I offered myself as an intermediary, and after some hesitation my friend yielded to my persuasions. But I hope that I have served your interests, too, for the slightest uncertainty even in the most trifling matter is always a worry, and when, as in this case, it can be easily dispelled, it is better that that should be done at once." "Thank you," said K. and he slowly rose to his feet, glanced at Fräulein Montag, then at the table, then out through the window—the sun was shining on the house opposite—and walked to the door. Fräulein Montag followed him for a few steps, as if she did not quite trust him. But at the door they had both to draw back, for it opened and Captain Lanz entered. This was the first time that K. had seen him close at hand. He was a tall man in the early forties with a tanned, fleshy face. He made a slight bow which included K. as well as Fräulein Montag, then went up to her and respectfully kissed her hand. His movements were easy. His politeness toward Fräulein Montag was in striking contrast to the treatment which she had received from K. All the same, Fräulein Montag did not seem to be offended with K., for she actually purposed, K. fancied, to introduce him to the Captain. But K. did not wish to be introduced, he was not in the mind to be polite either to the Captain or to Fräulein Montag, the hand-kissing had in his eyes turned the pair of them into accomplices who, under a cloak of the utmost amiability and altruism, were seeking to bar his way to Fräulein Bürstner. Yet he fancied that he could see even more than that, he recognized that Fräulein Montag had chosen a very good if somewhat two-edged weapon. She had exaggerated the importance of the connection between Fräulein Bürstner and K., she had exaggerated above all the importance of the interview he had asked for, and she had tried at the same time so to manipulate things as to make it appear that it was K. who was exaggerating. She would find that she was deceived, K. wished to exaggerate nothing, he knew that Fräulein Bürstner was an ordinary little typist who could not resist him for long. In coming to this conclusion he deliberately left out of account what Frau Grubach had told him about Fräulein Bürstner. He was thinking all this as he quitted the room with a curt word of leave-taking. He made straight for his own room, but a slight titter from Fräulein Montag, coming from the dining room behind him, put it into his head that perhaps he could provide a surprise for the pair of them, the Captain as well as Fräulein Montag. He glanced round and listened to make sure that no interruption was likely from any of the adjacent rooms, all was still, nothing was to be heard but a murmur of voices in the dining room and the voice of Frau Grubach coming from the passage leading to the kitchen. The opportunity seemed excellent, and K. went over to Fräulein Bürstner's door and knocked softly. When nothing happened he knocked again, but again no answer came. Was she sleeping? Or was she really unwell? Or was she pretending she wasn't there, knowing that it could only be K. who was knocking so softly? K. assumed that she was pretending and knocked more loudly, and at last, as his knocking had no result, cautiously opened the door, not without a feeling that he was doing something wrong and even more useless than wrong. There was nobody in the room. Moreover it had scarcely any resemblance now to the room which K. had seen. Against the wall two beds stood next to each other, three chairs near the door were heaped with dresses and underclothes, a wardrobe was standing open. Fräulein Bürstner had apparently gone out while Fräulein Montag was saying her piece in the dining room. K. was not very much taken aback, he had hardly expected at this stage to get hold of Fräulein Bürstner so easily, he had made this attempt, indeed, mainly to annoy Fräulein Montag. Yet the shock was all the greater when, as he was shutting the door again, he saw Fräulein Montag and the Captain standing talking together in the open door of the dining room. They had perhaps been standing there all the time, they scrupulously avoided all appearance of having been observing him, they talked in low voices, following K.'s movements only with the abstracted gaze one has for people passing when one is deep in conversation. All the same, their glances weighed heavily upon K., and he made what haste he could to his room, keeping close against the wall.

CHAPTER FIVE

The Whipper

A FEW evenings later K. was passing along the Bank corridor from his office to the main staircase—he was almost the last to leave, only two clerks in the dispatch department were still at work by the dim light of a glow lamp—when he heard convulsive sighs behind a door, which he had always taken to be the door of a lumber-room, although he had never opened it. He stopped in astonishment and listened to make sure that he had not been mistaken—all was still, yet in a little while the sighing began again. At first he thought of fetching one of the dispatch clerks, he might need a witness, but then he was seized by such uncontrollable curiosity that he literally tore the door open. It was, as he had correctly assumed, a lumber-room. Bundles of useless old papers and empty earthenware ink bottles lay in a tumbled heap behind the threshold. But in the room itself stood three men, stooping because of the low ceiling, by the light of a candle stuck on a shelf. "What are you doing here?" asked K., in great haste and agitation, but not loud. One of the men, who was clearly in authority over the other two and took the eye first, was sheathed in a sort of dark leather garment which left his throat and a good deal of his chest and the whole of his arms bare. He made no answer. But the other two cried: "Sir! We're to be flogged because you complained about us to the Examining Magistrate." And only then did K. realize that it was actually the warders Franz and Willem, and that the third man was holding a rod in his hand with which to beat them. "Why," said K., staring at them in astonishment, "I never complained, I only said what happened in my rooms. And, after all, your behavior there was not exactly blameless." "Sir," said Willem, while Franz openly tried to take cover behind him from the third man, "if you only knew how badly we are paid, you wouldn't be so hard on us. I have a family to feed and Franz here wants to get married, a man tries to make whatever he can, and you don't get rich on hard work, not even if you work day and night. Your fine shirts were a temptation, of course that kind of thing is forbidden to warders, it was wrong, but it's a tradition that body-linen is the warders' perquisite, it has always been the case, believe me; and it's understandable too, for what importance can such things have for a man who is unlucky enough to be arrested? But if he ventilates it openly, punishment is bound to follow." "I had no idea of all this, nor did I ever demand that you should be punished, I was only defending a principle." "Franz," Willem turned to the other warder, "didn't I tell you that the gentleman never asked us to be punished? Now you see that he didn't even know we should be punished." "Don't be taken in by what they say," remarked the third man to K., "the punishment is as just as it is inevitable." "Don't listen to him," said Willem, interrupting himself to clap his hand, over which he had got a stinging blow with the rod, to his mouth. "We are only being punished because you accused us; if you hadn't, nothing would have happened, not even if they had discovered what we did. Do you call that justice? Both of us, and especially myself, have a long record of trustworthy service as warders—you must yourself admit that, officially speaking, we guarded you quite well—we had every prospect of advancement and would certainly have been promoted to be Whippers pretty soon, like this man here, who simply had the luck never to be complained of, for a complaint of that kind really happens very seldom indeed. And all is lost now, sir, our careers are done for, we'll be set to do much more menial work than a warder's, and, besides that, we're in for a whipping, and that's horribly painful." "Can that birch-rod cause such terrible pain?" asked K., examining the switch, which the man waved to and fro in front of him. "We'll have to take off all our clothes first," said Willem. "Ah, I see," said K., and he looked more attentively at the Whipper, who was tanned like a sailor and had a brutal, healthy face. "Is there no way of getting these two off their whipping?" K. asked him. "No," said the man, smilingly shaking his head. "Strip," he ordered the warders. And he said to K.: "You mustn't believe all they say, they're so terrified of the whipping that they've already lost what wits they had. For instance, all that this one here"—he pointed to Willem—"says about his possible career is simply absurd. See how fat he is—the first cuts of the birch will be quite lost in fat. Do you know what made him so fat? He stuffs himself with the breakfasts of all the people he arrests. Didn't he eat up your breakfast too? There, you see, I told you so. But a man with a belly like that couldn't ever become a Whipper, it's quite out of the question." "There are Whippers just like me," maintained Willem, loosening his trouser belt. "No," said the Whipper, drawing the switch across his neck so that he winced, "you aren't supposed to be listening, you're to take off your clothes." "I'll reward you well if you'll let them go," said K., and without glancing at the Whipper again—such things should be done with averted eyes on both sides—he drew out his pocketbook. "So you want to lay a complaint against me too," said the Whipper, "and get me a whipping as well? No, no!" "Do be reasonable," said K. "If I had wanted these two men to be punished, I shouldn't be trying to buy them off now. I could simply leave, shut this door after me, close my eyes and ears, and go home; but I don't want to do that, I really want to see them set free; if I had known that they would be punished or even that they could be punished, I should never have mentioned their names. For in my view they are not guilty. The guilt lies with the organization. It is the high officials who are guilty." "That's so," cried the warders and at once got a cut of the switch over their backs, which were bare now. "If it was one of the high Judges you were flogging," said K., and as he spoke he thrust down the rod which the Whipper was raising again, "I certainly wouldn't try to keep you from laying on with a will, on the contrary I would pay you extra to encourage you in the good work." "What you say sounds reasonable enough," said the man, "but I refuse to be bribed. I am here to whip people, and whip them I shall." The warder Franz, who, perhaps hoping that K.'s intervention might succeed, had thus far kept as much as possible in the background, now came forward to the door clad only in his trousers, fell on his knees, and clinging to K.'s arm whispered: "If you can't get him to spare both of us, try to get me off at least. Willem is older than I am, and far less sensitive too, besides he's had a small whipping already, some years ago, but I've never been in disgrace yet, and I was only following Willem's lead in what I did, he's my teacher, for better or worse. My poor sweetheart is awaiting the outcome at the door of the Bank. I'm so ashamed and miserable." He dried his tear-wet face on K.'s jacket. "I can't wait any longer," said the Whipper, grasping the rod with both hands and making a cut at Franz, while Willem cowered in a corner and secretly watched without daring to turn his head. Then the shriek rose from Franz's throat, single and irrevocable, it did not seem to come from a human being but from some martyred instrument, the whole corridor rang with it, the whole building must hear it. "Don't," cried K.; he was beside himself, he stood staring in the direction from which the clerks must presently come running, but he gave Franz a push, not a violent one but violent enough nevertheless to make the half-senseless man fall and convulsively claw at the floor with his hands; but even then Franz did not escape his punishment, the birch-rod found him where he was lying, its point swished up and down regularly as he writhed on the floor. And now a clerk was already visible in the distance and a few paces behind him another. K. quickly slammed the door, stepped over to a window close by, which looked out on the courtyard, and opened it. The shrieks had completely stopped. To keep the clerks from approaching any nearer, K. cried: "It's me." "Good evening, Sir," they called back. "Has anything happened?" "No, no," replied K. "It was only a dog howling in the courtyard." As the clerks still did not budge, he added: "You can go back to your work." And to keep himself from being involved in any conversation he leaned out of the window. When after a while he glanced into the corridor again, they were gone. But he stayed beside the window, he did not dare to go back into the lumber-room, and he had no wish to go home either. It was a little square courtyard into which he was looking down, surrounded by offices, all the windows were dark now, but the topmost panes cast back a faint reflection of the moon. K. intently strove to pierce the darkness of one corner of the courtyard, where several hand-barrows were jumbled close together. He was deeply disappointed that he had not been able to prevent the whipping, but it was not his fault that he had not succeeded; if Franz had not shrieked—it must have been very painful certainly, but in a crisis one must control oneself—if he had not shrieked, then K., in all probability at least, would have found some other means of persuading the Whipper. If the whole lower grade of this organization were scoundrels, why should the Whipper, who had the most inhuman office of all, turn out to be an exception? Besides, K. had clearly seen his eyes glittering at the sight of the banknote, obviously he had set about his job in earnest simply to raise his price a little higher. And K. would not have been stingy, he was really very anxious to get the warders off; since he had set himself to fight the whole corrupt administration of this Court, it was obviously his duty to intervene on this occasion. But at the moment when Franz began to shriek, any intervention became impossible. K. could not afford to let the dispatch clerks and possibly all sorts of other people arrive and surprise him in a scene with these creatures in the lumber-room. No one could really demand such a sacrifice from him. If a sacrifice had been needed, it would almost have been simpler to take off his own clothes and offer himself to the Whipper as a substitute for the warders.* In any case the Whipper certainly would not have accepted such a substitution, since without gaining any advantage he would have been involved in a grave dereliction of duty, for as long as this trial continued, K. must surely be immune from molestation by the servants of the Court. Though of course ordinary standards might not apply here either. At all events, he could have done nothing but slam the door, though even that action had not shut out all danger. It was a pity that he had given Franz a push at the last moment, the state of agitation he was in was his only excuse.

He heard the steps of the clerks in the distance; so as not to attract their attention he shut the window and began to walk away in the direction of the main staircase. At the door of the lumber-room he stopped for a little and listened. All was as silent as the grave. The man might have beaten the warders till they had given up the ghost, they were entirely delivered into his power. K.'s hand was already stretched out to grasp the door-handle when he withdrew it again. They were past help by this time, and the clerks might appear at any moment; but he made a vow not to hush up the incident and to deal trenchantly, so far as lay in his power, with the real culprits, the high officials, none of whom had yet dared show his face. As he descended the outside steps of the Bank he carefully observed all the passers-by, but even in the surrounding streets he could perceive no sign of a girl waiting for anybody. So Franz's tale of a sweetheart waiting for him was simply a lie, venial enough, designed merely to procure more sympathy for him.

All the next day K. could not get the warders out of his head; he was absent-minded and to catch up on his work had to stay in his office even later than the day before. As he passed the lumber-room again on his way out he could not resist opening the door. And what confronted him, instead of the darkness he had expected, bewildered him completely. Everything was still the same, exactly as he had found it on opening the door the previous evening. The files of old papers and the ink bottles were still tumbled behind the threshold, the Whipper with his rod and the warders with all their clothes on were still standing there, the candle was burning on the shelf, and the warders immediately began to wail and cry out: "Sir!" At once K. slammed the door shut and then beat on it with his fists, as if that would shut it more securely. He ran almost weeping to the clerks, who were quietly working at the copying-presses and looked up at him in surprise. "Clear that lumber-room out, can't you?" he shouted. "We're being smothered in dirt!" The clerks promised to do so next day. K. nodded, he could hardly insist on their doing it now, so late in the evening, as he had originally intended. He sat down for a few moments, for the sake of their company, shuffled through some duplicates, hoping to give the impression that he was inspecting them, and then, seeing that the men would scarcely venture to leave the building along with him, went home, tired, his mind quite blank.

CHAPTER SIX

K's Uncle / Leni

ONE afternoon—it was just before the day's letters went out and K. was very busy—two clerks bringing him some papers to sign were thrust aside and his Uncle Karl, a small landowner from the country, came striding into the room. K. was the less alarmed by the arrival of his uncle since for a long time he had been shrinking from it in anticipation. His uncle was bound to turn up, he had been convinced of that for about a month past. He had often pictured him just as he appeared now, his back slightly bent, his panama hat crushed in his left hand, stretching out his right hand from the very doorway, and then thrusting it recklessly across the desk, knocking over everything that came in its way. His uncle was always in a hurry, for he was harassed by the disastrous idea that whenever he came to town for the day he must get through all the program he had drawn up for himself, and must not miss either a single chance of a conversation or a piece of business or an entertainment. In all this K., who as his former ward was peculiarly obliged to him, had to help him as best he could and also sometimes put him up for the night. "A ghost from the past," he was in the habit of calling him.

Immediately after his first greetings—he had no time to sit down in the chair which K. offered him—he begged K. to have a short talk with him in strict privacy. "It is necessary," he said, painfully gulping, "it is necessary for my peace of mind." K. at once sent his clerks out of the room with instructions to admit no one. "What is this I hear, Joseph?" cried his uncle when they were alone, sitting down on the desk and making himself comfortable by stuffing several papers under him without looking at them. K. said nothing, he knew what was coming, but being suddenly released from the strain of exacting work, he resigned himself for the moment to a pleasant sense of

indolence and gazed out through the window at the opposite side of the street, of which only a small triangular
section could be seen from where he was sitting, a slice
of empty house-wall between two shopwindows. "You sit
there staring out of the window!" cried his uncle, flinging up his arms. "For God's sake, Joseph, answer me. Is
it true? Can it be true?" "Dear Uncle," said K., tearing
himself out of his reverie. "I don't know in the least what
you mean." "Joseph," said his uncle warningly, "you've
always told the truth, as far as I know. Am I to take these
words of yours as a bad sign?" "I can guess, certainly,
what you're after," said K. accommodatingly. "You've
probably heard something about my trial." "That is so,"
replied his uncle, nodding gravely. "I have heard about
your trial." "But from whom?" asked K. "Erna wrote to
me about it," said his uncle. "She doesn't see much of you,
I know, you don't pay much attention to her, I regret to
say, and yet she heard about it. I got the letter this morning and of course took the first train here. I had no other
reason for coming, but it seems to be a sufficient one. I
can read you the bit from her letter that mentions you."
He took the letter from his pocketbook. "Here it is. She
writes: 'I haven't seen Joseph for a long time, last week
I called at the Bank, but Joseph was so busy that I
couldn't see him; I waited for almost an hour, but I had
to leave then, for I had a piano lesson. I should have liked
very much to speak to him, perhaps I shall soon have the
chance. He sent me a great big box of chocolates for my
birthday, it was very sweet and thoughtful of him. I for-

got to write and mention it at the time, and it was only your asking that reminded me. For I may tell you that chocolate vanishes on the spot in this boarding-school, hardly do you realize that you've been presented with a box when it's gone. But about Joseph, there is something else that I feel I should tell you. As I said, I was not able to see him at the Bank because he was engaged with a gentleman. After I had waited meekly for a while I asked an attendant if the interview was likely to last much longer. He said that that might very well be, for it had probably something to do with the case which was being brought against the Chief Clerk. I asked what case, and was he not mistaken, but he said he was not mistaken, there was a case and a very serious one too, but more than that he did not know. He himself would like to help Herr K., for he was a good and just man, but he did not know how he was to do it, and he only wished that some influential gentleman would take the Chief Clerk's part. To be sure, that was certain to happen and everything would be all right in the end, but for the time being, as he could see from Herr K.'s state of mind, things looked far from well. Naturally I did not take all this too seriously, I tried to reassure the simple fellow and forbade him to talk about it to anyone else, and I'm sure it's just idle gossip. All the same, it might be as well if you, dearest Father, were to inquire into it on your next visit to town, it will be easy for you to find out the real state of things, and if necessary to get some of your influential friends to intervene. Even if it shouldn't be necessary, and that is most likely, at least it will give your daughter an early chance of welcoming you with a kiss, which would please her.' A good child," said K.'s uncle when he had finished reading, wiping a tear from his eye. K. nodded, he had completely forgotten Erna among the various troubles he had had lately, and the story about the chocolates she had obviously invented simply to save his face before his uncle and aunt. It was really touching, and the theater tickets which he now resolved to send her regularly would be a very inadequate return, but he did not feel equal at present to calling at her boarding-school and chattering to an eighteen-year-old flapper. "And what have you got to say now?" asked his uncle, who had temporarily forgotten all his haste and agitation over the letter, which he seemed to be rereading. "Yes, Uncle," said K., "it's quite true." "True?" cried his uncle. "What is true? How on earth can it be true? What case is this? Not a criminal case, surely?" "A criminal case," answered K. "And you sit there coolly with a criminal case hanging round your neck?" cried his uncle, his voice growing louder and louder. "The cooler I am, the better in the end," said K. wearily. "Don't worry." "That's a fine thing to ask of me," cried his uncle. "Joseph, my dear Joseph, think of yourself, think of your relatives, think of our good name. You have been a credit to us until now, you can't become a family disgrace. Your attitude," he looked at K. with his head slightly cocked, "doesn't please me at all, that isn't how an innocent man behaves if he's still in his senses. Just tell me quickly what it is all about, so that I can help you. It's something to do with the Bank, of course?" "No," said K., getting up. "But you're talking too loudly, Uncle, I feel pretty certain the attendant is listening at the door, and I dislike the idea. We had better go out somewhere. I'll answer all your questions then as far as I can. I know quite well that I owe the family an explanation." "Right," cried his uncle, "quite right, but hurry, Joseph, hurry!" "I have only to leave some instructions," said K., and he summoned his chief assistant by telephone, who appeared in a few minutes. In his agitation K.'s uncle indicated to the clerk by a sweep of the hand that K. had sent for him, which, of course, was obvious enough. K., standing beside his desk, took up various papers and in a low voice explained to the young man, who listened coolly but attentively, what must be done in his absence. His uncle disturbed him by standing beside him round-eyed and biting his lips nervously; he was not actually listening, but the appearance of listening was disturbing enough in itself. He next began to pace up and down the room, pausing every now and then by the window or before a picture, with sudden ejaculations, such as: "It's completely incomprehensible to me" or "Goodness knows what's to come of this." The young man behaved as if he noticed nothing, quietly heard K.'s instructions to the end, took a few notes, and went, after having bowed both to K. and to his uncle, who, however, had his back to him just then and was gazing out of the window, flinging out his arms, and clutching at the curtains. The door had scarcely closed when K.'s uncle cried:

"At last that jackass has gone; now we can go too. At last!" Unluckily K. could find no means to make his uncle stop inquiring about the case in the main vestibule, where several clerks and attendants were standing about, while the Assistant Manager himself was crossing the floor. "Come now, Joseph," began his uncle, returning a brief nod to the bows of the waiting clerks, "tell me frankly now what kind of a case this is." K. made a few noncommittal remarks, laughing a little, and only on the staircase explained to his uncle that he had not wanted to speak openly before the clerks. "Right," said his uncle, "but get it off your chest now." He listened with bent head, puffing hastily at a cigar. "The first thing to grasp, Uncle," said K., "is that this is not a case before an ordinary court." "That's bad," said his uncle. "What do you mean?" asked K., looking at his uncle. "I mean that it's bad," repeated his uncle. They were standing on the outside steps of the Bank; as the doorkeeper seemed to be listening, K. dragged his uncle away; they were swallowed up in the street traffic. The uncle, who had taken K.'s arm, now no longer inquired so urgently about the case, and for a while they actually walked on in silence. "But how did this happen?" his uncle asked at last, stopping so suddenly that the people walking behind him shied off in alarm. "Things like this don't occur suddenly, they pile up gradually, there must have been indications. Why did you never write to me? You know I would do anything for you, I'm still your guardian in a sense and till now I have been proud of it. Of course I'll do what I can to help you, only it's very difficult when the case is already under way. The best thing, at any rate, would be for you to take a short holiday and come to stay with us in the country. You've got a bit thinner, I notice that now. You'd get back your strength in the country, that would be all to the good, for this trial will certainly be a severe strain on you. But besides that, in a sense you'd be getting away from the clutches of the Court. Here they have all sorts of machinery which they will automatically set in motion against you, depend on that; but if you were in the country they would have to appoint agents or get at you by letter or telegram or telephone. That would naturally weaken the effect, not that you would escape them altogether, but you'd have a breathing-space." "Still, they might forbid me to go away," said K., who was beginning to follow his uncle's line of thought. "I don't think they would do that," said his uncle reflectively, "after all, they wouldn't lose so much by your going away." "I thought," said K., taking his uncle's arm to keep him from standing still, "that you would attach even less importance to this business than I do, and now you are taking it so seriously." "Joseph!" cried his uncle, trying to get his arm free so as to be able to stand still, only K. would not let him, "you're quite changed, you always used to have such a clear brain, and is it going to fail you now? Do you want to lose this case? And do you know what that would mean? It would mean that you would be absolutely ruined. And that all your relatives would be ruined too or at least dragged in the dust.

Joseph, pull yourself together. Your indifference drives me mad. Looking at you, one would almost believe the old saying: 'Cases of that kind are always lost.' " "Dear Uncle," said K., "it's no use getting excited, it's as useless on your part as it would be on mine. No case is won by getting excited, you might let my practical experience count for something, look how I respect yours, as I have always done, even when you astonish me. Since you tell me that the family would be involved in any scandal arising from the case—I don't see myself how that could be so, but that's beside the point—I'll submit willingly to your judgment. Only I think going to the country would be inadvisable even from your point of view, for it would look like flight and therefore guilt. Besides, though I'm more hard-pressed here, I can push the case on my own more energetically." "Quite right," said his uncle in a tone of relief, as if he saw their minds converging at last, "I only made the suggestion because I thought your indifference would endanger the case while you stayed here, and that it might be better if I took it up for you instead. But if you intend to push it energetically yourself, that of course would be far better." "We're agreed on that, then," said K. "And now can you suggest what my first step should be?" "I'll have to do a bit of thinking about it, naturally," said his uncle, "you must consider that I have lived in the country for twenty years almost without a break, and my flair for such matters can't be so good as it was. Various connections of mine with influential persons who would probably know better than I how to tackle this affair have slackened in the course of time. I'm a bit isolated in the country, as you know yourself. Actually it's only in emergencies like this that one becomes aware of it. Besides, this affair of yours has come on me more or less unexpectedly, though strangely enough, after Erna's letter, I guessed at something of the kind, and as soon as I saw you today I was almost sure of it. Still that doesn't matter, the important thing now is to lose no time." Before he had finished speaking he was already on tiptoe waiting for a taxi, and now, shouting an address to the driver, he dragged K. into the car after him. "We'll drive straight to Huld, the lawyer," he said. "He was at school with me. You know his name, of course? You don't? That is really extraordinary. He has quite a considerable reputation as a defending counsel and a poor man's lawyer. But it's as a human being that I'm prepared to pin my faith to him." "I'm willing to try anything you suggest," said K., though the hasty headlong way in which his uncle was dealing with the matter caused him some perturbation. It was not very flattering to be driven to a poor man's lawyer as a petitioner. "I did not know," he said, "that in a case like this one could employ a lawyer." "But of course," said his uncle. "That's obvious. Why not? And now tell me everything that has happened up to now, so that I have some idea where we stand." K. at once began his story and left out no single detail, for absolute frankness was the only protest he could make against his uncle's assumption that the case was a terrible disgrace. Fräulein Bürstner's name he mentioned only once and in passing, but that did not detract from his frankness, since Fräulein Bürstner had no connection with the case. As he told his story he gazed out through the window and noted that they were approaching the very suburb where the Law Court had its attic offices; he drew his uncle's attention to this fact, but his uncle did not seem to be particularly struck by the coincidence. The taxi stopped before a dark house. His uncle rang the bell of the first door on the ground floor; while they were waiting he bared his great teeth in a smile and whispered: "Eight o'clock, an unusual time for clients to call. But Huld won't take it amiss from me." Behind a grille in the door two great dark eyes appeared, gazed at the two visitors for a moment, and then vanished again; yet the door did not open. K. and his uncle assured each other that they had really seen a pair of eyes. "A new maid, probably afraid of strangers," said K.'s uncle and knocked again. Once more the eyes appeared and now they seemed almost sad, yet that might have been an illusion created by the naked gas-jet which burned just over their heads and kept hissing shrilly but gave little light. "Open the door!" shouted K.'s uncle, banging upon it with his fists, "we're friends of Herr Huld." "Herr Huld is ill," came a whisper from behind them. A door had opened at the other end of the little passage and a man in a dressing-gown was standing there imparting this information in a hushed voice. K.'s uncle, already furious at having had to wait so long, whirled round shouting: "Ill? You say he's ill?" and bore down almost threateningly on the man as if he were the alleged illness in person. "The door has been opened," said the man, indicated the lawyer's door, caught his dressing-gown about him, and disappeared. The door really was open, a young girl—K. recognized the dark, somewhat protuberant eyes—was standing in the entrance hall in a long white apron, holding a candle in her hand. "Next time be a little smarter in opening the door," K.'s uncle threw at her instead of a greeting, while she sketched a curtsy. "Come on, Joseph," he cried to K., who was slowly insinuating himself past the girl. "Herr Huld is ill," said the girl, as K.'s uncle, without any hesitation, made toward an inner door. K. was still glaring at the girl, who turned her back on him to bolt the house door; she had a doll-like rounded face; not only were her pale cheeks and her chin quite round in their modeling, but her temples and the line of her forehead as well. "Joseph!" K.'s uncle shouted again, and he asked the girl: "Is it his heart?" "I think so," said the girl, she had now found time to precede him with the candle and open the door of a room. In one corner, which the candlelight had not yet reached, a face with a long beard was raised from a pillow. "Leni, who is it?" asked the lawyer, who, blinded by the candlelight, could not recognize his visitors. "It's your old friend Albert," said K.'s uncle. "Oh, Albert," said the lawyer, sinking back on his pillow again, as if there were no need to keep up appearances before this visitor. "Are you really in a bad way?" asked K.'s uncle, sitting down on the edge of the bed. "I can't believe it. It's one of your heart attacks and it'll pass over like all the others." "Maybe," said the lawyer in a faint voice, "but it's worse than it's ever been before. I find it difficult to breathe, can't sleep at all, and am losing strength daily." "I see," said K.'s uncle, pressing his panama hat firmly against his knee with his huge hand. "That's bad news. But are you being properly looked after? And it's so gloomy in here, so dark. It's a long time since I was here last, but it looked more cheerful then. And this little maid of yours doesn't seem to be very bright, or else she's concealing the fact." The girl was still standing near the door with her candle; as far as one could make out from the vague flicker of her eyes, she seemed to be looking at K. rather than at his uncle, even while the latter was speaking about her. K. was leaning against a chair which he had pushed near her. "When a man is as ill as I am," said the lawyer, "he must have quiet. I don't find it gloomy." After a slight pause he added: "And Leni looks after me well, she's a good girl." * But this could not convince K.'s uncle, who was visibly prejudiced against the nurse, and though he made no reply to the sick man he followed her with a stern eye as she went over to the bed, set down the candle on the bedside table, bent over her patient, and whispered to him while she rearranged the pillows. K.'s uncle, almost forgetting that he was in a sick-room, jumped to his feet and prowled up and down behind the girl; K. would not have been surprised if he had seized her by the skirts and dragged her away from the bed. K. himself looked on with detachment, the illness of the lawyer was not entirely unwelcome to him, he had not been able to oppose his uncle's growing ardor for his cause, and he thankfully accepted the situation, which had deflected that ardor without any connivance from him. Then his uncle, perhaps only with the intention of offending the nurse, cried out: "Fräulein, please be so good as to leave us alone for a while; I want to consult my friend on some personal business." The girl, who was still bending down over the sick man smoothing the sheet beside the wall, merely turned her head and said quite calmly, in striking contrast to the furious stuttering and frothing of K.'s uncle: "You see that my master is ill; he cannot be consulted about business." She had probably reiterated the phrase from sheer indolence; all the same it could have been construed as mockery even by an unprejudiced observer, and K.'s uncle naturally flared up as if he had been stung. "You damned—" he spluttered, but he was so furious as to be hardly intelligible. K. started up in alarm, though he had expected some such outburst, and rushed over to his uncle with the firm intention of clapping both hands over his mouth and so silencing him. Fortunately the patient raised himself up in bed behind the girl. K.'s uncle made a wry grimace as if he were swallowing some nauseous draught and he said in a smoother voice: "I assure you we aren't altogether out of our senses; if what I ask were impossible I should not ask it. Please go away now." The girl straightened herself beside the bed, turning full toward K.'s uncle, but with one hand, at least so K. surmised, she was patting the lawyer's hand. "You can discuss anything before Leni," said the lawyer in a voice of sheer entreaty. "This does not concern myself," said K.'s uncle, "it is not my secret." And he turned away as if washing his hands of the matter, although willing to give the lawyer a moment for reconsideration. "Then whom does it concern?" asked the lawyer in an exhausted voice, lying down again. "My nephew," said K.'s uncle, "I have brought him here with me." And he presented his nephew: Joseph K., Chief Clerk. "Oh," said the sick man with much more animation, stretching out his hand to K., "forgive me, I didn't notice you. Go now, Leni," he said to the nurse, clasping her by the hand as if saying good-by to her for a long time, and she went submissively enough. "So you haven't come," he said at last to K.'s uncle, who was now appeased and had gone up to the bed again, "to pay me a sick visit; you've come on business." It was as if the thought of a sick visit had paralyzed him until now, so rejuvenated did he look as he supported himself on his elbow, which must itself have been something of a strain; and he kept combing with his fingers a strand of hair in the middle of his beard. "You look much better already," said K.'s uncle, "since that witch went away." He broke off, whispered: "I bet she's listening," and sprang to the door. But there was no one behind the door and he returned again, not so much disappointed, since her failure to listen seemed to him an act of sheer malice, as embittered. "You are unjust to her," said the lawyer, without adding anything more in defense of his nurse; perhaps by this reticence he meant to convey that she stood in no need of defense. Then in a much more friendly tone he went on: "As for this case of your nephew's I should certainly consider myself very fortunate if my strength proved equal to such an excessively arduous task; I'm very much afraid that it will not do so, but at any rate I shall make every effort; if I fail, you can always call in someone else to help me. To be quite honest, the case interests me too deeply for me to resist the opportunity of taking some part in it. If my heart does not hold out, here at least it will find a worthy obstacle to fail against." K. could not fathom a single word of all this, he glanced at his uncle, hoping for some explanation, but with the candle in his hand his uncle was sitting on the bedside table, from which a medicine-bottle had already rolled on to the carpet, nodding assent to everything that the lawyer said, apparently agreeing with everything and now and then casting a glance at K. which demanded from him a like agreement. Could his uncle have told the lawyer all about the case already? But that was impossible, the course of events ruled it out. "I don't understand—" he therefore began. "Oh, perhaps I have misunderstood you?" asked the lawyer, just as surprised and embarrassed as K. "Perhaps I have been too hasty. Then what do you want to consult me about? I thought it concerned your case?" "Of course it does," said K.'s uncle, turning to K. with the question: "What's bothering you?" "Well, but how do you come to know about me and my case?" asked K. "Oh, that's it," said the lawyer, smiling. "I'm a lawyer, you see, I move in legal circles where all the various cases are discussed, and the more striking ones are bound to stick in my mind, especially one that concerns the nephew of an old friend of mine. Surely that's not so extraordinary." "What's bothering you?" K.'s uncle repeated. "You're all nerves." "So you move in those legal circles?" asked K. "Yes," replied the lawyer. "You ask questions like a child," said K.'s uncle. "Whom should I associate with if not with men of my own profession?" added the lawyer. It sounded incontrovertible and K. made no answer. "But you're attached to the Court in the Palace of Justice, not to the one in the attics," he wanted to say, yet could not bring himself actually to say it. "You must consider," the lawyer continued in the tone of one perfunctorily explaining something that should be self-evident, "you must consider that this intercourse enables me to benefit my clients in all sorts of ways, some of which cannot even be divulged. Of course I'm somewhat handicapped now because of my illness, but in spite of that, good friends of mine from the Law Courts visit me now and then and I learn lots of things from them. Perhaps more than many a man in the best of health who spends all his days in the Courts. For example, there's a dear friend of mine visiting me at this very moment," and he waved a hand toward a dark corner of the room. "Where?" asked K., almost rudely, in his first shock of astonishment. He looked round uncertainly; the light of the small candle did not nearly reach the opposite wall. And then some form or other in the dark corner actually began to stir. By the light of the candle, which his uncle now held high above his head, K. could see an elderly gentleman sitting there at a little table. He must have been sitting without even drawing breath, to have remained for so long unnoticed. Now he got up fussily, obviously displeased to have his presence made known. With his hands, which he flapped like short wings, he seemed to be deprecating all introductions or greetings, trying to show that the last thing he desired was to disturb the other gentlemen, and that he only wanted to be transported again to the darkness where his presence might be forgotten. But that privilege could no longer be his. "I may say you took us by surprise," said the lawyer in explanation, and he waved his hand to encourage the gentleman to approach, which he did very slowly and glancing around him hesitantly, but with a certain dignity. "The Chief Clerk of the Court—oh, I beg your pardon, I have not introduced you—this is my friend Albert K., this is his nephew Joseph K., and this is the Chief Clerk of the Court—who, to return to what I was saying, has been so good as to pay me a visit. The value of such a visit can really be appreciated only by the initiated who know how dreadfully the Clerk of the Court is overwhelmed with work. Yet he came to see me all the same, we were talking here peacefully, as far as my ill health permitted, we didn't actually forbid Leni to admit visitors, it was true, for we expected none, but we naturally thought that we should be left in peace, and then came your furious tattoo, Albert, and the Clerk of the Court withdrew into

the corner with his chair and his table, but now it seems
we have the chance, that is, if you care to take it, of
making the discussion general, since this case concerns us
all, and so we can get together.—Please, my dear Sir,"
he said with a bow and an obsequious smile, indicating an
armchair near the bed. "Unfortunately I can only stay
for a few minutes longer," said the Chief Clerk of the
Court affably, seating himself in the chair and looking at
his watch, "my duties call me. But I don't want to miss
this opportunity of becoming acquainted with a friend of
my friend here." He bowed slightly to K.'s uncle, who
appeared very flattered to make this new acquaintance,
yet, being by nature incapable of expressing reverent
feelings, requited the Clerk of the Court's words with a
burst of embarrassed but raucous laughter. An ugly
sight! K. could observe everything calmly, for nobody
paid any attention to him. The Chief Clerk of the Court,
now that he had been brought into prominence, seized
the lead, as seemed to be his usual habit. The lawyer,
whose first pretense of weakness had probably been intended simply to drive away his visitors, listened attentively, cupping his hand to his ear. K.'s uncle as candle-
bearer— he was balancing the candle on his thigh, the
lawyer often glanced at it in apprehension—had soon
rid himself of his embarrassment and was now delight-
edly absorbed in the Clerk of the Court's eloquence and
the delicate wavelike gestures of the hand with which he
accompanied it. K., leaning against the bedpost, was
completely ignored by the Clerk of the Court, perhaps

by deliberate intention, and served merely as an audience to the old gentleman. Besides, he could hardly follow the conversation and was thinking first of the nurse and the rude treatment she had received from his uncle, and then wondering if he had not seen the Clerk of the Court before, perhaps actually among the audience during his first interrogation. He might be mistaken, yet the Clerk of the Court would have fitted excellently into the first row of the audience, the elderly gentlemen with the brittle beards.

Then a sound from the entrance hall as of breaking crockery made them all prick up their ears. "I'll go and see what has happened," said K., and he went out, rather slowly, to give the others a chance to call him back. Hardly had he reached the entrance hall and was beginning to grope his way in the darkness, when a hand much smaller than his own covered the hand with which he was still holding the door and gently drew the door shut. It was the nurse, who had been waiting there. "Nothing has happened," she whispered. "I simply flung a plate against the wall to bring you out." K. said in his embarrassment: "I was thinking of you too." "That's all the better," said the nurse. "Come this way." A step or two brought them to a door paneled with thick glass, which she opened. "In here," she said. It was evidently the lawyer's office; as far as one could see in the moonlight, which brilliantly lit up a small square section of the floor in front of each of the two large windows, it was fitted out with solid antique furniture. "Here," said the nurse, pointing to a dark chest with a carved wooden back. After he had sat down K. still kept looking round the room, it was a lofty, spacious room, the clients of this "poor man's" lawyer must feel lost in it.* K. pictured to himself the timid, short steps with which they would advance to the huge table. But then he forgot all this and had eyes only for the nurse, who was sitting very close to him, almost squeezing him against the arm of the bench. "I thought," she said, "you would come out of your own accord, without waiting till I had to call you out. A queer way to behave. You couldn't keep your eyes off me from the very moment you came in, and yet you leave me to wait. And you'd better just call me Leni," she added quickly and abruptly, as if there were not a moment to waste. "I'll be glad to," said K. "But as for my queer behavior, Leni, that's easy to explain. In the first place I had to listen to these old men jabbering. I couldn't simply walk out and leave them without any excuse, and in the second place I'm not in the least a bold young man, but rather shy, to tell the truth, and you too, Leni, really didn't look as if you were to be had for the asking." "It isn't that," said Leni, laying her arm along the back of the seat and looking at K. "But you didn't like me at first and you probably don't like me even now." "Liking is a feeble word," said K. evasively. "Oh!" she said, with a smile, and K.'s remark and that little exclamation gave her a certain advantage over him. So K. said nothing more for a while. As he had grown used to the darkness in the room, he could now distinguish certain details of the furnishings. He was particularly struck by a large picture which hung to the right of the door, and bent forward to see it more clearly. It represented a man in a Judge's robe; he was sitting on a high thronelike seat, and the gilding of the seat stood out strongly in the picture. The strange thing was that the Judge did not seem to be sitting in dignified composure, for his left arm was braced along the back and the side-arm of his throne, while his right arm rested on nothing, except for the hand, which clutched the other arm of the chair; it was as if in a moment he must spring up with a violent and probably wrathful gesture to make some decisive observation or even to pronounce sentence. The accused might be imagined as standing on the lowest step leading up to the chair of justice; the top steps, which were covered with a yellowish carpet, were shown in the picture. "Perhaps that is my Judge," said K., pointing with his finger at the picture. "I know him," said Leni, and she looked at the picture too. "He often comes here. That picture was painted when he was young, but it could never have been in the least like him, for he's a small man, almost a dwarf. Yet in spite of that he had himself drawn out to that length in the portrait, for he's madly vain like everybody else here. But I'm a vain person, too, and very much upset that you don't like me in the least." To this last statement K. replied merely by putting his arm round her and drawing her to him; she leaned her head against his shoulder in silence. But to the rest of her remarks he answered: "What's the man's rank?" "He is an Examining Magistrate," she said, seizing the hand with which K. held her and beginning to play with his fingers. "Only an Examining Magistrate again," said K. in disappointment. "The higher officials keep themselves well hidden. But he's sitting in a chair of state." "That's all invention," said Leni, with her face bent over his hand. "Actually he is sitting on a kitchen chair, with an old horse-rug doubled under him. But must you eternally be brooding over your case?" she queried slowly. "No, not at all," said K. "In fact I probably brood far too little over it." "That isn't the mistake you make," said Leni. "You're too unyielding, that's what I've heard." "Who told you that?" asked K.; he could feel her body against his breast and gazed down at her rich, dark, firmly knotted hair. "I should give away too much if I told you that," replied Leni. "Please don't ask me for names, take my warning to heart instead, and don't be so unyielding in future, you can't fight against this Court, you must confess to guilt. Make your confession at the first chance you get. Until you do that, there's no possibility of getting out of their clutches, none at all. Yet even then you won't manage it without help from outside, but you needn't trouble your head about that, I'll see to it myself." "You know a great deal about this Court and the intrigues that prevail in it!" said K., lifting her on to his knee, for she was leaning too heavily against him. "That's better," she said, making herself at home on his knee by smoothing her skirt and pulling her blouse straight. Then she clasped both her hands round his neck, leaned back, and looked at him for a long time. "And if I don't make a confession of guilt, then you can't help me?" K. asked experimentally. "I seem to recruit women helpers," he thought almost in surprise; "first Fräulein Bürstner, then the wife of the usher, and now this little nurse who appears to have some incomprehensible desire for me. She sits there on my knee as if it were the only right place for her!" "No," said Leni, shaking her head slowly, "then I can't help you. But you don't in the least want my help, it doesn't matter to you, you're stiff-necked and never will be convinced." After a while she asked: "Have you got a sweetheart?" "No," said K. "Oh, yes, you have," she said. "Well, yes, I have," said K. "Just imagine it, I have denied her existence and yet I am actually carrying her photograph in my pocket." At her entreaty he showed her Elsa's photograph; she studied it, curled up on his knee. It was a snapshot taken of Elsa as she was finishing a whirling dance such as she often gave at the cabaret, her skirt was still flying round her like a fan, her hands were planted on her firm hips, and with her chin thrown up she was laughing over her shoulder at someone who did not appear in the photograph. "She's very tightly laced," said Leni, indicating the place where in her opinion the tight-lacing was evident. "I don't like her, she's rough and clumsy. But perhaps she's soft and kind to you, one might guess that from the photograph. Big strong girls like that often can't help being soft and kind. But would she be capable of sacrificing herself for you?" "No," said K. "She is neither soft nor kind, nor would she be capable of sacrificing herself for me. And up till now I have demanded neither the one thing nor the other from her. In fact I've never even examined this photograph as carefully as you have." "So she doesn't mean so very much to you," said Leni. "She isn't your sweetheart after all." "Oh, yes," replied K. "I refuse to take back my words." "Well, granted that she's your sweetheart," said Leni, "you wouldn't miss her very much, all the same, if you were to lose her or exchange her for someone else, me, for instance?" "Certainly," said K., smiling, "that's conceivable, but she has one great advantage over you, she knows nothing about my case, and even if she knew she wouldn't bother her head about it. She wouldn't try to get me to be less unyielding." "That's no advantage," said Leni. "If that's all the advantage she has over me I shan't give up hope. Has she any physical defect?" "Any physical defect?" asked K. "Yes," said Leni. "For I have a slight one. Look." She held up her right hand and stretched out the two middle fingers, between which the connecting web of skin reached almost to the top joint, short as the fingers were. In the darkness K. could not make out at once what she wanted to show him, so she took his hand and made him feel it. "What a freak of nature!" said K. and he added, when he had examined the whole hand: "What a pretty little paw!" Leni looked on with a kind of pride while K. in astonishment kept pulling the two fingers apart and then putting them side by side again, until at last he kissed them lightly and let them go. "Oh!" she cried at once. "You have kissed me!" She hastily scrambled up until she was kneeling openmouthed on his knees. K. looked up at her almost dumfounded; now that she was so close to him she gave out a bitter exciting odor like pepper; she clasped his head to her, bent over him, and bit and kissed him on the neck, biting into the very hairs of his head. "You have exchanged her for me," she cried over and over again. "Look, you have exchanged her for me after all!" Then her knees slipped, with a faint cry she almost fell on the carpet, K. put his arms round her to hold her up and was pulled down to her. "You belong to me now," she said.

"Here's the key of the door, come whenever you like," were her last words, and as he took his leave a final aimless kiss landed on his shoulder. When he stepped out on to the pavement a light rain was falling; he was making for the middle of the street so as perhaps to catch a last glimpse of Leni at her window, but a car which was waiting before the house and which in his distraction he had not even noticed suddenly emitted his uncle, who seized him by the arms and banged him against the house door as if he wanted to nail him there. "Joseph!" he cried, "how could you do it! You have damaged your case badly, which was beginning to go quite well. You hide yourself away with a filthy little trollop, who is obviously the lawyer's mistress into the bargain, and stay away for hours. You don't even seek any pretext, you conceal nothing, no, you're quite open, you simply run off to her and stay beside her. And all this time we three sit there, your uncle, who is doing his best for you, the lawyer, who has to be won over to your side, above all the Chief Clerk of the Court, a man of importance, who is actually in charge of your case at its present stage. There we sit, consulting how to help you, I have to handle the lawyer circumspectly, and the lawyer in turn the Clerk of the Court, and one might think you had every reason to give me at least some support. Instead of which you absent yourself. You were away so long that there was no concealing it; of course the two gentlemen, being men of the world, didn't talk about it, they spared my feelings, but finally even they could no longer ignore it, and as they couldn't mention it they said nothing at all. We sat there for minutes on end in complete silence, listening for you to come back at last. And all in vain. Finally the Chief Clerk of the Court, who had stayed much longer than he intended, got up and said good night, evidently very sorry for me without being able to help me, his kindness was really extraordinary, he stood waiting for a while longer at the door before he left. And I was glad when he went, let me tell you; by that time I felt hardly able to breathe. And the poor sick lawyer felt it even more, the good man couldn't utter a word as I took leave of him. In all probability you have helped to bring about his complete collapse and so hastened the death of a man on whose good offices you are dependent. And you leave me, your uncle, to wait here in the rain for hours and worry myself sick, just feel, I'm wet through and through!"

CHAPTER SEVEN

Lawyer / Manufacturer / Painter

ONE winter morning—snow was falling outside the window in a foggy dimness—K. was sitting in his office, already exhausted in spite of the early hour. To save his face before his subordinates at least, he had given his clerk instructions to admit no one, on the plea that he was occupied with an important piece of work. But instead of working he twisted in his chair, idly rearranged the things lying on his writing-table, and then, without being aware of it, let his outstretched arm rest on the table and went on sitting motionless with bowed head.

The thought of his case never left him now. He had often considered whether it would not be better to draw up a written defense and hand it in to the Court. In this defense he would give a short account of his life, and when he came to an event of any importance explain for what reasons he had acted as he did, intimate whether he approved or condemned his way of action in retrospect, and adduce grounds for the condemnation or approval. The advantages of such a written defense, as compared with the mere advocacy of a lawyer who himself was not impeccable, were undoubted. K. had no idea what the lawyer was doing about the case; at any rate it did not amount to much, it was more than a month since Huld had sent for him, and at none of the previous consultations had K. formed the impression that the man could do much for him. To begin with, he had hardly cross-questioned him at all. And there were so many questions to put. To ask questions was surely the main thing. K. felt that he could draw up all the necessary questions himself. But the lawyer, instead of asking questions, either did all the talking or sat quite dumb opposite him, bent slightly forward over his writing-table, probably because of his hardness of hearing, stroking a strand of hair in the middle of his beard and

gazing at the carpet, perhaps at the very spot where
K. had lain with Leni. Now and then he would give K.
some empty admonitions such as people hand out to children. Admonitions as useless as they were wearisome, for
which K. did not intend to pay a penny at the final
reckoning. After the lawyer thought he had humbled
him sufficiently, he usually set himself to encourage him
slightly again. He had already, so he would relate, won
many similar cases either outright or partially. Cases
which, though in reality not quite so difficult, perhaps,
as this one, had been outwardly still more hopeless. He
had a list of these cases in a drawer of his desk—at this
he tapped one of them—but he regretted he couldn't
show it, as it was a matter of official secrecy. Nevertheless the vast experience he had gained through all these
cases would now redound to K.'s benefit. He had started
on K.'s case at once, of course, and the first plea was
almost ready for presentation. That was very important,
for the first impression made by the Defense often determined the whole course of subsequent proceedings.
Though, unfortunately, it was his duty to warn K., it
sometimes happened that the first pleas were not read
by the Court at all. They simply filed them among the
other papers and pointed out that for the time being
the observation and interrogation of the accused were
more important than any formal petition. If the petitioner pressed them, they generally added that before
the verdict was pronounced all the material accumulated,
including, of course, every document relating to the case,

the first plea as well, would be carefully examined. But unluckily even that was not quite true in most cases, the first plea was often mislaid or lost altogether and, even if it were kept intact till the end, was hardly ever read; that was of course, the lawyer admitted, merely a rumor. It was all very regrettable, but not wholly without justification. K. must remember that the proceedings were not public; they could certainly, if the Court considered it necessary, become public, but the Law did not prescribe that they must be made public. Naturally, therefore, the legal records of the case, and above all the actual charge-sheets, were inaccessible to the accused and his counsel, consequently one did not know in general, or at least did not know with any precision, what charges to meet in the first plea; accordingly it could be only by pure chance that it contained really relevant matter. One could draw up genuinely effective and convincing pleas only later on, when the separate charges and the evidence on which they were based emerged more definitely or could be guessed at from the interrogations. In such circumstances the Defense was naturally in a very ticklish and difficult position. Yet that, too, was intentional. For the Defense was not actually countenanced by the Law, but only tolerated, and there were differences of opinion even on that point, whether the Law could be interpreted to admit such tolerance at all. Strictly speaking, therefore, none of the counsels for the Defense was recognized by the Court, all who appeared before the Court as councils being in reality merely in the position of pettifogging lawyers. That naturally had a very humiliating effect on the whole profession, and the next time K. visited the Law Court offices he should take a look at the lawyers' room, just for the sake of having seen it once in his life. He would probably be horrified by the kind of people he found assembled there. The very room, itself small and cramped, showed the contempt in which the Court held them. It was lit only by a small skylight, which was so high up that if you wanted to look out, you had to get some colleague to hoist you on his back, and even then the smoke from the chimney close by choked you and blackened your face. To give only one more example of the state the place was in—there had been for more than a year now a hole in the floor, not so big that you could fall through the floor, but big enough to let a man's leg slip through. The lawyers' room was in the very top attic, so that if you stumbled through the hole your leg hung down into the lower attic, into the very corridor where the clients had to wait. It wasn't saying too much if the lawyers called these conditions scandalous. Complaints to the authorities had not the slightest effect, and it was strictly forbidden for the lawyers to make any structural repairs or alterations at their own expense. Still, there was some justification for this attitude on the part of the authorities. They wanted to eliminate defending counsel as much as possible; the whole onus of the Defense must be laid on the accused himself. A reasonable enough point of view, yet nothing could be more erroneous than to deduce from this that accused persons had no need of defending counsel when appearing before this Court. On the contrary, in no other Court was legal assistance so necessary. For the proceedings were not only kept secret from the general public, but from the accused as well. Of course only so far as this was possible, but it had proved possible to a very great extent. For even the accused had no access to the Court records, and to guess from the course of an interrogation what documents the Court had up its sleeve was very difficult, particularly for an accused person, who was himself implicated and had all sorts of worries to distract him. Now here was where defending counsel stepped in. Generally speaking, he was not allowed to be present during the examination, consequently he had to cross-question the accused immediately after an interrogation, if possible at the very door of the Court of Inquiry, and piece together from the usually confused reports he got anything that might be of use for the Defense. But even that was not the most important thing, for one could not elicit very much in that way, though of course here as elsewhere a capable man could elicit more than others. The most important thing was counsel's personal connection with officials of the Court; in that lay the chief value of the Defense. Now K. must have discovered from experience that the very lowest grade of the Court organization was by no means perfect and contained venal and corrupt elements, whereby to some extent a breach was made in the water-tight system of justice. This was where most of the petty lawyers tried to push their way in, by bribing and listening to gossip, in fact there had actually been cases of purloining documents, at least in former times. It was not to be gainsaid that these methods could achieve for the moment surprisingly favorable results for the accused, on which the petty lawyers prided themselves, spreading them out as a lure for new clients, but they had no effect on the further progress of the case, or only a bad effect. Nothing was of any real value but respectable personal connections with the higher officials, that was to say higher officials of subordinate rank, naturally. Only through these could the course of the proceedings be influenced, imperceptibly at first, perhaps, but more and more strongly as the case went on. Of course very few lawyers had such connections, and here K.'s choice had been a very fortunate one. Perhaps only one or two other lawyers could boast of the same connections as Dr. Huld. These did not worry their heads about the mob in the lawyers' room and had nothing whatever to do with them. But their relations with the Court officials were all the more intimate. It was not even necessary that Dr. Huld should always attend the Court, wait in the Ante-room of the Examining Magistrates till they chose to appear, and be dependent on their moods for earning perhaps a delusive success or not even that. No, as K. had himself seen, the officials, and very high ones among them, visited Dr. Huld of their own accord, voluntarily providing information with great frankness or at least

in broad enough hints, discussing the next turn of the
various cases; more, even sometimes letting themselves
be persuaded to a new point of view. Certainly one
should not rely too much on their readiness to be persuaded, for definitely as they might declare themselves
for a new standpoint favorable to the Defense, they might
well go straight to their offices and issue a statement in the
directly contrary sense, a verdict far more severe on
the accused than the original intention which they claimed
to have renounced completely. Against that, of course,
there was no remedy, for what they said to you in private
was simply said to you in private and could not be
followed up in public, even if the Defense were not
obliged for other reasons to do its utmost to retain the
favor of these gentlemen. On the other hand it had also
to be considered that these gentlemen were not moved
by mere human benevolence or friendly feeling in paying
visits to defending counsel—only to experienced counsel,
of course; they were in a certain sense actually dependent
on the Defense. They could not help feeling the disadvantages of a judiciary system which insisted on
secrecy from the start. Their remoteness kept the officials
from being in touch with the populace; for the average
case they were excellently equipped, such a case proceeded almost mechanically and only needed a push now
and then; yet confronted with quite simple cases, or
particularly difficult cases, they were often utterly at a
loss, they did not have any right understanding of human
relations, since they were confined day and night to the

workings of their judicial system, whereas in such cases
a knowledge of human nature itself was indispensable.
Then it was that they came to the lawyers for advice,
with a servant behind them carrying the papers that
were usually kept so secret. In that window over there
many a gentleman one would never have expected to
encounter had sat gazing out hopelessly into the street,
while the lawyer at his desk examined his papers in
order to give him good advice. And it was on such
occasions as these that one could perceive how seriously
these gentlemen took their vocation and how deeply they
were plunged into despair when they came upon obstacles
which the nature of things kept them from overcoming.
In other ways, too, their position was not easy, and one
must not do them an injustice by regarding it as easy.
The ranks of officials in this judiciary system mounted
endlessly, so that not even the initiated could survey the
hierarchy as a whole. And the proceedings of the Courts
were generally kept secret from subordinate officials, consequently they could hardly ever quite follow in their
further progress the cases on which they had worked; any
particular case thus appeared in their circle of jurisdiction often without their knowing whence it came, and
passed from it they knew not whither. Thus the knowledge derived from a study of the various single stages of
the case, the final verdict and the reasons for that verdict
lay beyond the reach of these officials. They were forced
to restrict themselves to that stage of the case which was
prescribed for them by the Law, and as for what fol-

lowed, in other words the results of their own work, they generally knew less about it than the Defense, which as a rule remained in touch with the accused almost to the end of the case. So in that respect, too, they could learn much that was worth knowing from the Defense. Should it surprise K., then, keeping all this in mind, to find that the officials lived in a state of irritability which sometimes expressed itself in offensive ways when they dealt with their clients? That was the universal experience. All the officials were in a constant state of irritation, even when they appeared calm. Naturally the petty lawyers were most liable to suffer from it. The following story, for example, was current, and it had all the appearance of truth. An old official, a well-meaning, quiet man, had a difficult case in hand which had been greatly complicated by the lawyer's petitions, and he had studied it continuously for a whole day and night—the officials were really more conscientious than anyone else. Well, toward morning, after twenty-four hours of work with probably very little result, he went to the entrance door, hid himself behind it, and flung down the stairs every lawyer who tried to enter. The lawyers gathered down below on the landing and took counsel what they should do; on the one hand they had no real claim to be admitted and consequently could hardly take any legal action against the official, and also, as already mentioned, they had to guard against antagonizing the body of officials. But on the other hand every day they spent away from the Court was a day lost to them, and so a great deal depended on their getting in. At last they all agreed that the best thing to do was to tire out the old gentleman. One lawyer after another was sent rushing upstairs to offer the greatest possible show of passive resistance and let himself be thrown down again into the arms of his colleagues. That lasted for about an hour, then the old gentleman—who was exhausted in any case by his work overnight—really grew tired and went back to his office. The lawyers down below would not believe it at first and sent one of their number up to peep behind the door and assure himself that the place was actually vacant. Only then were they able to enter, and probably they did not dare even to grumble. For although the pettiest lawyer might be to some extent capable of analyzing the state of things in the Court, it never occurred to the lawyers that they should suggest or insist on any improvements in the system, while—and this was very characteristic—almost every accused man, even quite simple people among them, discovered from the earliest stages a passion for suggesting reforms which often wasted time and energy that could have been better employed in other directions. The only sensible thing was to adapt oneself to existing conditions. Even if it were possible to alter a detail for the better here or there—but it was simple madness to think of it—any benefit arising from that would profit clients in the future only, while one's own interests would be immeasurably injured by attracting the attention of the ever-vengeful officials. Anything rather than that! One must lie low, no matter how much it went against the grain, and try to understand that this great organization remained, so to speak, in a state of delicate balance, and that if someone took it upon himself to alter the disposition of things around him, he ran the risk of losing his footing and falling to destruction, while the organization would simply right itself by some compensating reaction in another part of its machinery—since everything interlocked—and remain unchanged, unless, indeed, which was very probable, it became still more rigid, more vigilant, severer, and more ruthless. One must really leave the lawyers to do their work, instead of interfering with them. Reproaches were not of much use, particularly when the offender was unable to perceive the full scope of the grounds for them; all the same, he must say that K. had very greatly damaged his case by his discourtesy to the Chief Clerk of the Court. That influential man could already almost be eliminated from the list of those who might be got to do something for K. He now ignored clearly on purpose even the slightest reference to the case. In many ways the functionaries were like children. Often they could be so deeply offended by the merest trifle—unfortunately, K.'s behavior could not be classed as a trifle—that they would stop speaking even to old friends, give them the cold shoulder, and work against them in all imaginable ways. But then, suddenly, in the most surprising fashion and without any particular reason, they would be moved to laughter by some small jest which you only dared to make because you felt you had nothing to lose, and then they were your friends again.

In fact it was both easy and difficult to handle them, you could hardly lay down any fixed principles for dealing with them. Sometimes you felt astonished to think that one single ordinary lifetime sufficed to gather all the knowledge needed for a fair degree of success in such a profession. There were dark hours, of course, such as came to everybody, in which you thought you had achieved nothing at all, in which it seemed to you that only the cases predestined from the start to succeed came to a good end, which they would have reached in any event without your help, while every one of the others was doomed to fail in spite of all your maneuvers, all your exertions, all the illusory little victories on which you plumed yourself. That was a frame of mind, of course, in which nothing at all seemed certain, and so you could not positively deny when questioned that your intervention might have sidetracked some cases which would have run quite well on the right lines had they been left alone. A desperate kind of self-assurance, to be sure, yet it was the only kind available at such times. These moods—for of course they were only moods, nothing more—afflicted lawyers more especially when a case which they had conducted satisfactorily to the desired point was suddenly taken out of their hands. That was beyond all doubt the worst thing that could happen to a lawyer. Not that a client ever dismissed his lawyer from a case, such a thing was not done, an accused man, once having briefed a lawyer, must stick to him whatever happened. For how could he keep going by himself, once he had called in someone to help him? So that never happened, but it did sometimes happen that the case took a turn where the lawyer could no longer follow it. The case and the accused and everything were simply withdrawn from the lawyer; then even the best connections with officials could no longer achieve any result, for even they knew nothing. The case had simply reached the stage where further assistance was ruled out, it was being conducted in remote, inaccessible Courts, where even the accused was beyond the reach of a lawyer. Then you might come home some day and find on your table all the countless pleas relating to the case, which you had drawn up with such pains and such flattering hopes; they had been returned to you because in the new stage of the trial they were not admitted as relevant; they were mere waste paper. It did not follow that the case was lost, by no means, at least there was no decisive evidence for such an assumption; you simply knew nothing more about the case and would never know anything more about it. Now, very luckily, such occurrences were exceptional, and even if K.'s case were a case of that nature, it still had a long way to go before reaching that stage. For the time being, there were abundant opportunities for legal labor, and K. might rest assured that they would be exploited to the uttermost. The first plea, as before mentioned, was not yet handed in, but there was no hurry; far more important were the preliminary consultations with the relevant officials, and they had already taken place. With varying success, as must be frankly admitted. It would be better for the time being not to divulge details which might have a bad influence on K. by elating or depressing him unduly, yet this much could be asserted, that certain officials had expressed themselves very graciously and had also shown great readiness to help, while others had expressed themselves less favorably, but in spite of that had by no means refused their collaboration. The result on the whole was therefore very gratifying, though one must not seek to draw any definite conclusion from that, since all preliminary negotiations began in the same way and only in the course of further developments did it appear whether they had real value or not. At any rate nothing was yet lost, and if they could manage to win over the Chief Clerk of the Court in spite of all that had happened —various moves had already been initiated toward that end—then, to use a surgeon's expression, this could be regarded as a clean wound and one could await further developments with an easy mind.

In such and similar harangues K.'s lawyer was inexhaustible. He reiterated them every time K. called on him. Progress had always been made, but the nature of the progress could never be divulged. The lawyer was always working away at the first plea, but it had never reached a conclusion, which at the next visit turned out to be an advantage, since the last few days would have been very inauspicious for handing it in, a fact which no one could have foreseen. If K., as sometimes happened, wearied out by the lawyer's volubility, remarked that, even taking into account all the difficulties, the case seemed to be getting on very slowly, he was met with the retort that it was not getting on slowly at all, although they would have been much further on by now had K. come to the lawyer in time. Unfortunately he had neglected to do so and that omission was likely to keep him at a disadvantage, and not merely a temporal disadvantage, either.

The one welcome interruption to these visits was Leni, who always so arranged things that she brought in the lawyer's tea while K. was present. She would stand behind K.'s chair, apparently looking on, while the lawyer stooped with a kind of miserly greed over his cup and poured out and sipped his tea, but all the time she was letting K. surreptitiously hold her hand. There was total silence. The lawyer sipped, K. squeezed Leni's hand, and sometimes Leni ventured to caress his hair. "Are you still here?" the lawyer would ask, after he had finished. "I wanted to take the tea-tray away," Leni would answer, there would follow a last handclasp, the lawyer would wipe his mouth and begin again with new energy to harangue K.

Was the lawyer seeking to comfort him or to drive him to despair? K. could not tell, but he soon held it for an established fact that his defense was not in good hands. It might be all true, of course, what the lawyer said, though his attempts to magnify his own importance were transparent enough and it was likely that he had never till now conducted such an important case as he imagined K.'s to be. But his continual bragging of his personal connections with the officials was suspicious. Was it so certain that he was exploiting these connections entirely for K.'s benefit? The lawyer never forgot to mention that these officials were subordinate officials, therefore officials in a very dependent position, for whose advancement certain turns in the various cases might in all probability be of some importance. Could they possibly employ the lawyer to bring about such turns in the case, turns which were bound, of course, to be unfavorable to the accused? Perhaps they did not always do that, it was hardly likely, there must be occasions on which they arranged that the lawyer should score a point or two as a reward for his services, since it was to their own interest for him to keep up his professional reputation. But if that were really the position, into which category were they likely to put K.'s case, which, as the lawyer maintained, was a very difficult, therefore important case, and had roused great interest in the Court from the very beginning? There could not be very much doubt what they would do. A clue was already provided by the fact that the first plea had not yet been handed in, though the case had lasted for months, and that according to the lawyer all the proceedings were still in their early stages, words which were obviously well calculated to lull the accused and keep him in a helpless state, in order suddenly to overwhelm him with the verdict or at least with the announcement that the preliminary examination had been concluded in his disfavor and the case handed over to higher authorities.

It was absolutely necessary for K. to intervene personally. In states of intense exhaustion, such as he experienced this winter morning, when all these thoughts kept running at random through his head, he was particularly incapable of resisting this conviction. The contempt which he had once felt for the case no longer obtained. Had he stood alone in the world he could easily have ridiculed the whole affair, though it was also certain that in that event it could never have arisen at all. But now his uncle had dragged him to this lawyer, family considerations had come in; his position was no longer quite independent of the course the case took, he himself, with a certain inexplicable complacence, had imprudently mentioned it to some of his acquaintances, others had come to learn of it in ways unknown to him, his relations with Fräulein Bürstner seemed to fluctuate with the case itself—in short, he hardly had the choice now to accept the trial or reject it, he was in the middle of it and must fend for himself. To give in to fatigue would be dangerous.

Yet there was no need for exaggerated anxiety at the moment. In a relatively short time he had managed to work himself up to his present high position in the Bank and to maintain himself in that position and win recognition from everybody; surely if the abilities which had made this possible were to be applied to the unraveling of his own case, there was no doubt that it would go well. Above all, if he were to achieve anything, it was essential that he should banish from his mind once and for all the idea of possible guilt. There was no such guilt. This legal action was nothing more than a business deal such as he had often concluded to the advantage of the Bank, a deal within which, as always happened, lurked various dangers which must simply be obviated. The right tactics were to avoid letting one's thoughts stray to one's own possible shortcomings, and to cling as firmly as one could to the thought of one's advantage. From this standpoint the conclusion was inevitable that the case must be withdrawn from Dr. Huld as soon as possible, preferably that very evening. According to him that was something unheard of, it was true, and very likely an insult, but K. could not endure that his efforts in the case should be thwarted by moves possibly originating in the office of his own representative. Once the lawyer was shaken off, the petition must be sent in at once and the officials be urged daily, if possible, to give their attention to it. This would never be achieved by sitting meekly in the attic lobby like the others with one's hat under the seat. K. himself, or one of the women, or some other messenger must keep at the officials day after day and force them to sit down at their desks and study K.'s papers instead of gaping out into the lobby through the wooden rails. These tactics must be pursued unremittingly, everything must be organized and supervised; the Court would encounter for once an accused man who knew how to stick up for his rights.

Yet even though K. believed he could manage all this, the difficulty of drawing up the petition seemed overwhelming. At one time, not more than a week ago, he had regarded the possibility of having to draw up his own plea with merely a slight feeling of shame; it never even occurred to him that there might be difficulties in the way. He could remember that one of those mornings, when he was up to his ears in work, he had suddenly pushed everything aside and seized his jotting-pad with the idea of drafting the plan of such a plea and handing it to Dr. Huld by way of egging him on, but just at that moment the door of the Manager's room opened and the Assistant Manager came in laughing uproariously. That had been a very painful moment for K., though, of course, the Assistant Manager had not been laughing at the plea, of which he knew nothing, but at a funny story from the Stock Exchange which he had just heard, a story which needed illustrating for the proper appreciation of the point, so that the Assistant Manager, bending over the desk, took K.'s pencil from his hand and drew the required picture on the page of the jotting-pad which had been intended for the plea.

Today K. was no longer hampered by feelings of shame; the plea simply had to be drawn up. If he could find no time for it in his office, which seemed very probable, then he must draft it in his lodgings by night. And if his nights were not enough, then he must ask for furlough. Anything but stop halfway, that was the most senseless thing one could do in any affair, not only in business. No doubt it was a task that meant almost interminable labor. One did not need to have a timid and fearful nature to be easily persuaded that the completion of this plea was a sheer impossibility. Not because of laziness or obstructive malice, which could only hinder Dr. Huld, but because to meet an unknown accusation, not to mention other possible charges arising out of it, the whole of one's life would have to be recalled to mind, down to the smallest actions and accidents, clearly formulated and examined from every angle. And besides how dreary such a task would be! It would do well enough, perhaps, as an occupation for one's second childhood in years of retirement, when the long days needed filling up. But now, when K. should be devoting his mind entirely to work, when every hour was hurried and crowded—for he was still in full career and rapidly becoming a rival even to the Assistant Manager—when his evenings and nights were all too short for the pleasures of a bachelor life, this was the time when he must sit down to such a task! Once more his train of thought had led him into self-pity. Almost involuntarily, simply to make an end of it, he put his finger on the button which rang the bell in the waiting-room. While he pressed it he glanced at the clock. It was eleven o'clock, he had wasted two hours in dreaming, a long stretch of precious time, and he was, of course, still wearier than he had been before. Yet the time had not been quite lost, he had come to decisions which might prove valuable. The attendants brought in several letters and two cards from gentlemen who had been waiting for a considerable time. They were, in fact, extremely important clients of the Bank who should on no account have been kept waiting at all. Why had they come at such an unsuitable hour?—and why, they might well be asking in their turn behind the door, did the assiduous K. allow his private affairs to usurp the best time of the day? Weary of what had gone before and wearily awaiting what was to come, K. got up to receive the first of his clients.

This was the jovial little man, a manufacturer whom K. knew well. He regretted having disturbed K. in the middle of important work and K. on his side regretted that he had kept the manufacturer waiting for so long. But his very regret he expressed in such a mechanical way, with such a lack of sincerity in his tone of voice, that the manufacturer could not have helped noticing it, had he not been so engrossed by the business in hand. As it was, he tugged papers covered with statistics out of every pocket, spread them before K., explained various entries, corrected a trifling error which his eye had caught even in this hasty survey, reminded K. of a similar transaction which he had concluded with him about a year before, mentioned casually that this time another bank was making great sacrifices to secure the deal, and finally sat in eager silence waiting for K.'s comments. K. had actually followed the man's argument quite closely in its early stages—the thought of such an important piece of business had its attractions for him too—but unfortunately not for long; he had soon ceased to listen and merely nodded now and then as the manufacturer's claims waxed in enthusiasm, until in the end he forgot to show

even that much interest and confined himself to staring at
the other's bald head bent over the papers and asking
himself when the fellow would begin to realize that all his
eloquence was being wasted. When the manufacturer
stopped speaking, K. actually thought for a moment that
the pause was intended to give him the chance of confessing that he was not in a fit state to attend to business.
And it was with regret that he perceived the intent look
on the manufacturer's face, the alertness, as if prepared
for every objection, which indicated that the interview
would have to continue. So he bowed his head as at a
word of command and began slowly to move his pencil
point over the papers, pausing here and there to stare at
some figure. The manufacturer suspected K. of looking
for flaws in the scheme, perhaps the figures were merely
tentative, perhaps they were not the decisive factors in
the deal, at any rate he laid his hand over them and shifting closer to K. began to expound the general policy behind the transaction. "It's difficult," said K., pursing his
lips, and now that the papers, the only things he had to
hold on to, were covered up, he sank weakly against
the arm of his chair. He glanced up slightly, but only
slightly, when the door of the Manager's room opened,
disclosed the Assistant Manager, a blurred figure who
looked as if veiled in some kind of gauze. K. did not seek
for the cause of this apparition, but merely registered
its immediate effect, which was very welcome to him.
For the manufacturer at once bounded from his chair
and rushed over to the Assistant Manager, though K.

could have wished him to be ten times quicker, since he was afraid the apparition might vanish again. His fear was superfluous, the two gentlemen met each other, shook hands, and advanced together toward K.'s desk. The manufacturer lamented that his proposals were being cold-shouldered by the Chief Clerk, indicating K., who under the Assistant Manager's eye had once more bent over the papers. Then as the two of them leaned against his desk, and the manufacturer set himself to win the newcomer's approval for his scheme, it seemed to K. as though two giants of enormous size were negotiating above his head about himself. Slowly, lifting his eyes as far as he dared, he peered up to see what they were about, then picked one of the documents from the desk at random, laid it flat on his open palm, and gradually raised it, rising himself with it, to their level. In doing so he had no definite purpose, but merely acted with the feeling that this was how he would have to act when he had finished the great task of drawing up the plea which was to acquit him completely. The Assistant Manager, who was giving his full attention to the conversation, merely glanced at the paper without even reading what was on it—for anything that seemed important to the Chief Clerk was unimportant to him—took it from K.'s hand, said: "Thanks, I know all that already," and quietly laid it back on the desk again. K. darted a bitter look at him, but the Assistant Manager did not notice that, or, if he did, was only amused; he laughed loudly several times, visibly disconcerted the manufacturer by a quick retort, only to counter it immediately himself, and finally invited the man into his private office, where they could complete the transaction together. "It is a very important proposal," he said to the manufacturer, "I entirely agree. And the Chief Clerk"—even in saying this he went on addressing himself only to the manufacturer—"will I am sure be relieved if we take it off his shoulders. This business needs thinking over. And he seems to be overburdened today; besides, there are some people who have been waiting for him in the anteroom for hours." K. had still enough self-command to turn away from the Assistant Manager and address his friendly but somewhat fixed smile solely to the manufacturer; except for this he did not intervene, supporting himself with both hands on the desk, bending forward a little like an obsequious clerk, and looked on while the two men, still talking away, gathered up the papers and disappeared into the Manager's room. In the very doorway, the manufacturer turned round to remark that he would not say good-by yet, for of course he would report the result of the interview to the Chief Clerk; besides, there was another little matter he had to mention.

At last K. was alone. He had not the slightest intention of interviewing any more clients and vaguely realized how pleasant it was that the people waiting outside believed him to be still occupied with the manufacturer, so that nobody, not even the attendant, could disturb him. He went over to the window, perched on the sill, holding on to the latch with one hand, and looked down on the square below. The snow was still falling, the sky had not yet cleared.

For a long time he sat like this, without knowing what

really troubled him, only turning his head from time to time with an alarmed glance toward the anteroom, where he fancied, mistakenly, that he heard a noise. But as no one came in he recovered his composure, went over to the washbasin, washed his face in cold water, and returned to his place at the window with a clearer mind. The decision to take his defense into his own hands seemed now more grave to him than he had originally fancied. So long as the lawyer was responsible for the case it had not come really home to him, he had viewed it with a certain detachment and kept beyond reach of immediate contact with it, he had been able to supervise it whenever he liked, but could also withdraw whenever he liked. Now, on the other hand, if he were to conduct his own defense he would be putting himself completely in the power of the Court, at least for the time being, a policy which would eventually bring about his absolute and definite acquittal, but would meanwhile, provisionally at least, involve him in far greater dangers than before. If he had ever doubted that, his state of mind today in his encounter with the Assistant Manager and the manufacturer would have been more than enough to convince him. What a stupor had overcome him, merely because he had decided to conduct his own defense! And what would develop later on? What days were lying in wait for him? Would he ever find the right path through all these difficulties? To put up a thoroughgoing defense—and any other kind would be a waste of time—to put up a thoroughgoing defense, did that not involve cutting himself off from every other activity? Would he be able to carry that through? And how was he to conduct his case from a Bank office? It was not merely the drawing up of a plea; that might be managed on a few weeks' furlough, though to ask for leave of absence just now would be decidedly risky; but a whole trial was involved, whose duration it was impossible to foresee. What an obstacle had suddenly arisen to block K.'s career!

And this was the moment when he was supposed to work for the Bank? He looked down at his desk. This the time to interview clients and negotiate with them? While his case was unfolding itself, while up in the attics the Court officials were poring over the charge papers, was he to devote his attention to the affairs of the Bank? It looked like a kind of torture sanctioned by the Court, arising from his case and concomitant with it. And would allowances be made for his peculiar position when his work in the Bank came to be judged? Never, and by nobody. The existence of his case was not entirely unknown in the Bank, though it was not quite clear who knew of it and how much they knew. But apparently the rumor had not yet reached the Assistant Manager, otherwise K. could hardly have failed to perceive it, since the man would have exploited his knowledge without any scruples as a colleague or as a human being. And the Manager himself? He was certainly well disposed to K. and as soon as he heard of the case would probably be willing enough to lighten K.'s duties as far as lay in his power, but his good intentions would be checkmated, for K.'s waning prestige was no longer sufficient to counterbalance the influence of the Assistant Manager, who was gaining a stronger hold on the Manager and exploiting the latter's invalid condition to his own advantage.* So what had K. to hope? It might be that he was only sapping his powers of resistance by harboring these thoughts; still, it was necessary to have no illusions and to view the position as clearly as the moment allowed.

Without any particular motive, merely to put off returning to his desk, he opened the window. It was difficult to open, he had to push the latch with both hands. Then there came into the room through the great window a blend of fog and smoke, filling it with a faint smell of burning soot. Some snowflakes fluttered in too. "An awful autumn," came the voice of the manufacturer from behind K.; returning from his colloquy with the Assistant Manager, he had entered the room unobserved. K. nodded and shot an apprehensive glance at the man's attaché case, from which doubtless he would now extract all his papers in order to inform K. how the negotiations had gone. But the manufacturer, catching K.'s eye, merely tapped his attaché case without opening it and said: "You would like to know how it has turned out? The final settlement is as good as in my pocket. A charming fellow, your Assistant Manager, but dangerous to reckon with." He laughed and shook K. by the hand, trying to make him laugh too. But now K.'s suspicions seized on the fact that the manufacturer had not offered to show him the papers, and he found nothing to laugh at. "Herr K.," said the manufacturer, "you're under the weather today. You look so depressed." "Yes," said K., putting his hand to his brow, "a headache, family troubles." "Ah, yes," said the manufacturer, who was a hasty man and could never listen quietly to anybody, "we all have our troubles." K. had involuntarily taken a step toward the door, as if to show the manufacturer out, but the latter said: "Herr K., there's another little matter I should mention to you. I'm afraid this isn't exactly the moment to bother you with it, but the last two times I've been here I forgot to mention it. And if I put off mentioning it any longer it will probably lose its point altogether. And that would be a pity, since my information may have some real value for you." Before K. had time to make any reply the man stepped up close to him, tapped him with one finger on the chest, and said in a low voice: "You're involved in a case, aren't you?" K. started back, crying out: "The Assistant Manager told you that." "Not at all," said the manufacturer. "How should the Assistant Manager know anything about it?" "How do you know about it?" asked K., pulling himself together. "I pick up scraps of information about the Court now and then," said the manufacturer, "and that accounts for what I have to mention." "So many people seem to be connected with the Court!" said K. with a bowed head, as he led the manufacturer back to the desk. They sat down as before and the manufacturer began: "Unfortunately it isn't much that I can tell you. But in these affairs one shouldn't leave the smallest stone unturned. Besides, I feel a strong desire to help you, no matter how modest the help. We have always been good business friends till now, haven't we? Well, then." K. wanted to excuse himself for his behavior that morning, but the manufacturer would not hear of it, pushed his attaché case firmly under his arm to show that he was in a hurry to go, and continued: "I heard of your case from a man called Titorelli. He's a painter, Titorelli is only his professional name, I don't know at all what his real name is. For years he has been in the habit of calling at my office from time to time, bringing little paintings for which I give him a sort of alms—he's almost a beggar. And they're not bad pictures, moors and heaths and so on. These deals—we have got into the way of them—pass off quite smoothly. But there was a time when he turned up too frequently for my taste, I told him so, we fell into conversation, I was curious to know how he could keep himself going entirely by his painting, and I discovered to my astonishment that he really earned his living as a portrait painter. He worked for the Court, he said. For what Court, I asked. And then he told me about this Court. With your experience you can well imagine how amazed I was at the tales he told me. Since then he brings me the latest news from the Court every time he arrives, and in this way I have gradually acquired a considerable insight into its workings. Of course Titorelli wags his tongue too freely, and I often have to put a stopper on him, not only because he's certainly a liar, but chiefly because a business man like myself has so many troubles of his own that he can't afford to bother much about other people's.

That's only by the way. Perhaps—I thought to myself—
Titorelli might be of some use to you, he knows many of
the Judges, and even if he can hardly have much influence himself, he can at least advise you how to get in touch
with influential men. And even if you can't take him as an
oracle, still it seems to me that in your hands his information might become important. For you are almost as
good as a lawyer yourself. I'm always saying: The Chief
Clerk is almost a lawyer. Oh, I have no anxiety about
your case. Well, would you care to go and see Titorelli?
On my recommendation he will certainly do all he can for
you; I really think you should go. It needn't be today, of
course, some time, any time will do. Let me add that you
needn't feel bound to go just because I advise you to, not
in the least. No, if you think you can dispense with
Titorelli, it's certainly better to leave him entirely out of
it. Perhaps you've a detailed plan of your own already
drawn up and Titorelli might spoil it. Well, in that case
you'd much better not go to see him. And it would certainly mean swallowing one's pride to go to such a fellow
for advice. Anyhow, do just as you like. Here is my letter
of recommendation and here is the address."

K. took the letter, feeling dashed, and stuck it in his
pocket. Even in the most favorable circumstances the advantages which this recommendation could procure him
must be outweighed by the damage implied in the fact
that the manufacturer knew about his trial and that the
painter was spreading news of it. He could hardly bring
himself to utter a few words of thanks to the manufac-

turer, who was already on his way out. "I'll go to see the man," he said as he shook hands at the door, "or write to him to call here, since I'm so busy." "I knew," said the manufacturer, "that you could be depended on to find the best solution. Though I must say I rather thought you would prefer to avoid receiving people like this Titorelli at the Bank, to discuss your case with him. Besides, it's not always advisable to let such people get their hands on letters of yours. But I'm sure you've thought it all over and know what you can do." K. nodded and accompanied the manufacturer a stage farther, through the waiting-room. In spite of his outward composure he was horrified at his own lack of sense. His suggestion of writing to Titorelli had been made merely to show the manufacturer that he appreciated the recommendation and meant to lose no time in making contact with the painter, but, left to himself, he would not have hesitated to write to Titorelli had he regarded the man's assistance as important. Yet it needed the manufacturer to point out the dangers lurking in such an action. Had he really lost his powers of judgment to that extent already? If it were possible for him to think of explicitly inviting a questionable character to the Bank in order to ask for advice about his case with only a door between him and the Assistant Manager, was it not also possible and even extremely probable that he was overlooking other dangers as well, or blindly running into them? There wasn't always someone at his side to warn him. And this was the moment, just when he intended to concentrate all his energies on the case, this was the moment for him to start doubting the alertness of his faculties! Must the difficulties he was faced with in carrying out his office work begin to affect the case as well? At all events he simply could not understand how he could ever have thought of writing to Titorelli and inviting him to come to the Bank.

He was still shaking his head over this when the attendant came up to him and indicated three gentlemen sitting on a bench in the waiting-room. They had already waited for a long time to see K. Now that the attendant accosted K. they sprang to their feet, each one of them eager to seize the first chance of attracting K.'s attention. If the Bank officials were inconsiderate enough to make them waste their time in the waiting-room, they felt entitled in their turn to behave with the same lack of consideration. "Herr K.," one of them began. But K. had sent for his overcoat and said to all three of them while the attendant helped him into it: "Forgive me, gentlemen, I'm sorry to tell you that I have no time to see you at present. I do apologize, but I have to go out on urgent business and must leave the building at once. You have seen for yourselves how long I have been held up by my last caller. Would you be so good as to come back tomorrow or at some other time? Or could we talk the matter over on the telephone, perhaps? Or perhaps you could inform me now, briefly, what your business is, and I shall give you a detailed answer in writing? Though it would certainly be much better if you made an appointment for some other time." These suggestions threw the three men, whose time had thus been wasted to no purpose at all, into such astonishment that they gazed at each other dumbly. "That's settled, then?" asked K., turning to the attendant, who was bringing him his hat. Through the open door of his room he could see that the snow was now falling more thickly. Consequently he put up his coat-collar and buttoned it high round his neck.

At that very moment the Assistant Manager stepped out of the next room, glanced smilingly at K. in his overcoat talking to the clients, and asked: "Are you going out, Herr K.?" "Yes," said K., straightening himself, "I have to go out on business." But the Assistant Manager had already turned to the three clients. "And these gentlemen?" he asked. "I believe they have already been waiting a long time." "We have settled what we are to do," said K. But now the clients could no longer be held in check, they clustered round K. protesting that they would not have waited for hours unless their business had been important, not to say urgent, necessitating immediate discussion at length, and in private at that. The Assistant Manager listened to them for a moment or two, meanwhile observing K., who stood holding his hat and dusting it spasmodically, then he remarked: "Gentlemen, there is a very simple solution. If you will accept me, I will gladly place myself at your disposal instead of the Chief Clerk. Your business must, of course, be attended to at once. We are businessmen like yourselves and know how valuable time is to a businessman. Will you be so good as to come with me?" And he opened the door which led to the waiting-room of his own office.

How clever the Assistant Manager was at poaching on the preserves which K. was forced to abandon! But was not K. abandoning more than was absolutely needful? While with the vaguest and—he could not but admit it— the faintest of hopes, he was rushing away to see an unknown painter, his prestige in the Bank was suffering irreparable injury. It would probably be much better for him to take off his overcoat again and conciliate at least the two clients waiting next door for their turn to receive the Assistant Manager's attention. K. might actually have attempted this if he had not at that moment caught sight of the Assistant Manager himself in K.'s own room, searching through his files as if they belonged to him. In great agitation K. approached the doorway of the room and the Assistant Manager exclaimed: "Oh, you're not gone yet." He turned his face toward K.— the deep lines scored upon it seemed to speak of power rather than old age—and immediately resumed his search. "I'm looking for a copy of an agreement," he said, "which the firm's representative says should be among your papers. Won't you help me to look?" K. took a step forward, but the Assistant Manager said: "Thanks, now I've found it," and carrying a huge package of documents, which obviously contained not only the copy of the agreement but many other papers as well, he returned to his office.

"I'm not equal to him just now," K. told himself, "but once my personal difficulties are settled he'll be the first to feel it, and I'll make him suffer for it, too." Somewhat soothed by this thought, K. instructed the attendant, who had been holding open the corridor door for a long time, to inform the Manager at any convenient time that he had gone out on a business call, and then, almost elated at the thought of being able to devote himself entirely to his case for a while, he left the Bank.

He drove at once to the address where the painter lived, in a suburb which was almost at the diametrically opposite end of the town from the offices of the Court. This was an even poorer neighborhood, the houses were still darker, the streets filled with sludge oozing about slowly on top of the melting snow. In the tenement where the painter lived only one wing of the great double door stood open, and beneath the other wing, in the masonry near the ground, there was a gaping hole out of which, just as K. approached, issued a disgusting yellow fluid, steaming hot, from which some rats fled into the adjoining canal. At the foot of the stairs an infant lay face down on the ground bawling, but one could scarcely hear its shrieks because of the deafening din that came from a tinsmith's workshop at the other side of the entry. The door of the workshop was open; three apprentices were standing in a half-circle round some object on which they were beating with their hammers. A great sheet of tin hanging on the wall cast a pallid light, which fell between two of the apprentices and lit up their faces and aprons. K. flung only a fleeting glance at all this, he wanted to finish off here as quickly as possible, he would merely ask the painter a few searching questions and return at once to the Bank. His work at the Bank for the rest of the day would benefit should he have any luck at all on this visit. When he reached the third floor he had to moderate his pace, he was quite out of breath, both the stairs and the stories were disproportionately high, and the painter was said to live quite at the top, in an attic. The air was stifling; there was no well for these narrow stairs, which were enclosed on either side by blank walls, showing only at rare intervals a tiny window very high up. Just as K. paused to take breath, several young girls rushed out of one of the flats and laughingly raced past him up the stairs. K. slowly followed them, catching up with one who had stumbled and been left behind, and as they ascended together he asked her: "Does a painter called Titorelli live here?" The girl, who was slightly hunchbacked and seemed scarcely thirteen years old, nudged him with her elbow and peered up at him knowingly. Neither her youth nor her deformity had saved her from being prematurely debauched. She did not even smile, but stared unwinkingly at K. with shrewd, bold eyes. K. pretended not to have noticed her behavior and asked: "Do you know the painter Titorelli?" She nodded and asked in her turn: "What do you want him for?" K. thought it a good chance to find out a little more about Titorelli while he still had time: "I want him to paint my portrait," he said. "To paint your portrait?" she repeated, letting her jaw fall open, then she gave K. a little slap as if he had said something extraordinarily unexpected or stupid, lifted her abbreviated skirts with both hands, and raced as fast as she could after the other girls, whose shrieks were already dying away in the distance. Yet at the very next turn of the stair K. ran into all of them. Obviously the hunchback had reported K.'s intention, and they were waiting there for him. They stood lined up on either side of the stairway, squeezing against the walls to leave room for K. to pass, and smoothing their skirts down with their hands. All their faces betrayed the same mixture of childishness and depravity which had prompted this idea of making him run the gauntlet between them. At the top end of the row of girls, who now closed in behind K. with spurts of laughter, stood the hunchback ready to lead the way. Thanks to her, he was able to make straight for the right door. He had intended to go on up the main stairs, but she indicated a side-stair that branched off toward Titorelli's dwelling. This stairway was extremely narrow, very long, without any turning, could thus be surveyed in all its length, and was abruptly terminated by Titorelli's door. In contrast to the rest of the stairway this door was relatively brightly lit by a little fan-light set on an angle above it, and was made of unpainted planks on which sprawled the name Titorelli in red, traced in sweeping brush-strokes. K. with his escort was hardly more than halfway up the stairs when someone above, obviously disturbed by the clatter of so many feet, opened the door a little way, and a man who seemed to be wearing nothing but a nightshirt appeared in the opening. "Oh!" he cried when he saw the approaching mob, and promptly vanished. The hunchback clapped her hands in joy, and the other girls crowded K. from behind to urge him on faster.

Yet they were still mounting toward the top when the painter flung the door wide open and with a deep bow invited K. to enter. As for the girls, he turned them off, he would not admit one of them, eagerly as they implored and hard as they tried to enter by force if not by permission. The hunchback alone managed to slip in under his outstretched arm, but he rushed after her, seized her by the skirts, whirled her once round his head, and then set her down before the door among the other girls, who had not dared meanwhile, although he had quitted his post, to cross the threshold. K. did not know what to make of all this, for they seemed to be on the friendliest terms together. The girls outside the door, craning their necks behind one another, shouted various jocular remarks at the painter which K. did not understand, and the painter was laughing too as he almost hurled the hunchback through the air. Then he shut the door, bowed once more to K., held out his hand, and said in introduction: "I'm the painter Titorelli." K. pointed at the door, behind which the girls were whispering, and said: "You seem to be a great favorite here." "Oh, those brats!" said the painter, trying unsuccessfully to button his nightshirt at the neck. He was barefooted and besides the nightshirt had on only a pair of wide-legged yellow linen trousers girt by a belt with a long end flapping to and fro. "Those brats are a real nuisance," he went on, while he desisted from fiddling with his nightshirt—since the top button had just come off—fetched a chair, and urged K. to sit down. "I painted one of them once—not any of those you saw—and since then they've all persecuted me. When I'm here

myself they only come in if I let them, but whenever I
go away there's always at least one of them here. They've
had a key made for my door, and they lend it round. You
can hardly imagine what a nuisance that is. For instance,
if I bring a lady here whom I want to paint, I unlock the
door with my own key and find, say, the hunchback over
there at the table, reddening her lips with my paint
brushes, while her little sisters, who she's supposed to
keep an eye on, are scampering over the whole place and
messing up every corner of the room. Or, and this actually
happened last night, I come home very late—by the way,
that's why I'm in this state of disrepair, and the room
too, please excuse it—I come home late, then, and start
climbing into bed and something catches me by the leg;
I look under the bed and haul out another of these pests.
Why they should make such a set at me I don't know,
you must have noticed yourself that I don't exactly
encourage them. And, of course, all this disturbs me in
my work. If it hadn't been that I have free quarters in
this studio I should have cleared out long ago." Just
then a small voice piped behind the door with anxious
cajolery: "Titorelli, can we come in now?" "No," replied
the painter. "Not even me?" the voice asked again. "Not
even you," said the painter, and he went to the door and
locked it.

Meanwhile K. had been looking round the room; it
would never have occurred to him that anyone could call
this wretched little hole a studio. You could scarcely
take two strides in any direction. The whole room, floor,

walls, and ceiling, was a box of bare wooden planks with cracks showing between them. Opposite K., against a wall, stood a bed with a variegated assortment of coverings. In the middle of the room an easel supported a canvas covered by a shirt whose sleeves dangled on the floor. Behind K. was the window, through which in the fog one could not see farther than the snow-covered roof of the next house.

The turning of the key in the lock reminded K. that he had not meant to stay long. Accordingly he fished the manufacturer's letter from his pocket, handed it to the painter, and said: "I heard of you from this gentleman, an acquaintance of yours, and have come here at his suggestion." The painter hastily read the letter through and threw it on the bed. If the manufacturer had not so explicitly claimed acquaintance with Titorelli as a poor man dependent on his charity, one might actually have thought that Titorelli did not know the manufacturer or at least could not remember him. On top of this he now asked: "Have you come to buy pictures or to have your portrait painted?" K. stared at him in amazement. What could have been in the letter? He had assumed as a matter of course that the manufacturer would tell Titorelli that he had come for no other purpose than to inquire about his case. He had been altogether too rash and reckless in rushing to this man. But he must make a relevant reply of some kind, and so he said with a glance at the easel: "You're working on a painting just now?" "Yes," said Titorelli, stripping the shirt from the easel and throwing it on the bed after the letter. "It's a portrait. A good piece of work, but not quite finished yet." K. was apparently in luck, the opportunity to mention the Court was being literally thrown at his head, for this was obviously the portrait of a Judge. Also it strikingly resembled the portrait hanging in the lawyer's office. True, this was quite a different Judge, a stout man with a black bushy beard which reached far up on his cheeks on either side; moreover the other portrait was in oils, while this was lightly and indistinctly sketched in pastel. Yet everything else showed a close resemblance, for here too the Judge seemed to be on the point of rising menacingly from his high seat, bracing himself firmly on the arms of it. "That must be a Judge," K. felt like saying at once, but he checked himself for the time being and approached the picture as if he wished to study the detail. A large figure rising in the middle of the picture from the high back of the chair he could not identify, and he asked the painter whom it was intended to represent. It still needed more detail, the painter replied, and fetched a crayon from a table, armed with which he worked a little at the outline of the figure, but without making it any more recognizable to K. "It is Justice," said the painter at last. "Now I can recognize it," said K. "There's the bandage over the eyes, and here are the scales. But aren't there wings on the figure's heels, and isn't it flying?" "Yes," said the painter, "my instructions were to paint it like that; actually it is Justice and the goddess of Victory in one." "Not a very good combination, surely," said K., smiling. "Justice must stand quite still, or else the scales will waver and a just verdict will become impossible." "I had to follow my client's instructions," said the painter. "Of course," said K., who had not wished to give any offense by his remark. "You have painted the figure as it actually stands above the high seat." "No," said the painter, "I have neither seen the figure nor the high seat, that is all invention, but I am told what to paint and I paint it." "How do you mean?" asked K., deliberately pretending that he did not understand. "It's surely a Judge sitting on his seat of justice?" "Yes," said the painter, "but it is by no means a high Judge and he has never sat on such a seat in his life." "And yet he has himself painted in that solemn posture? Why, he sits there as if he were the actual President of the Court." "Yes, they're very vain, these gentlemen," said the painter. "But their superiors give them permission to get themselves painted like that. Each one of them gets precise instructions how he may have his portrait painted. Only you can't judge the detail of the costume and the seat itself from this picture, unfortunately, pastel is really unsuited for this kind of thing." "Yes," said K., "it's curious that you should have used pastel." "My client wished it," said the painter, "he intends the picture for a lady." The sight of the picture seemed to have roused his ardor, he rolled up his shirt-sleeves, took several crayons in his hand, and as K. watched the delicate crayon-strokes a reddish shadow began to grow round the head of the Judge, a shadow which tapered off in long rays as it approached the edge of the picture. This play of shadow bit by bit surrounded the head like a halo or a high mark of distinction. But the figure of Justice was left bright except for an almost imperceptible touch of shadow; that brightness brought the figure sweeping right into the foreground and it no longer suggested the goddess of Justice, or even the goddess of Victory, but looked exactly like a goddess of the Hunt in full cry. The painter's activities absorbed K. against his will, and in the end he began to reproach himself for having stayed so long without even touching on the business that brought him. "What is the name of this Judge?" he asked suddenly. "I'm not allowed to tell," replied the painter, stooping over the picture and ostentatiously ignoring the guest whom at first he had greeted with such consideration. K. put this down to caprice and was annoyed that his time should be wasted in such a manner. "You're in the confidence of the Court, I take it?" he asked. The painter laid down his crayons at once, straightened himself, rubbed his hands, and looked at K. with a smile. "Come out with the truth," he said. "You want to find out something about the Court, as your letter of recommendation told me, I may say, and you started talking about my paintings only to win me over. But I don't take that ill, you could hardly know that that wasn't the right way to tackle me. Oh, please don't apologize!" he said sharply, as K. tried to make some excuse. And then he continued: "Besides, you were quite right in what you said; I am in the confidence of the Court." He paused, as if he wanted to give K. time to digest this fact. Now they could hear the girls behind the door again. They seemed to be crowding round the keyhole, perhaps they could see into the room through the cracks in the door as well. K. abandoned any attempt at apology, for he did not want to deflect the conversation, nor did he want the painter to feel too important, and so become in a sense inaccessible, accordingly he asked: "Is your position an official appointment?" "No," said the painter curtly, as if the question had cut him short. K., being anxious to keep him going, said: "Well, such unrecognized posts often carry more influence with them than the official ones." "That is just how it is with me," said the painter, knitting his brow and nodding. "The manufacturer mentioned your case to me yesterday, he asked me if I wouldn't help you; I said to him: 'Let the man come and see me some time,' and I'm delighted to see you here so soon. The case seems to lie very near your heart, which, of course, is not in the least surprising. Won't you take off your coat for a moment?" Although K. had it in mind to stay only for a short time, this request was very welcome to him. He had begun to feel the air in the room stifling, several times already he had eyed with amazement a little iron stove in the corner which did not seem even to be working; the sultry heat in the place was inexplicable. He took off his overcoat, unbuttoning his jacket as well, and the painter said apologetically: "I must have warmth. It's very cozy in here, isn't it? I'm well enough off in that respect." K. said nothing to this, for it was not the warmth that made him so uncomfortable, it was rather the stuffy, oppressive atmosphere; the room could not have been aired for a long time. His discomfort was still more intensified when the painter begged him to sit down on the bed, while he himself took the only chair in the room, which stood beside the easel. Titorelli also seemed to misunderstand K.'s reasons for sitting on the extreme edge of the bed, he urged him to make himself comfortable and actually pushed the reluctant K. deep down among the bedclothes and pillows. Then he returned to his chair again and at last put his first serious question, which made K. forget everything else. "Are you innocent?" he asked. "Yes," said K. The answering of this question gave him a feeling of real pleasure, particularly as he was addressing a private individual and therefore need fear no consequences. Nobody else had yet asked him such a frank question. To savor his elation to the full, he added: "I am completely innocent." "I see," said the painter, bending his head as if in thought. Suddenly he raised it again and said: "If you are innocent, then the matter is quite simple." K.'s eyes darkened, this man who said he was in the confidence of the Court was talking like an ignorant child. "My innocence doesn't make the matter any simpler," said K. But after all he could not help smiling, and then he slowly shook his head. "I have to fight against countless subtleties in which the Court indulges. And in the end, out of nothing at all, an enormous fabric of guilt will be conjured up." "Yes, yes, of course," said the painter, as if K. were needlessly interrupting the thread of his ideas. "But you're innocent all the same?" "Why, yes," said K. "That's the main thing," said the painter. He was not to be moved by argument, yet in spite of his decisiveness it was not clear whether he spoke out of conviction or out of mere indifference. K. wanted first to be sure of this, so he said: "You know the Court much better than I do, I feel certain, I don't know much more about it than what I've heard from all sorts and conditions of people. But they all agree on one thing, that charges are never made frivolously, and that the Court, once it has brought a charge against someone, is firmly convinced of the guilt of the accused and can be dislodged from that conviction only with the greatest difficulty." "The greatest difficulty?" cried the painter, flinging one hand in the air. "The Court can never be dislodged from that conviction. If I were to paint all the Judges in a row on one canvas and you were to plead your case before it, you would have more hope of success than before the actual Court." "I see," said K. to himself, forgetting that he merely wished to pump the painter.

Again a girl's voice piped from behind the door: "Titorelli, won't he be going away soon now?" "Quiet, there!" cried the painter over his shoulder. "Can't you see that I'm engaged with this gentleman?" But the girl, not to be put off, asked: "Are you going to paint him?" And when the painter did not reply she went on: "Please don't paint him, such an ugly man as that." The others yelled agreement in a confused jabbering. The painter made a leap for the door, opened it a little—K. could see the imploring, outstretched, clasped hands of the girls—and said: "If you don't stop that noise I'll fling you all down the stairs. Sit down here on the steps and see that you keep quiet." Apparently they did not obey him at once, for he had to shout in an imperious voice: "Down with you on the steps!" After that all was still.

"Excuse me," said the painter, returning to K. again. K. had scarcely glanced toward the door, he had left it to the painter to decide whether and in what manner he was to be protected. Even now he scarcely made a movement when the painter bent down to him and whispered in his ear, so that the girls outside might not hear: "These girls belong to the Court too." "What?" cried K., screwing his head round to stare at the painter. But Titorelli sat down again on his chair and said half in jest, half in explanation: "You see, everything belongs to the Court." "That's something I hadn't noticed," said K. shortly; the painter's general statement stripped his remark about the girls of all its disturbing significance. Yet K. sat gazing for some time at the door, behind which the girls were now sitting quietly on the stairs. One of them had thrust a blade of straw through a crack between the planks and was moving it slowly up and down.

"You don't seem to have any general idea of the Court yet," said the painter, stretching his legs wide in front of him and tapping with his shoes on the floor. "But since you're innocent you won't need it anyhow. I shall get you off all by myself." "How can you do that?" asked K. "For you told me yourself a few minutes ago that the Court was quite impervious to proof." "Impervious only to proof which one brings before the Court," said the painter, raising one finger as if K. had failed to perceive a fine distinction. "But it is quite a different matter with one's efforts behind the scenes; that is, in the consulting-rooms, in the lobbies or, for example, in this very studio." What the painter now said no longer seemed incredible to K., indeed it agreed in the main with what he had heard from other people. More, it was actually hopeful in a high degree. If a judge could really be so easily influenced by personal connections as the lawyer insisted, then the painter's connections with these vain functionaries were especially important and certainly not to be undervalued. That made the painter an excellent recruit to the ring of helpers which K. was gradually gathering round him. His talent for organization had once been highly praised in the Bank, and now that he had to act entirely on his own responsibility this was his chance to prove it to the uttermost. Titorelli observed the effect his words had produced upon K. and then said with a slight uneasiness: "Perhaps it strikes you that I talk almost like a jurist? It's my uninterrupted association with the gentlemen of the Court that has made me grow like that. I have many advantages from it, of course, but I'm losing a great deal of my *élan* as an artist." "How did you come in contact with the Judges to begin with?" asked K.; he wanted to win the painter's confidence first, before actually enlisting him in his service. "That was quite simple," said the painter. "I inherited the connection. My father was the Court painter before me. It's a hereditary post. New people are of no use for it. There are so many complicated and various and above all secret rules laid down for the painting of the different grades of functionaries that a knowledge of them is confined to certain families. Over there in that drawer, for instance, I keep all my father's drawings, which I never show to anyone. And only a man who has studied them can possibly paint the Judges. Yet even if I were to lose them, I have enough rules tucked away in my head to make my post secure against all comers. For every Judge insists on being painted as the great old Judges were painted, and nobody can do that but me." "Yours is an enviable situation," said K., who was thinking of his own post in the Bank. "So your position is unassailable?" "Yes, unassailable," replied the painter, proudly bracing his shoulders. "And for that reason, too, I can venture to help a poor man with his trial now and then." "And how do you do it?" asked K., as if it were not himself who had just been described as a poor man. But Titorelli refused to be sidetracked and went on: "In your case, for instance, as you are completely innocent, this is the line I shall take." The repeated mention of his innocence was already making K. impatient. At moments it seemed to him as if the painter were offering his help on the assumption that the trial would turn out well, which made his offer worthless. But in spite of his doubts K. held his tongue and did not interrupt the man. He was not prepared to renounce Titorelli's assistance, on that point he was decided; the painter was no more questionable as an ally than the lawyer. Indeed he very much preferred the painter's offer of assistance, since it was made so much more ingenuously and frankly.

Titorelli drew his chair closer to the bed and continued in a low voice: "I forgot to ask you first what sort of acquittal you want. There are three possibilities, that is, definite acquittal, ostensible acquittal, and indefinite postponement. Definite acquittal is, of course, the best, but I haven't the slightest influence on that kind of verdict. As far as I know, there is no single person who could influence the verdict of definite acquittal. The only deciding factor seems to be the innocence of the accused. Since you're innocent, of course it would be possible for you to ground your case on your innocence alone. But then you would require neither my help nor help from anyone."

This lucid explanation took K. aback at first, but he replied in the same subdued voice as the painter: "It seems to me that you're contradicting yourself." "In what way?" asked the painter patiently, leaning back with a smile. The smile awoke in K. a suspicion that he was now about to expose contradictions not so much in the painter's statements as in the Court procedure itself. However, he did not retreat, but went on: "You made the assertion earlier that the Court is impervious to proof, later you qualified that assertion by confining it to the public sessions of the Court, and now you actually say that an innocent man requires no help before the Court. That alone implies a contradiction. But, in addition, you said at first that the Judges can be moved by personal intervention, and now you deny that definite acquittal, as you call it, can ever be achieved by personal intervention. In that lies the second contradiction." "These contradictions are easy to explain," said the painter. "We must distinguish between two things: what is written in the Law, and what I have discovered through personal experience; you must not confuse the two. In the code of the Law, which admittedly I have not read, it is of course laid down on the one hand that the innocent shall be acquitted, but it is not stated on the other hand that the Judges are open to influence. Now, my experience is diametrically opposed to that. I have not met one case of definite acquittal, and I have met many cases of influential intervention. It is possible, of course, that in all the cases known to me there was none in which the accused was really innocent. But is not that improbable? Among so many cases no single case of innocence? Even as a child I used to listen carefully to my father when he spoke of cases he had heard about; the Judges, too, who came to his studio were always telling stories about the Court, in our circle it is in fact the sole topic of discussion; no sooner did I get the chance to attend the Court myself than I took full advantage of it; I have listened to countless cases in their most crucial stages, and followed them as far as they could be followed, and yet—I must admit it— I have never encountered one case of definite acquittal." "Not one case of acquittal, then," said K. as if he were speaking to himself and his hopes, "but that merely confirms the opinion that I have already formed of this Court. It is a pointless institution from any point of view. A single executioner could do all that is needed." "You mustn't generalize," said the painter in displeasure. "I have only quoted my own experience." "That's quite enough," said K. "Or have you ever heard of acquittals in earlier times?" "Such acquittals," replied the painter, "are said to have occurred. Only it is very difficult to prove the fact. The final decisions of the Court are never recorded, even the Judges can't get hold of them, consequently we have only legendary accounts of ancient cases. These legends certainly provide instances of acquittal; actually the majority of them are about acquittals, they can be believed, but they cannot be proved. All the same, they shouldn't be entirely left out of account, they must have an element of truth in them, and besides they are very beautiful. I myself have painted several pictures founded on such legends." "Mere legends cannot alter my opinion," said K., "and I fancy that one cannot appeal to such legends before the Court?" The painter laughed. "No, one can't do that," he said. "Then there's no use talking about them," said K., willing for the time being to accept the painter's opinions, even where they seemed improbable or contradicted other reports he had heard. He had no time now to inquire into the truth of all the painter said, much less contradict it, the utmost he could hope to do was to get the man to help him in some way, even should the help prove inconclusive. Accordingly he said: "Let us leave definite acquittal out of account, then; you mentioned two other possibilities as well." "Ostensible acquittal and postponement. These are the only possibilities," said the painter. "But won't you take off your jacket before we go on to speak of them? You look very hot." "Yes," said K., who had been paying no attention to anything but the painter's expositions, but now that he was reminded of the heat found his forehead drenched in sweat. "It's almost unbearable." The painter nodded as if he comprehended K.'s discomfort quite well. "Couldn't we open the window?" asked K. "No," replied the painter. "It's only a sheet of glass let into the roof, it can't be opened." Now K. realized that he had been hoping all the time that either the painter or he himself would suddenly go over to the window and fling it open. He was prepared to gulp down even mouthfuls of fog if he could only get air. The feeling of being completely cut off from the fresh air made his head swim. He brought the flat of his hand down on the feather bed and said in a feeble voice: "That's both uncomfortable and unhealthy." "Oh, no," said the painter in defense of his window. "Because it's hermetically sealed it keeps the warmth in much better than a double window, though it's only a simple pane of glass. And if I want to air the place, which isn't really necessary, for the air comes in everywhere through the chinks, I can always open one of the doors or even both of them." Somewhat reassured by this explanation, K. glanced round to discover the second door. The painter saw what he was doing and said: "It's behind you, I had to block it up by putting the bed in front of it." Only now did K. see the little door in the wall. "This is really too small for a studio," said the painter, as if to forestall K.'s criticisms. "I had to manage as best I could. Of course it's a bad place for a bed, just in front of that door. The Judge whom I'm painting just now, for instance, always comes in by that door, and I've had to give him a key for it so that he can wait for me in the studio if I happen to be out. Well, he usually arrives early in the morning, while I'm still asleep. And of course however fast asleep I am, it wakes me with a start when the door behind my bed suddenly opens. You would lose any respect you have for the Judges if you could hear the curses that welcome him when he climbs over my bed in the early morning. I could certainly take the key away from him again, but that would only make things worse. It is easy enough to burst open any of the doors here." All during these exchanges K. kept considering whether he should take off his jacket, but at last he realized that if he did not he would be incapable of staying any longer in the room, so he took it off, laying it, however, across his knee, to save time in putting it on again whenever the interview was finished. Scarcely had he taken off his jacket when one of the girls cried: "He's taken off his jacket now," and he could hear them all crowding to peer through the cracks and view the spectacle for themselves. "The girls think," said the painter, "that I'm going to paint your portrait and that's why you are taking off your jacket." "I see," said K., very little amused, for he did not feel much better than before, although he was now sitting in his shirt-sleeves. Almost morosely he asked: "What did you say the other two possibilities were?" He had already forgotten what they were called. "Ostensible acquittal and indefinite postponement," said the painter. "It lies with you to choose between them. I can help you to either of them, though not without taking some trouble, and, as far as that is concerned, the difference between them is that ostensible acquittal demands temporary concentration, while postponement taxes your strength less but means a steady strain. First, then, let us take ostensible acquittal. If you decide on that, I shall write down on a sheet of paper an affidavit of your innocence. The text for such an affidavit has been handed down to me by my father and is unassailable. Then with this affidavit I shall make a round of the Judges I know, beginning, let us say, with the Judge I am painting now, when he comes for his sitting tonight. I shall lay the affidavit before him, explain to him that you are innocent, and guarantee your innocence myself. And that is not merely a formal guarantee but a real and binding one." In the eyes of the painter there was a faint suggestion of reproach that K. should lay upon him the burden of such a responsibility. "That would be very kind of you," said K. "And the Judge would believe you and yet not give me a definite acquittal?" "As I have already explained," replied the painter. "Besides, it is not in the least certain that every Judge will believe me; some Judges, for instance, will ask to see you in person. And then I should have to take you with me to call on them. Though when that happens

the battle is already half won, particularly as I should
tell you beforehand, of course, exactly what line to take
with each Judge. The real difficulty comes with the Judges
who turn me away at the start—and that's sure to happen too. I shall go on petitioning them, of course, but
we shall have to do without them, though one can afford
to do that, since dissent by individual Judges cannot affect the result. Well then, if I get a sufficient number of
Judges to subscribe to the affidavit, I shall then deliver
it to the Judge who is actually conducting your trial. Possibly I may have secured his signature too, then everything will be settled fairly soon, a little sooner than usual.
Generally speaking, there should be no difficulties worth
mentioning after that, the accused at this stage feels su-
premely confident. Indeed it's remarkable, but true, that
people's confidence mounts higher at this stage than after
their acquittal. There's no need for them to do much more.
The Judge is covered by the guarantees of the other
Judges subscribing to the affidavit, and so he can grant
an acquittal with an easy mind, and though some formalities will remain to be settled, he will undoubtedly grant
the acquittal to please me and his other friends. Then
you can walk out of the Court a free man." "So then I'm
free," said K. doubtfully. "Yes," said the painter, "but
only ostensibly free, or more exactly, provisionally free.
For the Judges of the lowest grade, to whom my acquaintances belong, haven't the power to grant a final acquittal,
that power is reserved for the highest Court of all, which is
quite inaccessible to you, to me, and to all of us. What the

prospects are up there we do not know and, I may say in passing, do not even want to know. The great privilege, then, of absolving from guilt our Judges do not possess, but they do have the right to take the burden of the charge off your shoulders. That is to say, when you are acquitted in this fashion the charge is lifted from your shoulders for the time being, but it continues to hover above you and can, as soon as an order comes from on high, be laid upon you again. As my connection with the Court is such a close one, I can also tell you how in the regulations of the Law Court offices the distinction between definite and ostensible acquittal is made manifest. In definite acquittal the documents relating to the case are said to be completely annulled, they simply vanish from sight, not only the charge but also the records of the case and even the acquittal are destroyed, everything is destroyed. That's not the case with ostensible acquittal. The documents remain as they were, except that the affidavit is added to them and a record of the acquittal and the grounds for granting it. The whole dossier continues to circulate, as the regular official routine demands, passing on to the higher Courts, being referred to the lower ones again, and thus swinging backwards and forwards with greater or smaller oscillations, longer or shorter delays. These peregrinations are incalculable. A detached observer might sometimes fancy that the whole case had been forgotten, the documents lost, and the acquittal made absolute. No one really acquainted with the Court could think such a thing. No document is ever lost, the Court never forgets anything. One day—quite unexpectedly—

some Judge will take up the documents and look at them attentively, recognize that in this case the charge is still valid, and order an immediate arrest. I have been speaking on the assumption that a long time elapses between the ostensible acquittal and the new arrest; that is possible and I have known of such cases, but it is just as possible for the acquitted man to go straight home from the Court and find officers already waiting to arrest him again. Then, of course, all his freedom is at an end." "And the case begins all over again?" asked K. almost incredulously. "Certainly," said the painter. "The case begins all over again, but again it is possible, just as before, to secure an ostensible acquittal. One must again apply all one's energies to the case and never give in." These last words were probably uttered because he noticed that K. was looking somewhat collapsed. "But," said K., as if he wanted to forestall any more revelations, "isn't the engineering of a second acquittal more difficult than the first?" "On that point," said the painter, "one can say nothing with certainty. You mean, I take it, that the second arrest might influence the Judges against the accused? That is not so. Even while they are pronouncing the first acquittal the Judges foresee the possibility of the new arrest. Such a consideration, therefore, hardly comes into question. But it may happen, for hundreds of reasons, that the Judges are in a different frame of mind about the case, even from a legal viewpoint, and one's efforts to obtain a second acquittal must consequently be adapted to the changed circumstances, and in general must be every whit as energetic as those that secured the first one." "But this second acquittal isn't final either," said K., turning away his head in repudiation. "Of course not," said the painter. "The second acquittal is followed by the third arrest, the third acquittal by the fourth arrest, and so on. That is implied in the very conception of ostensible acquittal." K. said nothing. "Ostensible acquittal doesn't seem to appeal to you," said the painter. "Perhaps postponement would suit you better. Shall I explain to you how postponement works?" K. nodded. The painter was lolling back in his chair, his nightshirt gaped open, he had thrust one hand inside it and was lightly fingering his breast. "Postponement," he said, gazing in front of him for a moment as if seeking a completely accurate explanation, "postponement consists in preventing the case from ever getting any further than its first stages. To achieve that it is necessary for the accused and his agent, but more particularly his agent, to remain continuously in personal touch with the Court. Let me point out again that this does not demand such intense concentration of one's energies as an ostensible acquittal, yet on the other hand it does require far greater vigilance. You daren't let the case out of your sight, you visit the Judge at regular intervals as well as in emergencies and must do all that is in your power to keep him friendly; if you don't know the Judge personally, then you must try to influence him through other Judges whom you do know, but without giving up your efforts to secure a personal interview. If you neglect none of these things, then you can assume with fair certainty that the case will never pass beyond its first stages. Not that the proceedings are quashed, but the accused is almost as likely to escape sentence as if he were free. As against ostensible acquittal postponement has this advantage, that the future of the accused is less uncertain, he is secured from the terrors of sudden arrest and doesn't need to fear having to undergo—perhaps at a most inconvenient moment—the strain and agitation which are inevitable in the achievement of ostensible acquittal. Though postponement, too, has certain drawbacks for the accused, and these must not be minimized. In saying this I am not thinking of the fact that the accused is never free; he isn't free either, in any real sense, after the ostensible acquittal. There are other drawbacks. The case can't be held up indefinitely without at least some plausible grounds being provided. So as a matter of form a certain activity must be shown from time to time, various measures have to be taken, the accused is questioned, evidence is collected, and so on. For the case must be kept going all the time, although only in the small circle to which it has been artificially restricted. This naturally involves the accused in occasional unpleasantness, but you must not think of it as being too unpleasant. For it's all a formality, the interrogations, for instance, are only short ones; if you have neither the time nor the inclination to go, you can excuse yourself; with some Judges you can even plan your interviews a long time ahead, all that it amounts to is a formal recognition of your status as an accused man by regular appearances before your Judge." Already while these last words were being spoken K. had taken his jacket across his arm and got up. "He's getting up now," came the cry at once from behind the door. "Are you going already?" asked the painter, who had also got up. "I'm sure it's the air here that is driving you away. I'm sorry about it. I had a great deal more to tell you. I have had to express myself very briefly. But I hope my statements were lucid enough." "Oh, yes," said K., whose head was aching with the strain of forcing himself to listen. In spite of K.'s confirmation, the painter went on to sum up the matter again, as if to give him a last word of comfort: "Both methods have this in common, that they prevent the accused from coming up for sentence." "But they also prevent an actual acquittal," said K. in a low voice, as if embarrassed by his own perspicacity. "You have grasped the kernel of the matter," said the painter quickly. K. laid his hand on his overcoat, but could not even summon the resolution to put on his jacket. He would have liked best of all to bundle them both together and rush out with them into the fresh air. Even the thought of the girls could not move him to put on his garments, although their voices were already piping the premature news that he was doing so. The painter was anxious to guess K.'s intentions, so he said: "I take it that you haven't come to any decision yet on my suggestions. That's right. In fact, I should have advised you against it had you attempted an immediate decision. It's like splitting hairs to distinguish the advantages and disadvantages. You must weigh everything very carefully. On the other hand you mustn't lose too much time either." "I'll come back again soon," said K., in a sudden fit of resolution putting on his jacket, flinging his overcoat across his shoulders, and hastening to the door, behind which the girls at once began shrieking. K. felt he could almost see them through the door. "But you must keep your word," said the painter, who had not followed him, "or else I'll have to come to the Bank myself to make inquiries." "Unlock this door, will you?" said K., tugging at the handle, which the girls, as he could tell from the resistance, were hanging on to from outside. "You don't want to be bothered by the girls, do you?" asked the painter. "You had better take this way out," and he indicated the door behind the bed. K. was perfectly willing and rushed back to the bed. But instead of opening the bedside door the painter crawled right under the bed and said from down there: "Wait just a minute. Wouldn't you like to see a picture or two that you might care to buy?" K. did not want to be discourteous, the painter had really taken an interest in him and promised to help him further, also it was entirely owing to K.'s distractedness that the matter of a fee for the painter's services had not been mentioned, consequently he could not turn aside his offer now, and so he consented to look at the pictures, though he was trembling with impatience to be out of the place. Titorelli dragged a pile of unframed canvases from under the bed; they were so thickly covered with dust that when he blew some of it from the topmost, K. was almost blinded and choked by the cloud that flew up. "Wild Nature, a heathscape," said the painter, handing K. the picture. It showed two stunted trees standing far apart from each other in darkish grass. In the background was a many-hued sunset. "Fine," said K., "I'll buy it." K.'s curtness had been unthinking and so he was glad when the painter, instead of being offended, lifted another canvas from the floor. "Here's the companion picture," he said. It might be intended as a companion picture, but there was not the slightest difference that one could see between it and the other, here were the two trees, here the grass, and there the sunset. But K. did not bother about that. "They're fine prospects," he said. "I'll buy both of them and hang them up in my office." "You seem to like the subject," said the painter, fishing out a third canvas. "By a lucky chance I have another of these studies here." But it was not merely a similar study, it was simply the same wild heathscape again. The painter was apparently exploiting to the full this opportunity to sell off his old pictures. "I'll take that one as well," said K. "How much for the three pictures?" "We'll settle that next time," said the painter. "You're in a hurry today and we're going to keep in touch with each other anyhow. I may say I'm very glad you like these pictures and I'll throw in all the others under the bed as well. They're heathscapes every one of them, I've painted dozens of them in my time. Some people won't have anything to do with these subjects because they're too somber, but there are always people like yourself who prefer somber pictures." But by now K. had no mind to listen to the professional pronouncements of the peddling painter. "Wrap the pictures up," he cried, interrupting Titorelli's garrulity, "my attendant will call tomorrow and fetch them." "That isn't necessary," said the painter. "I think I can manage to get you a porter to take them along with you now." And at last he reached over the bed and unlocked the door. "Don't be afraid to step on the bed," he said. "Everybody who comes here does that." K. would not have hesitated to do it even without his invitation, he had actually set one foot plump on the middle of the feather bed, but when he looked out through the open door he drew his foot back again. "What's this?" he asked the painter. "What are you surprised at?" returned the painter, surprised in his turn. "These are the Law Court offices. Didn't you know that there were Law Court offices here? There are Law Court offices in almost every attic, why should this be an exception? My studio really belongs to the Law Court offices, but the Court has put it at my disposal." It was not so much the discovery of the Law Court offices that startled K.; he was much more startled at himself, at his complete ignorance of all things concerning the Court. He accepted it as a fundamental principle for an accused man to be always forearmed, never to let himself be caught napping, never to let his eyes stray unthinkingly to the right when his judge was looming up on the left—and against that very principle he kept offending again and again. Before him stretched a long passage, from which was wafted an air compared to which the air in the studio was refreshing. Benches stood on either side of the passage, just as in the lobby of the offices that were handling K.'s case. There seemed, then, to be exact regulations for the interior disposition of these offices. At the moment there was no great coming and going of clients.

A man was half sitting, half reclining on a bench, his face was buried in his arms and he seemed to be asleep; another man was standing in the dusk at the end of the passage. K. now stepped over the bed, the painter following him with the pictures. They soon found an usher— by this time K. recognized these men from the gold button added to the buttons on their ordinary civilian clothing— and the painter gave him instructions to accompany K. with the pictures. K. tottered rather than walked, keeping his handkerchief pressed to his mouth. They had almost reached the exit when the girls came rushing to meet them, so K. had not been spared even that encounter. The girls had obviously seen the second door of the studio opening and had made a detour at full speed, in order to get in. "I can't escort you any farther," cried the painter laughingly, as the girls surrounded him. "Till our next meeting. And don't take too long to think it over!" K. did not even look back. When he reached the street he hailed the first cab that came along. He must get rid of the usher, whose gold button offended his eyes, even though, likely enough, they escaped everyone else's attention. The usher, zealously dutiful, got up beside the coachman on the box, but K. made him get down again. Midday was long past when K. reached the Bank. He would have liked to leave the pictures in the cab, but was afraid that some day he might be required to recall himself to the painter by their means. So he had them carried into his office and locked them in the bottom drawer of his desk, to save them for the next few days at least from the eyes of the Assistant Manager.

CHAPTER EIGHT

Block, the Tradesman / Dismissal of the Lawyer

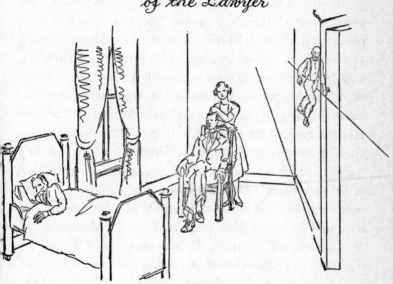

AT LONG last K. had made up his mind to take his case out of the lawyer's hands. He could not quite rid himself of doubts about the wisdom of this step, but his conviction of its necessity prevailed. To screw himself up to the decision cost him a lot of energy, on the day when he resolved to visit the lawyer his work lagged behind, he had to stay very late in the office, and so he did not reach the lawyer's door until well past ten o'clock. Before actually ringing the bell he thought it over once again; it might be better to dismiss the lawyer by telephone or by letter, a personal interview was bound to prove painful. Still, he did not want to lose the advantage of a personal interview, any other mode of dismissal would be accepted in silence or with a few formal words of acknowledgment, and unless he were to extract information from Leni he would never learn how the lawyer had reacted to the dismissal and what consequences for himself were likely to ensue according to the lawyer's opinion, which was not entirely negligible. Face to face with the lawyer, one could spring the dismissal on him as a surprise, and however guarded the man might be, K. would be easily able to learn from his demeanor all that he wanted to know. It was even possible that he might perceive the wisdom of leaving the case in the lawyer's hands after all and might withdraw his ultimatum.

The first ring at the lawyer's door produced, as usual, no result. "Leni could be a little quicker," thought K. But it was enough to be thankful for that no third party had come nosing in, as usually happened, the man in the dressing-gown, for instance, or some other interfering creature. K. glanced at the farther door as he pressed the button a second time, but on this occasion both doors remained firmly shut. At last a pair of eyes appeared at the peephole in the lawyer's door, but they were not

Leni's eyes. Someone shot back the bolt, but still blocked the way as a preliminary measure, calling back into the house: "It's him," and only then flinging the door open. K. had been pushing against the door, for he could already hear a key being hastily turned in the neighboring lock, and when it suddenly opened he was literally precipitated into the hall and caught a glimpse of Leni, for whom the warning cry must have been intended, rushing down the lobby in her shift. He peered after her for a moment and then turned to see who had opened the door. It was a dried-up little man with a long beard, he was holding a candle in one hand. "Are you employed here?" asked K. "No," said the man, "I don't belong to the house, I'm only the lawyer's client, I've come here on business." "In your shirt-sleeves?" asked K., indicating the man's inadequate attire. "Oh, excuse me," said the man, peering at himself by the light of the candle as if he had been unaware of his condition. "Is Leni your mistress?" inquired K. curtly. He was straddling his legs slightly, his hands, in which he was holding his hat, clasped behind his back. The mere possession of a thick greatcoat gave him a feeling of superiority over the meager little fellow. "Oh, God," said the other, raising one hand before his face in horrified repudiation, "no, no, what are you thinking of?" "You look an honest man," said K., smiling, "but all the same—come along." He waved him on with his hat, urging him to go first. "What's your name?" K. asked as they were proceeding. "Block, a tradesman," said the little man, turning round to introduce himself, but K. would not suffer him to remain standing. "Is that your real name?" went on K. "Of course," came the answer, "why should you doubt it?" "I thought you might have some reason for concealing your name," said K. He was feeling at ease now, at ease as one is when speaking to an inferior in some foreign country, keeping one's own affairs to oneself and discussing with equanimity the other man's interests, which gain consequence for the attention one bestows on them yet can be dismissed at will. As they came to the lawyer's study K. halted, opened the door, and called to the fellow, who was meekly advancing along the lobby: "Not so fast, show a light here." K. fancied that Leni might have hidden herself in the study; he made the tradesman shine the candle into all the corners, but the room was empty. In front of the Judge's portrait K. caught the fellow from behind by the braces and pulled him back. "Do you know who that is?" he asked, pointing upward at the picture. The man raised the candle, blinked up at the picture, and said : "It's a Judge." "A high Judge?" asked K., stationing himself beside the other to observe what impression the portrait made on him. The man gazed up with reverence. "It is a high Judge," he said. "You haven't much insight," said K., "that's the lowest of the low among the examining Judges." "Now, I remember," said the man, letting the candle sink. "I've been told that before." "But of course," cried K., "how could I forget, of course you must have heard it before." "But why, why must I?" asked the man, moving toward the door, for K. was propelling him from behind. When they were out in the lobby, K. said : "I suppose you know where Leni's hiding?" "Hiding?" said he. "No, she should be in the kitchen making soup for the lawyer." "Why didn't you tell me that at first?" asked K. "I was going to take you there, but you called me back," answered the man, as if bewildered by these contradictory demands. "You fancy you're being very sly," said K., "lead the way then!" K. had never yet been in the kitchen, and it was surprisingly large and well furnished. The cooking-stove alone was three times the size of an ordinary stove; the rest of the fittings could not be seen in detail since the sole light came from a small lamp hanging near the door. Leni was standing by the stove in a white apron, as usual, emptying eggs into a pan that stood over an alcohol flame. "Good evening, Joseph," she said, glancing over her shoulder. "Good evening," said K., waving the tradesman to a chair some distance away, on which the man obediently sat down. Then K. went quite close up behind Leni, leaned over her shoulder, and asked: "Who's this man?" Leni put her disengaged arm round K., stirring the soup with the other, and pulled him forward. "He's a miserable creature," she said, "a poor tradesman called Block. Just look at him." They both glanced round. The tradesman was sitting in the chair K. had indicated for him; having blown out the candle, which was no longer needed, he was snuffing the wick with his fingers. "You were in your shift," said K., turning Leni's head forcibly to the stove. She made no answer. "Is he your lover?" asked K. She reached for the soup pan, but K. imprisoned both her hands and said: "Give me an answer!" She said: "Come into the study and I'll explain everything." "No," said K., "I want you to tell me here." She slipped her arm into his and tried to give him a kiss, but K. fended her off, saying: "I don't want you to kiss me now." "Joseph," said Leni, gazing at him imploringly and yet frankly, "surely you're not jealous of Herr Block?" Then she turned to the tradesman and said: "Rudi, come to the rescue, you can see that I'm under suspicion, put that candle down." One might have thought that he had been paying no attention, but he knew at once what she meant. "I can't think what you have to be jealous about either," he said, with no great acumen. "Nor can I, really," replied K., regarding him with a smile. Leni laughed outright and profited by K.'s momentary distraction to hook herself on to his arm, whispering: "Leave him alone now, you can see the kind of creature he is. I've shown him a little kindness because he's one of the lawyer's best clients, but that was the only reason. What about yourself? Do you want to see the lawyer tonight? He's far from well today; all the same, if you like I'll tell him you're here. But you're certainly going to spend the night with me. It's such a long time since you were here last, even the lawyer has been asking after you. It won't do to neglect your case! And I've got some information for you, too, things I've found out. But the first thing is to get your coat off." She helped him out of his coat, took his hat from him, ran into the hall to hang them up, and then ran back to keep an eye on the soup. "Shall I announce you first or give him his soup first?" "Announce me first," said K. He felt irritated, for he had originally intended to discuss the whole case thoroughly with Leni, especially the question of dismissing the lawyer, and the tradesman's being there spoiled the situation. But again it struck him that his affairs were too important to allow of decisive interference by a petty tradesman, and so he called back Leni, who was already out in the lobby. "No, let him have his soup first," he said, "it'll strengthen him for his interview with me, and he'll need it." "So you're one of the lawyer's clients too," said the tradesman quietly from his corner, as if confirming a statement. His comment was but ill received. "What's that got to do with you?" said K., and Leni put in: "You be quiet." To K. Leni said: "Well, then, I'll take him his soup first," and she poured the soup into a bowl. "Only there's a risk that he might go to sleep immediately, he always falls asleep after food." "What I have to say to him will keep him awake all right," said K., who wanted to let it be known that his interview with the lawyer promised to be momentous; he wanted Leni to question him about it and only then would he ask her advice. But Leni merely followed out to the letter the orders he gave her. As she passed him with the bowl of soup she deliberately nudged him and whispered: "I'll announce you the minute he's finished his soup, so that I can have you back as soon as possible." "Get along," said K., "get along with you."

"Don't be so cross," she said, turning right round in the doorway, soup bowl and all.

K. stood gazing after her; now it was definitely settled that he would dismiss the lawyer, and it was just as well that he should have no chance of discussing it beforehand with Leni; the whole affair was rather beyond her scope and she would certainly have tried to dissuade him, possibly she might even have prevailed on him to put it off this time, and he would have continued to be a prey to doubts and fears until in the long run he carried out his resolve, since it was too imperative a resolve to be dropped. But the sooner it was carried out the less he would suffer. Perhaps, after all, the tradesman might be able to throw some light on the subject.

K. turned toward the man, who immediately gave a start as if to jump to his feet. "Keep your seat," said K., drawing a chair up beside him. "You're an old client of the lawyer's, aren't you?" "Yes," said the tradesman, "a very old client." "How long has he been in charge of your affairs?" asked K. "I don't quite know what affairs you mean," said the tradesman; "in my business affairs—I'm a grain dealer—the lawyer has been my representative since the very beginning, that must be for the past twenty years, and in my private case, which is probably what you are thinking of, he has been my lawyer also from the beginning, which is more than five years ago. Yes, well over five years now," he confirmed, drawing out an old pocketbook. "I have it all written down here. I can give you the exact dates if you like.

It's difficult to keep them in one's head. My case probably goes back further than I said, it began just after my wife's death, certainly more than five and a half years ago." K. moved his chair closer to the man. "So the lawyer has an ordinary practice as well?" he asked. This alliance between Court and jurisprudence seemed to him uncommonly reassuring. "Of course," said the tradesman, adding in a whisper: "They even say that he's better at ordinary law than at the other kind." Then apparently he regretted having ventured so far, for he laid a hand on K.'s shoulder and said: "Don't give me away, I implore you." K. patted him soothingly on the thigh and said: "No, I'm not an informer." "He's vindictive, you see," said Block. "Surely he wouldn't harm a faithful client like you?" said K. "Oh, yes," said Block, "once he's roused he draws no distinctions; besides, I'm not really faithful to him." "How is that?" asked K. "Perhaps I oughtn't to tell you," said Block doubtfully. "I think you can risk it," said K. "Well," said Block, "I'll tell you a certain amount, but in your turn you must tell me one of your secrets, so that we each have a hold over the other." "You're very cautious," said K., "but I'll entrust you with a secret that will allay all your suspicions. In what way, then, are you unfaithful to the lawyer?" "Well," said the tradesman hesitatingly, as if confessing something dishonorable, "I have other lawyers as well as him." "That's nothing very dreadful," said K., somewhat disappointed. "It's supposed to be," said the tradesman, who had not breathed freely since making his confession, but now gained a little confidence from K.'s rejoinder. "It's not allowed. And least of all is it allowed to consult pettifogging lawyers when one is the client of an official lawyer. And that's exactly what I've been doing, I have five pettifogging lawyers besides him." "Five!" cried K., amazed at the mere number, "five lawyers besides this one?" Block nodded: "I'm even negotiating with a sixth one." "But what do you need so many for?" asked K. "I need every one of them," said Block. "Tell me why, will you?" asked K. "With pleasure," said the tradesman. "To begin with, I don't want to lose my case, as you can well understand. And so I daren't ignore anything that might help me; if there's even the faintest hope of an advantage for myself I daren't reject it. That's why I've spent every penny I possess on this case of mine. For instance, I've drawn all the money out of my business; my business offices once filled nearly a whole floor of the building where now I need only a small back room and an apprentice. Of course it's not only the withdrawal of my money that has brought the business down, but the withdrawal of my energies. When you're trying to do anything you can to help your case along you haven't much energy to spare for other things." "So you've been working on your own behalf as well," interrupted K., "that's precisely what I wanted to ask you about." "There's not much to tell you," said the tradesman. "I did try my hand at it in the beginning, but I soon had to give it up. It's too exhausting, and the results are disappointing. Merely attending the Court to keep an eye on things proved too much, for me, at least. It makes you feel limp even to sit about and wait your turn. But you know yourself what the air's like." "How do you know I was ever up there?" asked K. "I happened to be in the lobby when you were passing through." "What a coincidence!" cried K., quite carried away and completely forgetting the ridiculous figure the tradesman had cut in his estimation. "So you saw me! You were in the lobby when I passed through. Yes, I did pass through the lobby once." "It's not such a coincidence as all that," said the tradesman, "I'm up there nearly every day." "I'm likely to be up there, too, often enough after this," said K., "only I can hardly expect to be received with such honor as on that occasion. Everyone stood up. I suppose they took me for a Judge." "No," said the tradesman, "it was the usher we stood up for. We knew you were an accused man. News of that kind spreads rapidly." "So you knew that already," commented K., "then perhaps you thought me somewhat high and mighty. Did no one comment on it?" "Not unfavorably," said the tradesman. "But it's all nonsense." "What's nonsense?" asked K. "Why do you insist on asking?" said the tradesman, irritably. "Apparently you don't know the people there yet and you might take it up wrongly. You must remember that in these proceedings things are always coming up for discussion that are simply beyond reason, people are too tired and distracted to think and so they take refuge in superstition. I'm as bad as anyone myself. And one of the superstitions is that you're supposed to tell from a man's face, especially the line of his lips, how his case is going to turn out. Well, people declared that judging from the expression of your lips you would be found guilty, and in the near future too. I tell you, it's a silly superstition and in most cases completely belied by the facts, but if you live among these people it's difficult to escape the prevailing opinion. You can't imagine what a strong effect such superstitions have. You spoke to a man up there, didn't you? And he could hardly utter a word in answer. Of course there's many a reason for being bewildered up there, but one of the reasons why he couldn't bring out an answer was the shock he got from looking at your lips. He said afterwards that he saw on your lips the sign of his own condemnation." "On my lips?" asked K., taking out a pocket mirror and studying them. "I can't see anything peculiar about my lips. Do you?" "I don't either," said the tradesman, "not in the least." "How superstitious these people are!" cried K. "Didn't I tell you so?" asked the other. "Do they meet each other so frequently, then, and exchange all these ideas?" queried K., "I've never had anything to do with them myself." "As a rule they don't mix much," said the tradesman, "it would be hardly possible, there are too many of them. Besides, they have few interests in common. Occasionally a group believes it has found a common interest, but it soon finds out its mistake. Combined action against the Court is impossible. Each case is judged on its own merits, the Court is very conscientious about that, and so common action is out of the question. An individual here and there may score a point in secret, but no one hears it until afterwards, no one knows how it has been done. So there's no real community, people come across each other in the lobbies, but there's not much conversation. The superstitious beliefs are an old tradition and increase automatically." "I saw all the people in the lobby," remarked K., "and thought how pointless it was for them to be hanging about." "It's not pointless at all," said Block, "the only pointless thing is to try taking independent action. As I told you, I have five lawyers besides this one. You might think—as I did once—that I could safely wash my hands of the case. But you would be wrong. I have to watch it more carefully than if I had only one lawyer. I suppose you don't understand that?" "No," said K., laying his hand appealingly on the other's to keep him from talking so fast, "I would only like to beg you to speak more slowly, all these things are extremely important to me and I can't follow so quickly." "I'm glad you reminded me," said the tradesman; "of course you're a newcomer, you're young in the matter. Your case is six months old, isn't it? Yes, I've heard about it. An infant of a case! But I've had to think these things out I don't know how many times, they've become a second nature to me." "I suppose you're thankful to think that your case is so far advanced," asked K., not liking to make a direct inquiry how the tradesman's case stood. But he received no direct answer either. "Yes, I've carried my burden for five long years," said Block, drooping his head, "it's no small achievement, that." Then he sat silent for a little. K. listened to hear if Leni were coming back. On the one hand he did not want her to come in just then, for he had many questions still to ask, nor did he want her to find him so deep in intimate conversation with the tradesman, but on the other hand he was annoyed because she was spending so much time with the lawyer while he was in the house, much more time than was needed for handing over a bowl of soup. "I can still remember exactly," the tradesman began again, and K. was at once all attention, "the days when my case was at much the same stage as yours is now. I had only this lawyer then, and I wasn't particularly satisfied with him." "Now I'm going to find out everything," thought K., nodding his head eagerly, as if that would encourage the tradesman to bring out all the right information. "My case," Block continued, "wasn't making any progress; there were of course interrogations, and I attended every one of them, I collected evidence, I even laid all my account books before the Court, which wasn't necessary at all, as I discovered later. I kept running to the lawyer, he presented various petitions——" "Various petitions?" asked K. "Yes, certainly," said Block. "That's an important point for me," said K., "for in my case he's still working on the first petition. He's done nothing at all yet. Now I see how scandalously he's neglecting me." "There might be several excellent reasons why the petition isn't ready yet," said Block. "Let me tell you that my petitions turned out later to be quite worthless. I even had a look at one of them, thanks to the kindness of a Court official. It was very learned but it said nothing of any consequence. Crammed with Latin in the first place, which I don't understand, and then whole pages of general appeals to the Court, then flattering references to particular officials, who weren't actually named but were easy enough for anyone versed in these matters to recognize, then self-praise of the lawyer himself, in the course of which he addressed the Court with a crawling humility, ending up with an analysis of various cases from ancient times that were supposed to resemble mine. I must say that this analysis, in so far as I could follow it, was very careful and thorough. You mustn't think that I'm passing judgment on the lawyer's work; that petition, after all, was only one of many; but at any rate, and this is what I'm coming to, I couldn't see that my case was making any progress." "What kind of progress did you expect to see?" asked K. "A good question," said the tradesman with a smile, "it's very rarely that progress in these cases is visible at all. But I didn't know that then. I'm a businessman, and I was much more of a businessman then than now, I wanted to see palpable results, the whole negotiation should be coming to a finish, I thought, or taking a regular upward course. Instead of that there were only ceremonial interviews, one after another, mostly of the same tenor, where I could reel off the responses like a litany; several times a week Court messengers came to my place of business or to my house or wherever I was to be found, and that, of course, was a nuisance (today I'm much better off in that respect, for telephone calls bother me less); and besides all that, rumors about my case began to spread among my business friends, but especially among my relatives, so that I was being injured on all sides without the slightest sign of any intention on the part of the Court to begin legal proceedings in the near future. So I went to the lawyer and made my complaint. He treated me to a lengthy explanation, but refused utterly to take action in my sense of the word, saying that nobody could influence the Court to appoint a day for hearing a case, and that to urge anything of the kind in a petition—as I wanted him to do—was simply unheard of and would only ruin myself and him. I thought: what this lawyer won't or can't do, another will and can. So I looked round for other lawyers. I may as well tell you now that not one of them ever prayed the Court to fix a day for the trial of my case, or managed to obtain such a trial; it is really an impossibility—with one qualification that I shall explain later—and the lawyer had not misled me there, although I found no cause for regretting having called in the other lawyers. I suppose Dr. Huld has told you plenty of things about the pettifogging lawyers, he has probably described them as contemptible creatures, and so they are, in a sense. All the same, in speaking of them and contrasting himself and his colleagues with them he always makes a small mistake, which I may as well call your attention to in passing. He always refers to the lawyers of his own circle as the 'great lawyers,' by way of contrast. Now that's untrue; any man can call himself 'great,' of course, if he pleases, but in this matter the Court tradition must decide. And according to the Court tradition, which recognizes both small and great lawyers outside the hole-and-corner lawyers, our lawyer and his colleagues rank only among the small lawyers, while the really great lawyers, whom I have merely heard of and never seen, stand as high above the small lawyers as these above the despised pettifogging lawyers." "The really great lawyers?" asked K. "Who are they, then? How does one get at them?" "So you've never heard of them," said Block. "There's hardly an accused man who doesn't spend some time dreaming of them after hearing about them. Don't you give way to that temptation. I have no idea who the great lawyers are and I don't believe they can be got at. I know of no single instance in which it could be definitely asserted that they had intervened. They do defend certain cases, but one cannot achieve that oneself. They only defend those whom they wish to defend, and they never take action, I should think, until the case is already beyond the province of the lower Court. In fact, it's better to put them out of one's mind altogether, or else one finds interviews with ordinary lawyers so stale and stupid, with their niggling counsels and proposals—I have experienced it myself—that one feels like throwing the whole thing up and taking to bed with one's face to the wall. And of course that would be stupider still, for even in bed one wouldn't find peace." "So you didn't entertain the thought of going to the great lawyers?" asked K. "Not for long," said Block, smiling again; "unfortunately one can never quite forget about them, especially during the night. But at that time I was looking for immediate results, and so I went to the pettifogging lawyers."

"How close you've got!" cried Leni, who had come back with the soup bowl and was standing in the doorway. They were indeed sitting so close to each other that they must have bumped their heads together at the slightest movement; Block, who was not only a small man but stooped forward as he sat, spoke so low that K. was forced to bend down to hear every word he said. "Give us a moment or two," cried K., warning Leni off; the hand which he still kept on the tradesman's hand twitched with irritation. "He wanted me to tell him about my case," the tradesman said to Leni. "Well, go on telling him," said she. Her tone in speaking to Block was kindly but a little condescending. That annoyed K.; the man, after all, as he had discovered, possessed a certain value, he had experiences and knew how to communicate them. Leni at least probably misjudged him. To K.'s further annoyance Leni removed the candle, which he had been grasping all this time, wiped his hand with her apron, and knelt down to scratch off some tallow which had dripped on his trousers. "You were going to tell me about pettifogging lawyers," said K., pushing Leni's hand away without comment. "What do you think you're doing?" she asked, giving K. a small slap and resuming her task. "Yes, the pettifogging lawyers," said Block, passing his hand over his brow as if in reflection. K. wanted to help him out and added: "You were looking for immediate results and so you went to the pettifogging lawyers." "That's right," said Block, but he did not continue. "Perhaps he doesn't want to talk of it before Leni," thought K., suppressing his impatience to hear the rest of the story at once and not urging the man any more.

"Did you announce me?" he asked Leni instead. "Of course," she said, "and the lawyer's waiting for you. Leave Block alone now, you can talk to him later, for he's staying here." K. still hesitated. "Are you staying here?" he asked the tradesman; he wanted the man to speak for himself, he disliked the way Leni discussed him as if he were absent, he was filled with obscure irritation today against Leni. And again it was Leni who did the speaking: "He often sleeps here." "Sleeps here?" cried K.; he had thought that the tradesman was waiting only till the interview with the lawyer was brought to a speedy conclusion, and that then they would go off together to discuss the whole business thoroughly in private. "Yes," said Leni, "everyone isn't like you, Joseph, getting an interview with the lawyer at any hour they choose. It doesn't even seem to strike you as surprising that a sick man like the lawyer should agree to see you at eleven o'clock at night. You take all that your friends do for you far too much as a matter of course. Well, your friends, or I at least, like doing things for you. I don't ask for thanks and I don't need any thanks, except that I want you to be fond of me." "Fond of you?" thought K., and only after framing the words did it occur to him: "But I am fond of her." Yet he said, ignoring the rest of her remarks: "He receives me because I'm his client. If I needed the help of others even to get an interview with my lawyer, I'd have to be bowing and scraping at every turn." "How difficult he is today, isn't he?" said Leni to the tradesman. "Now it's my turn to be treated as if I were absent," thought K., and his irritation extended to the tradesman too when the latter, copying Leni's discourtesy, remarked: "But the lawyer has other reasons for agreeing to see him. His is a much more interesting case than mine. Besides, it's only beginning, probably still at a hopeful stage, and so the lawyer likes handling it. You'll see a difference later on." "Yes, yes," said Leni, regarding the tradesman laughingly, "what a tongue-wagger!" Here she turned to K. and went on: "You mustn't believe a word he says. He's a nice fellow but his tongue wags far too much. Perhaps that's why the lawyer can't bear him. Anyhow, he never consents to see him unless he's in a good mood. I've tried my best to change that, but it can't be done. Only fancy, sometimes I tell the lawyer Block is here and he puts off seeing him for three days together. And then if Block isn't on the spot when he's called for, his chance is gone and I have to announce him all over again. That's why I let Block sleep here, for it has happened before now that he has been rung for in the middle of the night. So Block has to be ready night and day. It sometimes happens, too, that the lawyer changes his mind, once he has discovered that Block actually is on the spot, and refuses the interview." K. threw a questioning glance at the tradesman, who nodded and said, with the same frankness as before, or perhaps merely discomposed by a feeling of shame: "Yes, one becomes very dependent on one's lawyer in the course of time." "He's just pretending to complain," said Leni, "for he likes sleeping here, as he has often told me." She went over to a small door and pushed it open. "Would you like to see his bedroom?" she asked. K. followed her and gazed from the threshold into a low-roofed chamber with no window which had room only for a narrow bed. One had to climb over the bedposts to get into the bed. At the head of it, in a recess in the wall, stood a candle, an ink well, and a pen, carefully arranged beside a bundle of papers, probably documents concerning the case. "So you sleep in the maid's room?" asked K., turning to the tradesman. "Leni lets me have it," said he, "it's very convenient." K. gave him a long look; the first impression he had had of the man was perhaps, after all, the right one; Block was a man of experience, certainly, since his case had lasted for years, yet he had paid dearly for his experience. Suddenly K. could no longer bear the sight of him. "Put him to bed," he cried to Leni, who seemed not to comprehend what he meant. Yet what he wanted was to get away to the lawyer and dismiss from his life not only Huld but Leni and the tradesman too. Before he could reach the room, however, Block spoke to him in a low voice: "Herr K." K. turned round angrily. "You've forgotten your promise," said the tradesman, reaching out imploringly toward K. "You were going to tell me one of your secrets." "True," said K., casting a glance also at Leni, who was regarding him attentively, "well, listen then, though it's almost an open secret by this time. I'm going to the lawyer now to dismiss him from my case." "Dismiss him!" exclaimed the tradesman; he sprang from his seat and rushed round the kitchen with upraised arms, crying as he ran: "He's dismissing the lawyer!" Leni made a grab at K. but Block got in her way, and she requited him with her fists. Still clenching her fists, she chased after K., who was well ahead of her. He got inside the lawyer's room before she caught up with him; he tried to close the door behind him, but Leni put one foot in the crack and reached through it to grab his arm and haul him back. K. caught her wrist and squeezed it so hard that she had to loose her hold with a whimper. She did not dare to force her way right in, but K. made certain by turning the key in the lock.*

"I've been waiting a long time for you," said the lawyer from his bed, laying on the table a document which he had been reading by the light of a candle, and putting on a pair of spectacles through which he scrutinized K. sharply. Instead of apologizing K. said: "I shan't detain you long." This remark, as it was no apology, the lawyer ignored, saying: "I shall not see you again at such a late hour." "That agrees with my intentions," retorted K. The lawyer gave him a questioning look and said: "Sit down." "Since you ask me to," said K., pulling up a chair to the bedside table and seating himself. "I fancied I heard you locking the door," said the lawyer. "Yes," said K., "that was because of Leni." He was not thinking of shielding anyone, but the lawyer went on: "Has she been pestering you again?" "Pestering me?" asked K. "Yes," said the lawyer, chuckling until stopped by a fit of coughing, after which he began to chuckle once more. "I suppose you can't have helped noticing that she pesters you?" he asked, patting K.'s hand, which in his nervous distraction he had put on the bedside table and now hastily withdrew. "You don't attach much importance to it," went on the lawyer as K. remained silent. "So much the better. Or else I might have had to apologize for her. It's a peculiarity of hers, which I have long forgiven her and which I wouldn't mention now had it not been for your locking the door. This peculiarity of hers, well, you're the last person I should have to explain it to, but you're looking so bewildered that I feel I must, this peculiarity of hers consists in her finding nearly all accused men attractive. She makes up to all of them, loves them all, and is evidently also loved in return; she often tells me about these affairs to amuse me, when I allow her. It doesn't surprise me so much as it seems to surprise you. If you have the right eye for these things, you can see that accused men are often attractive. It's a remarkable phenomenon, almost a natural law. For of course the fact of being accused makes no alteration in a man's appearance that is immediately obvious and recognizable. These cases are not like ordinary criminal cases, most of the defendants continue in their usual vocations, and if they are in the hands of a good lawyer their interests don't suffer much. And yet those who are experienced in such matters can pick out one after another all the accused men in the largest of crowds. How do they know them? you will ask. I'm afraid my answer won't seem satisfactory. They know them because accused men are always the most attractive. It cannot be guilt that makes them attractive, for—it behooves me to say this as a lawyer, at least—they aren't all guilty, and it can't be the justice of the penance laid on them that makes them attractive in anticipation, for they aren't all going to be punished, so it must be the mere charge preferred against them that in some way enhances their attraction. Of course some are much more attractive than others. But they are all attractive, even that wretched creature Block."

By the time the lawyer finished this harangue K. had completely regained his composure, he had even nodded as if in complete agreement with the last words, whereas he was really confirming his own long-cherished opinion that the lawyer invariably attempted, as now, to bring in irrelevant generalizations in order to distract his attention from the main question, which was: how much actual work had been achieved in furthering the case? Presumably the lawyer felt that K. was more hostile than usual, for now he paused to give him the chance of putting in a word, and then asked, since K. remained silent: "Did you come here this evening for some specific reason?" "Yes," said K., shading the light of the candle a little with one hand so as to see the lawyer better. "I came to tell you that I dispense with your services as from today." "Do I understand you rightly?" asked the lawyer, half propping himself up in bed with one hand on the pillows. "I expect so," said K., sitting bolt upright as if on guard. "Well, that's a plan we can at least discuss," said the lawyer after a pause. "It's no plan, it's a fact," said K. "Maybe," said the lawyer, "but we mustn't be in too much of a hurry." He used the word "we" as if he had no intention of letting K. detach himself, as if he meant to remain at least K.'s adviser if not his official agent. "It's not a hurried decision," said K., slowly getting up and retreating behind his chair, "I have thought it well over, perhaps even for too long. It is my final decision." "Then allow me a few comments," said the lawyer, throwing off his feather quilt and sitting on the edge of the bed. His bare legs, sprinkled with white hairs, trembled with cold. He asked K. to hand him a rug from the sofa. K. fetched the rug and said: "It's quite unnecessary for you to expose yourself to a chill." "I have grave enough reasons for it," said the lawyer, wrapping the bed quilt round his shoulders and tucking the rug round his legs. "Your uncle is a friend of mine, and I've grown fond of you, too, in the course of time. I admit it freely. It's nothing to be ashamed of." This outburst of sentiment from the old man was most unwelcome to K., for it compelled him to be more explicit in his statements, which he would have liked to avoid, and disconcerted him too, as he frankly admitted to himself, although without in the least affecting his decision. "I am grateful for your friendly attitude," he said, "and I appreciate that you have done all you could do for what you thought to be my advantage. But for some time now I have been growing convinced that your efforts are not enough. I shall not, of course, attempt to thrust my opinions on a man so much older and more experienced than myself; if I have unwittingly seemed to do so, please forgive me, but I have grave enough reasons for it, to use your own phrase, and I am convinced that it is necessary to take much more energetic steps in this case of mine than have been taken so far." "I understand you," said the lawyer, "you are feeling impatient." "I'm not impatient," said K., a little irritated and therefore less careful in his choice of words, "you must have noticed on my very first visit here, when I came with my uncle, that I did not take my case very seriously; if I wasn't forcibly reminded of it, so to speak, I forgot it completely. Still my uncle insisted on my engaging you as my representative, and I did so to please him. One would naturally have expected the case to weigh even less on my conscience after that, since after all one engages a lawyer to shift the burden a little on to his shoulders. But the very opposite of that resulted. I was never so much plagued by my case as I have been since engaging you to represent me. When I stood alone I did nothing at all, yet it hardly bothered me; after acquiring a lawyer, on the other hand, I felt that the stage was set for something to happen, I waited with unceasing and growing expectancy for your intervention, and you did nothing whatever. I admit that you gave me information about the Court which I probably could not have obtained elsewhere. But that is hardly adequate assistance for a man who feels this thing secretly encroaching upon him and literally touching him to the quick." K. had pushed the chair away and now stood upright, his hands in his jacket pockets. "After a certain stage in one's practice," said the lawyer quietly in a low voice,* "nothing really new ever happens. How many of my clients have reached the same point in their cases and stood before me in exactly the same frame of mind as you and said the same things!" "Well," said K., "then they were all as much in the right as I am. That doesn't counter my arguments." "I wasn't trying to counter them," said the lawyer, "but I should like to add that I expected you to show more judgment than the others, especially as I have given you more insight into the workings of the Court and my own procedure than I usually give my clients. And now I cannot help seeing that in spite of everything you haven't enough confidence in me. You don't make things very easy for me." How the lawyer was humbling himself before K.! And without any regard for his professional dignity, which was surely most sensitive on this very point. Why was he doing it? If appearances spoke truly he was in great demand as a lawyer and wealthy as well, the loss of K. as a client or the loss of his fees could not mean much to such a man. Besides, he was an invalid and should himself have contemplated the advisability of losing clients. Yet he was clinging to K. with an insistence! Why? Was it personal affection for K.'s uncle, or did he really regard the case as so extraordinary that he hoped to win prestige either from defending K. or—a possibility not to be excluded—from pandering to his friends in the Court? His face provided no clue, searchingly as K. scrutinized it. One could almost suppose that he was deliberately assuming a blank expression, while waiting for the effect of his words. But he was obviously putting too favorable an interpretation on K.'s silence when he went on to say: "You will have noticed that although my office is large enough I don't employ any assistants. That wasn't so in former years, there was a time when several young students of the Law worked for me, but today I work alone. This change corresponds in part to the change in my practice, for I have been confining myself more and more to cases like yours, and in part to a growing conviction that has been borne in upon me. I found that I could not delegate the responsibility for these cases to anyone else without wronging my clients and imperiling the tasks I had undertaken. But the decision to cover all the work myself entailed the natural consequences: I had to refuse most of the cases brought to me and apply myself only to those which touched me nearly—and I can tell you there's no lack of wretched creatures even in this very neighborhood, ready to fling themselves on any crumb I choose to throw them. And then I broke down under stress of overwork. All the same, I don't regret my decision, perhaps I ought to have taken a firmer stand and refused more cases, but the policy of devoting myself single-mindedly to the cases I did accept has proved both absolutely necessary and has been justified by the results. I once read a very finely worded description of the difference between a lawyer for ordinary legal rights and a lawyer for cases like these. It ran like this: the one lawyer leads his client by a slender thread until the verdict is reached, but the other lifts his client on his shoulders from the start and carries him bodily without once letting him down until the verdict is reached, and even beyond it. That is true. But it is not quite true to say that I do not at all regret devoting myself to this great task. When, as in your case, my labors are as completely misunderstood, then, yes, then and only then, I come near to regretting it." * This speech, instead of convincing K., only made him impatient. He fancied that the very tone of the lawyer's voice suggested what was in store for him should he yield; the same old exhortations would begin again, the same references to the progress of the petition, to the more gracious mood of this or that official, while not forgetting the enormous difficulties that stood in the way—in short, the same stale platitudes would be brought out again either to delude him with vague false hopes or to torment him with equally vague menaces. That must be stopped once and for all, so he said: "What steps do you propose to take in my case if I retain you as my representative?" The lawyer meekly accepted even this insulting question and replied: "I should continue with those measures that I have already begun." "I knew it," said K., "well, it's a waste of time to go on talking." "I'll make one more attempt," said the lawyer, as if it were K. who was at fault and not himself. "I have an idea that what makes you so wrongheaded not only in your judgment of my legal assistance but also in your general behavior is the fact that you have been treated too well, although you are an accused man, or rather, more precisely, that you have been treated with negligence, with apparent negligence. There's a reason for the negligence, of course; it's often better to be in chains than to be free. But I'd like to show you how other accused men are treated, and perhaps you may learn a thing or two. I shall now send for Block; you'd better unlock the door and sit here beside the bed table." "With pleasure," said K., fulfilling these injunctions; he was always ready to learn. As a precaution, however, he asked once more: "You realize that I am dispensing with your services?" "Yes," said the lawyer, "but you may change your mind about it yet." He lay back in bed again, drew the quilt up to his chin, and turned his face to the wall. Then he rang the bell.

Almost at the same moment Leni was on the spot, darting quick glances to learn what was happening; she seemed to find it reassuring that K. was sitting so quietly beside the lawyer's bed. She nodded to him with a smile, but he gazed at her blankly. "Fetch Block," said the lawyer. Instead of fetching Block, however, she merely went to the door, called out: "Block! The lawyer wants you!" and then, probably because the lawyer had his face turned to the wall and was paying no attention to her, insinuated herself behind K., where she distracted him during all the rest of the proceedings by leaning over the back of his chair or running her fingers, gently and cautiously enough, through his hair and over his temples. In the end K. sought to prevent her by holding on to her hand, which after a little resistance she surrendered to him.

Block had answered the summons immediately, yet he hesitated outside the door, apparently wondering whether he was to come in or not. He raised his eyebrows and cocked his head as if listening for the summons to be repeated. K. could have encouraged the man to come in, but he was determined to make a final break not only with the lawyer but with all the persons in the house, and so he remained motionless. Leni too was silent. Block noticed that at least no one was turning him away, and he tiptoed into the room with anxious face and hands clutched behind him, leaving the door open to secure his retreat. He did not once look at K., but kept his eyes fixed on the humped-up quilt beneath which the lawyer was not even visible, since he had shifted close up to the wall. A voice, however, came from the bed, saying: "Is that Block?" This question acted like a blow upon Block, who had advanced a goodish way; he staggered, as if he had been hit on the chest and then beaten on the back, and, bowing deeply, stood still, answering: "At your service." "What do you want?" asked the lawyer. "You've come at the wrong time." "Wasn't I called for?" said Block, more to himself than to the lawyer, thrusting out his hands as if to guard himself, and preparing to back out. "You were called for," said the lawyer, "and yet you've come at the wrong time." After a pause he added: "You always come at the wrong time." From the moment when the lawyer's voice was heard Block averted his eyes from the bed and stood merely listening, gazing into a far corner, as if the sight of the lawyer were too dazzling to bear. But it was difficult for him even to listen, since the lawyer was speaking close to the wall and in a voice both low and quick. "Do you want me to go away?" asked Block. "Well, since you're here," said the lawyer, "stay!" One might have fancied that instead of granting Block his desire the lawyer had threatened to have him beaten, for the fellow now begin to tremble in earnest. "Yesterday," said the lawyer, "I saw my friend the Third Judge and gradually worked the conversation round to your case. Would you like to know what he said?" "Oh, please," said Block. Since the lawyer made no immediate reply, Block implored him again and seemed on the point of getting down on his knees. But K. intervened with a shout: "What's that you're doing?" Leni had tried to stifle his shout and so he gripped her other hand as well. It was no loving clasp in which he held her; she sighed now and then and struggled to free herself. But it was Block who paid the penalty for K.'s outburst; the lawyer shot the question at him: "Who is your lawyer?" "You are," said Block. "And besides me?" asked the lawyer. "No one beside you," said Block. "Then pay no heed to anyone else," said the lawyer. Block took the full force of these words; he gave K. an angry glare and shook his head violently at him. If these gestures had been translated into speech they would have made a tirade of abuse. And this was the man with whom K. had wished to discuss his own case in all friendliness! "I shan't interfere again," said K., leaning back in his chair. "Kneel on the floor or creep on all fours if you like, I shan't bother." Yet Block had some self-respect left, at least where K. was concerned, for he advanced upon him flourishing his fists and shouting as loudly as he dared in the lawyer's presence: "You're not to talk to me in that tone, it isn't allowed. What do you mean by insulting me? Before the lawyer, too, who admits us here, both of us, you and me, only out of charity? You're no better than I am, you're an accused man too and are involved in a case like me. If none the less you're a gentleman as well, let me tell you I'm as great a gentleman as you, if not a greater. And I'll have you address me as such, yes, you especially. For if you think you have the advantage of me because you're allowed to sit there at your ease and watch me creeping on all fours, as you put it, let me remind you of the old maxim: people under suspicion are better moving than at rest, since at rest they may be sitting in the balance without knowing it, being weighed together with their sins." K. said not a word, he merely stared in unwinking astonishment at this madman. What a change

had come over the fellow in the last hour! Was it his case
that agitated him to such an extent that he could not
distinguish friend from foe? Did he not see that the
lawyer was deliberately humiliating him, for no other
purpose on this occasion than to make a display of his
power before K. and so perhaps cow K. into acquiescence
as well? Yet if Block were incapable of perceiving this,
or if he were so afraid of the lawyer that he could not
allow himself to perceive it, how did it come about that
he was sly enough or brave enough to deceive the lawyer
and deny that he was having recourse to other lawyers?
And how could he be so foolhardy as to attack K., knowing that K. might betray his secret? His foolhardiness
went even further, he now approached the lawyer's bed
and laid a complaint against K. "Dr. Huld," he said, "did
you hear what this man said to me? His case is only a
few hours old compared with mine, and yet, though I have
been five years involved in my case, he takes it on himself
to give me advice. He even abuses me. Knows nothing
at all and abuses me, me, who have studied as closely
as my poor wits allow every precept of duty, piety, and
tradition." "Pay no heed to anyone," said the lawyer,
"and do what seems right to yourself." "Certainly," said
Block, as if to give himself confidence, and then with a
hasty side-glance knelt down close beside the bed. "I'm on
my knees, Dr. Huld," he said. But the lawyer made no
reply.* Block cautiously caressed the quilt with one hand.
In the silence that now reigned Leni said, freeing herself
from K.: "You're hurting me. Let go. I want to be with

Block." She went over and sat on the edge of the bed. Block was greatly pleased by her coming; he made lively gestures, though in dumb show, imploring her to plead his cause with the lawyer. Obviously he was urgently in need of any information which the lawyer might give, but perhaps he only wanted to hand it on to his other lawyers for exploitation. Leni apparently knew exactly the right way to coax the lawyer; she pointed to his hand and pouted her lips as if giving a kiss. Block immediately kissed the hand, repeating the performance twice at Leni's instigation. But the lawyer remained persistently unresponsive. Then Leni, displaying the fine lines of her taut figure, bent over close to the old man's face and stroked his long white hair. That finally evoked an answer. "I hesitate to tell him," said the lawyer, and one could see him shaking his head, perhaps only the better to enjoy the pressure of Leni's hand. Block listened with downcast eyes, as if he were breaking a law by listening. "Why do you hesitate?" asked Leni. K. had the feeling that he was listening to a well-rehearsed dialogue which had been often repeated and would be often repeated and only for Block would never lose its novelty. "How has he been behaving today?" inquired the lawyer instead of answering. Before providing this information Leni looked down at Block and watched him for a moment as he raised his hands toward her and clasped them appealingly together. At length she nodded gravely, turned to the lawyer, and said: "He has been quiet and industrious." An elderly businessman, a man with a long beard, begging a young girl to say a word in his favor! Let him make what private reservations he would, in the eyes of his fellow men he could find no justification. K. did not understand how the lawyer could ever have imagined that this performance would win him over. If the lawyer had not already succeeded in alienating him, this scene would have finished him once and for all. It was humiliating even to an onlooker. So the lawyer's methods, to which K. fortunately had not been long enough exposed, amounted to this: that the client finally forgot the whole world and lived only in hope of toiling along this false path until the end of his case should come in sight. The client ceased to be a client and became the lawyer's dog. If the lawyer were to order this man to crawl under the bed as if into a kennel and bark there, he would gladly obey the order. K. listened to everything with critical detachment, as if he had been commissioned to observe the proceedings closely, to report them to a higher authority, and to put down a record of them in writing. "What has he been doing all day?" went on the lawyer. "I locked him into the maid's room," said Leni, "to keep him from disturbing me at my work, that's where he usually stays, anyhow. And I could peep at him now and then through the ventilator to see what he was doing. He was kneeling all the time on the bed, reading the papers you lent him, which were spread out on the window sill. That made a good impression on me, since the window looks out on an air shaft and doesn't give much light. So the way Block stuck to his reading showed

me how faithfully he does what he is told." "I'm glad
to hear that," said the lawyer. "But did he understand
what he was reading?" All this time Block's lips were
moving unceasingly; he was obviously formulating the
answers he hoped Leni would make. "Well, of course,"
said Leni, "that's something I don't know with certainty.
At any rate, I could tell that he was thorough in his reading. He never got past the same page all day and he was
following the lines with his fingers. Whenever I looked
at him he was sighing to himself as if the reading cost
him a great effort. Apparently the papers you gave him
to read are difficult to understand." "Yes," said the
lawyer, "these scriptures are difficult enough. I don't believe he really understands them. They're meant only
to give him an inkling how hard the struggle is that I
have to carry on in his defense. And for whom do I
carry on this hard struggle? It's almost ridiculous to
put it into words—I do it for Block. He must learn
to understand what that means. Did he read without
stopping?" "Almost without a stop," answered Leni, "he
asked me only once for a drink of water, and I handed
it to him through the ventilator. Then at about eight
o'clock I let him out and gave him something to eat." Block
gave a fleeting glance at K. as if expecting to see him
impressed by this virtuous record. His hopes seemed to
be mounting, his movements were less constrained, and
he kept shifting his knees a little. It was all the more
noticeable that the lawyer's next words struck him rigid.
"You are praising him," said the lawyer. "But that

only makes it more difficult for me to tell him. For the Judge's remarks were by no means favorable either to Block or to his case." "Not favorable?" asked Leni. "How can that be possible?" Block was gazing at her as intently as if he believed her capable of giving a new and favorable turn to the words long pronounced by the Judge. "Not favorable," said the lawyer. "He was even annoyed when I mentioned Block. 'Don't speak about Block,' he said. 'But he's my client,' I said. 'You are wasting yourself on the man,' he said. 'I don't think his case is hopeless,' said I. 'Well, you're wasting yourself on him,' he repeated. 'I don't believe it,' said I, 'Block is sincerely concerned about his case and devotes himself to it. He almost lives in my house to keep in touch with the proceedings. One doesn't often find such zeal. Of course, he's personally rather repulsive, his manners are bad, and he is dirty, but as a client he is beyond reproach'—I said 'beyond reproach,' and it was a deliberate exaggeration. To that he replied: 'Block is merely cunning. He has acquired a lot of experience and knows how to keep on postponing the issue. But his ignorance is even greater than his cunning. What do you think he would say if he discovered that his case had actually not begun yet, if he were to be told that the bell marking the start of the proceedings hadn't even been rung?'—Quiet there, Block," said the lawyer, for Block was just rising up on trembling legs, obviously to implore an explanation. This was the first time the lawyer had addressed Block directly at any length. With lackluster eyes he looked down; his glance was partly vague and partly turned upon Block, who slowly sank back under it on his knees again. "That remark of the Judge's has no possible significance for you," said the lawyer. "Don't get into a panic at every word. If you do it again I'll never tell you anything. I can't begin a statement without your gazing at me as if your final sentence had come. You should be ashamed to behave like that before my client. And you're destroying his confidence in me. What's the matter with you? You're still alive, you're still under my protection. Your panic is senseless. You've read somewhere or other that a man's condemnation often comes unexpectedly from some chance person at some odd time. With many reservations that is certainly true, but it is equally true that your panic disgusts me and appears to betray a lack of the necessary confidence in me. All that I said was to report a remark made by a Judge. You know quite well that in these matters opinions differ so much that the confusion is impenetrable. This Judge, for instance, assumes that the proceedings begin at one point, and I assume that they begin at another point. A difference of opinion, nothing more. At a certain stage of the proceedings there is an old tradition that a bell must be rung. According to the Judge, that marks the beginning of the case, I can't tell you now all the arguments against him, you wouldn't understand them, let it be sufficient for you that there are many arguments against his view." In embarrassment Block sat plucking at the hair of the skin rug lying before the bed; his terror of the Judge's utterance was so great that it ousted for a while his subjection to the lawyer and he was thinking only of himself, turning the Judge's words round and surveying them from all sides. "Block," said Leni in a tone of warning, catching him by the collar and jerking him upward a little. "Leave the rug alone and listen to the lawyer."

This chapter was never completed.

CHAPTER NINE

In the Cathedral

AN ITALIAN colleague, who was on his first visit to the town and was one of the Bank's most influential clients, was to be taken in charge by K. and shown some of the town's art treasures and monuments. It was a commission that K. would once have felt to be an honor, but at the present juncture, now that all his energies were needed even to retain his prestige in the Bank, he accepted it reluctantly. Every hour that he spent away from the Bank was a trial to him; true, he was by no means able to make the best use of his office hours as once he had done, he wasted much time in the merest pretense of doing real work, but that only made made him worry the more when he was not at his desk. In his mind he saw the Assistant Manager, who had always spied upon him, prowling every now and then into his office, sitting down at his desk, running through his papers, receiving clients who had become almost old friends of K.'s in the course of many years, and luring them away from him, perhaps even discovering mistakes that he had made, for K. now saw himself continually threatened by mistakes intruding into his work from all sides which he was no longer able to circumvent. Consequently if he were charged with a mission, however honorable, which involved his leaving the office on business or even taking a short journey—and missions of that kind by some chance had recently come his way fairly often—then he could not help suspecting that there was a plot to get him out of the way while his work was investigated, or at least that he was considered far from indispensable in the office. Most of these missions he could easily have refused. Yet he did not dare do so, since, if there were even the smallest ground for his suspicions, a refusal to go would only have been taken as an admission of fear. For that reason he accepted every one of them with apparent equanimity, and on one occasion when he was expected to take an exhausting two days' journey he even said nothing about a severe chill he had, to avoid the risk of having the prevailing wet autumnal weather advanced as an excuse for his not going. When he came back from this journey with a racking headache, he discovered that he had been selected to act as escort next day for the Italian visitor. The temptation to refuse, for this once, was very great, especially since the charge laid upon him was not strictly a matter of business; still, it was a social duty toward a colleague and doubtless important enough, only it was of no importance to himself, knowing, as he did, that nothing could save him except work well done, in default of which it would not be of the slightest use to him in the unlikely event that the Italian were to find him the most enchanting companion; he shrank from being exiled from his work even for a single day, since he had too great a fear of not being allowed to return, a fear which he well knew to be exaggerated, but which oppressed him all the same. The difficulty on this occasion was to find a plausible excuse; his knowledge of Italian was certainly not very great, but it was at least adequate, and there was a decisive argument in the fact that he had some knowledge of art, acquired in earlier days, which was absurdly overestimated in the Bank owing to his having been for some time, purely as a matter of business, a member of the Society for the

Preservation of Ancient Monuments. Rumor had it that the Italian was also a connoisseur, and if so, the choice of K. to be his escort seemed the natural one.

It was a very wet and windy morning when K. arrived in his office at the early hour of seven o'clock, full of irritation at the program before him, but determined to accomplish at least some work before being distracted from it by the visitor. He was very tired, for he had spent half the night studying an Italian grammar as some slight preparation; he was more tempted by the window, where he had recently been in the habit of spending too much time, than by his desk, but he resisted the temptation and sat down to work. Unfortunately at that very moment the attendant appeared, reporting that he had been sent by the Manager to see if the Chief Clerk was in his office yet, and, if he was, to beg him to be so good as to come to the reception room; the gentleman from Italy had already arrived. "All right," said K., stuffed a small dictionary into his pocket, tucked under his arm an album for sightseers, which he had procured in readiness for the stranger, and went through the Assistant Manager's office into the Manager's room. He was glad that he had turned up early enough to be on the spot immediately when required; probably no one had really expected him to do so. The Assistant Manager's office, of course, was as empty as in the dead of night; very likely the attendant had been told to summon him too, and without result. When K. entered the reception room the two gentlemen rose from their deep armchairs.

The Manager smiled kindly on K., he was obviously delighted to see him, he performed the introduction at once, the Italian shook K. heartily by the hand and said laughingly that someone was an early riser. K. did not quite catch whom he meant, for it was an unfamiliar phrase the sense of which did not dawn on him at once. He answered with a few fluent sentences which the Italian received with another laugh, meanwhile nervously stroking his bushy iron-gray mustache. This mustache was obviously perfumed; one was almost tempted to go close up and have a sniff at it. When they all sat down again and a preliminary conversation began, K. was greatly disconcerted to find that he only partly understood what the Italian was saying. He could understand him almost completely when he spoke slowly and quietly, but that happened very seldom, the words mostly came pouring out in a flood, and he made lively gestures with his head as if enjoying the rush of talk. Besides, when this happened, he invariably relapsed into a dialect which K. did not recognize as Italian but which the Manager could both speak and understand, as indeed K. might have expected, considering that this Italian came from the very south of Italy, where the Manager had spent several years. At any rate, it became clear to K. that there was little chance of communication with the Italian, for the man's French was difficult to follow and it was no use watching his lips for clues, since their movements were covered by the bushy mustache. K. began to foresee vexations and for the moment gave up trying to follow the talk—while the Manager was present to understand all that was said it was an unnecessary effort to make—confining himself to morose observation of the Italian lounging so comfortably and yet lightly in his armchair, tugging every now and then at the sharply peaked corners of his short little jacket, and once raising his arms with loosely fluttering hands to explain something * which K. found it impossible to understand, although he was leaning forward to watch every gesture. In the end, as K. sat there taking no part in the conversation, only mechanically following with his eyes the see-saw of the dialogue, his earlier weariness made itself felt again, and to his horror, although fortunately just in time, he caught himself absent-mindedly rising to turn round and walk away. At long last the Italian looked at his watch and sprang to his feet. After taking leave of the Manager he pressed up to K. so close that K. had to push his chair back in order to have any freedom of movement. The Manager, doubtless seeing in K.'s eye that he was in desperate straits with this unintelligible Italian, intervened so cleverly and delicately that it appeared as if he were merely contributing little scraps of advice, while in reality he was briefly conveying to K. the sense of all the remarks with which the Italian kept on interrupting him. In this way K. learned that the Italian had some immediate business to attend to, that unfortunately he was pressed for time, that he had no intention of rushing round to see all the sights in a hurry, that he would much rather—of course only if K. agreed, the decision lay with K. alone—confine himself to inspecting the Cathedral, but to inspect that thoroughly. He was extremely delighted to have the chance of doing so in the company of such a learned and amiable gentleman—this was how he referred to K., who was trying hard to turn a deaf ear to his words and grasp as quickly as possible what the Manager was saying—and he begged him, if it were convenient, to meet him there in a couple of hours, say at about ten o'clock. He had hopes of being able to arrive there for certain about that time. K. made a suitable rejoinder, the Italian pressed the Manager's hand, then K.'s hand, then the Manager's hand again, and, followed by both of them, turning only half toward them by this time but still maintaining a flow of words, departed toward the door. K. stayed a moment or two with the Manager, who was looking particularly unwell that day. He felt that he owed K. an apology and said—they were standing intimately together—that he had at first intended to escort the Italian himself, but on second thoughts—he gave no definite reason—he had decided that K. had better go. If K. found that he could not understand the man to begin with he mustn't let that upset him, for he wouldn't take long to catch the sense of what was said, and even if he didn't understand very much it hardly mattered, since the Italian cared little whether he was understood or not. Besides, K.'s knowledge of Italian was surprisingly good and he would certainly acquit himself well. With that K. was dismissed to his room. The time still at his disposal he devoted to copying

from the dictionary various unfamiliar words which he
would need in his tour of the Cathedral. It was an unusually exasperating task; attendants came in with letters,
clerks arrived with inquiries, standing in the doorway
when they saw that K. was busy, yet not removing themselves until he answered, the Assistant Manager did not
miss the chance of making a nuisance of himself and appeared several times, taking the dictionary out of K.'s
hand and with obvious indifference turning the pages over;
even clients were dimly visible in the antechamber whenever the door opened, making deprecating bows to call attention to themselves, but uncertain whether they had
been remarked or not—all this activity rotated around
K. as if he were the center of it, while he himself was
occupied in collecting the words he might need, looking
them up in the dictionary, copying them out, practicing
their pronunciation, and finally trying to learn them by
heart. His once excellent memory seemed to have deserted
him, and every now and then he grew so furious with
the Italian who was causing him all this trouble that he
stuffed the dictionary beneath a pile of papers with the
firm intention of preparing himself no further, yet he
could not help seeing that it would not do to march
the Italian round the art treasures of the Cathedral in
dumb silence, and so with even greater rage he took the
dictionary out again.

Just at half past nine, as he was rising to go, the
telephone rang; Leni bade him good morning and asked
how he was; K. thanked her hastily and said he had no

time to talk to her, since he must go to the Cathedral. "To the Cathedral?" asked Leni. "Yes, to the Cathedral." "But why the Cathedral?" asked Leni. K. tried to explain briefly to her, but hardly had he begun when Leni suddenly said: "They're goading you." Pity which he had not asked for and did not expect was more than K. could bear, he said two words of farewell, but even as he hung up the receiver he murmured half to himself and half to the faraway girl who could no longer hear him: "Yes, they're goading me."

By now it was growing late, he was already in danger of not being in time for the appointment. He drove off in a taxicab; at the last moment he remembered the album which he had found no opportunity of handing over earlier, and so took it with him now. He laid it on his knees and drummed on it impatiently with his fingers during the whole of the journey. The rain had slackened, but it was a raw, wet, murky day, one would not be able to see much in the Cathedral, and there was no doubt that standing about on the cold stone flags would make K.'s chill considerably worse.

The Cathedral Square was quite deserted, and K. recollected how even as a child he had been struck by the fact that in the houses of this narrow square nearly all the window blinds were invariably drawn down. On a day like this, of course, it was more understandable. The Cathedral seemed deserted too, there was naturally no reason why anyone should visit it at such a time. K. went through both of the side aisles and saw no one but an old woman muffled in a shawl who was kneeling before a Madonna with adoring eyes. Then in the distance he caught sight of a limping verger vanishing through a door in the wall. K. had been punctual, ten o'clock was striking just as he entered, but the Italian had not yet arrived. He went back to the main entrance, stood there undecidedly for a while and then made the circuit of the building in the rain, to make sure that the Italian was perhaps not waiting at some side door. He was nowhere to be seen. Could the Manager have made some mistake about the hour? How could anyone be quite sure of understanding such a man? Whatever the circumstances, K. would at any rate have to wait half an hour for him. Since he was tired he felt like sitting down, went into the Cathedral again, found on a step a remnant of carpet-like stuff, twitched it with his toe toward a near-by bench, wrapped himself more closely in his greatcoat, turned up his collar, and sat down. By way of filling in time he opened the album and ran idly through it, but he soon had to stop, for it was growing so dark that when he looked up he could distinguish scarcely a single detail in the neighboring aisle.

Away in the distance a large triangle of candle flames glittered on the high altar; K. could not have told with any certainty whether he had noticed them before or not. Perhaps they had been newly kindled. Vergers are by profession stealthy-footed, one never notices them. K. happened to turn round and saw not far behind him the gleam of another candle, a tall thick candle fixed to a pillar. It was lovely to look at, but quite inadequate for illuminating the altarpieces, which mostly hung in the darkness of the side chapels; it actually increased the darkness. The Italian was as sensible as he was discourteous in not coming, for he would have seen nothing, he would have had to content himself with scrutinizing a few pictures piecemeal by the light of K.'s pocket torch. Curious to see what effect it would have, K. went up to a small side chapel near by, mounted a few steps to a low balustrade, and bending over it shone his torch on the altarpiece. The light from a permanent oil-lamp hovered over it like an intruder. The first thing K. perceived, partly by guess, was a huge armored knight on the outermost verge of the picture. He was leaning on his sword, which was stuck into the bare ground, bare except for a stray blade of grass or two. He seemed to be watching attentively some event unfolding itself before his eyes. It was surprising that he should stand so still without approaching nearer to it. Perhaps he had been set there to stand guard. K., who had not seen any pictures for a long time, studied this knight for a good while, although the greenish light of the oil-lamp made his eyes blink. When he played the torch over the rest of the altarpiece he discovered that it was a portrayal of Christ being laid in the tomb, conventional in style and a fairly recent painting. He pocketed the torch and returned again to his seat.

In all likelihood it was now unnecessary to wait any longer for the Italian, but the rain was probably pouring down outside, and since it was not so cold in the Cathedral as K. had expected, he decided to stay there for the present. Quite near him rose the great pulpit, on its small vaulted canopy two plain golden crucifixes were slanted so that their shafts crossed at the tip. The outer balustrade and the stonework connecting it with the supporting column were wrought all over with foliage in which little angels were entangled, now vivacious and now serene. K. went up to the pulpit and examined it from all sides; the carving of the stonework was very carefully wrought, the deep caverns of darkness among and behind the foliage looked as if caught and imprisoned there; K. put his hand into one of them and cautiously felt the contour of the stone; he had never known that this pulpit existed. By pure chance he noticed a verger standing behind the nearest row of benches, a man in a loose-hanging black garment with a snuffbox in his left hand; he was gazing at K. "What's the man after?" thought K. "Do I look a suspicious character? Does he want a tip?" But when he saw that K. had become aware of him, the verger started pointing with his right hand, still holding a pinch of snuff in his fingers, in some vaguely indicated direction. His gestures seemed to have little meaning. K. hesitated for a while, but the verger did not cease pointing at something or other and emphasizing the gesture with nods of his head. "What does the man want?" said K. in a low tone, he did not dare to raise his voice in this place; then he pulled out his purse and made his way along the benches toward him. But the verger at once made a gesture of refusal, shrugged his shoulders, and limped away. With something of the same gait, a quick, limping motion, K. had often as a child imitated a man riding on horseback. "A childish old man," thought K., "with only wits enough to be a verger. How he stops when I stop and peers to see if I am following him!" Smiling to himself, K. went on following him through the side aisle almost as far as the high altar; the old man kept pointing at something, but K. deliberately refrained from looking round to see what he was pointing at, the gesture could have no other purpose than to shake K. off. At last he desisted from the pursuit, he did not want to alarm the old man too much; besides, in case the Italian were to turn up after all, it might be better not to scare away the verger.

As he returned to the nave to find the seat on which he had left the album, K. caught sight of a small side pulpit attached to a pillar almost immediately adjoining the choir, a simple pulpit of plain, pale stone. It was so small that from a distance it looked like an empty niche intended for a statue. There was certainly no room for the preacher to take a full step backward from the balustrade. The vaulting of the stone canopy, too, began very low down and curved forward and upward, although without ornamentation, in such a way that a medium-sized man could not stand upright beneath it, but would have to keep leaning over the balustrade. The whole structure was designed as if to torture the preacher; there seemed no comprehensible reason why it should be there at all while the other pulpit, so large and finely decorated, was available.

And K. certainly would not have noticed it had not a lighted lamp been fixed above it, the usual sign that a sermon was going to be preached. Was a sermon going to be delivered now? In the empty church? K. peered down at the small flight of steps which led upward to the pulpit, hugging the pillar as it went, so narrow that it looked like an ornamental addition to the pillar rather than a stairway for human beings. But at the foot of it, K. smiled in astonishment, there actually stood a priest ready to ascend, with his hand on the balustrade and his eyes fixed on K. The priest gave a little nod and K. crossed himself and bowed, as he ought to have done earlier. The priest swung himself lightly on to the stairway and mounted into the pulpit with short, quick steps. Was he really going to preach a sermon? Perhaps the verger was not such an imbecile after all and had been trying to urge K. toward the preacher, a highly necessary action in that deserted building. But somewhere or other there was an old woman before an image of the Madonna; she ought to be there too. And if it were going to be a sermon, why was it not introduced by the organ? But the organ remained silent, its tall pipes looming faintly in the darkness.

K. wondered whether this was not the time to remove himself quickly; if he did not go now he would have no chance of doing so during the sermon, he would have to stay as long as it lasted, he was already behindhand in the office and was no longer obliged to wait for the Italian; he looked at his watch, it was eleven o'clock. But was there really going to be a sermon? Could K. represent the congregation all by himself? What if he had been a stranger merely visiting the church? That was more or less his position. It was absurd to think that a sermon was going to be preached at eleven in the morning on a weekday, in such dreadful weather. The priest—he was beyond doubt a priest, a young man with a smooth, dark face—was obviously mounting the pulpit simply to turn out the lamp, which had been lit by mistake.

It was not so, however; the priest after examining the lamp screwed it higher instead, then turned slowly toward the balustrade and gripped the angular edge with both hands. He stood like that for a while, looking around him without moving his head. K. had retreated a good distance and was leaning his elbows on the foremost pew. Without knowing exactly where the verger was stationed, he was vaguely aware of the old man's bent back, peacefully at rest as if his task had been fulfilled. What stillness there was now in the Cathedral! Yet K. had to violate it, for he was not minded to stay; if it were this priest's duty to preach a sermon at a certain hour regardless of circumstances, let him do it, he could manage it without K.'s support, just as K.'s presence would certainly not contribute to its effectiveness. So he began slowly to move off, feeling his way along the pew on tiptoe until he was in the broad center aisle, where he advanced undisturbed except for the ringing noise that his lightest footstep made on the stone flags and the echoes that sounded from the vaulted roof faintly but continuously, in manifold and regular progression. K. felt a little forlorn as he advanced, a solitary figure between the rows of empty seats, perhaps with the priest's eyes following him; and the size of the Cathedral struck him as bordering on the limit of what human beings could bear. When he came to the seat where he had left the album he simply snatched the book up without stopping and took it with him. He had almost passed the last of the pews and was emerging into the open space between himself and the doorway when he heard the priest lifting up his voice. A resonant, well-trained voice. How it rolled through the expectant Cathedral! But it was no congregation the priest was addressing, the words were unambiguous and inescapable, he was calling out: "Joseph K.!"

K. paused and stared at the ground before him. For the moment he was still free, he could continue on his way and vanish through one of the small, dark, wooden doors that faced him at no great distance. It would simply indicate that he had not understood the call, or that he had understood it and did not care. But if he were to turn round he would be caught, for that would amount to an admission that he had understood it very well, that he was really the person addressed, and that he was ready to obey. Had the priest called his name a second time K. would certainly have gone on, but as everything remained silent, though he stood waiting a long time, he could not help turning his head a little just to see what the priest was doing. The priest was standing calmly in the pulpit as before, yet it was obvious that he had observed K.'s turn of the head. It would have been like a childish game of hide-and-seek if K. had not turned right round to face him. He did so, and the priest beckoned him to come nearer. Since there was now no need for evasion, K. hurried back—he was both curious and eager to shorten the interview—with long flying strides toward the pulpit. At the first rows of seats he halted, but the priest seemed to think the distance still too great; he stretched out an arm and pointed with sharply bent forefinger to a spot immediately before the pulpit. K. followed this direction too; when he stood on the spot indicated he had to bend his head far back to see the priest at all. "You are Joseph K.," said the priest, lifting one hand from the balustrade in a vague gesture. "Yes," said K., thinking how frankly he used to give his name and what a burden it had recently become to him; nowadays people he had never seen before seemed to know his name. How pleasant it was to have to introduce oneself before being recognized! "You are an accused man," said the priest in a very low voice. "Yes," said K., "so I have been informed." "Then you are the man I seek," said the priest. "I am the prison chaplain." "Indeed," said K. "I had you summoned here," said the priest, "to have a talk with you." "I didn't know that," said K. "I came here to show an Italian round the Cathedral." "That is beside the point," said the priest. "What is that in your hand? Is it a prayer book?" "No," replied K., "it is an album of sights worth seeing in the town." "Lay it down," said the priest. K. threw it away so violently that it flew open and slid some way along the floor with disheveled leaves. "Do you know that your case is going badly?" asked the priest. "I have that idea myself," said K. "I've done what I could, but without any success so far. Of course, my petition isn't finished yet." "How do you think it will end?" asked the priest. "At first I thought it must turn out well," said K., "but now I frequently have my doubts. I don't know how it will end. Do you?" "No," said the priest, "but I fear it will end badly. You are held to be guilty. Your case will perhaps never get beyond a lower Court. Your guilt is supposed, for the present, at least, to have been proved." "But I am not guilty," said K.; "it's a mistake. And, if it comes to that, how can any man be called guilty? We are all simply men here, one as much as the other." "That is true," said the priest, "but that's how all guilty men talk." "Are you prejudiced against me too?" asked K. "I have no prejudices against you," said the priest. "Thank you," said K.; "but all the others who are concerned in these proceedings are prejudiced against me. They are influencing outsiders too. My position is becoming more and more difficult." "You are misinterpreting the facts of the case," said the priest. "The verdict is not suddenly arrived at, the proceedings only gradually merge into the verdict." "So that's how it is," said K., letting his head sink. "What is the next step you propose to take in the matter?" asked the priest. "I'm going to get more help," said K., looking up again to see how the priest took his statement. "There are several possibilities I haven't explored yet." "You cast about too much for outside help," said the priest disapprovingly, "especially from women. Don't you see that it isn't the right kind of help?" "In some cases, even in many I could agree with you," said K., "but not always. Women have great influence. If I could move some women I know to join forces in working for me, I couldn't help winning through. Especially before this Court, which consists almost entirely of petticoat-hunters. Let the Examining Magistrate see a woman in the distance and he knocks down his desk and the defendant in his eagerness to get at her." The priest leaned over the balustrade, apparently feeling for the first time the oppressiveness of the canopy above his head. What fearful weather there must be outside! There was no longer even a murky daylight; black night had set in. All the stained glass in the great window could not illumine the darkness of the wall with one solitary glimmer of light. And at this very moment the verger began to put out the candles on the high altar, one after another. "Are you angry with me?" asked K. of the priest. "It may be that you don't know the nature of the Court you are serving." He got no answer. "These are only my personal experiences," said K. There was still no answer from above. "I wasn't trying to insult you," said K. And at that the priest shrieked from the pulpit: "Can't you see one pace before you?" It was an angry cry, but at the same time sounded like the unwary shriek of one who sees another fall and is startled out of his senses.

Both were now silent for a long time. In the prevailing darkness the priest certainly could not make out K.'s features, while K. saw him distinctly by the light of the small lamp. Why did he not come down from the pulpit? He had not preached a sermon, he had only given K. some information which would be likely to harm him rather than help him when he came to consider it. Yet the priest's good intentions seemed to K. beyond question, it was not impossible that they could come to some agreement if the man would only quit his pulpit, it was not impossible that K. could obtain decisive and acceptable counsel from him which might, for instance, point the way, not toward some influential manipulation of the case, but toward a circumvention of it, a breaking away from it altogether, a mode of living completely outside the jurisdiction of the Court. This possibility must exist, K. had of late given much thought to it. And should the priest know of such a possibility, he might perhaps impart his knowledge if he were appealed to, although he himself belonged to the Court and as soon as he heard the Court impugned had forgotten his own gentle nature so far as to shout K. down.

"Won't you come down here?" said K. "You haven't got to preach a sermon. Come down beside me." "I can come down now," said the priest, perhaps repenting of his outburst. While he detached the lamp from its hook he said: "I had to speak to you first from a distance. Otherwise I am too easily influenced and tend to forget my duty."

K. waited for him at the foot of the steps. The priest stretched out his hand to K. while he was still on the way down from a higher level. "Have you a little time for me?" asked K. "As much time as you need," said the priest, giving K. the small lamp to carry. Even close at hand he still wore a certain air of solemnity. "You are very good to me," said K. They paced side by side up and down the dusky aisle. "But you are an exception among those who belong to the Court. I have more trust in you than in any of the others, though I know many of them. With you I can speak openly." "Don't be deluded," said the priest. "How am I being deluded?" asked K. "You are deluding yourself about the Court," said the priest. "In the writings which preface the Law that particular delusion is described thus: before the Law stands a doorkeeper. To this doorkeeper there comes a man from the country who begs for admittance to the Law. But the doorkeeper says that he cannot admit the man at the moment. The man, on reflection, asks if he will be allowed, then, to enter later. 'It is possible,' answers the doorkeeper, 'but not at this moment.' Since the door leading into the Law stands open as usual and the doorkeeper steps to one side, the man bends down to peer through the entrance. When the doorkeeper sees that, he laughs and says: 'If you are so strongly tempted, try to get in without my permission. But note that I am powerful. And I am only the lowest doorkeeper. From hall to hall, keepers stand at every door, one more powerful than the other. And the sight of the third man is already more than even I can stand.' These are difficulties which the man from the country has not expected to meet, the Law, he thinks, should be accessible to every man and at all times, but when he looks more closely at the doorkeeper in his furred robe, with his huge pointed nose and long thin Tartar beard, he decides that he had better wait until he gets permission to enter. The doorkeeper gives him a stool and lets him sit down at the side of the door. There he sits waiting for days and years. He makes many attempts to be allowed in and wearies the doorkeeper with his importunity. The doorkeeper often engages him in brief conversation, asking him about his home and about other matters, but the questions are put quite impersonally, as great men put questions, and always conclude with the statement that the man cannot be allowed to enter yet. The man, who has equipped himself with many things for his journey, parts with all he has, however valuable, in the hope of bribing the doorkeeper. The doorkeeper accepts it all, saying, however, as he takes each gift: 'I take this only to keep you from feeling that you have left something undone.' During all these long years the man watches the doorkeeper almost incessantly. He forgets about the other doorkeepers, and this one seems to him the only barrier between himself and the Law. In the first years he curses his evil fate aloud; later, as he grows old, he only mutters to himself. He grows childish, and since in his prolonged study of the doorkeeper he has learned to know even the fleas in his fur collar, he begs the very fleas to help him and to persuade the doorkeeper to change his mind. Finally his eyes grow dim and he does not know whether the world is really darkening around him or whether his eyes are only deceiving him. But in the darkness he can now perceive a radiance that streams inextinguishably from the door of the Law. Now his life is drawing to a close. Before he dies, all that he has experienced during the whole time of his sojourn condenses in his mind into one question, which he has never yet put to the doorkeeper. He beckons the doorkeeper, since he can no longer raise his stiffening body. The doorkeeper has to bend far down to hear him, for the difference in size between them has increased very much to the man's disadvantage. 'What do you want to know now?' asks the doorkeeper, 'you are insatiable.' 'Everyone strives to attain the Law,' answers the man, 'how does it come about, then, that in all these years no one has come seeking admittance but me?' The doorkeeper perceives that the man is nearing his end and his hearing is failing, so he bellows in his ear: 'No one but you could gain admittance through this door, since this door was intended for you. I am now going to shut it.' "

"So the doorkeeper deceived the man," said K. immediately, strongly attracted by the story. "Don't be too hasty," said the priest, "don't take over someone else's opinion without testing it. I have told you the story in the very words of the scriptures. There's no mention of deception in it." "But it's clear enough," said K., "and your first interpretation of it was quite right. The doorkeeper gave the message of salvation to the man only when it could no longer help him." "He was not asked the question any earlier," said the priest, "and you must consider, too, that he was only a doorkeeper, and as such fulfilled his duty." "What makes you think he fulfilled his duty?" asked K. "He didn't fulfill it. His duty might have been to keep all strangers away, but this man, for whom the door was intended, should have been let in." "You have not enough respect for the written word and you are altering the story," said the priest. "The story contains two important statements made by the doorkeeper about admission to the Law, one at the beginning, the other at the end. The first statement is: that he cannot admit the man at the moment, and the other is: that this door was intended only for the man. If there were a contradiction between the two, you would be right and the doorkeeper would have deceived the man. But there is no contradiction. The first statement, on the contrary, even implies the second. One could almost say that in suggesting to the man the possibility of future admittance the doorkeeper is exceeding his duty. At that time his apparent duty is only to refuse admittance and indeed many commentators are surprised that the suggestion should be made at all, since the doorkeeper appears to be a precisian with a stern regard for duty. He does not once leave his post during these many years, and he does not shut the door until the very last minute; he is conscious of the importance of his office, for he says: 'I am powerful'; he is respectful to his superiors, for he says: 'I am only the

lowest doorkeeper'; he is not garrulous, for during all
these years he puts only what are called 'impersonal questions'; he is not to be bribed, for he says in accepting a
gift: 'I take this only to keep you from feeling that you
have left something undone'; where his duty is concerned
he is to be moved neither by pity nor rage, for we are told
that the man 'wearied the doorkeeper with his importunity'; and finally even his external appearance hints at a
pedantic character, the large, pointed nose and the long,
thin, black, Tartar beard. Could one imagine a more
faithful doorkeeper? Yet the doorkeeper has other elements in his character which are likely to advantage anyone seeking admittance and which make it comprehensible
enough that he should somewhat exceed his duty in suggesting the possibility of future admittance. For it cannot be denied that he is a little simple-minded and consequently a little conceited. Take the statements he makes
about his power and the power of the other doorkeepers
and their dreadful aspect which even he cannot bear to
see—I hold that these statements may be true enough,
but that the way in which he brings them out shows that
his perceptions are confused by simpleness of mind and
conceit. The commentators note in this connection: 'The
right perception of any matter and a misunderstanding
of the same matter do not wholly exclude each other.'
One must at any rate assume that such simpleness and
conceit, however sparingly manifest, are likely to weaken
his defense of the door; they are breaches in the character
of the doorkeeper. To this must be added the fact that

the doorkeeper seems to be a friendly creature by nature, he is by no means always on his official dignity. In the very first moments he allows himself the jest of inviting the man to enter in spite of the strictly maintained veto aganist entry; then he does not, for instance, send the man away, but gives him, as we are told, a stool and lets him sit down beside the door. The patience with which he endures the man's appeals during so many years, the brief conversations, the acceptance of the gifts, the politeness with which he allows the man to curse loudly in his presence the fate for which he himself is responsible— all this lets us deduce certain feelings of pity. Not every doorkeeper would have acted thus. And finally, in answer to a gesture of the man's he bends down to give him the chance of putting a last question. Nothing but mild impatience—the doorkeeper knows that this is the end of it all—is discernible in the words: 'You are insatiable.' Some push this mode of interpretation even further and hold that these words express a kind of friendly admiration, though not without a hint of condescension. At any rate the figure of the doorkeeper can be said to come out very differently from what you fancied." "You have studied the story more exactly and for a longer time than I have," said K. They were both silent for a little while. Then K. said: "So you think the man was not deceived?" "Don't misunderstand me," said the priest, "I am only showing you the various opinions concerning that point. You must not pay too much attention to them. The scriptures are unalterable and the comments often enough merely express the commentators' despair. In this case there even exists an interpretation which claims that the deluded person is really the doorkeeper." "That's a far-fetched interpretation," said K. "On what is it based?" "It is based," answered the priest, "on the simple-mindedness of the doorkeeper. The argument is that he does not know the Law from inside, he knows only the way that leads to it, where he patrols up and down. His ideas of the interior are assumed to be childish, and it is supposed that he himself is afraid of the other guardians whom he holds up as bogies before the man. Indeed, he fears them more than the man does, since the man is determined to enter after hearing about the dreadful guardians of the interior, while the doorkeeper has no desire to enter, at least not so far as we are told. Others again say that he must have been in the interior already, since he is after all engaged in the service of the Law and can only have been appointed from inside. This is countered by arguing that he may have been appointed by a voice calling from the interior, and that anyhow he cannot have been far inside, since the aspect of the third doorkeeper is more than he can endure. Moreover, no indication is given that during all these years he ever made any remarks showing a knowledge of the interior, except for the one remark about the doorkeepers. He may have been forbidden to do so, but there is no mention of that either. On these grounds the conclusion is reached that he knows nothing about the aspect and significance of the interior, so that he is in a state of delusion. But he is deceived also about his relation to the man from the country, for he is inferior to the man and does not know it. He treats the man instead as his own subordinate, as can be recognized from many details that must be still fresh in your mind. But, according to this view of the story, it is just as clearly indicated that he is really subordinated to the man. In the first place, a bondman is always subject to a free man. Now the man from the country is really free, he can go where he likes, it is only the Law that is closed to him, and access to the Law is forbidden him only by one individual, the door-keeper. When he sits down on the stool by the side of the door and stays there for the rest of his life, he does it of his own free will; in the story there is no mention of any compulsion. But the doorkeeper is bound to his post by his very office, he does not dare go out into the country, nor apparently may he go into the interior of the Law, even should he wish to. Besides, although he is in the service of the Law, his service is confined to this one entrance; that is to say, he serves only this man for whom alone the entrance is intended. On that ground too he is inferior to the man. One must assume that for many years, for as long as it takes a man to grow up to the prime of life, his service was in a sense an empty formality, since he had to wait for a man to come, that is to say someone in the prime of life, and so he had to wait a long time before the purpose of his service could be fulfilled, and, moreover, had to wait on the man's pleasure, for the man came of his own free will. But the termination of his service also depends on the man's term of life, so that to the very end he is subject to the man. And it is emphasized throughout that the doorkeeper apparently realizes nothing of all this. That is not in itself remarkable, since according to this interpretation the doorkeeper is deceived in a much more important issue, affecting his very office. At the end, for example, he says regarding the entrance to the Law: 'I am now going to shut it,' but at the beginning of the story we are told that the door leading into the Law always stands open, and if it always stands open, that is to say at all times, without reference to the life or death of the man, then the doorkeeper cannot close it. There is some difference of opinion about the motive behind the doorkeeper's statement, whether he said he was going to close the door merely for the sake of giving an answer, or to emphasize his devotion to duty, or to bring the man into a state of grief and regret in his last moments. But there is no lack of agreement that the doorkeeper will not be able to shut the door. Many indeed profess to find that he is subordinate to the man even in knowledge, toward the end, at least, for the man sees the radiance that issues from the door of the Law while the doorkeeper in his official position must stand with his back to the door, nor does he say anything to show that he has perceived the change." "That is well argued," said K., after repeating to himself in a low voice several passages from the priest's exposition. "It is well argued, and I am inclined to agree that the doorkeeper is deceived. But that has not made me abandon my former opinion, since both conclusions are to some extent compatible. Whether the doorkeeper is clear-sighted or deceived does not dispose of the matter. I said the man is deceived. If the doorkeeper is clear-sighted, one might have doubts about that, but if the doorkeeper himself is deceived, then his deception must of necessity be communicated to the man. That makes the doorkeeper not, indeed, a deceiver, but a creature so simple-minded that he ought to be dismissed at once from his office. You mustn't forget that the doorkeeper's deceptions do himself no harm but do infinite harm to the man." "There are objections to that," said the priest. "Many aver that the story confers no right on anyone to pass judgment on the doorkeeper. Whatever he may seem to us, he is yet a servant of the Law; that is, he belongs to the Law and as such is beyond human judgment. In that case one must not believe that the doorkeeper is subordinate to the man. Bound as he is by his service, even only at the door of the Law, he is incomparably greater than anyone at large in the world. The man is only seeking the Law, the doorkeeper is already attached to it. It is the Law that has placed him at his post; to doubt his dignity is to doubt the Law itself." "I don't agree with that point of view," said K., shaking his head, "for if one accepts it, one must accept as true everything the doorkeeper says. But you yourself have sufficiently proved how impossible it is to do that." "No," said the priest, "it is not necessary to accept everything as true, one must only accept it as necessary." "A melancholy conclusion," said K. "It turns lying into a universal principle." *

K. said that with finality, but it was not his final judgment. He was too tired to survey all the conclusions arising from the story, and the trains of thought into which it was leading him were unfamiliar, dealing with impalpabilities better suited to a theme for discussion among Court officials than for him. The simple story had lost its clear outline, he wanted to put it out of his mind, and the priest, who now showed great delicacy of feeling, suffered him to do so and accepted his comment in silence, although undoubtedly he did not agree with it.

They paced up and down for a while in silence, K. walking close beside the priest, ignorant of his whereabouts. The lamp in his hand had long since gone out. The silver image of some saint once glimmered into sight immediately before him, by the sheen of its own silver, and was instantaneously lost in the darkness again. To keep himself from being utterly dependent on the priest, K. asked: "Aren't we near the main doorway now?" "No," said the priest, "we're a long way from it. Do you want to leave already?" Although at that moment K. had not been thinking of leaving, he answered at once: "Of course, I must go. I'm the Chief Clerk of a Bank, they're waiting for me, I only came here to show a business friend from abroad round the Cathedral." "Well," said the priest, reaching out his hand to K., "then go." "But I can't find my way alone in this darkness," said K. "Turn left to the wall," said the priest, "then follow the wall without leaving it and you'll come to a door." The priest had already taken a step or two away from him, but K.

cried out in a loud voice, "Please wait a moment." "I am waiting," said the priest. "Don't you want anything more from me?" asked K. "No," said the priest. "You were so friendly to me for a time," said K., "and explained so much to me, and now you let me go as if you cared nothing about me." "But you have to leave now," said the priest. "Well, yes," said K., "you must see that I can't help it." "You must first see who I am," said the priest. "You are the prison chaplain," said K., groping his way nearer to the priest again; his immediate return to the Bank was not so necessary as he had made out, he could quite well stay longer. "That means I belong to the Court," said the priest. "So why should I want anything from you? The Court wants nothing from you. It receives you when you come and it dismisses you when you go."

CHAPTER TEN

The End

ON THE evening before K.'s thirty-first birthday—it was about nine o'clock, the time when a hush falls on the streets—two men came to his lodging. In frock coats, pallid and plump, with top hats that were apparently irremovable. After some exchange of formalities re-

garding precedence at the front door, they repeated the
same ceremony more elaborately before K.'s door. Without having been informed of their visit, K. was sitting also
dressed in black in an armchair near the door, slowly
pulling on a pair of new gloves that fitted tightly over
the fingers, looking as if he were expecting guests. He
stood up at once and scrutinized the gentlemen with curiosity. "So you are meant for me?" he asked. The gentlemen bowed, each indicating the other with the hand that
held the top hat. K. admitted to himself that he had been
expecting different visitors. He went to the window and
took another look at the dark street. Nearly all the windows at the other side of the street were also in darkness;
in many of them the curtains were drawn. At one lighted
tenement window some babies were playing behind bars,
reaching with their little hands toward each other although not able to move themselves from the spot.
"Tenth-rate old actors they send for me," said K. to himself, glancing round again to confirm the impression.
"They want to finish me off cheaply." He turned abruptly
toward the men and asked: "What theater are you playing at?" "Theater?" said one, the corners of his mouth
twitching as he looked for advice to the other, who acted
as if he were a dumb man struggling to overcome a stubborn disability. "They're not prepared to answer questions," said K. to himself and went to fetch his hat.

While still on the stairs the two of them tried to take
K. by the arms, and he said: "Wait till we're in the street,
I'm not an invalid." But just outside the street door they

fastened on him in a fashion he had never before experienced. They kept their shoulders close behind his and instead of crooking their elbows, wound their arms round his at full length, holding his hands in a methodical, practiced, irresistible grip. K. walked rigidly between them, the three of them were interlocked in a unity which would have brought all three down together had one of them been knocked over. It was a unity such as can hardly be formed except by lifeless matter.

Under the street lamps K. attempted time and time again, difficult though it was at such very close quarters, to see his companions more clearly than had been possible in the dusk of his room. "Perhaps they are tenors," he thought, as he studied their fat double chins. He was repelled by the painful cleanliness of their faces. One could literally see that the cleansing hand had been at work in the corners of the eyes, rubbing the upper lip, scrubbing out the furrows at the chin.*

When that occurred to K. he halted, and in consequence the others halted too; they stood on the verge of an open, deserted square adorned with flower beds. "Why did they send you, of all people!" he said; it was more a cry than a question. The gentlemen obviously had no answer to make, they stood waiting with their free arms hanging, like sickroom attendants waiting while their patient takes a rest. "I won't go any farther," said K. experimentally. No answer was needed to that, it was sufficient that the two men did not loosen their grip and tried to propel K. from the spot; but he resisted them.

"I shan't need my strength much longer, I'll expend all the strength I have," he thought. Into his mind came a recollection of flies struggling away from the flypaper till their little legs were torn off. "The gentlemen won't find it easy."

And then before them Fräulein Bürstner appeared, mounting a small flight of steps leading into the square from a low-lying side-street. It was not quite certain that it was she, but the resemblance was close enough. Whether it were really Fräulein Bürstner or not, however, did not matter to K.; the important thing was that he suddenly realized the futility of resistance. There would be nothing heroic in it were he to resist, to make difficulties for his companions, to snatch at the last appearance of life by struggling. He set himself in motion, and the relief his warders felt was transmitted to some extent even to himself. They suffered him now to lead the way, and he followed the direction taken by the girl ahead of him, not that he wanted to overtake her or to keep her in sight as long as possible, but only that he might not forget the lesson she had brought into his mind. "The only thing I can do now," he told himself, and the regular correspondence between his steps and the steps of the other two confirmed his thought, "the only thing for me to go on doing is to keep my intelligence calm and analytical to the end. I always wanted to snatch at the world with twenty hands, and not for a very laudable motive, either. That was wrong, and am I to show now that not even a year's trial has taught me anything? Am I to leave this world as a

man who has no common sense? Are people to say of me
after I am gone that at the beginning of my case I wanted
to finish it, and at the end of it I wanted to begin it again?
I don't want that to be said. I am grateful for the fact
that these half-dumb, senseless creatures have been sent
to accompany me on this journey, and that I have been
left to say to myself all that is needed."

Fräulein Bürstner meanwhile had gone round the
bend into a side-street, but by this time K. could do without her and submitted himself to the guidance of his
escort. In complete harmony all three now made their way
across a bridge in the moonlight, the two men readily
yielded to K.'s slightest movement, and when he turned
slightly toward the parapet they turned, too, in a solid
front. The water, glittering and trembling in the moonlight, divided on either side of a small island, on which
the foliage of trees and bushes rose in thick masses, as if
bunched together. Beneath the trees ran gravel paths,
now invisible, with convenient benches on which K. had
stretched himself at ease many a summer. "I didn't mean
to stop," he said to his companions, shamed by their
obliging compliance. Behind K.'s back the one seemed to
reproach the other gently for the mistaken stop they had
made, and then all three went on again.*

They passed through several steeply rising streets, in
which policemen stood or patrolled at intervals; sometimes a good way off, sometimes quite near. One with a
bushy mustache, his hand on the hilt of his saber, came
up as of set purpose close to the not quite harmless-looking

group. The two gentlemen halted, the policeman seemed to be already opening his mouth, but K. forcibly pulled his companions forward. He kept looking round cautiously to see if the policeman were following; as soon as he had put a corner between himself and the policeman he started to run, and his two companions, scant of breath as they were, had to run beside him.

So they came quickly out of the town, which at this point merged almost without transition into the open fields. A small stone quarry, deserted and desolate, lay quite near to a still completely urban house. Here the two men came to a standstill, whether because this place had been their goal from the very beginning or because they were too exhausted to go farther. Now they loosened their hold of K., who stood waiting dumbly, took off the top hats and wiped the sweat from their brows with pocket handkerchiefs, meanwhile surveying the quarry. The moon shone down on everything with that simplicity and serenity which no other light possesses.

After an exchange of courteous formalities regarding which of them was to take precedence in the next task—these emissaries seemed to have been given no specific assignments in the charge laid jointly upon them—one of them came up to K. and removed his coat, his waistcoat, and finally his shirt. K. shivered involuntarily, whereupon the man gave him a light, reassuring pat on the back. Then he folded the clothes carefully together, as if they were likely to be used again at some time, although perhaps not immediately. Not to leave K. standing motionless, exposed to the night breeze, which was rather chilly, he took him by the arm and walked him up and down a little, while his partner investigated the quarry to find a suitable spot. When he had found it he beckoned, and K.'s companion led him over there. It was a spot near the cliffside where a loose boulder was lying. The two of them laid K. down on the ground, propped him against the boulder, and settled his head upon it. But in spite of the pains they took and all the willingness K. showed, his posture remained contorted and unnatural-looking. So one of the men begged the other to let him dispose K. all by himself, yet even that did not improve matters. Finally they left K. in a position which was not even the best of the positions they had already tried out. Then one of them opened his frock coat and out of a sheath that hung from a belt girt round his waistcoat drew a long, thin, double-edged butcher's knife, held it up, and tested the cutting edges in the moonlight. Once more the odious courtesies began, the first handed the knife across K. to the second, who handed it across K. back again to the first. K. now perceived clearly that he was supposed to seize the knife himself, as it traveled from hand to hand above him, and plunge it into his own breast. But he did not do so, he merely turned his head, which was still free to move, and gazed around him. He could not completely rise to the occasion, he could not relieve the officials of all their tasks; the responsibility for this last failure of his lay with him who had not left him the remnant of strength necessary for the deed. His glance fell on the top story of the house adjoining the quarry. With a flicker as of a light going up, the casements of a window there suddenly flew open; a human figure, faint and insubstantial at that distance and that height, leaned abruptly far forward and stretched both arms still farther. Who was it? A friend? A good man? Someone who sympathized? Someone who wanted to help? Was it one person only? Or was it mankind? Was help at hand? Were there arguments in his favor that had been overlooked? Of course there must be. Logic is doubtless unshakable, but it cannot withstand a man who wants to go on living. Where was the Judge whom he had never seen? Where was the High Court, to which he had never penetrated? He raised his hands and spread out all his fingers.*

But the hands of one of the partners were already at K.'s throat, while the other thrust the knife deep into his heart and turned it there twice. With failing eyes K. could still see the two of them immediately before him, cheek leaning against cheek, watching the final act. "Like a dog!" he said; it was as if the shame of it must outlive him.

APPENDIX
POSTSCRIPTS
TRANSLATOR'S NOTE

I

THE UNFINISHED CHAPTERS

ON THE WAY TO ELSA

ONE day, just as he was about to leave the Bank, K. was rung up on the telephone and summoned to come to the Law Court at once. He was warned against disobedience. All his unprecedented statements: that the judicial examinations were unnecessary, that they led to no result and never could, that in the future he would refuse to appear, that he would ignore all summonses, whether by telephone or in writing, and would send any messengers packing—all those statements had been duly filed and had already done him considerable harm. And why should he refuse to obey? Was it not true that, regardless of time and money, every effort was being made to clarify his complicated case? Did he really wish to obstruct this wantonly and allow those violent measures to take their course from which he had so far been spared? Today's summons was his last chance. Let him act as he pleased, but let him remember that the High Court of Justice could not permit itself to be treated with contempt.

As it happened K. had announced a visit to Elsa for that evening, reason enough for not attending at Court. He was glad to be able to justify his nonappearance in this way, though he would naturally never make use of it as an excuse and would probably not have gone even if the evening had been entirely free and completely at his own disposal. Nevertheless, conscious of his own rights, he asked through the telephone what would happen if he failed to put in an appearance. "We shall know where to find you," was the answer. "And shall I be punished for not having come of my own accord?" asked K., and smiled in anticipation of the reply. "No," was the answer. "Splendid," said K., "then what motive could I have for complying with this summons?" "It is not usual to bring the powers of the Court upon one's own head," said the voice, becoming fainter and finally dying away. "It is very rash not to do so," thought K. as he hung up; "for after all one should try to find out what those powers are."

Without hesitation he drove off to Elsa. Leaning back comfortably in the corner of the carriage, his hands in his coat-pockets—for it was already getting chilly—he surveyed the bustling streets. With a certain satisfaction he reflected that, if the Court were really sitting, he was causing it considerable inconvenience. He had not said outright whether he were coming or not. So the Judge would be waiting and perhaps a whole assembly as well; and only K., to the disappointment of the gallery in particular, would not be there. Unperturbed by the

Court, he was going where he wanted to go. Just for a moment he was uncertain whether he had not absent-mindedly given the coachman the address of the Court, so he called out Elsa's address loudly. The coachman nodded his head; that was the address he had been given. From then onward K. gradually put the Court out of his mind and thoughts of the Bank began to preoccupy him exclusively as they had been wont to do.

JOURNEY TO HIS MOTHER

Suddenly, at lunch, it occurred to him that he wanted to visit his mother. Spring was nearly over now, which made it three years since he had seen her last. On that occasion she had begged him to come to her on his birthday; in spite of a good many difficulties he had complied and had even promised to spend all his future birthdays with her, a promise which, it must be owned, he had already broken twice. To make up for this, he decided not to wait for his birthday, although it was only a fortnight off, but to go at once. Yet, as he told himself, there was no particular reason to go at the actual moment; on the contrary, the news which he received regularly every two months from a cousin, who owned a business in the little town and administered the money K. sent for his mother, was more reassuring than ever before. It is true that his mother's eyesight was failing; but then K. had expected that for many years from the doctors' reports; and her general health had improved. Several of the disabilities of old age, instead of becoming more noticeable, were less so, or at least she complained less. His cousin was of the opinion that this was possibly connected with her excessive piety during the last few years. K. had noticed slight signs of that on his last visit with something like repugnance; and in one of his letters his cousin had described very vividly how the old lady, who used to drag herself along with such difficulty, now stepped out quite vigorously when he gave her his arm on the way to church. And K. could believe his cousin implicitly, for he was an alarmist as a rule and apt to exaggerate the bad rather than the good side in his reports.

But be that as it might, K. had now decided to go. Among other distressing manifestations he had lately noticed a certain plaintiveness in himself, a tendency to give way without a struggle to all his desires. Well, in this case that failing at least served a good purpose.

He went to the window in order to collect his thoughts. He then ordered the meal to be cleared away at once and sent the attendant off to Frau Grubach to announce his departure and to fetch his suitcase packed with whatever she thought necessary. After that he gave Kühne a few instructions to cover the time of his absence; and on this occasion it hardly even vexed him that Kühne, in an ill-mannered fashion that had now become habitual, received the directions with averted head, as if he knew perfectly well what he had to do and only put up with

K.'s injunctions as a pure formality. Finally K. went to the Manager. When he asked the latter for two days' leave to go and see his mother, the Manager naturally asked if she were ill. "No," said K. without further explanation. He was standing in the middle of the room, his hands crossed behind his back and frowning as he thought it over. Had he perhaps been too precipitate in his preparations for departure? Wouldn't it have been better to stay here? Why did he want to go? Was sentimentality the cause of the journey? And might not such sentimentality result in something important missed, an opportunity to intervene, which might after all occur any day, any hour, now that his trial had apparently been at a standstill for weeks, and hardly one definite piece of news had reached him? Besides, might he not frighten the old lady, which was naturally not his intention, but which might very easily happen against his will, since so many things were happening now against his will? And his mother was not clamoring to see him; on the contrary. In the past his cousin's letters had been full of her repeated urgent invitations; but not for a long time now. So he was not going for his mother's sake; that much was clear. But if he were going for his own sake, cherishing any kind of hopes, then he was an irreclaimable fool, and he would be repaid for his folly there by the resultant despair. But, as if all these doubts were not his own, but were being insinuated into his mind by others, he came out of his trance and adhered to his resolution. Meanwhile the Manager, either by chance or more probably out of respect for K.'s silence, had been bending over a news-paper. He now looked up and, rising, shook hands with K., wishing him a pleasant journey without further questions.

K. then waited in his office for the return of the attendant, pacing up and down and monosyllabically warding off the Assistant Manager, who came in several times to inquire the reason for his departure. When at last the suitcase arrived, he hastened down at once to the cab which had been ordered earlier. He was already halfway down when at the last moment the official Kullich appeared at the head of the stairs holding a letter he had begun to write and obviously anxious for instructions. K. waved him away; but the fair-haired, chuckleheaded young man misunderstood the gesture and waving the paper came dashing down after K. in perilous leaps and bounds. The latter was so much incensed by this that, when Kullich overtook him on the outside staircase, he snatched the letter from him and tore it up. He looked back when he had got into the cab, and there stood Kullich, who had probably not even yet realized what he had done amiss, rooted to the spot and staring after the departing cab, while the porter beside him saluted deferentially. So K. was still one of the highest officials in the Bank; if he tried to deny it, the porter would contradict him. As for his mother, whatever he could say to the contrary, she believed him to be the Bank Manager and had done so for years. He would not sink in her estimation, whatever other injury his prestige had suffered. Perhaps it was a good sign that he had convinced himself just as he was leaving that he could snatch a letter away from an official who actually had some connection with the Court and tear it up without any kind of apology and without reprisals.

Deleted from here on.

. . . On the other hand he had not been able to do what he would have liked to do most of all: administer two ringing blows on Kullich's pale round cheeks. From another point of view this is just as well; for K. hates Kullich, and not Kullich alone, but Rabensteiner and Kaminer too. He believes that he has hated them from the beginning. Their appearance in Fräulein Bürstner's room had, it is true, first brought them to his notice; but his hatred is older. And latterly K. has been almost sick with that hatred, for he cannot satisfy it. It is so difficult to get at them. They are now the lowest of all the officials; and as they are all three completely inferior, they will never get promotion except through the pressure of their years of seniority and even then more slowly than anyone else. So that it is next to impossible to hinder their careers. No hindrance engineered by anyone else can ever be as great as Kullich's stupidity, Rabensteiner's laziness, and Kaminer's cringing and repulsive modesty. The only thing one could attempt against them would be to have them dismissed; and as a matter of fact that would be very easy to compass. A word from K. to the Manager would be enough. But K. shrinks from that. Perhaps he might do it, if the Assistant Manager, who openly or in secret favors everything K. hates, were to take their part. But oddly enough the Assistant Manager makes an exception in this case and wants the same thing as K.

PROSECUTING COUNSEL *

In spite of his knowledge of men and the experience of the world which K. had acquired during his long service in the Bank, the company he met at dinner in the evenings had always impressed him as particularly calculated to inspire respect and he never denied in his inmost thoughts that it was a great honor for him to belong to such a society. It consisted almost exclusively of judges, prosecuting counsel, and lawyers, although a few quite young officials and lawyers' clerks were also admitted; but they sat right at the bottom of the table and were only allowed to take part in the debates when questions were addressed to them directly, such questions being nearly always put in order to divert the rest of the company. Hasterer in particular, a prosecuting counsel who generally sat next to K., loved to embarrass the young men in this way. When he spread out his great hairy hand in the middle of the table and turned toward

* This fragment would have followed immediately after the seventh chapter of the novel. It is begun on the same sheet of paper on which the last sentences of that chapter are transcribed. M. B. But see translator's note, p. 339.

the lower end, everyone sat up and took notice. And if one of those below the salt took up the question and could not make head or tail of it, or stared thoughtfully into his mug of beer, or opened and shut his jaws instead of speaking; or even—and that was worst of all—championed an erroneous or discredited opinion in an endless flood of words, then the older men turned round smiling in their chairs and really began to enjoy themselves. The solidly serious professional conversations were their exclusive prerogative.

K. had been introduced into this society by a lawyer who was the legal representative of the Bank. At one time K. had been obliged to hold long conferences with this lawyer lasting late into the evening; and so it had come about quite naturally that he had taken his supper at the lawyer's table and had enjoyed the society he met there. He found himself among a whole company of learned and eminent men who wielded a certain power and whose recreation consisted in exerting themselves to find the solution of thorny problems which had only the slightest connection with everyday life. K. himself could naturally take little part in all this; but it enabled him to learn a good deal which sooner or later might profit him in the Bank; and besides, there was the possibility of establishing personal relations with the Court, which were always useful. Moreover the members of the dining club seemed to like his society. He was soon accepted as an authority on business matters, and his opinion on such questions was accepted as incontrovertible, although with some ironical reservations. It frequently happened that when two of the diners could not agree on a point of commercial law they appealed to K. for his opinion on the facts of the case, and his name was then bandied about in all the retorts and counterretorts and even figured in the most abstruse speculations long after he had ceased to follow the trend of the argument. Gradually however many obscurities were cleared up, for he had a helpful counselor by his side in the person of Hasterer, the prosecuting counsel, who became very friendly with him. He even frequently accompanied him home at night; and it took K. a long time to get used to walking arm in arm with this giant of a man who could have completely concealed him in the folds of his cloak.

In the course of time they became so intimate that all distinctions of education, profession, and age were obliterated; they associated with each other as if they had always belonged together; and if sometimes one of them seemed superficially superior to the other, then it was not Hasterer, but K., whose practical experience generally proved right in the end, because it had been acquired at first hand, which is never the case at a lawyer's desk.

Of course this friendship was soon common knowledge among the members of the dining club; they began to forget who K.'s original sponsor had been; for in any case it was now Hasterer who stood surety for him, and he would have had every right, had anyone ever questioned his title to a seat at that table, to refer the doubter to

Hasterer. This gave K. a peculiarly privileged position, for Hasterer was respected as much as he was feared. Granted the force and ingenuity of his legal arguments, still many others were at least his equals in that respect; but no one could compete with him in the ferocity with which he defended his opinions. K. had the impression that when Hasterer failed to convince an opponent, he managed at least to intimidate him, for many recoiled as soon as he stretched out a finger in their direction. It almost seemed at such times as if the opponent were on the point of forgetting that he was among friends and colleagues, that after all it was only a theoretical discussion and that in reality nothing could possibly happen to him; for he would fall silent and it needed courage even to shake his head. Everyone felt apprehensive when the opponent was seated at a considerable distance and Hasterer, realizing that he was too far off to make him see reason, pushed back his plate and got up slowly in order to get into contact with him. Those seated near him bent their heads back the better to see his face. On the other hand such incidents were relatively rare, for it was only legal questions which really had the power to rouse him, especially those about trials which he had conducted or was conducting himself. When such questions were not involved, he was a quiet and friendly person, with an amiable way of laughing and a passion for the good things of the table. It could even happen at times that, paying no heed to the general conversation, he would turn to K., and with his arm along the back of his friend's

chair, would question him in a lowered voice about the
Bank and then talk about his own work or about his lady-
friends, who were almost as troublesome as the Law Courts.
With no one else at the table was he ever seen to speak
like this; and in fact if Hasterer were to be asked for
a favor—generally in order to reconcile him with a colleague—K. was often approached first to act as mediator,
a task he always undertook willingly and with ease and
brought to a successful conclusion. Altogether, far from
exploiting his relationship with Hasterer in such matters,
he was very courteous and modest with everyone; and
(much more important than modesty and courtesy) he
knew how to differentiate correctly between the various
grades in the legal hierarchy and to treat everyone according to his rank. This admittedly was due to Hasterer,
who never tired of instructing him in the art. It was the
only set of rules which he himself never broke even in
the stormiest debate. That was why he only addressed the
young men at the bottom of the table, who had hardly as
yet achieved a rank, in general terms, treating them, not
as individuals, but as a conglomerate mass. Yet it was
just those men who showed him the greatest respect; and
when he rose up from the table at about eleven o'clock
to go home, one of them was immediately by his side to
help him on with his heavy coat, and another to hold the
door open for him with a low bow, and to keep it open
of course for K. when he left the room with Hasterer.

At the beginning of their friendship K. had accompanied Hasterer part of the way home, or else Hasterer

had done the same by K.; but as time went on the evenings generally ended by Hasterer inviting K. to come back home with him and stay a while. They would then often sit together for an hour over brandy and cigars. Those evenings were so much to Hasterer's taste that he could not bring himself to forgo them even when he had a woman called Helen living with him for a few weeks. She was a fat female of uncertain age with yellowish skin and dark curls clustering round her forehead. At first K. never saw her except in bed, shamelessly sprawling, reading a serial novel and paying no heed to their conversation. Only when it was getting late, she would stretch and yawn or even throw one of her serial numbers at Hasterer if she could not attract his attention in any other way. The latter would then get up smiling and K. would take his leave. But later, when Hasterer was beginning to tire of Helen, she became a very disturbing influence. She was now fully clad when they arrived, generally in a dress which she doubtless thought highly becoming and stylish, actually an old ball-dress bedizened with trimmings and draped with several rows of conspicuously unsightly fringes. K. had no idea what this dress really looked like, for he could hardly bring himself to glance at her, and would sit for hours on end with lowered lids while she walked up and down the room swaying her hips or sat down near him. Later, as her position became increasingly precarious, she made desperate efforts to arouse Hasterer's jealousy by openly preferring K. It was only misery and not malice which made her lean across the table, exposing her bare, fat, rounded back, in order to bring her face into close proximity with K.'s and force him to look at her. All she gained from that was K.'s refusal to go to Hasterer next time he was asked; and when he did return after an interval, Helen had been sent packing for good and all. K. took that as a matter of course. They remained together for an unusually long time that evening and at Hasterer's instigation they drank the pledge of brotherhood. Indeed on going home he was next door to being fuddled with all the smoking and drinking.

The very next morning in the course of a business conversation the Bank Manager remarked that he believed he had seen K. the evening before. If he were not mistaken, K. had been walking arm in arm with Hasterer, the prosecuting counsel. The Manager seemed to think this so extraordinary that he named the church alongside which, close to the fountain, the encounter had taken place. Although this was typical of his usual accuracy, still, if he had been describing a *fata morgana*, he could hardly have made more of it. K. thereupon explained to him that the prosecuting counsel was a friend of his and agreed that they had in fact passed by the church the evening before. Smiling in astonishment, the Manager asked K. to sit down. This was one of the moments which so much endeared him to K.; moments in which a certain anxiety for K.'s welfare and his future made itself felt on the part of a man who was a confirmed invalid with a chronic cough and in addition overburdened with work of the utmost responsibility. It was certainly possible to label this solicitude cold and superficial (as other officials did who had experienced something similar), nothing but a stratagem by which to attach valuable assistants to his person for years at the sacrifice of a few moments of his time; but, be that as it might, K. was subjugated by the Manager in such moments. Perhaps too the Manager used a rather different tone to K. than to the others. He did not, for instance, forget his position of authority in order to be on the level with K., a regular practice of his in ordinary business intercourse; on the contrary at such times he seemed actually to have forgotten K.'s position in the Bank and spoke to him as if he were a child or an ignorant young man applying for a post who, for some obscure reason, had aroused the Manager's good will. K. would certainly never have tolerated such a method of address from anyone else, nor from the Manager himself, if the solicitude of the latter had not seemed genuine, or rather if the mere possibility of the solicitude revealed in such moments had not completely disarmed him. He realized that this was a weakness; its cause was possibly to seek in the fact that in this respect there really was something childish about him still, because he had never known a father's care, his own having died very young. K. had left home early and had always repelled rather than invited the tenderness of his mother, who still lived, half blind, in the sleepy little town and whom he had last visited about two years ago.

"I knew nothing whatsoever about this friendship,"

said the Manager; and only a faint friendly smile softened the severity of the words.

THE HOUSE

Without any very definite purpose at first K. had tried on several occasions to find out where the office was situated which had sent out the first notification of his case. He discovered it without difficulty. Both Titorelli and Wolfahrt told him the exact number of the house as soon as he asked them. Later Titorelli completed the information with a smile which he always had ready for any private plans not submitted for his approval. This, he declared, was the office which, more than any other, was entirely negligible. It only executed the commissions entrusted to it, being merely the most remote agent of the great Court of Impeachment. It was true that this latter was not accessible to defendants, and that if one of them wanted something from the Court of Impeachment —there were naturally many such wishes, although it was not always wise to express them—then admittedly he would have to apply to the above-named subordinate court. Nevertheless, neither would he penetrate to the real Court of Impeachment by doing so, nor would he ever succeed in bringing his wishes to its notice.

K. already knew the painter's technique; he therefore did not contradict him, nor did he pursue his inquiries, he merely nodded his head and stored up the information. It seemed to him, and not for the first time, that as far as tormenting went, Titorelli was more than a match for the lawyer, the only difference being that K. was not so much at Titorelli's mercy, and could shake him off without more ado if and when he had a mind to. Besides Titorelli was extremely communicative, not to say garrulous, although less so of late; and finally K. had it in his power to plague Titorelli himself.

And plague him he did in connection with the matter in hand, often speaking of that house in a tone which implied that he was keeping something back from Titorelli; hinting that he was in contact with the office situated there, but that his connection with it had not yet progressed far enough to be made known with impunity. But if Titorelli thereupon pressed him for more detailed disclosures, K. would change the subject abruptly and not refer to it again for a long time. Little triumphs of this sort procured him moments of pleasure. At such times he believed that he now understood the people in the proximity of the Court much better than before and could make them dance to his piping. He felt that he had almost become one of them, or at least that he shared in flashes the clearer view which their position on the first step leading up to the Court somehow assured them. What matter then if in the end he should after all lose his position down here? Even then there was still a possibility of salvation there. He need only slip into their ranks; and, if they had been unable to help him with his case because they were too lowly placed or for any other reason, they could still shelter him and hide him. Indeed if he did it circumspectly and secretly, they were in no position to refuse him this service, especially not Titorelli, whose close acquaintance and benefactor he had after all become.

It was not every day that K. nourished such hopes as this. As a rule he was still clear-sighted enough and on his guard against overlooking or overleaping any kind of obstacle. But in moments of absolute exhaustion, generally in the evening when the day's work was done, he took comfort from the most trifling incidents, and equivocal ones into the bargain, which the day had brought forth. Lying as a rule full length on the sofa in his office— he could no longer leave his office without resting for an hour on his sofa—he would mentally piece his observations together. He did not restrict himself narrowly to those persons who were connected with the Court; in his half-sleeping state they all mingled together. He then forgot the tremendous tasks which the Court had to fulfill; he thought of himself as the only defendant and of all the others as officials and lawyers thronging the corridors of a law court; even the dullest walked with bowed heads, pursed lips, and the fixed gaze induced by weighty thoughts. In these visions Frau Grubach's lodgers always made their appearance as a closed group. They stood shoulder to shoulder with open mouths, like an accusing chorus. There were many unfamiliar faces among them, for it was long enough since K. had taken the slightest interest in the affairs of the boarding-house; and because of the many unknown faces he felt uncomfortable when scrutinizing the group. But this had to be done sometimes when he was searching for Fräulein Bürstner among them. For instance, glancing rapidly along the group he would suddenly encounter a pair of totally unfamiliar eyes shining into his own and arresting his attention. Then of course he could not see Fräulein Bürstner; but, in order to make assurance doubly sure, he looked again, and there she was, right in the middle, her arms round two men standing beside her. He could hardly have cared less, especially as there was nothing new about the scene, it being merely the indelible impression made upon him by a photograph taken at the seaside which he had once seen in Fräulein Bürstner's room. All the same it had the effect of making him avoid the group; and although he often returned to the place, he now hastened through the building, up and down, with long strides. He knew his way about all the rooms very well; remote passages he could never have seen in his life seemed as familiar to him as if he had always lived there, and details kept on impressing themselves on his mind with painful clarity. For instance there was a foreigner strolling about in the antechamber dressed like a bullfighter, with a wasp's waist and an abbreviated little coat of coarse yellow lace standing out stiffly; this man, without pausing for a moment in his perambulations, allowed K.'s astonished gaze to follow him unremittingly. Stooping low, K. circled round him, gaping at him with wide-open eyes. He knew all the patterns of the lace, all the torn fringes, all the oscillations of the little coat, and still he couldn't see enough of it. Or rather, he had seen enough of it long ago; or, better still, he had never wanted to look at it at all, and yet he couldn't tear himself away. "What masquerades foreign countries provide," he thought, and opened his eyes wider still. And he kept on following this man about until he flung himself round on the sofa and pressed his face into the leather upholstery.

Deleted from here onward.

He lay like this for a long time and really rested now. He still went on thinking, but it was in the dark and undisturbed. Best of all he liked to think of Titorelli. Titorelli was sitting in an armchair and K. was kneeling beside him, stroking his arms and cajoling him in every possible way. The painter knew quite well what K. was aiming at, but he pretended not to know and this tormented K. a little. Yet K. for his part knew that he would finally succeed; for Titorelli was a frivolous person and easy to win over, being without a strict sense of duty, so that it was a mystery how the Court had come to have any dealings with a man like that. Here if anywhere, he realized, it would be possible to break through. He was not disconcerted by Titorelli's shameless smile, directed with lifted head into empty space; he persisted in his request and even went so far as to stroke Titorelli's cheeks. He did this slackly, almost sluggishly, taking an inordinate pleasure in prolonging the situation, for he was certain of success. How easy it was to outwit the Court! Finally, as if he were obeying a law of nature, Titorelli bent down toward him and took K.'s hand in a firm clasp, while a slow and friendly lowering of his eyelids showed that he was ready to grant K.'s desire. K. rose to his feet; he naturally felt rather solemn; but Titorelli would have nothing more to do with solemnity. He seized hold of K. and started to run, pulling K. after him. In the twinkling of an eye they were in the Law Courts and flying along the stairs, upward and downward too, without the slightest effort, gliding along as easily as a buoyant craft through water. And at the very moment when K. looked down at his feet and came to the conclusion that this lovely motion had no connection with the humdrum life he had led until now—at that very moment over his bent head the transformation occurred. The light which until then had been behind them changed and suddenly flowed in a blinding stream toward them. K. looked up, Titorelli nodded assent and turned him round. He was in the corridor of the Law Courts again, but everything was quieter and simpler and there were no conspicuous details. He took it all in at a glance, detached himself from Titorelli, and went his way. He was wearing a new long dark suit which comforted him by its warmth and weight. He knew what had happened to him; but he was so happy about it that he could not bring himself to acknowledge it. In the corner of one of the passages he found his other clothes in a heap: the black jacket, the pin-striped trousers, and on the top the shirt stretched out with crumpled sleeves.

One morning K. felt much fresher and more resilient than usual. Thoughts of the Court hardly intruded at all; or when they did, it seemed as if it would be easy enough to get a purchase on this immeasurably vast organism by means of some hidden lever which admittedly he would first have to grope for in the dark; but that then it would be child's play to grasp it, uproot the whole thing, and shatter it. This unwonted state of mind actually induced K. to invite the Assistant Manager to his room in order to discuss a business matter which had been pending for some time. On such occasions the Assistant Manager always acted as if his relationship with K. had not altered in the least during the last months. He came in as calmly as he used to do in the earlier days of his incessant rivalry with K.; he listened calmly to K.'s expositions, showed his sympathetic interest by little remarks of a confidential indeed comradely nature, and only put him out of countenance, although not necessarily with intent, by refusing to be diverted by a hair's breadth from the matter in hand. It was no exaggeration to say that he concentrated his whole mind on this; whereas K.'s thoughts, faced with such a model of conscientiousness, began to stray in all directions and forced him to leave the matter in question almost without a struggle to the Assistant Manager. On one occasion he had been woolgathering to such an extent that he only began to take notice when the Assistant

Manager suddenly got up and went back to his office in silence. K. had no idea what had happened. It was possible that the conference had come to a normal end; but it was equally possible that the Assistant Manager had broken it off because K. had unwittingly offended him, or because he had been talking nonsense, or because the Assistant Manager had realized that he was not attending and that his thoughts were elsewhere. But worse than that, it might well be that K. had made some ludicrous proposal or that his adversary had wormed one out of him and was now hastening to put it into execution to K.'s detriment. On the other hand, no further mention was made of this particular matter. K. was unwilling to bring it up and the Assistant Manager remained uncommunicative; meanwhile there had at least so far been no visible repercussions. At all events K. had not been frightened off by this incident. Let a suitable opportunity present itself, and let him but feel at all equal to it, and there he would be at the Assistant Manager's door either to go in to him or to invite him to his office. The time had passed for lying low as he had done before. He no longer hoped for an early decisive victory which would free him at one blow from all his anxieties and restore his previous relationship with the Assistant Manager. K. realized that he must persist; for should he bow to the facts and retreat, then there was the danger that never again in all probability would he be able to advance. The Assistant Manager must not be allowed to continue in the belief that K. was dead and done for; he must not be permitted to sit quietly in his office secure in that belief; his peace of mind must be attacked. He must be made to realize as often as possible that K. was still alive, and that like all living things he might yet one day astonish the world with new potentialities, however little danger there seemed of that just now. K. sometimes told himself, it is true, that in adopting this method he was simply and solely fighting for his honor; for it could surely profit him nothing to keep on opposing the Assistant Manager in all his weakness, thus increasing the latter's sense of power and giving him the opportunity to observe the present state of affairs accurately and take his measures accordingly. But K. could not have altered his conduct had he wished to do so; he was the victim of self-delusion; at times he was absolutely convinced that the psychological moment had come to measure himself against the Assistant Manager, and the most unfortunate experiences never taught him better. What he had not achieved in ten cases, he believed that he would accomplish in the eleventh, although everything without exception had always turned out to his disadvantage. When after such encounters he was left exhausted, bathed in sweat, and drained of thought, he never knew whether it had been hope or despair which had impelled him into the presence of his enemy. Yet the next time it was hope again and nothing but hope with which he hastened to the Assistant Manager's door.

The passage in square brackets was deleted by the author.

[On that morning the hope seemed to be particularly

the little pillars back into the appropriate hol
at was the most ticklish part of the whole operati
e Assistant Manager got to his feet and tried to fo
balustrade back into position with both hands; t
how he might, he did not succeed. While reading
ort and elaborating it as he went on, K. had or
uely noticed that his companion had stood up. A
ugh he had rarely quite lost sight of the latte
teur carpentry, still he took it for granted that tl
upt movement was somehow also connected with I
ort. So he got up too and, with one finger underlinir
roup of figures, he held out a sheet of paper to tl
istant Manager. But in the meantime the other ha
ized that his hands alone would never do the tric
therefore, taking a sudden decision, he sat dow
his whole weight on the balustrade. Success certainl
ned this effort. The little pillars went crashing bac
their holes, but one of them broke in the proces
the delicate upper strip split in two. "Rotten wood,
the Assistant Manager crossly.

A FRAGMENT

was drizzling when they came out of the theater. K
lready tired out by the play and the poor perform
; and the thought that he would have to put up hi
for the night depressed him profoundly. For today

well founded. The Assistant Manager came in slowly,
his hand to his head and complaining of a headache. K.'s
first reaction was to reply to this, but then he thought
better of it, and embarked immediately on business without paying the slightest attention to his opponent's headache. Now, whether the pains were not very acute, or
whether his interest in the subject under discussion allayed
them for the moment; whatever the reason, the Assistant
Manager removed his hand from his forehead during the
course of the conversation and answered in his usual
style, promptly and almost without stopping to think,
like one of those model pupils who answer before the
question is well out of the master's mouth. This time K.
was able to meet him on his own ground and refute him
several times. But the thought of the Assistant Manager's
headache kept on nagging at him, as if it told in his
enemy's favor instead of against him. He bore and
mastered his pains so admirably! Sometimes he would
smile irrespective of what he was saying, as if he were
boasting of the fact that, though he had a headache, this
did not hinder his mental processes. They were speaking
of quite other things, but at the same time a soundless
dialogue was taking place between them, in which the
Assistant Manager, without denying the violence of his
headache, kept on hinting that the pains were harmless
and therefore quite different from those K. was accustomed
to have. And however much K. contradicted him, the way
in which the Assistant Manager dealt with his pains gave
K. the lie. But at the same time it was an example to him.

He too could barricade himself against all those carking cares which had nothing to do with his profession. He need only stick more closely to his work than ever before and introduce new methods into the Bank whose establishment and maintenance would provide him with a permanent occupation; he must also strengthen his slightly slackened ties with the world of commerce by visits and journeys, report more frequently to the Manager, and try to obtain special commissions from him.]

It was the same again today. The Assistant Manager came in at once, then remained standing near the door, polished his pince-nez (a new habit of his), and looked first at K. and then, in order not to occupy himself too conspicuously with the Chief Clerk, he surveyed the whole room carefully. It seemed as if he were seizing the opportunity to test his eyesight. K. withstood this byplay and even smiled slightly as he asked the Assistant Manager to be seated. He sat down himself in his armchair, moving it as close to the Assistant Manager as possible, took up the relevant papers at once, and began his report. At first his vis-à-vis hardly seemed to be listening. Round the top of K.'s desk ran a little carved balustrade. The desk was a piece of excellent workmanship and the balustrade too was firmly attached to the wood. But the Assistant Manager made a show of discovering just at that moment that it was loose, and he tried to repair the damage by tapping it with his forefinger. K. thereupon offered to interrupt his report, but the other would not consent to this, declaring that he could hear and follow everything

perfectly. In the meantime, however, K. coul[d] a single factual observation from him, w[ith] balustrade seemed to demand extraordinary me[asures] the Assistant Manager now brought out hi[s] and, using K.'s ruler as a lever, he tried to balustrade, evidently in order the better to thru[st] In his report K. had embodied a proposal of new kind which, he assured himself, could not press the Assistant Manager greatly; and as he to this proposal he could hardly pause to ta[ke] enthralled as he was by his own production, uplifted by the consciousness, daily becoming he still had a part to play in the Bank and tha[t] had the power to vindicate him. Perhaps indee[d] the best way to defend himself, and not only in but in his trial too, a far better way probably other line of defense he had so far adopted o[r contem-] plated. Reading at top speed, K. could not spar[e] to ask the Assistant Manager in so many word[s] from his labors at the balustrade; all he coul[d] while he was reading was to run his hand rea[dily] along the balustrade, almost unconsciously indic[ating] there was nothing wrong with it; and that eve[n] were, listening was more important at the mo[ment] also more befitting than any attempt to put But this manual task had roused the other's zea[l] happens with energetic persons whose occupati[on] clusively mental. One piece of the balustrade been successfully levered up, and the problem w[as]

of all days he had set his heart on a talk with F[räulein] B[ürstner], and perhaps there might have been an opportunity to get hold of her, but his uncle's presence put it entirely out of the question. Actually there was a night train which his uncle could catch; but there seemed not the slightest chance of persuading him to leave today when he was so much preoccupied with K.'s trial. However K. made the attempt, although without much hope of success. "My dear uncle," he said, "I'm afraid that I shall really need your help in the near future. I can't quite see yet in what connection; but I shall certainly need it." "You can count on me," said his uncle; "for I can think of nothing else but how to help you." "That's just like you," said K.; "only I'm afraid that my aunt will be vexed if I have to ask you to return here in a day or two." "Your trial is more important than annoyances of that sort." "I can't quite agree with you there," said K., "but whether or no, I don't want to deprive my aunt of your society more than is necessary; and as it looks as if I shall want you in the course of the next few days, what about going home in the meantime?" "Tomorrow?" "Yes, tomorrow," said K., "or perhaps even now with the night train; that might be best."

II

THE PASSAGES DELETED BY THE AUTHOR

PAGE *14*

The interrogation seems to be limited to looks, thought K.; well, I'll give him a few minutes' grace. I wish I knew what kind of an official body it can be which goes in for such elaborate arrangements in a case like mine which, from the official point of view, offers no prospects of any kind. For elaborate is the only word to use for this whole setup. Three people already wasted on me, two rooms not belonging to me disarranged, and over there in the corner another three young men are standing and looking at Fräulein Bürstner's photographs.

PAGE *16*

As someone said to me—I can't remember now who it was—it is really remarkable that when you wake up in the morning you nearly always find everything in exactly the same place as the evening before. For when asleep and dreaming you are, apparently at least, in an essentially different state from that of wakefulness; and therefore, as that man truly said, it requires enormous

presence of mind or rather quickness of wit, when opening
your eyes to seize hold as it were of everything in the
room at exactly the same place where you had let it go
on the previous evening. That was why, he said, the
moment of waking up was the riskiest moment of the day.
Once that was well over without deflecting you from your
orbit, you could take heart of grace for the rest of the day.

PAGE *17*

As you know, employees always know more than their
employers.

PAGE *24*

The thought that by doing this he was perhaps making
it easier for them to keep his own person under observation, which they had possibly been instructed to do, seemed
to him such a ludicrous notion, that he buried his head in
his hands and remained like that for several minutes in
order to come to his senses. "A few more ideas like that,"
he said to himself, "and you really will go mad." Then he
raised his rather grating voice all the louder.

PAGE *30*

A soldier was doing sentry duty up and down before
the house. So now they had even put a watch on the house.
K. had to lean out very far to see him, for he was walking
close to the wall. "Hallo!" he called out to him, but not
loud enough for the man to hear. However it soon became
apparent that he was only waiting for a servant girl who

319

had gone across the road to a public house to fetch some beer, for she now appeared in the lighted doorway. K. asked himself if he had believed even for a moment that the sentry had been meant for him. He could not answer the question.

PAGE *34*

"What a tiresome person you are; it's impossible to tell whether you are serious or not." "There's something in that," said K., delighted to be chatting with a pretty girl; "there's something in that. I am never serious, and therefore I have to make jokes do duty both for jest and earnest. But I was arrested in earnest."

PAGE *48*

Instead of "local political meeting," "socialist meeting" was originally used.

PAGE *58*

All K. could see was that her blouse was unbuttoned and hanging round her waist, that a man had dragged her into a corner and was pressing her body to his, she being bare from the waist up except for her vest.

PAGE *72*

K. had just been going to catch hold of the woman's hand which she was obviously if timorously stretching out to him, when the student's words caught his attention. He was a voluble, overbearing young man, so that perhaps it would be possible to get more precise information from him about the charges brought against K. And if only K. had this information then undoubtedly he could put a stop to the whole proceedings immediately with one wave of his hand to everyone's dismay.

PAGE *110*

Yes, it was even certain that he would also have rejected this proposal even if it had been combined with bribery, which would probably have offended him still more. For, as long as his case was pending, K.'s person must surely be inviolable to all the officials connected with the case.

PAGE *125*

Even this praise left the girl unmoved, nor did it seem to make any real impression on her when K.'s uncle replied: "Maybe. All the same I'll send a nurse round to you, if possible today. If she does not prove satisfactory, you can always dismiss her; but give her trial to please me. These surroundings and the oppressive silence you are living in are enough to finish anyone off." "It's not always so quiet here," said the lawyer; "I'll only agree to that hospital nurse if I must." "You must," said K.'s uncle.

PAGE *133*

The desk, which took up almost the whole length of the room, stood near the windows and was placed in such a way that the lawyer had his back to the door, so that a visitor was obliged to cross the whole width of the room like the veriest intruder before he could see the lawyer's face, unless indeed the latter were kind enough to turn round toward him.

PAGE *168*

No, K. had nothing whatsoever to hope for if his trial became common knowledge. Anyone who did not rise up as a judge to condemn him out of hand would certainly try to humiliate him at the very least, that being now such an easy thing to do.

PAGE *228*

It was quite dark in the room; there were probably heavy stuff curtains at the windows which allowed no shimmer of light to shine through. Slightly stimulated because he had been running, K. automatically took several long strides. Then he came to a halt and realized that he had no idea which part of the room he was in. The lawyer was obviously asleep and his breathing was inaudible because it was his habit to creep right under the feather quilt.

PAGE *233*

. . . as if he were waiting for a sign of life from the accused. . . .

PAGE *235*

"You are not speaking frankly to me, and you never have spoken frankly to me. So that if, at least in your own opinion, you are being misjudged, you have only your-self to blame. I am not afraid of being misjudged, be-cause I am being frank with you. You have pounced upon my case as if I were quite free; and it almost seems to me now as if you had not only conducted it badly, but as if, omitting to take any serious steps, you had also tried to conceal the state of the case from me, thus ob-structing any intervention on my part, so that one day, somewhere, in my absence, judgment will be pronounced. I do not say that you meant to do all that. . . ."

PAGE *240*

It would have been very tempting now to laugh at Block. Leni took advantage of K.'s absent-mindedness and, since he was holding her hands, she rested her el-bows on the back of his armchair and began to rock it gently. At first K. paid no attention to this, but watched Block cautiously lifting up the feather quilt, obviously in order to find the lawyer's hands, which he wished to kiss.

PAGE *252*

. . . if one did not know what he was talking about, one would have taken it, at first sight at least, to be the falling of water into the basin of a fountain.

PAGE *276*

When he had said that, he faltered. It came home to him that he had been talking about a legend and judging it and yet that he knew nothing whatsoever about its source of origin and that he was equally in the dark about the interpretations. He had been drawn into a train of thought which was totally foreign to him. So after all this priest was like all the others? Only willing to speak about K.'s case allusively, in order to mislead him perhaps and finally fall silent? Revolving these thoughts, K. had neglected the lamp, which began to smoke, although he only noticed this when the smoke was eddying round his chin. Then he tried to turn the lamp down and it went out. He stood still. It was quite dark and he had no idea which part of the church he was in. As there was no sound anywhere near him either, he asked: "Where are you?" "Here," said the priest and took his hand. "Why did you let the lamp go out? Come with me and I'll take you to the vestry where there is a light."

K. was glad enough to be able to leave the Cathedral proper. The height and breadth of the space around him oppressed him, impenetrable as it was to his gaze except for a tiny circumference. More than once, although well aware of the futility of doing so, he had looked up, and darkness, nothing but darkness, had literally flown toward him from all sides. Led by the priest, he hastened after him.

A lamp was burning in the vestry, a still smaller lamp than the one K. was carrying; and it hung down so low that it hardly illuminated anything but the floor of the vestry which, though narrow, was probably as lofty as the Cathedral itself. "It's so dark everywhere," said K.

and put his hand over his eyes as if they were aching from the strain of finding his way about.

PAGE 281

Their eyebrows looked as if they had been stuck on to their foreheads, and they danced up and down independently of the movements made in walking.

PAGE 283

They went along several paths mounting upward. There were policemen about here and there, either standing or strolling, sometimes in the distance, sometimes very near. One of them with a bushy mustache, his hand on the hilt of the saber entrusted to him by the state, strode up, purposefully it seemed, toward the rather suspect-looking group. "The state is offering to come to my assistance," whispered K. into the ear of one of the men. "What if I transferred the trial into the domain where the writ of the state law runs? The outcome might very well be that I would have to defend you two gentlemen against the state!"

PAGE 286   ORIGINAL VERSION OF THE LAST SENTENCES IN THE PENULTIMATE PARAGRAPH.

. . . were there arguments in his favor that had been overlooked? Of course there must be. Logic is doubtless unshakable, but it cannot withstand a man who wants to go on living. Where was the Judge? Where the High Court of Justice? I have something to say. I lift up my hands.

POSTSCRIPT TO THE FIRST EDITION

(1925)

ALL Franz Kafka's utterances about life were profound
and original, and so too was his attitude toward his own
work and to the question of publication altogether. It
would be impossible to overrate the gravity of the problems with which he wrestled in this connection, and which
for that reason must serve as a guide for any publication
of his posthumous works. The following indications may
help to give at least an approximate idea of his attitude.

I wrested from Kafka nearly everything he published
either by persuasion or by guile. This is not inconsistent
with the fact that he frequently during long periods of his
life experienced great happiness in writing, although he
never dignified it by any other name than "scribbling."
Anyone who was ever privileged to hear him read his own
prose out loud to a small circle of intimates with an in-
toxicating fervor and a rhythmic verve beyond any actor's
power, was made directly aware of the genuine irrepres-
sible joy in creation and of the passion behind his work.

If he nevertheless repudiated it, this was firstly because certain unhappy experiences had driven him in the direction of a kind of self-sabotage and therefore also toward nihilism as far as his own work was concerned; but also independently of that because, admittedly without ever saying so, he applied the highest religious standard to his art; and since this was wrung from manifold doubts and difficulties, that standard was too high. It was probably immaterial to him that his work might nevertheless greatly help many others who were striving after faith, nature, and wholeness of soul; for in his inexorable search for his own salvation, his first need was to counsel, not others, but himself.

That is how I personally interpret Kafka's negative attitude toward his own work. He often spoke of "false hands" beckoning to him while he was writing; and he also maintained that what he had already written, let alone published, interfered with his further work. There were many obstacles to be overcome before a volume of his saw the light of day. All the same, the sight of the books in print gave him real pleasure, and occasionally, too, the impression they made. In fact there were times when he surveyed both himself and his works with a more benevolent eye, never quite without irony, but with friendly irony; with an irony which concealed the infinite pathos of a man who admitted of no compromise in his striving for perfection.

No will was found among Kafka's literary remains. In his desk among a mass of papers lay a folded note written in ink and addressed to me. This is how it runs:

DEAREST MAX, my last request: Everything I leave behind me (in my bookcase, linen-cupboard, and my desk both at home and in the office, or anywhere else where anything may have got to and meets your eye), in the way of diaries, manuscripts, letters (my own and others'), sketches, and so on, to be burned unread; also all writings and sketches which you or others may possess; and ask those others for them in my name. Letters which they do not want to hand over to you, they should at least promise faithfully to burn themselves.

> Yours,
>
> FRANZ KAFKA

A closer search produced an obviously earlier note written in pencil on yellowed paper, which said:

DEAR MAX, perhaps this time I shan't recover after all. Pneumonia after a whole month's pulmonary fever is all too likely; and not even writing this down can avert it, although there is a certain power in that.

For this eventuality therefore, here is my last will concerning everything I have written:

Of all my writings the only books that can stand are these: *The Judgment, The Stoker, Metamorphosis, Penal Colony, Country Doctor* and the short story: *Hunger-Artist*. (The few copies of *Meditation* can remain. I do not want to give anyone the trouble of pulping them; but nothing in that volume must be printed again.) When I say that those five books and the short story can stand, I do not mean that I wish them to be reprinted and handed down to posterity. On the contrary, should they disappear altogether that would please me best. Only, since they do exist, I do not wish to hinder anyone who may want to, from keeping them.

But everything else of mine which is extant (whether in journals, in manuscript, or letters), everything without exception in so far as it is discoverable or obtainable from the addressees by request (you know most of them yourself; it is chiefly . . . and whatever happens don't forget the couple of notebooks in . . .'s possession)—all these things, without exception and preferably unread (I won't absolutely forbid you to look at them, though I'd far rather you didn't and in any case no one else is to do so)—all these things without exception are to be burned, and I beg you to do this as soon as possible.

Franz

If, in spite of these categorical instructions, I nevertheless refuse to perform the holocaust demanded of me by my friend, I have good and sufficient reasons for that.

Some of them do not admit of public discussion; but in my opinion those which I can communicate are themselves amply sufficient to explain my decision.

The chief reason is this: when in 1921 I embarked on

a new profession, I told Kafka that I had made my will in which I had asked him to destroy this and that, to look through some other things, and so forth. Kafka thereupon showed me the outside of the note written in ink which was later found in his desk, and said: "My last testament will be quite simple—a request to you to burn everything." I can still remember the exact wording of the answer I gave him: "If you seriously think me capable of such a thing, let me tell you here and now that I shall not carry out your wishes." The whole conversation was conducted in the jesting tone we generally used together, but with the underlying seriousness which each of us always took for granted in the other. Convinced as he was that I meant what I said, Franz should have appointed another executor if he had been absolutely and finally determined that his instructions should stand.

I am far from grateful to him for having precipitated me into this difficult conflict of conscience, which he must have foreseen, for he knew with what fanatical veneration I listened to his every word. Among other things, this was the reason why, during the whole twenty-two years of our unclouded friendship, I never once threw away the smallest scrap of paper that came from him, no, not even a post card. Nor would I wish the words "I am far from grateful" to be misunderstood. What does a conflict of conscience, be it never so acute, signify when weighed in the balance against the inestimable blessing I owe to his friendship which has been the mainstay of my whole existence!

Other reasons are: the instructions in the penciled note were not followed by Franz himself; for later he gave the explicit permission to reprint parts of *Meditation* in a journal; and he also agreed to the publication of three further short stories which he himself brought out, together with *Hunger-Artist*, with the firm Die Schmiede. Besides, both sets of instructions to me were the product of a period when Kafka's self-critical tendency was at its height. But during the last year of his life his whole existence took an unforeseen turn for the better, a new, happy, and positive turn which did away with his self-hatred and nihilism. Then, too, my decision to publish his posthumous work is made easier by the memory of all the embittered struggles preceding every single publication of Kafka's which I extorted from him by force and often by begging. And yet afterwards he was reconciled with these publications and relatively satisfied with them. Finally in a posthumous publication a whole series of objections no longer applies; as, for instance, that present publication might hinder future work and recall the dark shadows of personal grief and pain. How closely non-publication was bound up for Kafka with the problem of how to conduct his life (a problem which, to our immeasurable grief, no longer obtains) could be gathered from many of his conversations and can be seen in this letter to me:

. . . I am not enclosing the novels. Why rake up old efforts? Only because I have not burned them yet? . . . Next time I come I hope to do so. Where is the sense in keeping such work which is "even" bungled from the aesthetic point of view? Surely not in the hope of piecing a whole together from all these fragments, some kind of justification for my existence, something to cling to in an hour of need? But that, I know, is impossible; there is no help for me there. So what shall I do with the things? Since they can't help me, am I to let them harm me, as must be the case, given my knowledge about them?

I am well aware that something remains which would prohibit publication to those of outstandingly delicate feelings. But I believe it to be my duty to resist the very insidious lure of such scruples. My decision does not rest on any of the reasons given above but simply and solely on the fact that Kafka's unpublished work contains the most wonderful treasures, and, measured against his own work, the best things he has written. In all honesty I must confess that this one fact of the literary and ethical value of what I am publishing would have been enough to decide me to do so, definitely, finally, and irresistibly, even if I had had no single objection to raise against the validity of Kafka's last wishes.

Unhappily Kafka performed the function of his own executor on part of his literary estate. In his lodgings I found ten large quarto notebooks—only the covers remained; their contents had been completely destroyed. In addition to this he had, according to reliable testimony, burned several writing pads. I only found one file in his lodgings (about a hundred aphorisms on religious subjects), an autobiographical sketch which must remain unpublished for the moment, and a pile of papers which I am now putting in order. I hope that among them several finished or almost finished short stories may be found. I was also entrusted with an incompleted beast-tale and a sketchbook.

The most valuable part of the legacy consists in those works which were removed before the author's grim intentions could be fulfilled and conveyed to a place of safety. These are three novels. "The Stoker," a story already published, forms the first chapter of a novel whose scene is laid in America; and, as the concluding chapter is extant, there is probably no essential gap in the story. This novel is in the keeping of a woman-friend of the author. I obtained possession of the two others, *The Trial* and *The Castle*, in 1920 and 1923; and this is a great consolation to me now. For these works will reveal the fact that Kafka's real significance, which has been thought until now with some reason to lie in his specialized mastery of the short story, is in reality that of a great epic writer.

These works will probably fill about four volumes of the posthumous edition; but they are far indeed from rendering the whole magic of Kafka's personality. The time has not yet come for the publication of his letters, each single one of which shows the same truth to nature and intensity of feeling as his literary work; but meanwhile a small circle of Kafka's friends will see to it that all the utterances of this incomparable human being which remain in their memory shall be collected forthwith. To give only one instance: how many of the works which, to my bitter disappointment, were not to be found in his lodgings, were read out to me by my friend, or read at least in part, and their plots sketched in part. And what unforgettable, entirely original, and profound thoughts he communicated to me! As far as my memory and my strength permit, nothing of all this shall be lost.

I took the manuscript of *The Trial* into my keeping in June 1920 and immediately put it in order. The manuscript has no title; but Kafka always called it *The Trial* in conversation. The division into chapters as well as the chapter headings are his work; but I had to rely on my own judgment for the order of the chapters. However, as my friend had read a great part of the novel to me, memory came to the aid of judgment. Franz regarded the novel as unfinished. Before the final chapter given here a few more stages of the mysterious trial were to have been described. But as the trial, according to the author's own statement made by word of mouth, was never to get as far as the highest Court, in a certain sense the novel could never be terminated—that is to say, it could be prolonged into infinity. At all events, the completed chapters taken in conjunction with the final chapter which rounds them off, reveal both the meaning and the form with the most convincing clarity; and anyone ignorant of the fact that the author himself intended to go

on working at it (he omitted to do so because his life
entered another phase) would hardly be aware of gaps.
My work on the great bundle of papers which at that
time represented this novel was confined to separating the
finished from the unfinished chapters. I am reserving the
latter for the final volume of the posthumous edition; they
contain nothing essential to the development of the action. One of these fragments, under the title "A Dream,"
was included by the author himself in the volume called
A Country Doctor. The completed chapters have been
united here and arranged in order. Only one of the unfinished chapters, which was obviously very nearly complete, has been inserted as Chapter viii with a slight
transposition of four lines. I have of course altered nothing
in the text. I have only expanded the numerous contrac-
tions (for instance, "Fräulein Bürstner" for "F. B."
and "Titorelli" for "T."), and I have corrected a few
little slips which had obviously only been left in the
manuscript because the author had never subjected it to a
final revision.

MAX BROD

POSTSCRIPT TO THE SECOND EDITION

(*1935*)

THIS, the second edition of Kafka's great novel-fragments, has a different aim and is guided by different laws from the first (now historical) edition. The overriding purpose then was to render accessible an autonomous poetical world, baffling in its nature and not a perfect whole. Everything which might have accentuated its fragmentary character and made it more difficult of approach was therefore avoided. Today, when Kafka's work is gaining in appeal year by year and has also arrested the attention of theologians, psychologists, and philosophers, it is now desirable to work as far as possible toward a critical edition with variant readings.

The difficulty facing Kafka philologists is unusually great. For, although his style is only comparable with J. P. Hebel's or Kleist's, still its unique charm is heightened by the presence of Prague and generally speaking Austrian elements in the run of the sentence and its cadence. In the present edition an effort has therefore been made to approximate the punctuation, style, and syntax to the accepted German usage; but only so far as seemed compatible with the distinctive melody of the author's speech. The guiding rule of this method therefore was not grammatical; it was based on a repeated recital of the sentences and paragraphs in question until evidence of correctness had been obtained. As the manuscript in its extant form was not intended for publication, and would therefore have undergone a final revision by the author, there is also some uncertainty about the passages deleted by him. Some of them would probably have been replaced after a further revision. Nevertheless, the intention of the author in the context of the novel has been rigorously respected. Those deletions which represent an enrichment of the work either in form or in content have been given in an appendix and completed by the chapters which had to be eliminated from the first edition as too fragmentary.

Contrary to the practice of the first edition, the order of the words as well as the repetition of the same word two or three times in the same sentence have been faithfully adhered to on principle throughout, except when a slip of the author's could be established with absolute certainty. Only quite obvious mistakes in the manuscript have been corrected.

In the first edition the eighth chapter was brought to a conclusion by means of a slight change of position of four lines. These have been replaced in their original context, and the chapter appears, as in the original, incomplete.

MAX BROD

POSTSCRIPT TO THE THIRD EDITION

(*1946*)

A FURTHER scrutiny of the manuscript undertaken recently makes it appear not impossible that Kafka intended the episode now designated as the fifth chapter to be in fact the second. Although Kafka gave titles to the chapters, he did not number them. I put them in order on internal evidence; and I was also guided by special indications, as for instance the repetition of the last words of one chapter on the first page of the next. This must have been the original form. Later Kafka separated the single chapters from each other, and each time he added the above-mentioned final words at the end of each chapter in a very abbreviated copy, often written in his personal shorthand. Such duplicate passages at least prove that chapters marked in this way originally belonged together. Whether it was the author's intention to retain this order or to relinquish it must forever remain doubtful.

Tel Aviv, 1946   MAX BROD

TRANSLATOR'S NOTE

IN connection with Max Brod's third postscript, it is interesting to consider various suggestions made by Professor Herman Uyttersprot in a monograph entitled *"Zur Struktur von Kafka's 'Der Prozess.' Versuch einer Neuordnung,"* Brussels, 1953. In the first place he points out that Chapter v could not possibly have been intended to be the second chapter, since it refers to events in Chapter ii. He also contends that, despite Max Brod's footnote to the unfinished chapter "Prosecuting Counsel," the reference at the end to the two years since K. had last visited his mother makes it clear that this chapter must have been destined for the beginning of the novel, perhaps as a prologue to it, or even as Chapter i, since there is no hint in it that the trial has begun. From this Uyttersprot goes on to consider the structure of the novel as a whole and bases his scheme for a different ordering of the chapters on two kinds of internal evidence. He follows the progress of the seasons during the trial-year, the last year of Joseph K.'s life, beginning with his arrest in the late spring or early summer on his thirtieth birthday and ending with his execution on the day before his thirty-first. There is also the progressive demoralization of K. as the trial goes on, symbolized by the conflict between his work at the bank and his preoccupation with the case. Uyttersprot's analysis of this psychological deterioration has enabled him to place the unfinished chapters in their probable positions in the whole. There is a good deal to be said in favor of his scheme, not the least being that it makes the novel appear less episodic and more of an organic whole. The two most controversial suggestions are: the hypothesis that "Prosecuting Counsel" opens the book, which, as Uyttersprot himself points out, is æsthetically unsatisfactory, since the first chapter makes a far better beginning; and secondly the placing of "Cathedral" before "Lawyer—Manufacturer—Painter." Here again the internal evidence supports Uyttersprot's suggestion; and the æsthetic objection is not so strong; for although it does seem as if the scene in the cathedral were working up to an imminent metaphysical catastrophe, still Kafka himself told Max Brod that several episodes were to intervene between "Cathedral" and the end.

Brod's Order	Uyttersprot's Order
	Fragments
	Prosecuting Counsel
I. *Arrest* . . .	1 (I)
II. *First Interrogation*	2 (IV)
III. *Empty Courtroom* . . .	3 (II)

N.B.—Brod's order is given in Roman numerals and Uyttersprot's in Arabic numerals.

E. M. BUTLER

MODERN LIBRARY GIANTS

A series of full-sized library editions of books that formerly were available only in cumbersome and expensive sets.
THE MODERN LIBRARY GIANTS REPRESENT A SELECTION OF THE WORLD'S GREATEST BOOKS

These volumes contain from 600 to 1,400 pages each
